Buying and Owning your own AIRPLANE

Buying and Owning your own AIRPLANE

THIRD EDITION

James E. Ellis

Aviation Supplies & Academics, Inc.
Newcastle, Washington

James E. Ellis is a systems engineering manager for L-3 Titan Corporation near Hanscom AFB, Massachusetts, and a retired Air Force Reserve lieutenant colonel. With over 2,200 flying hours logged, he holds a single-engine commercial land and sea license with an instrument rating plus a commercial hot air balloon rating. He has flown nearly 200 different aircraft including the Piper Cub, most of the Piper Cherokee series and most Cessna single-engine aircraft, and new types including the Lancair Columbia, the Cirrus SR22, and the Diamond DA-40. He has owned and flown a Cherokee 180 for 30 years. He conducts EAA Young Eagles flights to inspire a new generation of pilots, and he has flown hot air balloons at festivals in the United States, Canada, France, and New Zealand. He also lectures, writes for a monthly aviation newspaper and balloon magazines, and serves on the Aero Club of New England Cabot Award selection committee.

Buying and Owning Your Own Airplane
by James E. Ellis

© 2006 Aviation Supplies & Academics, Inc.
All rights reserved.
Third edition 2004 by Blackwell Publishing. Second Printing (of Third Ed.) 2006 ASA, Inc.

Published 2006 by
Aviation Supplies & Academics, Inc.
7005 132nd Place SE • Newcastle, WA 98059
Website: www.asa2fly.com • Email: asa@asa2fly.com

Cover photo courtesy of Diamond Aircraft.

Printed in the United States of America

2009   2008   2007   2006   9 8 7 6 5 4 3 2

ISBN 1-56027-629-0
        978-1-56027-629-6
ASA-BUY-OWN

Library of Congress Cataloging-in-Publication Data:
Ellis, James E.
        Buying and owning your own airplane / James E. Ellis.—3rd. ed.
            p.   cm.
        Includes index.
        1. Airplanes—Purchasing. I. Title.
TL671.E44 2004
629.133'340422—dc22   2004000855

To Dale and Alan Klapmeier of Cirrus Design, Lance Neibauer of Lancair, and visionaries at Diamond Aircraft, who produced a new generation of aircraft that redefined the state-of-the-art in General Aviation despite the advice of experts who said there was no market for their aircraft. And to all of the pilots and aircraft owners who persevere in maintaining the freedom to fly in the United States in the face of increasingly unreasonable restrictions imposed on our liberties in the post-9/11 era. And finally, to my wife Susan A. Sparks who keeps me flying in airplanes, hot air balloons, and occasionally even in blimps.

Contents

THIS BOOK is sold with the understanding that the author is not engaged in the manufacture, sale, inspection, or maintenance of aircraft, or in rendering legal or other professional services. If expert assistance in the selection and acquisition of an aircraft is required, the services of a competent professional should be sought.

The purpose of this book is to complement, amplify, and supplement other texts and sources. Anyone contemplating the purchase of a new or used aircraft should familiarize themselves with all appropriate materials, including Federal Aviation Administration Service Difficulty Reports and Airworthiness Directives, the manufacturer's service bulletins and other publications, information on the specific make and model of the aircraft from the Aircraft Owners and Pilots Association, and from clubs and associations devoted to the dissemination of information on that type of aircraft. And no one contemplating the purchase of an aircraft should ever purchase it without a complete and thorough pre-purchase inspection by an FAA-licensed mechanic.

Every effort has been made to make this book as complete and accurate as possible. However, some errors and omissions may exist in this text, and this book can only contain information on general aviation aircraft and the aviation marketplace that was up-to-date as of the date of publication. The author accepts no liability for any person or entity with respect to any injury, loss, or damage alleged to be caused by the information contained in this book.

Preface

First edition

Systems engineers like to approach major decisions systematically. You gather all the data you can, study it, organize it, analyze it, prioritize it, and eventually reach a conclusion. When the thought occurred to me that I could actually go out and buy my own airplane, I quite naturally attacked the problem with a systems engineering approach. I wasn't about to spend thousands of dollars without having some idea of what owning an airplane was all about.

I ended up reaching an unexpected conclusion. The only good information on the subject of buying and owning an airplane existed in magazine articles. No good books. Just magazine articles. Sure, books on the subject were available. They told me how to buy the airplane. Owning it? Maintenance? Government paperwork? Forget looking for that information!

Five years and three airplanes later, I was tired of giving other pilots the same repetitive advice about owning an airplane and I decided to write it all down. This book is the result. It is intended to cover all of the pilots who dream of owning their own airplanes. It's intended first and foremost for the average student or private pilot who is slightly bewildered by it all, who doesn't realize how much there is to know, and who can't pay cash for a brand-new Bonanza!

Second edition

Ten years after the first edition of this book was published, I realized that my vision had been too narrow. When I first wrote the book, my methodical systems engineering approach told me that I could never afford a fast, powerful, retractable aircraft. So in a perverse kind of reverse snobbery, I excluded a whole category of wonderful aircraft.

I've learned over the years that if you really want something enough, you can make it happen. If you have a dream, you can make it a reality. The new version of *Buying and Owning Your Own Airplane* doesn't neglect the little guy who wants more than anything else to fly. It just recognizes that even the pilot who aspires to own a modest little airplane may someday aspire to something bigger and faster ... and that he or she will make it happen if the dream is vivid enough!

Third edition

Big changes have happened since the second edition has been published. None is bigger than the growth of the Internet and its entry squarely into the lives of almost all educated Americans. It had given the second edition of *Buying and Owning Your Own Airplane* a new life after normal sales had declined after the first five years of publication. It also changed forever the way information was exchanged and made available, and General Aviation is no exception. If you want to buy a used airplane now, if you don't follow the Web sites carrying airplanes for sale on an almost daily basis it is likely that by the time print advertising appears the plane you want will be long gone, sold to an Internet-savvy buyer.

Other significant changes have occurred in General Aviation. A new liability law has been passed, not very good, but good enough to bring Cessna back into the market. New planes are once again being produced, although at outrageously expensive prices. Cirrus, Lancair, and Diamond have brought truly new aircraft into the market. And there apparently are pilots out there fortunate enough to be able to afford airplanes with quarter-million dollar price tags, even if for most of us it is just a dream. And GPS and other advanced avionics have brought previously unheard of capabilities to General Aviation aircraft at a price even the owners of 40-year-old airplanes can afford.

The Internet also told the publisher that while the second edition of *Buying and Owning Your Own Airplane* was perceived as excellent by its target market, after more than ten years from its publication it was becoming dated. That word came from buyer feedback on sites such as Amazon.com and barnesandnoble.com. The publisher paid attention, and approached me to bring out a third edition. How could I say no?

Acknowledgments

It is truly hard to believe, in looking back on the effort involved in original-ly writing and publishing this book, how many people assisted me. My orig-inal aircraft partner and crew chief Steve Stetson was particularly helpful, providing a fresh outlook that focused my ideas, often at late hours in a cold hangar while we tried to fix some broken widget on our bird.

I owe much to those who made the original edition of the book possi-ble, including J. A. Diblin, of AVCO-Lycoming (now retired), whose AVCO-Lycoming Flyer was an authoritative source of aircraft engine knowledge; Warren Hupper, Fixed Base Operator at Tew-Mac Airport, who gave con-structive criticism and other assistance; Bill Toomey, a working mechanic who gave me his honest view of aircraft owners; Link Noble of the Multibank Aviation Division of South Shore Bank, who supplied informa-tion on the policies of a bank specializing in aircraft financing; and a won-derful group of people at Analytical Systems Engineering Corporation who furnished much-needed material and moral support, including ASEC President James Henderson, Senior Technical Illustrator Mark Hayes, and then-secretaries Claire Peterson and Sheila MacLean.

More than ten years later, it was time to update and expand the book, and again I found almost everyone I asked for information, photographs, or support cooperative and encouraging. Among those who willingly gave use-ful and authoritative information were Terry Lee Rogers, hardworking founder of the Cherokee Pilots' Association, who allowed me to reprint comprehensive information on sources of maintenance data originally pub-lished in Cherokee Hints and Tips; Ben Owen, of the Experimental Aircraft Association, who supplied extensive information on the EAA's autogas STC program as well as on rules and limitations that apply to home-built and kit-built aircraft; autogas expert Todd L. Petersen, of Petersen Aviation, Inc., who furnished his list of aircraft and engines STC'd for autogas; and William J. Barton, president of Monarch Air & Development, who provided information on his company's line of leak-resistant fuel caps and plastic fuel tanks to solve fuel system problems on Cessna single-engine aircraft.

Aircraft manufacturers and their representatives were very helpful in furnishing photographs of their aircraft. I would like to express my appreciation to Aerospatiale General Aviation; American General Aircraft Corporation; Beech Aircraft Corporation; the Wallace Aircraft Division of Cessna Aircraft Company; Classic Aircraft Corporation; Pick Point Air, Inc., New England dealer for Maule Air, Inc.; Mooney Aircraft Corporation; and Piper Aircraft Corporation.

The third edition was done in the age of the Internet. The Internet provides a wealth of information with, for better or for worse, little personal contact and therefore a lot less people to acknowledge and thank. I would like to thank Stu Mann and Jim Jackson of Lancair Northeast for an outstanding demonstration flight in the Lancair, Dave Mueller and Bill Vaccaro for an equally outstanding demonstration flight in the Cirrus SR22, Tim Tower of LMT Aviation for a great flying introduction to the Diamond DA-40-180, and Ken Dono of Columbia Aircraft Sales for the chance to fly the New Piper Archer III.

Buying and Owning your own AIRPLANE

Can I?
Should I?

It takes a little while for the reality to sink in. This airplane you are flying is yours! Not a rental, not a club airplane, but yours! It just doesn't seem possible at first. You look at the older style instrument panel; at the older radios; at the faded, slightly scratched paint on the wings; and it still doesn't quite sink in. I *own* this airplane!

You begin to realize it when you see a beautiful valley just beyond the next ridge. Do you have time to fly over it? You check your watch ... and then realize that you don't have to get *this* plane back until you feel like it! The awareness grows on a warm summer day when you taxi *your* plane to a tie-down along a fence lined with wishful, adoring kids watching with a mixture of reverence and envy. And you remember the pride you felt that day when everyone else was on a tight schedule and you said casually, "Oh, that's OK, I'll fly my plane."

You realize it too when the radio dies, and you receive the $1,500 repair bill. Or when you learn a $5,000 lesson in the meaning of Airworthiness Directive. Every silver lining has its cloud. And that too is yours!

Ownership has become a way of life for you now. It is not exactly what you expected, but you know you wouldn't trade owning your old bird for a chance to fly a fleet of brand-new Cessnas, Pipers, or even Cirruses. This is *your* airplane, and you wouldn't have it any other way!

The "crazy idea"

Thoughts of owning an airplane probably first occur to the average general aviation pilot during student pilot days. Just a crazy idea though. After all, a Porsche Carrera, or maybe a 36-foot cabin cruiser, or a jet-set summer on the Riviera are fun to daydream about, too—and are probably in the same league financially as those shiny new airplanes the fixed base operator (FBO) flies and *Flying* magazine advertises. Oh well, who needs his or her own airplane anyway? The FBO's airplanes are clean and well maintained and always available for student lessons. Airplane ownership is just another interesting daydream.

You face a different world as a private pilot. Those airplanes you flew as a student never seem to be available when the weather is good. Or they are only available for one-hour blocks, or at odd hours. Then there was that day you arrived at the airport only to find the airplane you had scheduled had been "borrowed" by an instructor for a lesson when the radio went out in "his" bird. "Nobody called you? We sure are sorry about that!"

There are airplanes available on a rental or club basis—Cessna Skyhawks and 182s; Piper Warriors, Archers, and Arrows; Trinidads and Tobagos; and maybe even an occasional Mooney, Bonanza, or Cirrus. A minimum of two hours flying required per day, of course—three hours on Saturdays, Sundays, and holidays. Over three hundred dollars a day! Are you buying the damn thing or just flying it?

By now you have read the bulletin boards at small airports, leafed through a copy or two of *Trade-A-Plane*, and even checked some Web sites advertising airplanes for sale. That crazy idea comes back again. Could I really own my very own plane? The idea grows slowly, but it does grow. The impossible dream seems less out of reach, less improbable, and finally, maybe, just maybe, possible!

Can I afford it?

The most crucial question facing the prospective buyer is, Can I afford it? Surprisingly enough, the average, active private pilot can afford to own an airplane. The emphasis is on "active." If you fly rental aircraft 50 to 75 hours per year at a typical cost of $75 to $125 per hour, you are spending between $3,750 and almost $10,000 per year. You must be able to afford it because you are spending that much!

The cost of an airplane can be divided into two categories: the cost of acquisition and the cost of ownership and operation. The cost of acquiring a good used airplane varies with the sizes and capabilities of the choices. A good 15- to 30-year-old, four-seat VFR aircraft of modern construction, such as the Piper Warrior or the Cessna Skyhawk, will cost approximately twice as much as a basic 10-, 20-, 30-year-old or older two-seat trainer, such as a Cessna 150 or 152, a Piper Tomahawk, or an Ercoupe. A good 15- to 30-year-old, four-seat minimum IFR airplane—the Piper Warrior and the Cessna Skyhawk being prime examples—will cost about three times as much as the basic VFR two-seater. *Trade-A-Plane* can be used as a handy guide to estimate what any particular type or category will cost.

Yearly expenses can best be demonstrated by presenting a sample calculation of the cost of owning and operating a typical aircraft. For this purpose an airplane capable of carrying two adults, two children, and a small amount of baggage (such as a Piper Warrior or a Cessna Skyhawk) and costing $50,000 will be assumed. A typical aircraft would have 1,000 hours left before major overhaul on a 2,000-hour time between overhaul (TBO) Lycoming O-320 engine, would burn 9 gallons per hour in cruising flight, would be equipped with one 720/200-channel full capability nav/comm, one 720/200-channel comm or nav backup radio, and a basic IFR or good VFR GPS, and would be capable of limited IFR flying. It is assumed that the aircraft is to be purchased with a $10,000 down payment and five-year repayment of a loan for the remaining $40,000. For purposes of simplification, an interest rate of 10 percent is assumed to be paid in equal sums over each of the five years, with no allowance being made for factors such as interest charges going down as the loan is paid off.

The cost of owning and operating an airplane is further broken down into two categories. The first (indirect expense) is independent of the number of hours flown. The second (direct expense) is the actual cost of operation. There would be no direct expenses if the plane were never flown.

INDIRECT EXPENSES. The indirect expenses that might be encountered in a typical year fall into two groups. The first includes expenses that would be typical after the aircraft loan was paid off, such as insurance, tie-down, annual

Figure 1.1. If you are an active pilot, aircraft ownership is the "possible dream."

inspection, unscheduled maintenance, taxes, and fees. The second includes costs directly attributable to those associated with the loan, such as interest, repayment of principal, and additional insurance.

Insurance costs are estimated at $1,000. This assumes liability coverage of $1 million and hull coverage for ground incidents or accidents only (including those in motion). This means that the owner could not recover any losses suffered between the start of the takeoff roll and the completion of the landing roll. The cost of in-flight hull coverage is substantial and many owners choose to fly without it. (More detailed information on aircraft insurance is presented in Chapter 6.)

Tie-down costs may be $900, or $75 per month. This is typical of a tie-down on a paved surface at a medium-size, tower-controlled field. Grass tie-downs at smaller fields may run as low as $50 per month. In most cases, hangar fees will be too high for the average individual owner, running from $125 per month at small fields to over $250 per month at medium-size, tower-controlled fields.

An annual inspection, required yearly by the FAA for all active registered aircraft, generally costs approximately $5 per horsepower for the basic inspection—for our example, $750. The repair of any problems found during inspection will be at the shop rate, and costs are in addition to the charge for basic inspection. While annuals can be obtained more cheaply at less reputable shops, this is not the time or the place to look for cut-rate deals. Shoddy maintenance practices will cost you more in the long run at best, and at worst they could kill you. This is probably a good time to have any marginal items taken care of as well, since the aircraft will already be in the shop and opened up for inspection. Repairs and marginal items may cost about $1,000, for a total annual inspection cost of $1,750.

Oil changes, which are scheduled by engine tach time rather than by the calendar, and unscheduled maintenance are assumed to cost $1,500. Unscheduled maintenance consists of those nasty surprises associated with aircraft operation, like sticking or broken carburetor or cabin heat control cables, burned-out rotating beacon bulbs, rapidly deteriorating nosewheel shimmy dampeners, or any number of other things capable of wiping away your smile. Twenty hours of labor at $50 per hour and $500 for parts and supplies combine to make up the $1,500 figure. This would probably be adequate for a typical year. However, the first year of ownership of a used airplane is generally a time for correcting numerous inherited problems, large and small. It is also a time of making minor modifications to make it "yours." A wise buyer of a used aircraft probably should set aside 10 percent of the purchase price for correction of real and imagined first-year problems.

State and local registration fees and taxes will probably cost at least $200 per year.

Total yearly indirect operating expenses, not including loan repayment and associated charges, come to $5,350. Repayment of the $40,000 loan and interest, plus $500 to cover the cost of additional in-flight hull insurance (which a lending institution would insist on), adds $12,500 per year. Total yearly indirect expenses, to be paid before the prop ever turns, come to $17,850. These costs are summarized below:

Insurance (ground hazards only)	$1,000
Tie-down ($75/month)	900
Annual inspection	1,750
Unscheduled maintenance	1,500
Taxes, fees	200
	$5,350
Interest on loan (10%)	$4,000
Repayment on principal	8,000
Additional insurance (hull)	500
	$12,500
Total	$17,850

DIRECT EXPENSES. Direct expenses for the sample airplane are the sum of gasoline costs and a set-aside fund for a future major overhaul. At $3.00 per gallon of gasoline, burned at a rate of 9 gallons per hour, hourly gasoline costs are approximately $27.00. A wise owner will establish a reserve fund based upon the number of hours flown, the cost of a major overhaul, and the amount of time remaining on the engine. The sample airplane has 1,000 hours remaining on the engine. Typical major overhaul costs for the Lycoming O-320 are assumed to be $12,000. Therefore, the owner must set aside $12 per flying hour to have the money available when the "major" is due. (If the airplane is sold before it is due for the major overhaul, no set-aside would be required. Nothing is free, of course. An aircraft sold with a high-time engine will simply not sell for as high a price as a similar one with lower engine time.) Finally, to compute the total direct cost, add the cost of gasoline to the set-aside for major overhaul, which results in total direct costs of $39.00 per hour.

To compare the cost of owning an airplane to that of renting, it is necessary to know the total price per hour. To compute this figure, the yearly indirect cost is divided by the number of hours the plane is flown per year, and this figure is added to the direct cost per hour. Table 1.1 shows the hourly expenses of operating the sample airplane for 50, 100, 150, 200, 250, and 300 hours per year. Operating costs are shown independent of those resulting from repayment of the loan. For 100 hours per year of utilization, indirect operating expenses ($5,350) are divided by 100, then added to the direct expenses ($39.00) to arrive at a cost per hour of $92.50. Loan expenses ($12,500) are likewise divided by 100 and added to the $92.50 to bring the total cost per hour to $217.50.

It is apparent from Table 1.1 that the cost per hour of operating the airplane goes down as utilization goes up. While the direct operating expenses will remain constant regardless of the number of hours flown, the impact of the indirect operating expenses on the cost per hour will decrease as the number of hours increases. If it is assumed that the cost of renting an airplane of similar capabilities is $100 per hour, it is apparent that the breakeven point for renting versus owning, independent of loan expenses, falls between 75 and 100 hours flown annually. If loan expenses are taken into account, the airplane would have to be flown at least 250 hours to approach break even.

Table 1.1. Hourly expenses for operating an airplane

	Operating Expenses			Loan Expenses, Indirect	Overall Total
Hours	Indirect	Direct	Total		
50	$107.00	$39.00	$146.00	$250.00	$396.00
100	$53.50	$39.00	$92.50	$125.00	$217.50
150	$35.67	$39.00	$74.67	$83.33	$158.00
200	$26.75	$39.00	$65.75	$62.50	$128.25
250	$21.40	$39.00	$60.40	$50.00	$110.40
300	$17.83	$39.00	$56.83	$41.67	$98.50

Prospective buyers should not assume they will fly significantly more hours a year as owners than they would as renters. Readier access to the airplane will often be offset by an increase in the boredom with local flying. The real impact will be in the area of freedom. Freedom to go to a variety of places "just for the hell of it"—to fly to a lake or beach, forest or mountains, or to visit family or friends just to spend a day. This intangible will often be the deciding factor. Using your airplane to fly to a location one hour or two hours flying time away will not significantly add to the number of hours flown. But it may just become a way of life, widening immensely the circle of places to go and things to see that will be available to you on any weekend.

ALTERNATIVES TO OWNING. The only real way to significantly lower the indirect costs of owning an airplane, as well as the initial cost of acquisition, is to buy and operate it in partnership with one or more other pilots. This route may open doors to ownership that would otherwise remain financially closed to many prospective buyers. Partnerships, however, should be approached with caution. Marriage is probably the only partnership requiring more tact and diplomacy in its consummation than a partnership of aircraft owners. Leaseback arrangements and club memberships are other alternatives to renting. However, these should not be viewed as ownership. They are, in effect, business arrangements with their own advantages and drawbacks. Fractional ownership arrangements are an innovation of the new millennium, offering high-cost partial share ownership of new aircraft. All of these options will be discussed in Chapter 2.

So, we return to the crucial question. Can I afford it? Can I afford it alone? If not, can I afford it with one or more partners?

Which airplane?

If you have decided you can afford to own an airplane, you are ready for the second crucial question: Which one are you going to buy? This should translate not only into, What do you want? but also into, What really suits your needs? There is probably no single factor more responsible for turning first-time owner-pilots into bitter ex-owner-pilots than buying an unrealistic first airplane. Forget the big old Navion you saw. Forget the 400 Comanche. Forget the out-of-production twin with the high-time engines that seemed like a real bargain. Forget all those big, complicated airplanes! Exotic birds may be a bargain when you buy them, but finding parts and a knowledgeable mechanic may be like a Crusader's search for the Holy Grail.

For your first airplane, think small and think common. Airplanes more than six or seven years old, if properly maintained, seldom depreciate. If your first airplane turns out to be too small or too slow, you can always move up. And when you do, you will move up with the knowledge of the ins and outs of aircraft ownership that has been acquired by hard experience but at a relatively low price commensurate with the small size of your plane. Start big or exotic and you will see big and exotic maintenance bills and end up convinced that airplane ownership must be only for the Rockefellers, the Gateses, and the Gettys.

What kind of speed and range do you want? If your typical trip is 150 miles, the difference in en route time between an aircraft like the Piper

Warrior or the Cessna Skyhawk compared with bigger, faster, and more complicated aircraft like the Piper Arrow or the Cessna 182 is less than 15 minutes. Is that worth paying an initial price that is $25,000 higher, or $10 more an hour for aviation gas (avgas), or $15,000 more for a major overhaul? If you fly mostly VFR, do you really need an airplane with a 1,000-mile range just to do away with one 15-minute fuel stop? The airplane may outlast your bladder!

How many seats do you need? Check your logbook again and see how many times you flew with only one other person. It is probably much more often than the number of times you took your whole family. More than two small children? Better settle on a two-seater. You won't be able to afford a six-seater and who would you leave behind? On the whole, it is a relatively simple matter to find an economical, reliable airplane that will carry two couples or a family of four with a minimal amount of baggage. This is the key to the success of the Skyhawk and the Warrior, and the Cherokee 140 can fill the bill better than most pilots realize. But for more than four seats the price goes out of sight for many of us.

Do you intend to use the airplane for business flying? Better check with your boss. Many employers, for good reasons or no reasons, prohibit the use of personal aircraft for company business, or they impose odd and limiting restrictions.

Will you use the airplane for training? Better check with an aircraft insurance agent. Your plans to teach in your own airplane may not look so bright when you find out your insurance premium doubles if you want your student's first solo to be covered, or you may not be able to get coverage at all.

Figure 1.2. Taildraggers are fun to fly but should be approached with caution by pilots trained in tricycle gear aircraft.

Going to rent your plane to friends? Back to the insurance agent. Your prospective insurance company may define your airplane as a commercial operation and up your rates by 100 percent the moment you accept the first penny or even the first gallon of avgas. And how about hull coverage? How would you like to sue your buddy when he or she makes a dumb mistake and totals your bird? You only carried ground hazard coverage, remember? The insurance company certainly will!

Are you going to fly IFR? Older radios may be obsolete, not meeting FCC frequency tolerance standards and having too few frequencies, and no maintenance or spare parts available. On the other hand, new radios cost a bundle. Installation costs can be outrageous. And don't expect to get a bargain. Even if you find cut-rate prices on new radios, the avionics manufacturer may have the funny idea that you have no warranty unless the installation was done at an "approved" shop.

So after you have weighed all these factors, you will have defined what you want. It may even approximate what you need, and more importantly, what you can afford to own!

Now let's look at some interesting but less important questions. Should you buy a high-wing or low-wing aircraft? How about a taildragger? What about older airplanes—ones that are no longer in production, like Ercoupes or Piper Colts? If simple aircraft are better, what about the simplest of all, the ultralights? And what about home-builts, the new cutting edge of general aviation technology?

The merits of high-wingers versus low-wingers have probably been debated around airports since the first designer tried one wing instead of two. There are really no compelling reasons for favoring one over the other.

High-wing aircraft obviously offer a better view of the ground while flying over it. However, for budding amateur photoreconnaissance types, the strut supporting the high wing often cancels out any inherent advantage this type may have. The strut seems to have a habit of sneaking into whatever corner of the photo your camera's viewfinder leaves out. High-wing aircraft generally have two doors, allowing for easier ground access. The high wing also makes a great umbrella if a cloudburst should hit before you get that last door closed. And if the engine's fuel pump should fail, gravity can take over if you are not in the midst of some insane (and probably prohibited) maneuver.

The crucial advantage of low-wing aircraft lies in its increased visibility into those places above, from which the threat of a collision is most likely. The pilots of low-wingers don't have to do a frantic dance on the taxiway to assure that they are not taking the runway away from someone cutting short their base-to-final turn. And in the landing pattern, the wing toward the runway drops on a downwind-to-base turn. Very helpful if some idiot is hedge-hopping his or her way to a long, low, straight-in landing. As for what that other wing is blocking out ... who cares? You are already turning away from that direction! A ready-made evasion maneuver. A low-winger is also conducive to properly checking fuel tank caps and is a godsend to the service crew. But perhaps the low-winger's greatest advantage is in the daydream mode. After all, did the Flying Tigers sit on the wing or hang under it? Remember, even illustrious fighter aces got wet climbing out of their planes in a rainstorm!

With the exception of J-3 Cubs and Cessna 170s, which have now become expensive classics, and new production Huskys or Maules, taildraggers can be some of the lowest-priced aircraft available. According to the pilots who own and fly them, they also can be some of the most fun aircraft to own. Taildragger pilots will be quick to assure any listener in sight that only they fly their planes. People with the extra wheel up front drive theirs! Anyone trained in tricycle gear airplanes (and who isn't these days?) should be very careful when making the transition to taildraggers. Taildraggers have an inherent tendency to weathervane, pointing their noses in whatever direction the wind is coming from. Makes life interesting if there is a crosswind or if there are variable and gusty winds! The results for a pilot who does not concentrate at all times during the landing and takeoff roll, or even while taxiing, can be and have been enough to make a grown man or woman cry. Taildraggers surpass their more modern nose-legged relatives on short grass strips, rough gravel strips, or skis. They are a natural for the free spirited, so if you long for the good old days away from towers, terminal control areas (formerly TCAs, now Cat B airspace), and two-mile runways, a taildragger may be ideal.

Most taildraggers on the used market will be older aircraft, which as a group present their own unique rewards, challenges, and problems. Older aircraft (which for purposes of this book are those built before 1960) can be some of the real bargains on the market in terms of acquisition price. Unlike automobiles, which generally are considered to have outlived their usefulness when 10 years old, well-maintained aircraft can have an almost indefinite lifetime. An older airplane can be an object of pride to an owner willing to invest the time and money required to keep it in top-notch condition.

The long-term costs of maintaining an older airplane at many large metropolitan fields may far exceed the cost of maintaining a 10-, 20-, or 30-year-old version still in production. A variety of factors are involved. Older aircraft may have been built with different construction methods, such as wood or steel tube and fabric, not used in most modern production types. It may be difficult to find mechanics who are capable of making high-quality repairs to wood or fabric-covered planes. Even if contemporary construction techniques are used, mechanics may be unfamiliar with the model. You will end up paying for the time a mechanic takes to learn the subtle differences in your airplane. However, maintenance of specific older types may be much less expensive at smaller fields where the mechanics may have the specialized knowledge and skills required. One fairly reliable indicator is the number of similar aircraft at the field. If Cubs, Champions, Huskys, and other ragwings abound, your odds are pretty good that there is a mechanic around who "knows fabric."

Parts availability for older aircraft may be another problem. A classic case is the Franklin engine used in beautiful old Stinsons and other old planes. The complete and total rights to the Franklin engine line were sold to a Polish firm. Do you really want to rely on any new parts coming all the way from Poland, even if the parts are available from U.S. distributors? Parts availability for older aircraft is generally not hopeless, however. Specialized parts suppliers like Univair in Colorado, Wag-Aero in Wisconsin, and a variety of other companies advertising in *Trade-A-Plane* carry an extensive line of parts for many out-of-production aircraft.

Older aircraft may present other problems. If you want IFR capability, you should be aware that panels in older planes were not designed for the extensive complement of radio equipment found in even the average modern IFR trainer. Significant modification or replacement of an instrument panel can be a very costly undertaking. Insurance costs also may be higher for older aircraft, due to increased parts and repair costs. Taildraggers may have even higher insurance rates, reflecting a history of minor and major

Figure 1.3. The Piper Cherokee 140 is an excellent first aircraft.

landing accidents. Insurance companies may require minimum checkout times with an instructor familiar with the aircraft. If the previous owner is not an instructor, you could have difficulty complying with this requirement.

Another problem with older aircraft is that most have engines designed for 80/87-octane avgas. Continuous use of 100-octane, low-lead gasoline (100LL) in these engines will generally result in lead-fouled spark plugs and lead buildup around the valves. Older Continental engines, including the O-200 used in Cessna 150s and the O-300 used in Cessna 170s and 1967-and-older 172s, are particularly susceptible to 100LL problems. It is not unusual for one of these engines run regularly on 100LL to require replacement of valves in at least one cylinder every 250 hours. New-design valves and seats have helped but not eliminated this problem. Lycoming engines, generally found in older Piper aircraft, are less susceptible to 100LL problems but still generally require at least one top overhaul between major overhauls if 100LL avgas is used regularly in them.

Fortunately, there is an answer for most older aircraft with engines designed to run on 80/87 gasoline. Largely through the efforts of the Experimental Aircraft Association (EAA), which in 1982 conducted more than 700 hours of flight testing using automobile gas (autogas) in a Cessna 150, objections by the FAA and engine manufacturers to the use of autogas in 80/87 octane-burning aircraft engines have been largely overcome. Supplemental type certificates (STCs) are available from the EAA and through Petersen Aviation in Minden, Nebraska, to allow almost any aircraft certificated to operate on 80/87 avgas to use autogas. Another answer is to use TCP, a fuel additive marketed by Alcor, which acts as a lead scavenger to prevent the buildup of lead on valves, valve seats, and spark plugs.

If simple airplanes are best, are ultralights an answer to the prospective aircraft owner's dreams? Unfortunately, no. Ultralights seem to fall into two categories, neither one particularly desirable to a pilot wanting to safely experience and share the joys of owning and flying his or her own airplane.

Many original ultralights were unregulated and dangerous aircraft with all-too-flimsy "aluminum lawn chair" construction. Parts were used that weren't aircraft quality, and all too often key structural parts or fittings subject to corrosion and wear were buried beneath fabric, making good preflight inspection impossible. The inevitable result was reflected in a National Transportation Safety Board report issued in late 1984 showing that between March 1983 and September 1984, 88 out of 177 ultralight accidents studied were fatal, with an airframe failure rate six times that of certificated single-engine aircraft.

Many ultralights have become stronger and better since then, but FAR Part 103 makes the best of them severely and artificially constrained miniature versions of "real airplanes." An ultralight is limited to a maximum empty weight of 254 pounds; it must be a one-person machine, have a maximum speed of 55 knots, and a maximum fuel capacity of 5 U.S. gallons. If you live in a large metropolitan area, you'll have quite a drive to get to where you can legally fly it, because you can't fly one over those congested areas depicted by all those yellow patches on the Sectionals. You'll be flying an aircraft with light wing loading, so you should not plan on flying in winds much over 10 mph. (And if you do, you won't go very far against the wind anyway!) You'll also have a two-cycle engine requiring an overhaul after about only 200 hours of operation (but considering the limitations of the vehicle, that may be several years).

In 1988, a *Private Pilot* magazine survey of ultralights showed a cost of ultralight kits starting at about $5,000 and going up from there. If you want it put together, ready to fly, figure to pay at least $10,000. In 2003, good used ultralight aircraft were still selling for not much more than $10,000, a bargain considering how the prices of other aircraft have increased over the years.

If the thought crosses your mind that maybe a used one will do, remember that this is not a certificated aircraft. Unlike certificated aircraft, a used ultralight will come with a totally unknown maintenance history, in which an aircraft mechanic has to at least put his or her reputation on the line as to the aircraft's airworthiness once a year. Cheap to fly and maintain? Not necessarily. The dacron or nylon wings are susceptible to ultraviolet deterioration, requiring hangaring or wing covers and an outdoor tie-down. Some ultralights can be readily disassembled for ground transportation and storage, but most cannot, despite manufacturers' claims. The best source of reliable information on ultralights is likely to be an ultralight club specializing in the operation and maintenance of this kind of aircraft.

An Aeronca Champ or a J-3 Cub will do almost everything most ultralights will do. The difference is that when you're tired of slowly circling near your home field, you can push in the throttle and go somewhere. And you can even take somebody with you! Curiously enough, both the Aeronca Champ and the J-3 Cub will meet the new Sport Pilot limitations. The Sport Pilot rating is likely to create an entire new series of light two-seat aircraft. It may also make most ultralights obsolete, because many ultralight pilots were older pilots who had experienced medical problems, "lost their medicals," and didn't want to put up with the hassles of regaining the FAA's blessing to fly again. The Sport Pilot rating should open the door to these pilots and others to be able to buy and fly respectable small two-seat aircraft once again without worrying about the every-other-year crises at the Medical Examiner's office.

Are home-builts an answer to aircraft ownership? If all you can afford is a used aircraft, probably not. The home-built and kit-built aircraft movement today is on the forefront of general aviation progress, but one price of progress is that poor designs are just as prevalent as good ones in the marketplace. When dealing with home-builts, one should keep in mind that these are uncertificated aircraft. Their stall speeds can be more than the 61-knot maximum imposed by FAR 23 on certificated aircraft; they may or may not have had extensive structural and in-flight testing; and they may well have very strange handling characteristics. The price of the aircraft will be inexpensive only compared to a new certificated aircraft. It is not unusual for the price of an excellent kit-built aircraft like a Vans RV-series airplane or a Lancair with a 160- to 200-hp engine and full avionics instrumentation to exceed $50,000 or even $100,000 without even considering the value of the builder's time. The finished aircraft will never be able to be flown for compensation or hire, and if you want to sell it, you will find an uncertain market and be faced with the threat of a liability suit if the purchaser ever has a crash. After all, you are the builder.

Obviously, there must be some advantages to home-builts or there wouldn't be so many of them. The November 2003 edition of the EAA's *Sport Aviation* magazine announced that the number of home-builts registered in the United States exceeds 25,000, approximately 15 percent of the single-engine piston-powered fleet. Home-built aircraft can be ideal for the person who has the skills required to work with the particular materials the aircraft is to be made of, be it wood, aluminum, fiberglass, or more exotic composite materials. For the person who builds his or her own aircraft, the result can be an aircraft exceeding the capabilities of any "off-the-shelf" aircraft. The builder will know the intimate details of the aircraft and will have the latitude to do far more of his or her own maintenance than the certificated aircraft owner could ever think of. Certification as a "repairman" in accordance with FAA Advisory Circular 65-23 can even enable the primary aircraft builder to do major airframe and engine maintenance normally done by certificated mechanics, provided the work is done only on his or her aircraft. This includes doing annual "condition inspections" in accordance with FAR Part 43, Appendix D inspection guidelines.

How about buying an already built home-built or kit-built? Unless you know the builder and have watched the aircraft being built, you will have little or no guarantee of the quality of the workmanship that went into the aircraft. Because the FAA now only requires one FAA inspection before the first flight of the aircraft, you cannot be sure that a used home-built aircraft is even structurally sound or safe. A very close inspection of the construction logs, however, can provide reassurance that the aircraft was well constructed and that EAA inspectors have conducted recommended supplemental inspections prior to the FAA inspection. AC 20-27C, "Certification and Operation of Amateur-Built Aircraft," recommends standards for detailed construction logs and precover inspections by EAA inspectors during the building of home-built and kit-built aircraft. If you are considering buying these types of aircraft, you should become familiar with this advisory circular as well as with AC 65-23. And you should definitely join the EAA and become familiar with the extensive material they have available on building and owning home-builts.

A buyer of a home-built or kit-built aircraft can work on the aircraft during the course of the year just as if he or she were the builder, according to EAA sources. This can be a significant advantage for an aircraft owner who is mechanically adept but doesn't have the time to build his or her own aircraft. However, an annual inspection or an annual "condition inspection" will be required and the new owner will not be able to be certificated as the repairman for purposes of this inspection because he or she is not the primary builder of the aircraft. If the aircraft has been maintained by its builder, the builder who holds a certificate and who is selling you the aircraft can continue to do the annual "condition inspections." If you plan to base the aircraft near the original owner or builder, it may be a good idea to see if you can make this a condition of the purchase. Otherwise, you are likely to have to engage the services of a certificated aircraft mechanic who knows little or nothing of the unique construction details of an aircraft for which no airframe maintenance manuals are likely to exist. Because of the limitations on the repairman's certificate, if you are capable of working on the aircraft yourself and have lots of spare time, you may be better off building your own rather than buying one built by someone else.

One option for anyone who is handy enough to build their own aircraft but who can't afford the price of the kits, engines and instrumentation is to consider rebuilding an old fabric-covered aircraft like a Champ or a Taylorcraft. The EAA also has many members who are into rebuilding old aircraft rather than building new ones, and can provide a wealth of information to a person wishing to try this route to ownership. Keep in mind, of course, that your work will have to be monitored and signed off by a cooperative mechanic. Rebuilding a certificated aircraft does not eliminate FAA requirements that apply to the maintenance of all certificated aircraft.

Ownership is possible

Ownership is not beyond the reach of the average, active general aviation pilot who is willing to sacrifice other luxuries for the pleasure of owning an airplane and is content to settle for a simple, unsophisticated type. The cost is high enough that if a prospective owner and his or her family can only afford one expensive hobby, they must be willing to make the plane the one. A spouse's likes or dislikes also should be considered in the decision to buy an airplane and which one to buy. And a buyer should remember that acquisition costs and the fixed expenses of ownership can be made more acceptable by sharing the aircraft with one or more partners. A bleak financial picture can become much brighter when costs are divided by two or three.

A readily affordable aircraft should be simple to operate, easily maintained, and readily insurable. It should be 10 or more years old so the owner will not be faced with depreciation losses. Good modern-design airplanes available with a low purchase price are two-seat trainer aircraft, including the Cessna 150 and 152, and the Piper Tomahawk. Even older Rotax versions of the modern two-seat Diamond Katana may be available at an affordable price. Older Piper Cherokees and Warriors and Cessna 172s are good affordable four-seaters. Even older two-seat aircraft can be good buys if the owner understands and is willing to accept the problems and limitations of such aircraft. Good examples in this category are the Aeronca Champ, Taylorcraft, Luscombe, Piper Colt, and Ercoupe.

Maximum simplicity and the assurance of readily available parts and knowledgeable mechanics are more likely to be obtained when buying an older version of an aircraft currently in production or for which parts are still being produced by the original manufacturer. By buying an older version of a fixed tricycle gear, fixed-pitch prop, two-to-four seat aircraft similar to one the pilot is currently renting, the purchaser will also have the advantage of knowing the aircraft (and the added advantage of lower insurance rates). The trap of "buying what you trained in" should be avoided like the plague, however. Familiarity with a single line of aircraft can blind a prospective owner to other excellent models of both old and new designs.

Even if you are one of those fortunate individuals who has made more money than the average person ever dreams of without winning the lottery, don't be too ambitious with your first aircraft. A simple but capable aircraft like the fixed-gear Piper 161 or 181, a Tiger Aircraft Tiger, or the Aerospatiale Tobago will be a good first-time aircraft. Learn about the complexities of owning an aircraft with a "bullet-proof" design first, before moving up to faster and more exotic varieties like Bonanzas, Cirruses, Lancairs, Mooneys, and Lakes.

To avoid many possible pitfalls, a buyer must be knowledgeable in a wide range of areas associated with aircraft operation and maintenance—how to select a good airplane; how to select the right home field; paperwork from and for a variety of government agencies and a confusing tangle of requirements cropping up every six months, every year, every two years, every five years; insurance coverage; top overhauls; major overhauls; and modifications. The following chapters, while not all-encompassing, are intended to provide the average owner or prospective buyer with at least the minimum knowledge required to make the experience of buying and owning an airplane a satisfying one rather than a costly nightmare.

Partnerships, clubs, fractional ownership, and leasebacks

2

For the person who flies over 100 hours per year and can afford to buy, operate, and maintain an airplane, there is no substitute for outright, single-party ownership. But what if you cannot afford the price of a good used aircraft? What if you fly only five or six hours a month and realize that so little time does not justify spending so much money? You would like to own an airplane, but it really doesn't seem realistic to spend so much money for so little flying. Having one or more partners would cut your costs and make for more realistic utilization of the plane. You have seen clubs advertised in newspaper want ads and general aviation publications, promising excellent aircraft at bargain rates. You've seen how timeshare ownership has transformed the business jet market, and you've heard that fractional shares of new Skyhawks, Archers, Cirruses, and Diamonds might be available, too. And how about those magazine articles on leasebacks? Can you really get a fixed base operation (FBO) to buy a late-model airplane for you merely by letting them use it for a year or two?

You love flying, and you are sick of the uncertainty and the high prices of renting from the FBOs. You can afford to be an active pilot. So what is the best alternative? The appeal of being the one and only owner of an airplane is obvious, but so are the drawbacks. What about partnerships, clubs, fractional ownership, or leasebacks? Are they viable alternatives? And if so, which one is the best for you?

Full partnership

Partnerships have several definite advantages over sole ownership for the average prospective aircraft owner. Splitting the purchase price may make half or partial ownership possible for someone who could not afford to raise the full amount. This arrangement may also allow purchase of an airplane with greater capabilities—IFR instead of VFR; retractable instead of fixed gear; or maybe just a more recent, lower-time version of the same plane. Indirect costs of ownership are shared as well, including small items like tie-downs and state fees and taxes, and larger items like insurance and annual inspections. For the person who wants to own an airplane but would probably fly it no more than 100 hours a year, a partnership will also result in its more frequent use. Aircraft, like many other mechanical objects, last longer and require less expensive maintenance if they are frequently used, rather than allowed to remain idle for long periods.

But having a partnership means that you are involved in one more human relationship. From the moment you buy the airplane until the distant day you sell it or trade it, every significant decision concerning it must be shared with another person. Choosing partners for aircraft ownership and operation should be done with the same care taken in seeking a marriage partner (or more, if divorce statistics are any indication). Like marriage, aircraft partnership involves a significant financial and emotional commitment. Perhaps only boat owners and sports car fanatics become as emotionally committed to an inanimate object as a pilot-owner is to an airplane. So caution is advised. You are going to lose some of the freedom you would have as sole owner, and you are entering a pact involving heavy commitment.

The most common partnership is established when two or more pilots who have met at an aero club or FBO or through some other means decide to "go in together" on the purchase and operation of an airplane. Or one person defines specific needs and then seeks partners, possibly through newspaper want ads. This latter method has the severe drawback of making it necessary not only to determine compatibility of finances but of personality, desires, and operating philosophies in one or two short meetings before firm commitments are established.

Once a decision has been made to enter into a partnership, other decisions must be made before the aircraft is purchased. A discussion of these partnership considerations follows.

WHICH AIRCRAFT AND AIRPORT. The first decision is what kind of airplane to purchase. Two seats or four? High wing or low? IFR or VFR? Tricycle gear or taildragger? Fixed gear or retractable? All the factors involved in choosing are shared decisions now. And where will the plane be based? Nearer to one partner or the other? At a large field or small? Hangar or tie-down? Is an IFR approach needed or available?

SCHEDULING POLICY. A scheduling arrangement must be established. The best is probably to have each partner control the aircraft for a certain period, usually one week. For that week, one partner will be free to use the airplane without consulting the other or others. If any other partner wants to use the airplane that week, permission must be obtained from the "controlling partner." This arrangement is usually quite effective, sharing the feeling of ownership and the burden of scheduling among all the partners. Some problems can arise that may not be anticipated, however. For example, what happens if the airplane is down for maintenance through all of one partner's week? Will the schedule of assigned weeks be slipped for all? Or what if one partner wants to take the plane for a two-week vacation? How much advance notice, if any, will be required? And will that person have to pay back an extra week as controlling partner for the two-week privilege? Do vacation trips or business trips have scheduling priority? While it may seem unnecessary to dwell on such details, these matters should be worked out in advance. Small differences between partners can cause a great deal of bitterness, and "who has the bird when" is a prime area for such misunderstandings to develop.

OPERATIONAL POLICY. How will the airplane be used? May an instructor-pilot use it for training? How about letting students solo in it? Will the instructor-partner pay the greatly increased insurance premium to cover such use? Will nonpartners ever be allowed to borrow the aircraft? If so, who? What must their minimum qualifications be? What part of the operating expenses will they be expected to share?

MAINTENANCE AND MODIFICATIONS POLICIES. Maintenance policy should be established and adhered to. Will only annual inspections be performed, or will 100-hour (nonmandatory except for the commercial operation) inspections be performed as well? Where will the maintenance be done? In the ultra-reliable but high-priced shop at the large field, or in the cheaper single-mechanic repair shop at the dirt strip up the valley? Will every malfunction be repaired immediately, or will items not related to safety be allowed to wait until a major item also needs repair? If some items will not be fixed immediately, where do you draw the line? (This decision can be particularly applicable to IFR birds with dual nav/comms, GPS, automatic direction finder {ADF}, transponder, and other equipment. Do you really need the ADF? Both communications transmitters?) Will maintenance be split equally regardless of hours flown? Or prorated by hours flown? How much owner-performed maintenance will be done? When? If individuals cannot make the work parties, can they pay a certain sum into the maintenance kitty? Should they? Will they?

Who decides what modifications will be performed? What if one partner wants an item and the others don't? Can the partner who wants the item have it installed and personally pay for it?

FINANCIAL INVOLVEMENTS. A policy should be established concerning damage to the aircraft. Will you have a "fault" or a "no-fault" policy concerning damage caused by a partner which is not covered by the insurance (such as the deductible)? Does the partner damaging the aircraft pay for it all? Or do you accept that "it could have happened to any of us" and split the expenses? What if one partner misses payments for any of the expenses? Will any sanctions be taken? Can any be taken? How long and for how large an amount will the other partners cover for the delinquent?

Policy also should be established regarding the sale of a partner's share. Do those remaining have an option to buy? Do they have the right to veto the sale to a potential buyer deemed to be an unsuitable prospective partner?

"LEGAL PAPER". It should be readily apparent that strong disagreements in a partnership would result not only in hurt feelings but in serious legal complications as well. When all prospective partners have arrived at an agreement on the many questions arising from the purchase, operation, and sale of an airplane, the services of a lawyer should be retained to record this understanding on "legal paper." Each partner should clearly know the individual rights and responsibilities within the partnership and be bound to them.

Limited partnership

The prospective owner who can afford the entire cost of an airplane but who wants to cut down indirect expenses such as insurance, maintenance, and tie-down fees has another alternative that is halfway between sole ownership and a true partnership. A limited partnership arrangement can be established where the owner retains full title but grants operating rights to a qualified partner in exchange for expense sharing.

One example of such an arrangement would work like this: The "limited" partner pays the owner half of the insurance costs, tie-down, and maintenance expenses as well as a set-aside fee toward major overhaul of the engine based on engine time and the cost of a major. In exchange for these payments, the partner receives the same rights to use the airplane as if it were actually owned by both pilots. If the owner's circumstances change, the arrangement can be terminated merely by making an equitable adjustment of shared expenses with the partner.

There are two basic advantages for an owner from such an arrangement. First, the indirect costs are split in half, making them considerably easier to bear. Second, utilization is increased, with only one other person of presumably known capabilities sharing the airplane. The advantage to the limited partner is also obvious—enjoying all the advantages of full partnership without the required capital investment. The arrangement can be very beneficial to both parties.

Special handling through a reputable insurance broker will be required to find an aviation insurer who will write a policy incorporating the specific terms required by this arrangement. The typical insurance company will define this type of partnership as "commercial rental," which carries a higher rate and will not adequately protect the partner. A specialized insurance policy can and should be obtained, stating that the partner, in addition to the owner, is covered by the policy to fly the airplane and that the insurance company waives its rights of subrogation against the partner if that person were involved in a crash.

Figure 2.1. Having a mechanic as your partner can be mutually beneficial.

This type of arrangement, like a conventional partnership, still requires considerable agreement between the owner and the second party. The arrangement works best if the participant really feels like a real partner. While the owner will have the final say in what type of aircraft is acquired and how it is equipped, mutual agreement should determine policies for scheduling, maintenance, and the like. These matters must be handled in exactly the same way as in a true partnership if the arrangement is to be successful.

Perhaps the ultimate arrangement is one where the limited partner is an airframe and powerplant (A&P) mechanic with access to maintenance facilities. In a typical case the owner pays for parts and avionics repairs and the mechanic-partner is responsible for the annual and unscheduled airframe and engine maintenance. Insurance and tie-down fees are still shared, and a set-aside toward a major overhaul is still maintained.

Many young A&P mechanics are also private pilots—but seldom in a financial position to buy an airplane—and would welcome an opportunity to have the ready access to one that this type of arrangement can provide. The owner receives the extra satisfaction of knowing that the mechanic, as a partner, has a reason for putting just a little extra effort into the airplane. It is a partnership arrangement that can be highly satisfying.

The limited partnership arrangement may seem like a short step away from allowing friends to use your airplane, and then paying your expenses. But lending your plane is a bad practice that should be avoided. Insurance is the major reason. Many standard aircraft insurance policies do not cover use for which any compensation is received. Even filling up the tanks after a flight may be considered a payment. And even if sharing expenses is allowed, the borrower may not be covered for hull damage unless the policy states that the person, by name, is granted a waiver of subrogation. Without such a waiver, the owner would be paid for any damage in the event of a crash, but the borrower-pilot could be sued by the insurance company for those damages. This, of course, assumes that in-flight hull coverage was in force. Any owner who lends an airplane without such coverage is a complete fool!

Flying clubs

Flying clubs (or aero clubs) range from small groups of individuals banded together in what is little more than an extended partnership, on up to organizations with several hundred members which rival and even surpass FBOs as combined flight school and aircraft rental organizations. In some cases, clubs are run as a part of an FBO, with renters trading off an initiation fee and monthly dues for lower per-hour rental costs.

The smallest flying clubs probably grew out of, or even are, partnerships. A typical situation may be one in which four individuals buy an aircraft in partnership and successfully operate it and maintain it for a number of years. At some point, however, the desire to move up is shared by the partners. But new airplanes, particularly well-equipped ones, are very expensive. Perhaps the idea begins to grow that with more partners, say four or even eight more, an IFR plane could be acquired and the present aircraft could have its engine overhauled and be retained as a VFR bird. The idea takes hold, becomes reality, and the four-member partnership is now a twelve-member club.

The idea of continued growth to more members and more aircraft is tantalizing. But it usually doesn't work. Scheduling the club aircraft, which formerly consisted of making a few phone calls among members, becomes a serious procedural chore when 20, 30, or even more people are involved. Four partners meeting on a sunny Saturday morning to wash and wax the bird was easy. Getting 20 members out to work on four or five airplanes is nearly impossible. Policy meetings that used to occur casually in one partner's den become formal and require renting a meeting room. And inevitably differences of opinions arise over a variety of issues—scheduling policy, the price of maintenance, who is or isn't contributing to do-it-yourself work parties. Large doesn't necessarily mean better in an informal flying club operation.

At the other end of the spectrum are the large flying clubs with 100, 200, or even more members and from a half-dozen airplanes to a dozen or more. These clubs are no longer participatory democracies. They are business organizations established to run a flight school and rent out aircraft, and they are run by one or more paid professionals who are literally and figuratively in charge. Whether they are member-owned, military, or FBO-connected, these clubs parallel FBOs in their operations, methods, and policies.

A good independent flying club will have a variety of aircraft available solely to club members. There will be no more than 10 to 12 members per plane. A sufficient range in the aircraft capabilities should be available to allow a member to choose anything from a two-seat VFR trainer to a modest four-place retractable IFR bird. The aircraft may all be from one manufacturer (to obtain the economies of maintenance compatibility) or from a variety of manufacturers to allow members to sample many different models. The club will usually have its own lounge, scheduling area, and manager's office, much like an FBO. It may combine flying with social functions such as fly-ins, hangar breakfasts, and flying poker rallies.

Ordinarily, a member joins a club by paying a onetime initiation fee. In many clubs this fee is like a share of stock which may be sold by the initial club member to another person, thus transferring club membership rights. The basic fee may entitle the member to fly basic two-seat trainers only. Additional assessments may have to be paid to obtain rights to larger and more complex types such as four-seat VFR aircraft, four-seat IFR birds, and 200-hp retractables. In addition to the initial fees, monthly dues must ordinarily be paid to retain membership rights. In exchange for these fees and dues, the member obtains the right to rent club aircraft at hourly rates typically 10 to 20 percent below FBO rental rates.

Whether it is more economical to rent from an FBO or through club membership depends on how many hours the pilot flies per month, how large the dues are, and how big the difference is between FBO and club rental rates for similar aircraft. (The initiation fee is assumed to be transferable and therefore not a factor in the rental cost.) Assume an FBO rents a four-seat aircraft for $100 per hour and an aero club with $100 per month dues rents the same type of aircraft for $75 per hour. Table 2.1 shows that a renter-pilot would be better off renting the aircraft from an FBO and paying no dues if flying only three hours per month. However, if the same pilot flies six hours per month, the per hour savings in rental cost are greater than the dues, and club flying is cheaper. It is apparent that a pilot flying infrequently or on very short flights may be better off sticking to rental from an FBO. A pilot who flies regularly or on long flights will probably be better off renting through an aero club.

Many FBOs originally felt that flying clubs were unfair competition, renting aircraft similar to their own fleet at prices well below any they could match. Eventually, FBOs began setting up club plans as an integral part of their operation. Just as for the independent flying clubs, members pay an initiation fee and then pay monthly fees to retain membership. Unlike the independent clubs, however, the FBO clubs are intended to be profit-making operations. The aircraft available are usually the same as the ones available for ordinary rentals. Social functions are seldom found in FBO clubs, which

Table 2.1. Aero Club vs. FBO Rental

Aero Club		FBO Rental	
3 hr./month @ $75/hr.	$225.00	3 hr./month @ $100/hr.	$300.00
Dues	$100.00		
	$325.00		$300.00
6 hr./month @ $75/hr.	$450.00	6 hr./month @ $100/hr.	$600.00
Dues	$100.00		
	$550.00		$600.00

in effect offer little more than a different type of rental arrangement. One additional function, however, may be to interest club members in the purchase of a used airplane. This of course can be a significant advantage to the prospective buyer as well as to the FBO. Having firsthand knowledge of an aircraft's maintenance history as well as individual handling peculiarities can be a definite asset to a pilot interested in purchasing it.

The use of the same aircraft for both club plan use and ordinary rentals could predispose an unscrupulous FBO to make planes available to ordinary renters rather than to club members in the event of a scheduling conflict between the two. The FBO already has the initiation fee and monthly dues of the club member and would be renting at a discount compared to what the nonclub pilot would pay. While giving priority to renter-pilots over club pilots as a regular policy would probably destroy the club in the long run, it would have obvious advantages to the FBO over a short period.

Military aero clubs

For active duty, ready reserve, and retired military personnel as well as civil service personnel working at military bases, military aero clubs offer another alternative to aircraft rentals from FBOs. Being based in military buildings, having low-interest or no-interest government loans available for aircraft acquisition, and being able to purchase avgas that is not subject to state and federal taxes, military aero clubs have a definite advantage in offering reasonably priced flying to members.

This low-cost flying does not come without a hidden price, however—living with the multitiered military bureaucracy that must be satisfied if the clubs are to exist. Military aero clubs must meet not only federal aviation regulations but also those of the particular service governing the club operation and very often, base or post regulations imposed by the local commander as well. Attendance at monthly safety meetings is mandatory. Night checkouts in aero club aircraft may take up to four hours. All aircraft checkouts make those conducted by most FBOs seem lax. Annual recertification rides, roughly equivalent to the FAA's biennial flight reviews, are required. Aero clubs are also subject to inspection by military teams, whose members often have little or no experience with the safe and economical operation of general aviation aircraft. Air Force aero clubs are particularly plagued by this problem—visiting inspection teams seem to believe that Cessna 152s and Piper Warriors should be operated and maintained in precisely the same manner as B-1Bs, C-5s, and F-15Es.

For a person familiar with the military way of life and tolerant of it, these aero clubs can offer a very reasonably priced alternative to civilian club and FBO flying. But it is also an alternative with inherent restrictions and frustrations unknown in civilian general aviation activities.

Fractional ownership

Fractional ownership has transformed the executive jet market, with far more companies buying shares of executive jets than ever owned and operated their own corporate aircraft. The idea of fractional ownership has trickled down to the light (but hardly inexpensive) single-engine general aviation market. It offers the alternative of new aircraft ownership to those who could afford to buy a good 20- to 25-year-old used aircraft outright, but who prefer to fly a new aircraft without coming up with two or three hundred thousand dollars. Like all other forms of aircraft ownership, fractional ownership has its advantages as well as its risks and disadvantages.

Two large organizations, OurPLANE (www.ourplane.com) and AirSharesElite (www.airshareselite.com), and other smaller FBO-based operations such as SharePlus (www.skyworksaviation.com) at Reid Hillview Airport in San Jose, California, have been leaders in offering fractional share ownership of single-engine aircraft. Typically, the fractional shares owner buys a one-eighth interest in an aircraft with a large up-front payment. There are also monthly management fees plus hourly fees for actual use of the aircraft.

OurPLANE and AirSharesElite both charge a high up-front buy-in fee of approximately $40,000 to $60,000 for a one-eighth share, plus a monthly fee of approximately $500 to $750 for insurance, hangar, GPS update, and management expenses. An hourly fee, which includes avgas, is also charged. For this investment, the fractional share owner gets to fly 75 to 100 hours per year.

OurPLANE was founded by a pair of Canadians in the Toronto area in 1998. In 2003 it offered shares in Cessna Skylanes, Piper Archer IIIs, and Cirrus SR20s and SR22s, with more than 80 owners flying over a dozen airplanes in Toronto and Vancouver, Canada; Oxford, Connecticut; San Diego and San Francisco in California; and Houston, Texas. In 2003 the company was also actively marketing shares in Los Angeles, California, and White Plains, New York (in the New York City area). OurPLANE may only have a single aircraft per location, and the location may be subject to change if a majority of the owners agree to moving the airplane. OurPLANE owners are not true owners, but their interest is protected by an FAA lien filed at buy-in.

In 2002 OurPLANE was charging an hourly wet rate of $116 per hour. If a fractional OurPLANE share owner flew 100 hours per year, the hourly cost would be $176 per hour, not counting interest or lost investment value of the $40,000 upfront fee. (Compare this to total indirect and direct operating expenses shown in Table 1.1 for operating an older $50,000 four-seat aircraft 100 hours of less than $100 per hour.) OurPLANE's ownership term is five years, at which time the aircraft is sold at market value and the proceeds are divided among the shareholders to cash out or to buy into a new aircraft. One potentially big advantage to OurPLANE owners is that an OurPLANE owner traveling to another OurPLANE location can fly the aircraft located there. Of course, it is only an advantage if you will be traveling to an OurPLANE location, but if the network grows so will the benefit.

AirSharesElite, the other large fractional ownership organization, specializes in the Cirrus SR22. Unlike OurPLANE, it strives to have a minimum of two aircraft and usually a small fleet at each location, offering greater availability as long as an owner doesn't insist on flying "his" or "her" own aircraft. AirSharesElite started in Atlanta, and in 2002 had expanded to Birmingham, Alabama; Chicago, Illinois; and White Plains, New York, and Caldwell, New Jersey, in the New York City area. The company plans to expand to a total of 20 locations. Unlike OurPLANE, AirSharesElite owners are real owners and their names appear on the aircrafts' titles. AirSharesElite shares are for 75 hours per year, and in 2003 AirSharesElite was charging an hourly wet rate of $60 per hour. If a fractional AirSharesElite share owner flew 75 hours per year, the hourly cost would be $135 per hour plus the monthly maintenance fee, not counting interest or lost investment value of the $60,000 upfront fee for a one-eighth share. This is closer to, but still more expensive than, the hourly cost of owning an older airplane, as shown in Table 1.1. AirSharesElite deals are for four-year terms, at which point the fractional share owners can cash out the value of their initial investment or roll it over into a new airplane, minus a 7 percent broker's fee retained by AirSharesElite.

The FAA published new regulations for Fractional Aircraft Ownership programs in 2003; the final rule took effect on November 17, 2003. Fortunately for light General Aviation, the FAA's definition of fractional ownership is aimed at the corporate jet programs. If trained flight crews aren't furnished in the package, you don't need to worry about the new rule. As far as the FAA is concerned, the AirSharesElite and OurPLANE programs aren't Fractional Aircraft Ownership programs, at least not as the FAA defines them.

The advantages of fractional ownership are that you get to fly a new airplane with the "smell of new" and the latest avionics. If you choose a plan with an aircraft like the Cirrus, you get the very latest in general aviation aircraft and not just a warmed-over older design. (Before you buy in, be sure to fly the Cirrus and see if you like it. You may just decide you like the way the warmed-over old designs like the Archer IIIs and the Skylanes fly better than the sleek new beauties.) You get to buy a realistic amount of time in the 50-, 75-, or 100-hour annual increments most pilots actually fly. The management organization takes care of annoying details individual owners have to deal with such as insurance, maintenance, hangaring, washing and cleaning the airplane, and nasty surprises like Airworthiness Directives. They also insulate you from having to deal directly with your partners. AirSharesElite and some of the others may also offer other nearly identical aircraft to fly if yours is down for maintenance or otherwise unavailable.

But there are also significant disadvantages. One is that you have to live near an airport where the fractional ownership airplanes are available. Like rental or club flying, there is likely to be limited availability on weekends and at other peak times. The biggest disadvantage is the expense. There is a high up-front buy-in fee plus high monthly fees. The cost per hour is definitely higher than the cost of flying an older aircraft you own or share with one or two other partners. And you also are relying on the stability of the fractional ownership management company. If the company goes out of business, you probably will get your buy-in fee back, but you will be back to looking for an airplane to fly.

Is fractional ownership for you? It may be if you can afford to buy and want to fly a new airplane, but can't justify paying a purchase price of two or three hundred thousand dollars or more to fly a limited number of hours per year. It also may be for you if you have the money to own an airplane and want a more exclusive arrangement than rental or flying clubs, but you don't want to be bothered with all the hassles that can be involved in owning and taking care of your own airplane. Just as with any aircraft purchase, you should also be sure to fly the type of aircraft you will be buying a share in before committing significant amounts of money. You don't want to put down $60,000 and then find out that you really don't like the Cirrus SR22. But if you really want to own your own airplane, fractional ownership is probably not the answer.

The average aspiring aircraft owner should wish the fractional ownership companies good fortune. With their policy of selling off their aircraft and buying new ones every four to five years, they are helping assure the long-term availability of good used aircraft.

Leasebacks

Leasebacks are seen by some pilots as an easy means of acquiring a good, late-model airplane at little or no cost. Like Santa Claus and the Tooth Fairy, the idea makes a nice story, but the average pilot with dreams of personally owning an airplane might just as well depend on one of those two fictional characters.

In theory the leaseback owner provides capital that is invested in the new aircraft. The FBO, through rentals, provides the owner with a revenue-producing means of offsetting the cost of the purchase and operating expenses. In the rose-colored glasses of theory, the FBO has a new airplane to use for two or three years (the length of the leaseback agreement) without large capital investment, and the owner derives income to pay all the expenses for that time, eventually resulting in sole ownership of a nearly paid-off, late-model airplane. Unfortunately, in real life the leaseback is a risky arrangement for the owner, who must continue to make payments whether any income is produced or not. Furthermore, the Tax Reform Act of 1986 ended the practice of writing off leaseback losses against all of the owner's other sources of income. This had been the primary advantage of the arrangement for airplane lovers with excess income to shelter from taxes. Leasebacks are not the golden path to aircraft ownership for the average pilot, but they could very easily be the road to financial ruin.

Let's look at two possible arrangements to illustrate how leasebacks work.

The first type of leaseback arrangement is one in which the FBO is responsible for most of the costs of aircraft operation and maintenance. The FBO's relatively small payments to the aircraft owner are offset by a smaller percentage of expenses for which the aircraft owner is responsible. With this type of arrangement, the owner's payments are limited to making payments on the aircraft, paying for half of the insurance, and some unscheduled maintenance. The FBO is responsible for the potentially costly 100-hour and annual inspections and other routine maintenance; half of the insurance; and fuel, oil, and tie-down fees.

For an aircraft renting for $120 from the FBO, the owner may receive only one-third, or $40. If the owner has yearly airplane loan payments of $30,000 per year for five years, and the owner's half of a $5,000 annual insurance bill is $2,500, the owner's annual expenses will be $32,500 per year plus any unscheduled maintenance charges. With an hourly income of $40 per hour, the aircraft will have to be rented out for more than 800 hours per year, or nearly 70 hours per month, for the owner to break even on income versus outgo. And this figure does not include a set-aside for major overhaul, which would be an additional expense for the prudent owner who intends to keep the airplane after termination of the leaseback arrangement.

This arrangement benefits the owner in that it is to the FBO's advantage to keep down the costs of 100-hour and annual inspections. The downside of the arrangement is that the FBO may skimp and take undesirable shortcuts with such scheduled maintenance, and may limit the inspections to the minimum work required and not bother to fix small problems that are found.

The second and more typical leaseback arrangement requires the owner to provide for nearly all expenses, including insurance, all maintenance (including 100-hour and annual inspections), fuel and oil, and tie-down fees. The FBO in effect acts as a rental agent, taking 20 to 25 percent of the hourly rental rate and giving the owner 75 to 80 percent. An example of typical yearly costs for such an arrangement is shown in the following cost summary, based on an assumed rental price of $120 per hour with 80 percent going to the owner, and an assumed annual income from 600 flying hours per year used for fuel, oil, and 100-hour inspection estimates.

Aircraft payments	$30,000
Insurance	5,000
Annual inspection	2,500
100-hour inspections (5 × $750)	3,750
Gasoline ($2.50/gal, 10 gal/hr)	15,000
Tie-down ($75/mo)	900
Total Expenses	$57,150
Annual income from 600-hour operation at $96/hr:	$57,600

Although this arrangement looks promising, the owner is vulnerable to "getting the shaft" from the FBO. While the owner is responsible for the maintenance and seemingly in control of maintenance expenses, in reality it is not unusual for the FBO to require that maintenance be done in their maintenance shop. Under this type of arrangement, the owner could be overcharged for parts and labor, have unnecessary or unauthorized work performed, or be charged for work not accomplished. In many instances, supposedly in the interests of efficiency (keeping the plane on the line and in the air), maintenance will be performed by the FBO without the explicit authorization of the owner, despite prior agreements requiring such an authorization before work is performed. If the owner is required to have the work performed at the FBO's shop, he or she really has no control over maintenance expenses. And to make matters worse, since the FBO is making money on the maintenance, it has no incentive to assure that the airplane is not abused or rented to unqualified pilots.

It is obvious that with either arrangement, it is crucial to find a scrupulously honest FBO. In a business where all too many FBOs come and go, or die and get resurrected with new names every year or two, this will be very difficult to do.

So let's say that you've found the ideal airplane, the ideal deal, and a squeaky clean FBO that's been in business at the same field for twenty years. Why not give it a try? The major problem is that the owner needs to have money coming in from rental of the airplane, with nearly 50 hours per month required just to break even. There is no guarantee that the airplane will fly even 40 hours per month, let alone 50 hours or more. Many problems can conspire to ground your plane or severely limit the number of hours it flies—bad weather, unscheduled maintenance tying up your aircraft for unexpectedly long periods, an accident causing damage that takes time to fix, financial or administrative problems with the FBO or its instructor staff, a drop in the local or national economy, or some seemingly irrational directive from the TSA grounding all the aircraft at your airport for some period of time.

Another fact of life which the owner should be aware of is that the airplane may have a limited useful life of only two to three years on the typical FBO rental line. Even if the FBO is willing to keep the aircraft on the line for a longer period, fickle renter-pilots are likely to desert an older aircraft for similar new, zero-timed, or even repainted and refurbished models that other leaseback owners have provided. This will mean reduced rental hours and thus reduced income from your no-longer-new-looking bird. Of course there are some exceptions to the rule. If your airplane is unique on the line and remains so (such as a Waco aerobatic biplane, a Lake amphibian, or even the only IFR trainer or twin), your rental income may not necessarily decrease as the plane ages. But if your airplane is a VFR Skyhawk or Archer, you had better count on it!

Before the Tax Reform Act of 1986, it was possible to offset significant losses from a leaseback by write-offs against an owner's entire taxable income. This could then be depended on to lower federal taxes by a sufficient amount to offset any expenses involved in the leaseback which were not covered by income from rental of the aircraft. Depreciation of a new aircraft could be counted on to provide substantial, deductible tax losses. A wealthy leaseback owner paying taxes in a 50-percent tax bracket could do very well indeed, converting a losing proposition into a winning one.

But today, leaseback losses are defined as "passive losses," which cannot be written off against earned income or portfolio income from stocks, bonds, or savings accounts. Leaseback losses can only be written off against gains from other "passive" activities. But one thing hasn't really changed at all: leasebacks can still be a money-making proposition for those who have money, and are likely to be a losing proposition for those who don't.

Leasebacks are somewhat like investments in the stock market. The financial risk involved in such an arrangement is sufficiently high that the only money a person should invest is money he or she can afford to lose. And like the stock market, those who already have money are those most likely to make money.

One last caution—if you get involved in a leaseback, don't fall in love with the airplane. If you want pride of ownership and a machine with a personality to love, don't try to find it in an aircraft that will be subject to abuse by uncaring strangers. And a successful leaseback aircraft with a lot of rental hours will be getting lots of opportunity for renter abuse! While it is on leaseback, it is a piece of business machinery, no more or no less.

Is a leaseback arrangement a good way to buy an airplane? Perhaps it can be if you can already afford to buy the airplane without the arrangement and if you can coldheartedly look at the airplane as nothing more than another business asset. But for the average pilot-owner or for any pilot-owner who loves his or her airplane? Definitely not!

Selecting a
home field

3

One step of great importance when becoming an airplane owner, almost totally ignored in aviation books and magazine articles on aircraft ownership, is the selection of a home field and maintenance facility.

Important considerations

Almost all prospective owners know that it is good common sense to have a mechanic check over any airplane they are interested in before purchasing it. But how many personally know a mechanic? How many know what maintenance facility will perform the inspection? If the airplane is purchased, where will it be hangared or tied down? One thing that would certainly wipe out the warm glow of a brand-new, first-time owner would be to find out upon landing at the intended home field that there is a waiting list for tie-downs. So how do you go about selecting a home field?

DRIVING DISTANCE. The most obvious consideration in selecting a home field is to pick one within a reasonable driving distance for you and any partners. But the nearest may not be the best airfield for you. If the nearest airfield is also the only one within 50 miles, the selection process is probably totally irrelevant. Most major metropolitan areas will have several large and small airports within a 20-mile radius. But in smaller towns or rural areas there may be only a single airfield located within a reasonable driving radius.

FIELD CHARACTERISTICS. The field must be suited to your aircraft. A short grass strip may be ideal for a Piper J-3 Cub being flown by a single pilot. A Piper Cherokee, if it succeeded in landing in that same field, might not be successful in taking off. Gravel strips may be suitable for high-wing tail-draggers but may result in nicked props and dented flaps for low-wing tri-cycle gear aircraft. And the field should also be suited to your flying needs and capabilities. If despite long hours of practice, your crosswind landing technique still leaves something to be desired, the small airport with a narrow runway may not be for you. If you live in an area where IFR conditions are not an unusual occurrence and you intend to rely on your airplane for dependable transportation, you are probably better off basing it at a larger tower-controlled field with a variety of instrument approaches available than at an uncontrolled airfield with one nondirectional beacon (NDB) approach (although GPS overlay approaches have improved the situation at many airports which had only a VOR or NDB approach in the past).

TIE-DOWN OR HANGAR SPACE. Availability and price of tie-downs or hangar space must be considered. In some areas, particularly near major western cities, there may be as much as a six-month waiting list for tie-down spaces.

Figure 3.1. Large fields offer more services but with a bigger price tag attached.

Prices for light, single-engine aircraft start as low as $50 per month for grass tie-down spots at small rural strips and go up to as much as $125 a month for hard-surface locations at major general aviation airports near large cities.

Hangar rent may run anywhere from $75 per month for an unheated T-hangar with a dirt floor at an uncontrolled field to over $250 per month for a single-engine aircraft in a heated hangar at a larger controlled field. If you are considering keeping your airplane in a large heated hangar where it will be one of many, you should also determine the size of the service fee to have your plane pulled in or out of the hangar for you. It could be very frustrating to jockey your airplane around several others in the hangar every time you want to use it, particularly if the others are large and difficult to move.

CLASS B, C, AND D AIRSPACE. The location of the airport in relation to Class B airspace (formerly known as Terminal Control Areas or TCAs), Class C airspace (formerly known as Airport Radar Service Areas or ARSAs), and Class D airspace (airports with control towers) may affect your decision on where to base your aircraft. If you have a classic J-3 Cub which has no electrical system, you may not want to have to install a transponder with an altitude encoder, required below Class B airspace floors or to enter or exit Class C airspace. A field farther from a major metropolitan area may be a better choice, if you have the option. Sometimes small uncontrolled fields lie on the edge of a larger controlled field's airport traffic area, constraining the possible approaches to the smaller field. Check carefully the location and airspace limitations of an airport when considering it as a home field.

COLD-WEATHER SERVICES. If you live in an area where winter snows and cold temperatures are a way of life, determine what cold-weather services are available at your prospective home field and how much they cost. These services include clearing snow from your tie-down, engine preheat, jump starts, electricity available at tie-downs for engine heaters, and short-term hangaring to melt ice and snow off the wings and control surfaces. If possible, talk to pilots who have flown out of the field during the winter months to determine how effectively the airport operator's snow removal plan is implemented.

If you are considering keeping your plane at a grass strip or on a grass tie-down, you should be aware that generally solid surfaces can become a sea of viscous mud in a spring thaw or during prolonged spring or summer rains.

Figure 3.2. The small field has a distinctive personality at a lower price.

MAINTENANCE AVAILABILITY. Maintenance capabilities are another important consideration in choosing a home field. Larger controlled fields will usually have one or more good facilities for aircraft and engine repairs. There will usually be an avionics installation and repair shop available as well. However, labor rates at the larger fields are usually higher to cover the greater overhead costs that these maintenance shops must pay. Maintenance facilities at small uncontrolled fields may be limited to a simple one-mechanic operation located in a small hangar. Labor rates, reflecting lower overhead, are likely to be less at the smaller airport maintenance shops.

Specialized skills such as woodworking or fabric covering are also more likely to be found at small airports, where craftsmanship in a variety of areas may still be considered more important than the speed and efficiency of an FBO maintenance facility at a larger airport. If you are considering the purchase of an old wooden-wing or fabric-covered aircraft, this could be a crucial consideration.

Maintenance shops at large metropolitan airports seldom have the capability or inclination to do fabric or wood work. These shops, geared to working on Cessna, Piper, Beechcraft, or Mooney aluminum construction, are often high-overhead, high-volume operations similar in management philosophy to Ford, Chevrolet, or Toyota auto dealerships. No time can be spared for teaching young mechanics low-priority, low-volume finer points like fabric work. And young mechanics are not sufficiently trained in fabric and wood techniques in school. An instructor at a large northeastern mechanics school put it this way: "These kids only get three weeks of fabric and wood techniques in a year-and-a-half course of study. That just isn't enough to make them any good at it." A rookie needs a period of apprenticeship with an older mechanic as a mentor, a real hands-on experience, to learn the art of wood and fabric work. And usually this can happen only at small airfields.

How can you tell if the maintenance shop at your intended home base has mechanics who are capable in the "lost arts" of wood and fabric? One tip-off is the number of fabric-covered aircraft at the field. If there are a lot of old Cubs, Taylorcrafts, and Champs around, odds are that somebody there knows how to care for them. If you want to be sure, talk to other aircraft owners as well as the mechanic at the field.

You should also investigate shop and airport policy regarding owner-performed maintenance. At some facilities, pilot-performed maintenance is encouraged, with hangar space and A&P mechanic supervision provided for a reasonable fee. At other fields, any maintenance activities by the owner, including oil changes at the tie-down, are strictly prohibited. If you are mechanically inclined and expect to reduce your expenses by doing as much owner-performed maintenance as regulations allow, you should be assured that the field where you base your airplane and the mechanic who will be signing off on the maintenance will encourage or at least tolerate your efforts.

Another interesting challenge may be to find mechanics capable of repairing composite aircraft with fully integrated avionics including certificated production aircraft like the Cirrus, Lancair, and Diamonds, or sleek homebuilts that are also available.

If your airplane is a type still in production, it will also be to your advantage to base it at a field that has a dealer affiliated with the make you own. Availability of parts and a mechanic knowledgeable in your plane's oddities will make maintenance a more tolerable experience. A truly forlorn pilot is one who tries to get his Piper Cherokee fixed at a small field where 80 percent of the aircraft are Cessnas (and the rest are an odd conglomeration of everything except Pipers)!

FUEL AVAILABILITY. Availability of the appropriate fuel for your airplane is another critical factor to be considered. Both Continental and Lycoming have acknowledged that 100-octane, low-lead gasoline causes frequent spark plug fouling as well as the erosion of or lead buildup on valves and valve seats of engines designed for use with 80/87-octane aviation gasoline.

Relatively few aircraft built before 1975 which are within the price range of the average pilot-owner have engines built to use 100-octane gasoline. Therefore, the availability of 80/87 avgas or autogas on the field, or the ability to freely transport autogas to an aircraft on the field, can be a serious concern.

The Continental O-200 engines used in Cessna 150s and the Continental O-300 engines used in some Temco Swifts, Cessna 170s, and older 172s are particularly susceptible to these problems. Smaller Continental engines including 65-, 85-, and 90-hp engines powering Ercoupes, Luscombes, Cessna 120s and 140s, Aeroncas, and Taylorcrafts are also susceptible. Lycoming engines designed for 80/87-octane use, if operated with proper leaning techniques, appear less susceptible to 100LL problems than the small Continentals, but they are still unable to match the excellent maintenance records of which they were capable if used solely with 80/87-octane gasoline. Grumman-American Tr-2s and Travelers; 1968-1976 Cessna 172s; Beechcraft Musketeers and Sports; and Piper Tri-Pacers, Colts, Cherokee 140s, 150s, 235s, and 151 Warriors are powered by Lycoming engines designed for 80/87-octane operation. Larger Continental engines designed for 80/87-octane operation, like the O-470 engines used in aircraft like pre-1976 Cessna 182s and early Beechcraft Debonairs and Bonanzas, also perform better on 80/87 than on 100LL.

Fortunately, with 80/87-octane avgas becoming extinct, autogas STCs are available from the EAA and Petersen Aviation for nearly all aircraft with engines designed for 80/87-octane avgas and for many with 91/93 rated engines. Not all FBOs carry autogas, however, and not all airport operators will allow the private owner to bring autogas to the aircraft from ordinary gas stations without severe restrictions. While anyone transporting gasoline should do so with great care, municipal airport authorities in particular may be so rigorous in enforcing fire prevention codes as to make it totally impractical for you to transport gasoline from an off-airport service station to your aircraft. If you are going to own and operate an aircraft with an engine designed to use 80/87-octane avgas, availability of autogas should certainly be a key criteria in selecting a home field.

A French company, SMA, is leading other aircraft engine manufacturers in developing and certificating a practical aerodiesel engine. The SMA SR305 produces a maximum of 230 horsepower, and a 300-hp engine was in development in 2003. The company is aiming at the retrofit market with the engine intended for use in Cessna 182s and other production aircraft. Owners of aircraft with these engines, which use Jet A rather than avgas, will have to base their aircraft at medium- and large-size airports capable of supporting and servicing jets or will have to carry diesel fuel to the airport. They are likely to be unable to refuel at smaller general aviation airports too small for jet operations.

TAXES. State and local taxes may also have a bearing on where you will want to base your airplane. States, or even counties and localities within a state, may have significantly differing policies on taxes on private aircraft. For anyone who lives near state or municipal boundaries, it may be possible to save a significant amount of money every year by basing your plane at an airport in the state or municipality with the most reasonable tax structure. In many instances, these taxes will be determined by where the aircraft is based rather than where the owner resides.

Military fields

For active duty, ready reserve (including National Guard), or retired military personnel, another attractive option may be military fields that have active aero clubs. At many of these facilities, club members who own private aircraft are allowed to keep them at club tie-downs and to use the military facility as their home field. Only a nominal charge is ordinarily made beyond the normal club initiation fees and dues. The most significant advantage to basing the aircraft on a military facility is that maintenance can usually be performed by the owner under the direction of the club mechanic or can be done directly by the mechanic in the club's maintenance shop. (The private owner, however, must pay the mechanic directly for his or her time.) The possibility of having maintenance performed at the aero club facility, however, is largely dependent on the willingness of the mechanic. The aero club, justifiably, will insist that any work the mechanic performs on a member's private aircraft be done only after all work on the club fleet is complete.

There are certain drawbacks to keeping a privately owned aircraft at a military facility. Any time the plane is on the base or in the airspace controlled by it, the member must abide not only by FAA regulations but also by explicit regulations of the military service and even by the distinct wishes and desires of the base or post commander as expressed verbally or in local regulations or policy letters. Also, be aware that military alerts or exercises might close the field with little or no warning, making it impossible to take your plane out or bring it back in until the alert or exercise is over. If you are a commercial pilot, the aero club may ask you to volunteer to act as a clearance official on weekends or holidays when the regular manager is not on duty. Liability insurance in excess of that which the average private owner might carry will be required, and agreements must be signed releasing the military service from all liability incurred in connection with the owner's use of the military facility. Another serious drawback is that it may be impossible to buy parts, gasoline, or even oil through military or aero club supply channels.

Despite the problems and limitations of military basing, prospective owners who are presently associated with the military or compatible with that way of life should look into the possibilities of basing their aircraft at a military aero club. For a civilian with skills desired by Reserve or National Guard units, participation in a military reserve program could not only provide access to aero club facilities but also provide a part-time job bringing in additional income to support the expensive aerial habit. For the prospective owner living near a military base, the combined advantages of low-cost basing and maintenance and income from participation in a military reserve unit could make the difference between aircraft ownership being a reality or an idle dream. But be sure to remember the lesson taught by Desert Storm, Afghanistan, and Operation Iraqi Freedom. When you join the Reserves or the National Guard, you are ultimately agreeing to fight and die for your country.

The final choice

You have narrowed the selection of a home field to two or three possibilities based on objective factors such as runway length, distance from your home, and tie-down availability and price. It is time to make your choice based on intangibles. Spend time around possible home airfields and get to know some of the people who hang around, including FBO personnel and other pilot-owners. While large airports are often coldly impersonal, small fields usually are more intimate. Some small fields are friendly, but others take their personality from an "in" crowd that is not receptive immediately to newcomers.

Keep in mind that not all your time around the airport will be spent actually engaged in real, "in-the-air" flying activities. "Hangar flying," that glorious pastime in which pilots engage in the aeronautical version of telling traditional American tall tales, is one of the benefits of being a pilot. An airport with a lounge equipped with well-worn furniture and a welcome, friendly look can be much more satisfying than a mega-FBO's plush but coldly impersonal, all-business, high-efficiency corporate jet-jock lounge.

Try to get to know the mechanics at the field. Approach them to make arrangements for inspecting the airplane you are considering purchasing and ask for their advice. Remember, though, that the time the mechanic takes to talk to you is interrupting his or her work. Offer to buy coffee or some donuts at the morning break or extend an invitation to have lunch or dinner. Remember to approach the mechanic with humility. Whether you are a doctor or a lawyer or a janitor, you need the mechanic's service. The mechanic doesn't need yours! Keep in mind that these people are probably in the business of repairing small airplanes because they love the work. Any good mechanic could probably earn considerably more money working for the airlines or a corporate flight department or even repairing upscale automobiles. The mechanic is going to be independent, so respect this independence! Establish a good working relationship from the beginning and your future problems won't seem so great. Make an enemy of the same mechanic, and you might as well look for another home field.

If you have any doubts about your ability to handle specific conditions at a prospective home field, take a dual ride in an airplane similar to the one you intend to purchase. Go when field conditions are less than ideal. Find out ahead of time whether the field is too short on a hot day, or too narrow in a crosswind, or too turbulent when the winds are strong and gusty. You may change your mind not only about the home field but also about the airplane you want to buy!

When you make your final decision, it is a good idea to arrange as soon as possible with the FBO for basing your airplane at the field. While it may seem strange to be contracting for a tie-down before you own a plane, it is much better to pay a month's fee for an empty spot than to be shut out of the field when you finally complete the purchase arrangements. If the field you desire has a waiting list, enter your name as soon as possible. With luck, an opening may be available by the time you take delivery of your airplane. Firm arrangements should also be made with the local maintenance facility for the inspection of the aircraft you are considering.

Anyone who intends to base an airplane at a military facility should also be aware that it could be as long as two or three months after purchase before the plane is actually allowed on the field. Ordinarily, a request must be approved by the facility commander and proof of insurance is generally part of the package. This also effectively rules out pre-purchase inspection by the aero club mechanic at the club maintenance facilities on the base. Therefore, anyone who intends to keep an airplane at a military facility should also plan to base it at a civilian field for the first two or three months of ownership and have any pre-purchase inspections performed at the civilian field as well.

Selecting your airplane

4

The decisive moment has arrived. It is time to locate the airplane. You (and your partner or partners) have defined what you will be looking for, taking into account number of seats, range, speed, maintainability, and preference for high or low wings. You have decided how much you can afford, allowing 10 percent of the purchase price for first-year maintenance and modifications if you're buying a used airplane. And you have selected a home field where you will base the bird and have it checked out with your interests in mind before you buy it.

Where do you look for a really good used airplane?

Now you have a mental picture of your dream aircraft. If it's your first airplane, it probably won't be new, but it will be very special to you. You are already having trouble sleeping because of the anticipation and excitement of the decision you've made to really do it! But how are you going to locate it?

THE LOCAL SCENE. Don't overlook the obvious! Even in the Internet age the old fashioned ways may still find you your dream plane. Bulletin boards at your home field and at airports in your local flying area will be filled with notices about a variety of used aircraft for sale. And almost all of them will be located nearby. Some will be real dogs. Many will be old, out-of-production types that have seen better days. Ragwings and trainers will abound and may be a good choice if adequate maintenance and parts are readily available in your area. Maybe, just maybe, you will find the plane of your dreams right under your nose! If you rent airplanes for short weekend flights, make a habit of stopping at one or more different airports each weekend. Strike up conversations with other pilots at airport snack bars and ask if they know of any airplanes for sale that may meet your needs. If you have a specific make and model in mind, make up your own 3x5 cards with a description of exactly what you want and the price range you are willing to consider. Put your cards on the airport bulletin boards and leave them with FBOs in your area. You may not find your dream plane this way, but for the small time and effort involved it would be a shame not to try a quick search of your own backyard!

AVIATION PUBLICATIONS AND WEBSITES. Like most aircraft buyers (or, for that matter, car or boat buyers), when you have been bitten by the bug, you will not be satisfied until you have found that fantastic first airplane. Against all common sense and your better judgment you will want the airplane soon, if not now! Your frantic search of a variety of aviation advertising publications and Web sites will be under way.

More than half a dozen aviation advertising publications exist. Some have been around a long time or are owned by big publishers, like the *Controller*, while others may be a neat, new idea that won't be around a year from now. Some are aimed primarily at the corporate high rollers, advertising primarily jets and turboprops and top-of-the-line singles, while others are more attuned to typical flight schools and individual private owners. Almost all aviation advertising publications now have Web sites with information on the same aircraft that are advertised for sale in their publications. The *Controller*'s Web site (www.controller.com), for example, has an excellent database of aircraft. The *Controller*'s database is slanted toward the high-priced side of the market, and you will have to search through aircraft from all over the country.

While most print publications list a subscription price, several are provided free to current aircraft owners and are available to serious buyers for the asking. Any prospective aircraft buyer should inquire about a free subscription to these publications, or at least a free complimentary copy, before sending in any money. Also check online to see if you need to subscribe to the print publication to have access to their Web site.

Trade-A-Plane (www.trade-a-plane.com), published on yellow paper in a tabloid format, is the Old Faithful of used aircraft advertising publications. Covering the entire nation, *Trade-A-Plane* has enough aircraft advertised to give even the most avid searcher eyestrain, particularly when seeking the gems embedded in the seemingly endless columns of small-print classified ads. Of course, now with a subscription you also get access to the *Trade-A-Plane* Web site so you can also spend hours staring at your computer screen.

Trade-A-Plane ads can serve a very useful function for the buyer who is willing to expend some effort charting prices. Realistic price ranges for the desired aircraft can be found by rigorously reviewing the classifieds and listing or even graphing prices and years. The prices listed for any given airplanes range from very low-priced, high-time VFR dogs to high-priced, newly majored or low-time, always-hangared IFR beauties. Blue book prices may be fine for dealers, but you will be better off charting asking prices in *Trade-A-Plane*. These are the prices being asked for real, not "average," airplanes. The publication is also a national clearinghouse for all manner of aircraft-related goods and services. Parts, accessories, instruments, overhauls— all these and more are in *Trade-A-Plane*. Any prospective owner will spend worthwhile hours becoming familiar with the invaluable wealth of information in this paper.

The primary drawback of *Trade-A-Plane* for the aircraft buyer is its coverage of the entire United States in a single edition. The first-time owner should probably limit the hunting grounds to a realistic search radius of 500 miles, which is the maximum distance that could easily be covered in a one-day round trip in a borrowed or rented club or FBO aircraft, or that could reasonably be driven in a weekend. A bargain 2,000 miles from home may not seem like such a find after adding on the costs of an airline ticket, rental car, motel, meals, and even lost work time needed to inspect it. If the "real find" turns out to be a dog, congratulations! You have just spent nearly a thousand dollars for nothing. So probably three-fourths of all the ads in *Trade-A-Plane* (and other national advertising publications) are nearly worthless, unless you are looking for a Beech Staggerwing or one of Pappy Boyington's Corsairs and are willing to go anywhere to get it. To help locate aircraft that are not unrealistically far away, the intrepid explorer of *Trade-A-Plane* should keep the national map of telephone area codes (found in the front of most phone books) handy, because most of the classified ads will give a telephone number but may not include an address. If you don't need the national map, *Trade-A-Plane* includes a list of telephone area codes near the front of the classified listings.

Regionally oriented publications offer the advantage of limiting the search to a reasonable distance. Publications which contain both dealers' display ads and private-owner classifieds are the most valuable, allowing the buyer to compare dealer versus private-owner asking prices. They also allow the owner to find out quickly and easily what is available within the recommended 500 miles from home. Regional aviation newspapers usually contain both dealer and private-owner classifieds. The *Pacific Flyer* (www.pacificflyer.com) is a monthly aviation newspaper covering the Pacific coast, while its northeastern clone, the *Atlantic Flyer* (www.aflyer.com) covers the East coast with an emphasis on New England and the northeast. Prospective buyers in New England and the middle Atlantic states also have another good monthly magazine/advertising publication in the *Aviation Digest* (www.avdigest.net). The *Atlantic Flyer*, the *Pacific Flyer*, and the *Aviation Digest* all offer the bonus of aviation articles and stories which are interesting and informative but which would never see the light of day in the slick, glossy national magazines with their paid staff writers. A national aviation newspaper, also offering good aviation articles in addition to advertising, is *GA* (General Aviation) *News*. *GA News* has a pink classifieds section in the middle of the paper. It also has a good Web site (www.GeneralAviationNews.com) with aviation classified ads, allowing searches by single-engine or multi-engine and by manufacturer.

Most aviation trade publications, particularly in the central, southern, and western United States, are oriented almost exclusively to dealer ads, with few or no private-owner classifieds. Included in this category are the *Controller*, available in eastern, central, and western editions, and the slick and colorful *A/C Flyer* (www.aircraftbuyer.com), aimed at the top of the market anywhere in the country. Most of these publications are of little value to average first-time airplane buyers, except for daydreaming. The more affluent aircraft buyer, including small business owners looking for an owner-flown, high-performance retractable single or twin, should definitely not overlook these sources. One odd exception is the *AeroTrader* (www.aerotrader.com), available monthly at convenience stores for $3.99. *AeroTrader* is chock-full of classified and dealer ads from all over the country. Unlike most aviation advertising publications which have Web sites often as good or better than the print publication, the *AeroTrader* Web site is noticeably inferior to the print version.

There are also a handful of Web sites with airplane classified ads which are not directly connected to any print publication. The best of these is Aircraft Shopper Online (www.aso.com), which allows you to select from an extensive list of different aircraft so you don't have to look through a lot of listings you aren't interested in. The excellent aviation Web publication AvWeb also has an excellent aircraft classifieds section online, although you will have to go through an annoying (although free) sign-up procedure to obtain access. The Aircraft Owners and Pilots Association Web site (www.aopa.org) also includes aircraft classifieds, but their format presents all available aircraft in a single large listing, forcing you to search through the entire set of listings for the aircraft you are interested in.

SCANNING THE ADS. As a serious prospective buyer, you should obtain sample copies of all available aircraft advertising publications and subscribe to those best suited to your home region. You should also have a list of Web sites for the publications and subscribe to those that require subscriptions. Plans should be formulated for inspection trips. Finances should be put in order, and sufficient funds should be made available to provide an immediate down payment when you are ready to buy. If you plan to have the airplane inspected at your home field, you should let the mechanic know that you will be seriously looking for a plane. (The mechanic has heard many people daydreaming out loud, so let him or her know you are serious.)

Your print media search should move into high gear early in the month when the advertising publications arrive. Your online search of Web sites can literally begin anytime, although some of the databases may be updated in conjunction with the associated print publication. As you go through the ads, list all aircraft that meet your requirements within your price range. Based on the limited information in the ads, rate those available on how well they meet your specifications.

Desirable aircraft may be sold within days of being advertised. As a general rule, the serious buyer should be prepared to make a move as soon as the advertisement appears. You should already know what you want. If you don't, you are not yet a serious buyer. You are, however, a good candidate for somebody looking for a sucker to buy their semi-airworthy 1947 SuperWingwalker Special or that "bargain twin" with the worn-out engines that will cost twice the asking price of the airplane to replace! Aircraft spotted on a bulletin board or from an FBO's flight line may not require quite as fast a response, because the number of potential buyers who know about it will not be as great. However, a good deal won't last forever. If you found out about it, somebody else will, too.

The first phone call

Few, if any, ads will contain even half the information you will need to decide whether a particular used airplane is even worth looking at. The next step is to make a telephone call or e-mail request to get a better description of the plane being sold. You should have a checklist developed before you make any phone calls or send out any e-mail requests to ensure that you obtain all the information you need, keep your phone bill from reaching astronomical proportions, or have to keep bugging the prospective seller with repeated e-mails. Questions you should ask include:

- Total time—airframe and engine
- Time since major overhaul, if done
  - Number of times the engine has been overhauled, if known
  - Was the overhaul performed to factory-new tolerances or service-limit (minimum acceptable) tolerances?
  - Shop at which the overhaul was performed
  - Chrome rebuilt cylinders?
  - New cylinders?
- Time since top overhaul, if done
  - Shop at which the overhaul was performed
  - Chrome cylinders?
  - New cylinders?
- Compression reading for each cylinder at last annual or at any more recent compression check
- Time since prop overhaul (constant-speed props)
- Time since turbocharger overhaul or replacement (if applicable)
- Are all Airworthiness Directives complied with?
  - If not, which ones? Why not?
- Does the aircraft have any major or minor damage history?
- Description of avionics
  - If there is a panel mount GPS, is it IFR enroute and approach certified? WAAS capable?
- Condition of fabric (if applicable)
  - Type of fabric
  - Date and reading of latest fabric strength test
  - Date of last re-covering
- Date of last annual
  - Where was last annual performed?
- Date of last static/altimeter check (IFR only)
- Date of last transponder check
- Special features or options
- Known defects or anomalies, if any
- Overall interior and exterior appearance
- Price

Inspecting the candidates

The information obtained in phone calls or e-mail will be most useful in eliminating any unacceptable aircraft from consideration. While you should be quick to act in seeking out and purchasing the airplane you want, at the same time you should be patient and not be hurried into buying one that is marginal or undesirable. Eliminate these from your list as soon as possible, then forget them completely! After you have crossed off the undesirables, you should again rate the remaining candidates. Arrangements should be made to inspect the planes remaining on your list and, if possible, to fly them and review their logbooks. (Difficulty in traveling to an inspection will probably be a criterion for deciding which of two otherwise equally desirable airplanes is best for you.)

If the airplane is being sold privately, it should be possible to convince the owner to fly it to your home field for inspection by you and your mechanic. Refusal to do so might even be considered a reason to doubt the desirability of the airplane, particularly if you offer to top the tanks or at least contribute to the fuel costs incurred in making the flight (which you should). If the owner won't fly it to you, why not? Is the capability of the airplane questionable? (Here again, however, is another reason to limit your search radius to one day's reasonable flying distance. You shouldn't fault a Cessna 150 or Tomahawk owner for not wanting to fly halfway across the country just to show the airplane to a possible buyer!) You should also make arrangements with your local mechanic to assist in inspecting the aircraft and the logbooks, and the seller should be advised that a mechanic will be participating in the inspection. Any reluctance on the seller's part to allow a mechanic to inspect the aircraft and the logbooks should be viewed with deep suspicion!

If the aircraft is being sold by a dealer (generally an FBO), you will probably have to go to the dealer's field to inspect the plane, unless the aircraft you are interested in is a new or high-performance late model aircraft. While the purchase of a used airplane that costs $40,000 is no small matter to you, the profit to be made on that amount may not allow a dealer sufficient margin to spend the time and money required to show it to you at your home field. And you should realize that any money such as travel expenses that the dealer incurs to show the airplane will reduce your bargaining power if you decide to buy it. A reputable dealer is not going to take a loss on a good airplane and will go just so far in meeting your demands when it comes time to complete the sale.

You may also find that a dealer may be almost totally unwilling to bargain with you if other potential buyers have expressed a strong interest in the airplane you want. Used aircraft, like any other commodity, are subject to the economic law of supply and demand. The general aviation manufacturing slump in the 1980s through the 1990s did not help the supply of "middle-aged used aircraft," so the demand for some good late-model used aircraft may keep a dealer's price high.

If you can arrange it, take a mechanic along to assist you in the inspection. Again, you should be suspicious of any reluctance on the part of the dealer to allow a mechanic to inspect the aircraft or its logbooks.

General condition of the airplane

WHAT TO LOOK FOR, Whether you check out an aircraft alone or with a mechanic, the same basic items should be covered. The inspection will generally consist of three phases: the general condition of the airplane, the logbooks, and a flight check. While these can be done in any order, it is best to familiarize yourself with the airplane before inspecting the logbooks. Then carefully review the logbooks. Repairs or unusual conditions noted in the logs can be inspected during the preflight check. (Inspecting the aircraft and the logbooks first will also allow you to decide if it is really safe to go up for a flight check at all!) You should also be sure to have available any information you were given by the owner or the dealer on the phone. By comparing the actual airplane with the description you received earlier, you will be able to get an indication not only as to the condition of the aircraft, but also as to the honesty and integrity of the seller.

When checking out an airplane you might buy, look for the following:

- Fuselage, wings, and tail
  - Check for wrinkles, paint mismatches, or sprung rivets that could indicate damage.
  - Check for corrosion under the fuselage. Remove inspection panels to check for corrosion or damage inside the wings and fuselage. (Aluminum corrosion will appear to be a white powder or scaly buildup on the aluminum surface.)
  - Check all radio antennas for tightness of mountings.
  - Check around fuel tanks and seams near tanks for fuel stains and discolorations, which indicate fuel tank leaks.
  - Check wing struts for bends, damage, or loose fittings. (Struts can be damaged by lazy, overweight owners checking fuel caps by climbing on the struts.)
  - Check wing and tail leading edges and tips for dents, cracks, and other damage.
  - Check for cracks and metal fatigue, particularly around the cowling, which could indicate excessively hard use.
  - Check fabric coverings for peeling tape or paint or "ringworms" in the finish. Have the fabric on wings and fuselage tested using a fabric-punch tester.
  - Check controls for free and easy movement. Check ailerons for movement. Check hinges for rust and corrosion.
  - Check control cables for wear and for secure attachment at control horns.
  - Check flaps for smooth, even extension and retraction.

- Landing gear
  - Check oleo struts for leaks, pitting, and scoring. Check strut extension against manufacturer's recommendations.
  - Check nose gear mechanism for excessive play in steering and/or retraction linkages. (Cessna 150s, 172s, and 182s are particularly susceptible to shimmy caused by nose gear looseness.)
  - Check main gear strut housings and scissor links for fatigue cracks, particularly on Piper Cherokees (PA-28 and PA-32 series aircraft).
  - Check main gear retraction mechanisms and gear doors for excessive play or fatigue cracks.
  - Check spring-steel or fiberglass fixed main gear (Cessna and Grumman-American singles, Piper Tomahawk, Beech Skipper) fuselage attachment points for wrinkles or bends, which could be a sign of very hard landings.
  - Check brake lines and hydraulic retraction mechanism lines for leaks.
  - Check brake pads for excessive wear, particularly on Grumman-American and other singles which use differential braking for ground steering.
  - Check shock cords (bungees) on aircraft like the Piper Cub and Tri-Pacer for fraying or for oil or dirt that could cause deterioration.
  - Check tires for tread, cracks, "weatherchecking," and uneven wear or random bald spots (which could be caused by uneven hard braking).
- Engine and propeller
  - Check for engine oil leaks, particularly around pushrod housings, oil pan gaskets, and accessory section gaskets.
  - Check fuel lines, carburetor, and intake gaskets for leaks, which will show up as areas discolored by the dye in the grade of fuel used by that engine.
  - Check for exhaust manifold/exhaust gasket leaks, which will show up as a whitish, ashy discoloration around the lower cylinder heads and lower spark plugs. If a leak is noted, be sure it is merely a blown gasket and not an eroded area of the cylinder around the exhaust port.
  - Check for distorted, bent, or broken cooling fins or baffle plates. Improper air cooling could cause hot spots in cylinders, shortening engine life.
  - Check engine controls for free, easy motion by observing their movement while someone in the cabin manipulates the controls.
  - Check wiring harnesses and other electrical connections for brittleness, discoloration, fraying, or wear.
  - Check oil and air hoses and tubing for fraying, wear, chafing, and excessively tightened clamps.
  - Check exhaust manifolds and mufflers for cracks or dents.
  - Have lower spark plugs removed from each cylinder. Oily plugs could be a sign of broken rings. A normal plug should be a light grayish tan.

Sooty, black plugs may mean an engine running too rich, and a lead buildup could also be a warning sign that the valves could be suffering from "100LL blues."

– Check the inside of the exhaust pipe. Any excessive buildup could indicate excessive oil use, which in turn could indicate worn cylinders or pistons or broken rings.

– Check engine mounts for security of the mounting bolts and be sure mounts are free of bends or fatigue cracks, which could indicate very serious problems.

– Check engine for crankcase cracks using a magnifying glass. Check closely around accessory attachment points, particularly on Continental O-520 series engines.

Figure 4.1. Cessna 150s and 172s are notorious for nose-wheel shimmy problems.

– Check prop for cracks and nicks that have not been properly dressed down.
– Check constant-speed props for excessive play or oil leaks.
– Check the spinner and spinner mounting ring for fatigue cracks, particularly on Cessna 150s.

- Cabin
  – Check seat upholstery for rips or fraying. Check for collapsed springs or padding.
  – Check for cracks in plastic on the instrument panel, ceiling, and doors. (Single-engine Cessnas have an excessive amount of interior plastic, and broken plastic on areas like armrests can quickly become very irritating.)
  – Check the door seal and latching mechanism. (Piper Cherokees are known for having leaky door seals. Wet carpet behind the copilot's seat is usually a fact of life in older Cherokees left out in the rain, particularly if no canopy cover was used.)
  – Check seat belts for excessive wear and attachment points for security.
  – Check control wheels and trim for free, easy movement with no catching or binding.
  – Move all knobs and levers. Check for free movement and proper operation.
  – Check seats for security and easy movement in adjusting (particularly on single-engine Cessnas).
  – Check windshield and side windows for cracks, cloudiness, or crazing.

No used aircraft is going to be flawless. But a good used airplane should have received regular maintenance. It should not have been abused and should have no serious faults that have not been attended to. While the airplane should be reasonably clean, you should not put too much emphasis on flaws such as faded paint or worn carpets. This is particularly true of IFR aircraft. If the logs show good maintenance, with regular oil changes and up-to-date static/altimeter and transponder checks, fraying carpeting and faded paint might merely be an indication that the owner was placing emphasis (and money) on capabilities rather than appearance. With this in mind, the next step in considering a used aircraft is the inspection of the logbooks.

LOGBOOKS. Inspection of the logbooks should be performed at a desk or table where you can spread out engine and airframe records, as well as other pertinent paperwork, to compare items and get a complete and thorough picture of the airplane's history. This is no time for haste. Don't let the impatience of the owner or the FBO hurry you.

Go through the logbooks at least twice. The first review should be done with the aim of getting a general impression of the kind of use (or abuse) the airplane has seen as well as the kind of maintenance performed.

- How long has the plane been used as a trainer? One-hundred-hour inspections any less than three months apart probably indicate training use. Private owners seldom fly more than 200 or 300 hours a year, and they are not required to have 100-hour inspections performed unless the aircraft was used for commercial purposes (even use for private transportation on business trips does not constitute commercial use).
- How many owners has the airplane had? If it has changed hands often, why?
- Where has it been based? An airplane in the salt-air environment of the island of Nantucket could be expected to have more serious corrosion problems than one from the dry desert environment of Tucson.
- How often were oil changes performed? Were engine manufacturer's standards met?
- How thorough were the annuals? A fastidious owner may use the annual as an opportunity to clear up minor deficiencies, whereas nothing but basic annuals may indicate minimum acceptable maintenance only.
- Where was the maintenance performed? Do the shops noted in the logs have reputations for high-quality work, or are they cut-rate outfits specializing in "pencil-whipping" the logs?
- If the nav/comms are old 360-channel types, have they been modified with upgrade kits to the FCC 0.003% frequency tolerance requirement? (Upgrade kits were produced for Bendix/King KX-170, 170A, 175, and 195s; Narco Com 10, 11, 110, 111, 11-B, and 111-Bs; by Sigma Tek for Cessna/Arc RT-308C, 328C, and 528E-1s; and by Aero-Sciences Inc. for EDO-Aire RT-551, 553, and 661 radios.)

The second review of the logs should be conducted in detail. Using a list of Airworthiness Directives (ADs) obtained from a mechanic with an inspection authorization (IA) or from an FAA website (www2.faa.gov: Click on Regulations & Policies; click on Airworthiness Directives; click on Current AD by Make), check to be sure that all ADs applying to this aircraft have been complied with. Check for any damage history, which should (but won't always) show up on FAA Form 337s (record of major alteration or repair). Be especially suspicious of prop removals or replacements recorded in the engine log. If sheet metal repairs show up in the airframe log in the same time period, it is almost a sure indication of damage history. If you are buying a retractable, be particularly wary of prop removal or replacement coinciding with the installation of avionics. Significant sheet metal repairs to the belly (as might result from a wheels-up landing) may be hidden in an innocuous "installed transponder and GPS antennas" entry.

If a major or top overhaul has been performed, how many times and what parts were replaced? (Too frequent cylinder work can be a sign of an owner that abuses the engine.) Were the cylinders chromed, replaced with new cylinders, or merely rebored? Was the overhaul done to new or service-limit tolerances? Was the overhaul performed by a known, reputable firm? (Be aware, however, that excellent overhauls can be accomplished by conscientious individual mechanics in seemingly tiny shops.)

If you intend to use the aircraft for IFR operation, note when the transponder and static system/altimeter were last checked. These must be tested and proper log notations made for legal IFR operation. Also note if the omni nav receivers/indicators have been recently checked.

When you have finished reviewing the logbooks, you should have an even better idea of whether you are still interested in buying the airplane. If it appears to be poorly maintained, and the logbooks give the same impression, forget this plane. There are more out there. If there were minor problems in the log, such as recurring AD noncompliance, low compression readings, or IFR system checks not performed, you may not want to give up on the airplane just yet. Keep the problems in mind, though, when you discuss the price you are willing to pay.

THE TEST FLIGHT. When you have inspected the airplane and its logbooks on the ground, you are finally ready to take it for a flight check. (Assuming, of course, you are still confident it will actually fly!)

Objectively, the flight check is probably not as important a step in the final selection process as the rigorous inspection of the plane and the logbooks. If your ground inspection and the logbook review were as thorough as they should have been, you are not likely to pick up any serious problems with the airplane in the air. It is hoped that you have eliminated any aircraft with really serious problems from consideration at this point. The flight check, however, serves two very useful functions. The first is to check all operating systems for any malfunctions. Lights, radios, and instruments must be operating to be properly evaluated. And the second, and probably the most important function of the flight check, is to give you an opportunity to see how this bird feels to you. It is time for the intangible, the subtle little things—does it feel right to you? And this is no small item. After all, you are about to spend a great deal of money on what has probably been a lifelong dream. If you're a real pilot, this is more than just a working tool. It's a piece of machinery that will seem to acquire a personality of its own. And now is the time to make sure that it is one you can live with.

Before you fly the aircraft, go over the owner's manual with the seller. Familiarize yourself with the layout of the instrument panel before starting the engine. Unless the airplane is identical to those you are checked out and current in, be sure the owner remains capable of taking control at any stage of the flight.

During your preflight, check all lights, strobes, and beacons for proper operation. During start-up, note whether the starter turns over the engine smoothly, and check the oil and fuel gauges for quick, proper indication of pressure. If the aircraft has an auxiliary fuel pump, shut it off on the ground and check to ensure that the fuel pressure remains firmly "in the green." Listen to the gyro instruments run up and verify that all sound smooth, without the roughness or scratchiness that would indicate worn bearings and an upcoming expensive instrument overhaul or replacement. Run through the standard preflight checklist, verifying proper carb heat operation, mag drop, propeller pitch control, and smooth control response. Run the trim adjustment from stop to stop to check for smooth cable travel. If a VOR test facility (VOT) exists on the field, verify that the omni receivers/indicators are within allowable tolerances. Ask the unicom or ground control on the field how the communications radios sound. If the plane has a GPS, now is the time to ask the owner to show you that the set is fully functional. Have him or her program in navigation functions you can check during the flight as you follow along in the owner's manual. Program in one or two verifiable waypoints (like VORs or other airports) you can check on the test flight. During engine run-up, check the toe brakes and the parking brake.

During the takeoff roll, check the tachometer (in an aircraft with a fixed-pitch prop), or the tachometer and the manifold pressure gauge to assure that the RPM and manifold pressure values are reaching those specified in the owner's manual. Check the vacuum gauge during the takeoff roll, when it should indicate that the vacuum system is developing the maximum pressure the regulator setting allows. As the speed builds up, note any tendency for nosewheel shimmy.

In the air get the feel of the airplane by performing basic maneuvers such as straight and level flight, climbs, descents, stalls, and steep turns. For the average buyer, there is no need to perform any really exotic maneuvers. What you really want to know is if you like the way the airplane feels in normal flight. Does it respond quickly and smoothly to control pressures? Is it in trim? Or is it a sluggish, unresponsive dog?

If you are checking out an IFR-equipped airplane, try to find a tower-controlled field with an instrument landing system (ILS) approach. By flying one practice approach, it is possible to check out almost an entire basic IFR package. Both navigation receivers should be tuned to the ILS frequency. Both should be checked for proper indications and compared to verify that both have nearly identical readings. Proper indication of the glide slope receiver/indicator can be checked simultaneously. If it still has an automatic direction finder (ADF), it should be tuned to the outer marker frequency and its indications checked throughout the approach, but particularly as the outer marker is overflown. The marker beacon receiver/indicator can be checked as the airplane flies over the outer and middle markers. A GPS can be set to check its stability and accuracy against key points in the approach including the final approach fix, the outer marker, the middle marker, and the airport runway. It is also likely that there will be a GPS overlay approach matching or close to the ILS approach.

The communication portion of the radios can also be exercised. Tune one radio to approach control and the second to the tower. Listen for audio quality and talk over each of the radios, both with and without a headset plugged in, if jacks are available. Use right and left jacks if both are installed. If the approach is made in radar-controlled airspace, ask approach control for a check of the transponder and altitude encoder. And again, note how the airplane feels during the approach. Is it a solid, stable instrument platform? Are the radios installed so that all are easily tuned and adjusted, or are some nearly out of reach? Is the panel arranged in a manner that permits easy reading of the gauges and indicators used during an instrument approach?

Flaps, particularly manual flaps, should be checked on the approach to a landing. Does the detent handle firmly hold each notch of flaps added, or is there a tendency for the flaps to "pop out" of one or more settings due to a worn detent? Upon landing, check for any "bottoming out" of oleo struts and check again for any nosewheel shimmy. On rollout, check the brakes for firm, even pedal pressure. When you have completed the flight check of the airplane, make a list of any problems noted.

Is this the one?

With the ground and logbook inspections and flight check complete, you should have sufficient information to decide if you want this airplane, and if so, on what terms and at what price. Is the seller's asking price reasonable? As is? With all deficiencies corrected? With certain large faults corrected? How much would the seller have to decrease the price to make the airplane attractive to you?

How you answer these questions will depend on many factors. First, of course, is the seller's willingness to correct any deficiencies or else to lower the price. But most important, how strongly do you want the airplane? If you have several different aircraft in mind, it would be unwise to jump at buying any one unless it seemed ideal. However, if the aircraft is in demand and is the only one available that meets your requirements, you may have to decide without comparing it to others available.

If more than one airplane is available, how do you decide which you want to buy? Standard wisdom might suggest, "Buy the newest, lowest-time, least expensive aircraft." Unfortunately, even this advice may be completely wrong. It just isn't that easy, as the following example will demonstrate.

Two Piper Warriors are available. One is a 1981 with 2,000 hours total time on the airframe and 1,000 hours since major overhaul on the engine. It is equipped with one King KX-170B nav/comm radio and a Mode C transponder with altitude encoder, and is priced at $40,000. It has no GPS installed, because the owner probably had a VFR-only handheld GPS he or she used on a yoke mount. The second, a 1977, has 3,700 hours total time on the airframe and 1,500 hours since major overhaul on the engine. It has a UPS Aviation Technologies IFR approach-certified GX-60 GPS/comm, a Bendix/King KX-155 nav/comm with glide slope, a Mode C transponder with altitude encoder, and an audio panel with a three-light marker beacon (3LMB) receiver. It is priced at $50,000.

Assuming that both aircraft are similar in their general interior and exterior condition and have similar use and maintenance histories, which is the better buy? Standard wisdom would say the 1981 aircraft. It is newer, lower time, and less expensive. But is it really the better buy?

If a VFR airplane is desired, you probably will get more for your money with the 1981 model. But if an IFR plane is your choice, the price required to equip the 1981 Warrior to the same capability as the 1977 model would probably make the older airplane the better buy.

The expenses for upgrading the 1981 airplane to a configuration basically identical to the 1977 model are summarized below:

Install UPSAT GX-60	$7,500
Replace KX-170B with	
reconditioned KX-155 with glideslope	$4,000
Install Audio Panel with 3LMB	$1,000
Avionics Upgrade Total	$12,500
500 hr closer to overhaul	+$4,000
Advantage for newer, lower-time aircraft	−$3,500
	$500
Aircraft asking price (1981)	$40,000
Plus adjusted cost of upgrades (see above)	+$13,000
Equivalent Price	$53,000

The example assumes that the airplane will end up with nearly identical equipment. A cost of $16,000 for a major overhaul of the 2,000-hour TBO engine gives the 1977 model an additional $4,000 advantage in addition to the cost of the added equipment, because it has 500 hours more "left" on the engine. Since the 1981 model is newer and has lower time, it is given a $3,500 advantage. As the example shows, the 1981 airplane, after being modified and even allowing for an adjustment for it being a newer aircraft, would be $3,000 more expensive than the IFR 1977 model. And this does not reflect small costs like transponder and static/altimeter checks, which probably would already be included in the price of the IFR 1977 airplane. It also doesn't reflect the time and hassle of finding a reliable avionics shop to do the work and the downtime to have the work done. Unless you are buying a stripped VFR aircraft with the intention of putting in a specific line of brand-new avionics like the Garmin full-color GPS map 530s and 430s, an existing well-equipped airplane will be a better buy than modifying a similar VFR model after the purchase.

Figure 4.2. If you want a good used IFR aircraft, it's usually cheaper to buy it equipped.

Bargaining strategy

When you have located a suitable airplane, how do you go about clinching the deal? What kind of terms should you insist on? How hard a bargain should you try to drive?

Surprisingly enough, it is usually shortsighted to try to bargain with the seller for the lowest possible price. Over the long run, it is often better to pay the asking price and insist that all deficiencies be corrected than it is to drive a hard bargain, only to be beset by a never-ending string of expensive maintenance bills after the airplane is yours. At the very least, the terms of the sale should include a fresh annual inspection. While this is no guarantee that the airplane will be problem free, it does mean that a mechanic has to certify that it is at least airworthy. And it will relieve you of worrying about one large maintenance bill for the first 12 months of ownership.

Your chances of getting the best possible deal on a used airplane are probably greatest when dealing with a private owner, who usually will not be worrying, as a dealer or FBO might be, about profit and loss statements but will just be interested in receiving a ballpark price. You should have more latitude in dealing with the private owner, who may be more interested in accomplishing the sale than in getting a specific price, since the costs he or she will have to continue to pay on the unsold aircraft such as insurance and tie-downs are usually not tax deductible. For the FBO, these are tax-deductible business expenses. The private owner will also be less likely to insist that the annual be performed at a specific maintenance shop, allowing you the option of having it done by a mechanic of your choice.

Almost all used aircraft will have some malfunctions or defects. It is probably better to insist that these be repaired than it is to bargain for a lower selling price. If you find the aircraft you want being sold by a private owner, offer to pay the asking price plus the basic price of the annual inspection at a maintenance facility of your choice. Then specify that all nonairworthy or nonfunctioning items, all ADs requiring compliance, and all service bulletins affecting the aircraft are to be paid for by the seller as a condition of the sale. While you will pay the asking price plus the basic price of the annual, the seller will pay for the repair of any defects. You will end up with an airplane you can count on, blessed by a mechanic you trust. It is, of course, advisable to put all details of this kind of agreement in a signed and notarized conditional sales contract before the annual is begun. The seller may insist on an escape clause, wherein if the price of repairs is excessive, the seller pays for the basic annual and keeps the airplane. In this case, you lose nothing but time and irritation, and the seller still has a certified airworthy, if imperfect, airplane.

Buying an aircraft from an FBO will not leave you as much flexibility in negotiating either price or conditions. The FBO will stick strictly to profit margins based on adjusted blue book prices, limiting the bargaining range to how much or how little profit the facility decides it must have. Unlike the private owner, the FBO may feel much less pressure to sell the airplane. Operating expenses are tax deductible as business expenses, and the FBO may be using the aircraft you want in the income-producing rental fleet. Another problem associated with buying from an FBO is that while a fresh annual may be readily agreed to as a condition of the sale, it may be performed in the FBO shop to only the minimum standards necessary to certify that the plane is airworthy. The FBO will probably not be very cooperative if you request that the annual be performed in a shop of your choice. Generally, when dealing with an FBO, it is advisable to expect to pay full price but to drive a hard bargain on clearing up marginal areas. One possible advantage, however, is in acquiring the aircraft with better equipment or in better condition than the asking price reflects. If you are willing to pay more than the asking price, the FBO may agree to install avionics or a newly majored engine at their cost. If you can afford it, this could be an excellent opportunity to have the extras added at a cost substantially below what you would be charged later.

Many older aircraft sold by FBOs will be planes that are being brokered. Buying a brokered aircraft presents many of the same advantages and disadvantages of buying one owned by the FBO. However, there is one additional disadvantage to the buyer. Ordinarily, brokered airplanes are still owned by private sellers, who pay the FBO a fee or commission to make the sale. The prospective buyer, therefore, is dealing with a broker whose real interest is in keeping the price up, particularly when the broker is receiving a percentage of the selling price rather than a fixed fee. The private owner/seller still has the last word on the selling price of the airplane. But that owner now must consider the broker's fee and certainly will not drop the price or give in on other considerations to the extent that may have been possible in a direct seller-buyer deal. Therefore, buying through a broker must be considered the least desirable arrangement for a private individual purchasing a used airplane. Unfortunately, this is becoming the most prevalent method for buying and selling older used aircraft.

Buying a new airplane

If you are fortunate enough to be able to afford the $200,000 or more that most new airplanes cost, you are presented with different (although similar) problems and opportunities than if you choose to buy a used airplane. The first step is still to decide which plane is right for you. Make a rational study of how you want to use the aircraft. Check the manufacturer's Web site as well as the Web sites of type clubs for the aircraft you are considering. Read all the information you can find on the aircraft you are considering in aviation magazines. Even if you are not a subscriber to *Aviation Consumer* magazine, log onto their Web site (www.aviationconsumer.com/airplanereviews) and see if they have one of their uniquely unbiased reports on the airplane you want to buy. Considering the amount of money you are about to spend, paying $12.95 to download one of their reports could be one of your best investments.

If you are buying a new version of an aircraft you have already flown, you already know the airplane's characteristics. But if you are selecting the airplane from magazine articles, manufacturer's literature, and Web site information, and the airplane is one that seems to make sense but is one you have never flown, be sure to arrange for a long demonstration flight in which you get to fly the airplane. If this is going to be your personal aircraft, you will have a lot of pride wrapped up in it, and you will grow to love it or hate it. And unlike the buyer of a used airplane, you are likely to have to face depreciation losses which become even tougher to face if you decide you don't like the airplane after you buy it.

Buying a new airplane isn't as easy as buying a car. Some manufacturers sell direct from the factory to eliminate dealer costs. Others sell through dealers. Some do both. With very low volume production, the manufacturers may be experimenting with the best way to sell their product line, and the new aircraft sales organization may change from year to year or even month to month. When you are ready to seriously investigate the purchase of a new aircraft, find the manufacturer's number or e-mail address from an ad in an airplane magazine. If their Web site doesn't give you the information you need, send the manufacturer an e-mail or call their sales department directly to determine how they handle new sales.

Be prepared to wait up to six months or a year for delivery of your airplane. Most general aviation aircraft are produced in limited quantities and it may be possible that this year's entire production is already sold out. (Although your dealer making a deal with another dealer who bought this year's models on speculation may still be possible ... but you may have to pay a hefty markup if you want it now!) Other aircraft may not be produced until the order and a 10 percent down payment is received. In some cases, you may get to pretend you are American Airlines or Delta, arranging for the rights to a "delivery position," just like the big guns do with Boeing or Airbus. Or you may be able to make arrangements with a dealer or another prospective owner to purchase the rights to a delivery position he or she already has paid for, but you will probably pay a premium. Other than the pride of owning "new," the main advantage to buying a new aircraft is that it should either be problem free or any problems should be covered under warranty. Be sure that you know exactly how any problems with your new airplane will be fixed, and where. The big advantage to buying from a company like Cessna or New Piper with an established dealer network is that established FBOs are likely to be close by if you need warranty work. Don't be overly impressed by added bonuses like free maintenance and a free annual inspection for the first year you own the airplane until you find out where the work will be done. If you have to fly a thousand miles to the nearest repair station or back to the manufacturer's factory, your costs to get the airplane there could exceed the cost of the free work.

Most manufacturers will offer specialized training on their aircraft free with the purchase of a new aircraft. Some manufacturers may even insist on it as a condition of sale to reduce their potential liability from an unqualified pilot buying and then crashing one of their aircraft. These programs are usually very worthwhile, even if you have to take a week off to go to the factory or another aviation simulator center for the training. It will make you a better and much safer pilot, and besides, your insurance company will probably insist that you go, particularly if the aircraft you are buying is more complex than what you are flying now. If you have partners in the purchase of the aircraft, they should take the training program too, whether the insurance company requires it or not.

When it comes time to take delivery of your new aircraft, be sure to insist on a preacceptance checkout flight for your assurance that everything is in working order. The recommendations contained in "The Test Flight" section earlier in this chapter are just as applicable to a preacceptance flight test of a new aircraft as they are to a checkout of a used aircraft. This is obviously not the time, however, to decide that you don't like the way this type of airplane flies. You should have made up your mind about that on an extended demo flight long before you placed your order for this aircraft. Of course, if your new airplane doesn't seem to fly the way the demo aircraft flew, that could be an indication of a problem with your new airplane.

Make sure you don't sign the final papers accepting the aircraft until after the flight test. If you traveled to the factory or a delivery center, be prepared to spend an extra day or two in the area to allow for the repair of small problems found on the flight test. For $200,000 or more, your airplane should be flawless when you fly it home.

Decision time

You know what is available. You know what you can afford. This is not a time for rash decisions. But it is a time to make some decision. Are you serious about owning your own airplane? Or spending the money to move up to a newer or even a brand-new airplane?

It's your move!

Taking possession: paper and red tape

5

The actual purchase of a used aircraft should not be, and seldom is, a "hand the seller a check and fly it away" operation. When you decide to buy an airplane, you have taken only the first step toward actually making the purchase. The aircraft should undergo and pass an annual inspection as a condition of the sale, and any items not functioning properly should be repaired before you take possession. This will take time. And you will need this time to arrange for a title search, obtain insurance coverage, and probably arrange for a loan. And don't overlook renting a tie-down or hangar space at your intended home field, if you have not already made the arrangements (a good idea if there is a waiting list).

Conditional sales contract

To "stake your claim," you will probably have to provide the seller with a deposit (down payment) of $1,000 or more, depending on the price of the aircraft. You should also have a conditional sales contract drawn up and signed by both you and the seller. This contract should delineate clearly the responsibilities of both parties. It should include a description of the airplane, including the serial number and registration (N) number; a description of radios and other equipment (will headsets, external power cables, and other accessories go with the aircraft?); and a clear and concise description of the expected condition at delivery (either with all equipment functioning or with known deficiencies as agreed to in advance). If an annual inspection is to be performed as a condition of the sale, the contract should clearly spell out who will be responsible for the basic cost and repair of any malfunctions found, and it may include a statement specifying at which shop the annual will be performed.

The contract should clearly state the conditions under which your deposit may be returned. The seller should have clear title to the aircraft, with no liens or encumbrances outstanding at an agreed upon delivery date. If the seller cannot produce clear title, you should obviously get your deposit back. Other reasons for the return of the deposit may include an unwillingness on the part of the seller to repair faults discovered during the annual inspection or an unwillingness to reduce the selling price because of the faults. You should be aware, however, that you have no right to have your deposit returned if you back out of the deal, as long as the seller has lived up to the agreement. After all, the seller may be expending considerable time, effort, and expense to meet obligations. As with any transaction involving sizable sums of money, it may be advisable to consult a lawyer to review the documents before you sign them.

If the deposit involves a substantial sum of money, you may want to consider placing the deposit in an escrow account, with the money not being released to the seller, broker, or dealer until the aircraft has been delivered. The Aircraft Owners and Pilots Association (AOPA) offers an escrow service (1-800-711-0087, www.aopa.org/info/certified/tne/escrow.htm), or you can consult your lawyer about arranging to have an escrow account set up.

Title search

The next step in purchasing the airplane is to have a title search made to assure that the seller really owns the aircraft which you wish to purchase. Does the seller have partners you haven't heard about? Is the seller behind on payments to the bank and trying to stay one step (and one state line) ahead of repossession? Did a divorce decree award the airplane to an ex-husband or ex-wife? Is a disgruntled mechanic just waiting for the aircraft to show up for a chance to remove the propeller until that bill for last year's annual is paid?

While there is a legal question in some states on whether other state or locally filed liens may be valid, it is generally recognized that lien instruments placed on record at the FAA Aircraft Registry in Oklahoma City preempt all other filings and recordings (including your attempt to register the aircraft in your name). A title search can be performed by one of the title search services operating in Oklahoma City in close proximity to the FAA Aircraft Registry. FAA AC 8050-55, accessible online at http://registry/faa.gov/docs/8050-55.pdf, provides a list of title search companies. Names of title search companies can also be found in *Trade-A-Plane*, and occasionally in the classified sections of nationally distributed flying magazines. Most title searches for private owners today are conducted by the AOPA, which maintains a title search office in Oklahoma City to provide the service to its members and nonmembers. AOPA title search services are accessible by calling 1-800-654-4700 or online at www.aopa.org/info/certified/tne/title-search.htm. A simple title search ordered online from the AOPA office costs $59; nonmembers are charged $10 more. AOPA also offers additional information search packages. The AOPA Essential Plan includes a title search and damage history research, including the FAA/NTSB Accident/Incident Report and FAA 337 copies, for $139. The AOPA Comprehensive Plan adds a brief listing of FAA Airworthiness Directives and service difficulty reports for $60 more.

AOPA membership is highly recommended for all aircraft owners. While often accused of speaking out too stridently or being a powerful special-interest lobby in Washington, the AOPA is probably the single most effective general aviation lobbying organization in the United States. While their positions can sometimes be exasperating, they are the only ones who can speak for you with clout if you have an aviation-related problem with a government bureaucracy. They also were the most effective force in returning general aviation pilots to the skies after 9/11 and in dealing with the ever-changing dictates of the Transportation Safety Administration in the years that followed.

Now, what happens if an aircraft has a lien against it? It can be cleared by the lien holder who files a properly executed release with the FAA Aircraft Registry. If you are buying an airplane encumbered by a lien, you should never turn over the final payment to the seller without having the release form in your hand. But be aware of this vicious circle: you won't pay the seller until you receive the release form. But the seller can't afford to pay off the lien holder until your payment is received. And of course, the lien holder won't grant the release until the debt is paid. Still interested in the airplane? You may be able to work something out, but be very careful. And if you haven't retained the services of a lawyer, you had better do so now! First-time buyers of used aircraft, however, would usually be well advised to insist on the return of their deposits if things get this tricky. After all, how unique is any Cessna Skyhawk or Piper Warrior?

Obtaining a loan

If you are in the same financial circumstances as most private pilots who dream of owning an airplane, you will have to obtain a loan to turn that dream into a reality. An aircraft loan will generally be obtained from a bank or lending institution specializing in such loans. Bankers are notoriously conservative. The average bank loan officer probably has never flown in anything smaller than a Boeing 737. You say you found a 1977 Skyhawk with a recent AVCON conversion to a 180-hp Lycoming engine, with a top-line new Garmin avionics package, and the price is a steal? Great! But the average bank officer sees private airplanes as, at best, equivalent to automobiles and, at worst, as dangerous and expensive toys. And this one is over twenty years old? AVCON conversion? Garmin avionics package? You might as well say it in Chinese!

Some banks and lending institutions have pilots in executive positions who are not only knowledgeable but even specialize in the aircraft loan field. These institutions usually advertise in the used aircraft publications described in Chapter 4 and listed in Appendix A. Typical loan terms are given below:

• The loan is based on the *wholesale* price, adjusted to take into account engine hours and extra radios and other equipment.
• The interest rate is approximately 3 percent above prime rate, with a term of from 60 months to as much as 15 years.
• A title search would be conducted by the lending institution. The cost would be charged to the borrower and built into the loan.
• The aircraft would normally be the only collateral required.
• Loans may be processed in as little as 24 hours.

If you are purchasing the airplane from a large, established FBO, the FBO may be able to arrange the financing through its own credit sources. AOPA offers an aircraft financing program accessed by calling 800-627-5263 or through the AOPA Web site www.aopa.org/info/certified/afp.html.

Insurance coverage

The next critical item that must be taken care of before you take possession is insurance. Aircraft coverage, unlike automobile insurance, is not required by most states. However, it would be financial insanity to operate an airplane without liability coverage at the very least. A crash subjecting you to lawsuits could wipe out all your assets, not just your airplane. If your plane is purchased with a loan, lending institutions will insist upon hull coverage as well to protect their interest.

The first step in obtaining aircraft insurance is to define your requirements. Will you be the only pilot? Do you intend to lend or rent the aircraft to friends? Will you be taking any money from anyone, even gas money from friends, when you fly? All these items will determine the specific coverage you need. Unless you intend to buy your airplane outright, operate it as the sole pilot, and take no money from anyone, you will have to have a policy tailored to your specific needs. (The complex ins and outs of aircraft insurance coverage will be covered in detail in Chapter 6.)

Almost all owners, regardless of their specific circumstances, opt for liability coverage to protect their overall financial assets. A $1 million, single-limit liability coverage (including medical payments and property damage) would be recommended for a typical two-seat to four-seat airplane. Some pilots who own their own aircraft carry only ground hazards hull coverage, which effectively ceases to exist when the aircraft is on the runway or in the air and may reduce the price of the total insurance package by more than 40 percent compared to that including in-flight hull (crash) hazards. This option will not be open to you if you have an outstanding loan on the airplane and should not be considered by any owner who intends to allow any other pilot to fly it.

When you have decided on your insurance requirements, it is time to contact insurance underwriters or brokers to ask for quotations. You should emphasize getting the needed coverage and terms, with the lowest price a secondary consideration. Saving $500 a year on the premium would certainly be false economy if you damage your airplane and find out that the small print in your bargain policy contains exclusions. Surprise, it is your $10,000 in damage, not theirs! Information you should provide to the underwriters and brokers when seeking an insurance quote will include a range of items pertinent to both the aircraft and the pilots involved. Data will include the aircraft's age, make and model, horsepower, number of engines, number of seats, type of landing gear, and estimated value. Information on each pilot to be specifically insured will include a description of the pilot's ratings, total flying hours, and a breakdown of the total hours into a variety of categories including dual, solo, multiengine, retractable, and most important, time in the specific make and model of aircraft for which the policy is sought. In addition, the home field and whether or not the aircraft will be hangared should be specified.

The decision to obtain your insurance from a direct underwriter or from an insurance broker will be largely a matter of preference. If your policy will be simple and straightforward, dealing with a direct underwriter may be the best. However, if you have any special terms or conditions you want written into the policy (for example, partnership arrangements or use by other pilots), it will be to your advantage to deal with a knowledgeable, reputable broker. Such a person will have a wealth of information available on aircraft insurance and should be willing to advise you as to exactly the kind of policy that is best. If you find a broker who is unwilling to take the time to explain the many policy options available to you, maybe you should find someone else. By now you should also not be surprised to learn that AOPA offers excellent insurance coverage through the AOPA insurance agency (888-462-2672, www.aopaia.com).

Taking possession

The preliminaries are over. You have located the airplane, determined that the present owner has clear title, and have arranged for a loan to pay for it and for insurance to cover future unspeakable possibilities. You are about to become an aircraft owner.

Before signing the final paper to make your dream come true, and before turning over that big check to the seller, be sure you inspect the aircraft closely inside and out. Check any conditions that were supposed to have been corrected to make certain that the repairs were actually made. Use the checklists provided in Chapter 4 to ensure that the entire aircraft is in the condition you expect. If all systems cannot be checked on the ground, insist on a check flight. Check the aircraft logbooks. Are all repairs properly signed off? AD notes? Annual inspection? Have the static system and altimeter been tested and the results noted in the log? How about the transponder check?

When you are certain that the airplane and the logbooks are acceptable, it is time for you to take possession. The documents you should expect to receive from the seller are listed below:

• Bill of Sale (FAA Form 8050-2)
• Standard Airworthiness Certificate (FAA Form 8100-2)
• Airframe and engine logbooks or other maintenance records
• Equipment list
• Weight and balance data
• Airplane flight manual or operating limitations
• Maintenance manuals, service letters, warranties (optional)

When you have completed the transaction and taken possession of your airplane, the federal government will be happy to provide you with experience in filling out forms. You must send the Aircraft Bill of Sale (FAA Form 8050-2; see Figure 5.1) along with the green and white copies of the Aircraft Registration Application (FAA Form 8050-1; see Figure 5.2) and $5 to the Federal Aviation Administration Aircraft Registry, Mike Monroney

FORM APPROVED
OMB NO. 2120-0042

UNITED STATES OF AMERICA

U.S. DEPARTMENT OF TRANSPORTATION FEDERAL AVIATION ADMINISTRATION

AIRCRAFT BILL OF SALE

FOR AND IN CONSIDERATION OF $ 1+OVC THE UNDERSIGNED OWNER(S) OF THE FULL LEGAL AND BENEFICIAL TITLE OF THE AIRCRAFT DESCRIBED AS FOLLOWS:

UNITED STATES REGISTRATION NUMBER **N** 1234A

AIRCRAFT MANUFACTURER & MODEL Piper PA-28-180C

AIRCRAFT SERIAL No. 24-2468

DOES THIS 30th DAY OF Feb. 20 04 HEREBY SELL, GRANT, TRANSFER AND DELIVER ALL RIGHTS, TITLE, AND INTERESTS IN AND TO SUCH AIRCRAFT UNTO:

Do Not Write In This Block
FOR FAA USE ONLY

PURCHASER

NAME AND ADDRESS
(IF INDIVIDUAL(S), GIVE LAST NAME, FIRST NAME, AND MIDDLE INITIAL.)

Ellis, James E.
28 Normal Avenue
Somewhere, XZ 01234

DEALER CERTIFICATE NUMBER

AND TO SINGULARLY THE SAID AIRCRAFT FOREVER, AND WARRANTS THE TITLE THEREOF. EXECUTORS, ADMINISTRATORS, AND ASSIGNS TO HAVE AND TO HOLD

IN TESTIMONY WHEREOF HAVE SET HAND AND SEAL THIS DAY OF 20

SELLER	NAME (S) OF SELLER (TYPED OR PRINTED)	SIGNATURE (S) (IN INK) (IF EXECUTED FOR CO-OWNERSHIP, ALL MUST SIGN.)	TITLE (TYPED OR PRINTED)
	Joe Seller		Seller

ACKNOWLEDGMENT (NOT REQUIRED FOR PURPOSES OF FAA RECORDING: HOWEVER, MAY BE REQUIRED BY LOCAL LAW FOR VALIDITY OF THE INSTRUMENT.)

ORIGINAL: TO FAA

AC Form 8050-2 (9/92) (NSN 0052-00-629-0003) Supersedes Previous Edition

Figure 5.1. Aircraft bill of sale.

FORM APPROVED
OMB No. 2120-0042

UNITED STATES OF AMERICA DEPARTMENT OF TRANSPORTATION
FEDERAL AVIATION ADMINISTRATION-MIKE MONRONEY AERONAUTICAL CENTER
AIRCRAFT REGISTRATION APPLICATION

CERT. ISSUE DATE

UNITED STATES
REGISTRATION NUMBER **N** 1234A

AIRCRAFT MANUFACTURER & MODEL
PIPER PA-28-180C

AIRCRAFT SERIAL No.
24-2468

FOR FAA USE ONLY

TYPE OF REGISTRATION (Check one box)

☒ 1. Individual   ☐ 2. Partnership   ☐ 3. Corporation   ☐ 4. Co-owner   ☐ 5. Gov't.   ☐ 8. Non-Citizen Corporation

NAME OF APPLICANT (Person(s) shown on evidence of ownership. If individual, give last name, first name, and middle initial.)

Ellis, James E.

TELEPHONE NUMBER: (999) 111-2222

ADDRESS (Permanent mailing address for first applicant listed.)

Number and street: 28 Normal Avenue

Rural Route: P.O. Box:

| CITY Somewhere | STATE XZ | ZIP CODE 01234 |

☐ **CHECK HERE IF YOU ARE ONLY REPORTING A CHANGE OF ADDRESS**
ATTENTION! Read the following statement before signing this application.
This portion MUST be completed.

A false or dishonest answer to any question in this application may be grounds for punishment by fine and / or imprisonment (U.S. Code, Title 18, Sec. 1001).

CERTIFICATION

I/WE CERTIFY:

(1) That the above aircraft is owned by the undersigned applicant, who is a citizen (including corporations) of the United States.

(For voting trust, give name of trustee: _____), or:

CHECK ONE AS APPROPRIATE:

a. ☐ A resident alien, with alien registration (Form 1-151 or Form 1-551) No. _____

b. ☐ A non-citizen corporation organized and doing business under the laws of (state) _____
and said aircraft is based and primarily used in the United States. Records or flight hours are available for inspection at _____

(2) That the aircraft is not registered under the laws of any foreign country; and

(3) That legal evidence of ownership is attached or has been filed with the Federal Aviation Administration.

NOTE: If executed for co-ownership all applicants must sign. Use reverse side if necessary.

TYPE OR PRINT NAME BELOW SIGNATURE

	SIGNATURE	TITLE	DATE
EACH PART OF THIS APPLICATION MUST BE SIGNED IN INK.		Owner	2/30/04
	SIGNATURE	TITLE	DATE
	SIGNATURE	TITLE	DATE

NOTE   Pending receipt of the Certificate of Aircraft Registration, the aircraft may be operated for a period not in excess of 90 days, during which time the PINK copy of this application must be carried in the aircraft.

AC Form 8050-1 (12/90) (0052-00-628-9007) Supersedes Previous Edition

Figure 5.2. Application for aircraft registration.

Aeronautical Center, P.O. Box 25504, Oklahoma City, OK 73125. The pink copy of the aircraft registration form should be retained in the airplane as the temporary registration until the permanent certificate (FAA Form 8050-3) is received, hopefully within 90 days.

There is good news and bad news relating to Federal Communications Commission requirements. Every prospective aircraft owner flying any aircraft with radio transmitters used to have to obtain an Aircraft Radio Station License at a cost of $35. The good news is that if you don't fly outside the United States, you are not required to have a Radio Station License. The bad news is that if you intend to travel to a foreign destination you need to obtain an Aircraft Station License good for 10 years for a $100 fee plus a lifetime Operators License available for an additional $50. "Foreign destinations" include Canada, Mexico, and the Bahamas, so unless your plane is a modest little underpowered two-seater that you won't fly over 100 miles, you probably will need the Aircraft Station License and the Operators License sooner or later.

FCC Form 605 has replaced the old Forms 404 and 404A. To obtain an Aircraft Station License, prepare for a serious adventure in bureaucratic form filling and filing. First, you will need to obtain an FCC Registration Number (FRN). You could do this by filling out and submitting an FCC Form 160 and waiting who knows how long, or you can get one by filing online at the FCC Universal Licensing System at http://wireless.fcc.gov/uls/. For the Operators License you will need to fill out another FCC 605-Main Form and FCC 605-Schedule E. Then you will need to fill out FCC 605-Schedule C for the Aircraft Radio Station License. And of course you have to pay your fee. This requires filling out your FCC Remittance Advice Form, FCC Form 159. Things get fun when you get to the "Payment Type Code." There are separate payment codes for your Operators License and your Aircraft Radio Station License. You have to find these in the FCC Filing Fee Guide or on the FCC Form 1070Y. Use Form 1070Y. The FCC Form 1070Y dated September 2002 listed the "Payment Code Type" for the General Radio Operators License as "PADM" and the "Payment Code Type" for Aircraft Radio Services as "PAAR." Enter these onto the Form 159, and remember that the Operator License fee is $50 and the Aircraft Radio Station License is $100. You would probably be well advised to pay by credit card, which the Form 159 allows. Applications other than renewals should be mailed to the Federal Communications Commission, Wireless Bureau Applications, P.O. Box 358130, Pittsburgh, PA 15251-5130.

Depending on the state you live in and will base the aircraft in, you may also have to register your aircraft with the state and pay a state registration fee. And you may also get a nasty surprise if your state has a sales tax and you didn't pay one yet! Some states insist that you pay the sales tax when you register. Think you'll just skip the whole thing? You'd probably better not, particularly if you live in a state like Massachusetts, where the Massachusetts Aeronautics Commission checks FAA aircraft registration lists against their state registration lists. With computers, it's "you pay me now, or you'll really pay me later"! The AOPA Web site contains up-to-date information on states requiring aircraft registration and their phone numbers so you can check with your state aviation authorities.

Pilot-owner obligations

When you acquired your dream airplane, you also inherited a complex set of statutory obligations that must be fulfilled at a bewildering conglomeration of time intervals. The more complex the airplane, the more complex the obligations. Annual inspections; static, altimeter, and altitude reporting system checks; transponder checks; expiration date of the emergency locator transmitter (ELT) battery pack—all these and more are yours with the aircraft. Of course, as a pilot you already have a similar set of obligations on your winged body and soul. Currency of your medical certificate, biennial

Figure 5.3. Now it's yours! And so is the paperwork!

flight reviews, landings and takeoffs in the last 90 days, instrument currency—all these, and more, and more, and seemingly more. But now you dis-
cover, that was only the beginning.

A checklist of statutory obligations which must be met to keep you flying legally is presented in Table 5.1. Descriptions of these requirements follow.

Each active, registered aircraft in the United States is required to have
an airframe and engine inspection by a mechanic with an Inspection
Authorization, unless the owner has set up and obtained approval for a pro-
gressive inspection schedule (very unusual and seldom a bargain for personal aircraft). The annual inspection is good until a year from the last day of
the month in which the inspection was performed. (If you have an annual
inspection signed off on April 15, you can legally fly your aircraft without
another annual up to and including April 30 of the following year.)

The transponder must have been tested within the last 24 months by a
certificated repair station or by the manufacturer if the transponder is newly
installed. The check can be either a bench test with the transponder removed
from the aircraft or a ramp test with it operating installed. The test is current up to and including the last day of the twenty-fourth month after the
test was performed.

For IFR operation, or for all aircraft with a functioning altitude reporting capability (Mode C), the static system, altimeter, and altitude reporting
system (ordinarily a second altimeter with a built-in encoder but with no
cockpit readout) must have been tested by an appropriately rated and certificated repair station within the last 24 months. Many certificated shops
will insist on having the altimeter either calibrated or replaced by a recently
calibrated altimeter. Sending out the altimeter for calibration is less expensive but may take up to two weeks, whereas replacing it with a recently calibrated instrument may be accomplished in less than a day.

Table 5.1. Obligations required to keep your plane in the air

Item	5 yr	24 mo	12 mo	30 days	100 hr	50 hr	Other
Annual inspection			X				
Transponder test		X					
Static/altimeter check		X					
ELT batteries							X
State registration							X*
Aircraft insurance		X					
Airworthiness Directive			X		X	X	X
VOR check (IFR)				X			
100-hour inspection					X		

* Varies from state to state.

Emergency locator transmitter batteries must be replaced when the ELT has more than one hour of accumulated use, or when 50 percent of the manufacturer's specified useful battery life has expired. The expiration date will be marked on the outside of the battery case. Most ELT batteries are good for 18 months. But no differentiation is made between shelf life and installed life, so be sure that any replacement battery you buy has been recently manufactured.

To remain legal to fly from a base airport in a given state, it may be necessary to regularly renew your state aircraft registration or to pay state taxes and fees. Check with the AOPA Web site or your state aviation authorities to determine the recurring requirements that apply to you.

Aircraft insurance is another item that usually comes up regularly for renewal. Most insurance policies are written for one year and must be renewed annually. The policy should be reviewed two to three months prior to the date of renewal each year to ensure that any changes you may desire are incorporated in the renewal.

Airworthiness Directives, the curse of aircraft owners, may have a wide range of compliance times ranging from immediate correction of serious safety hazards to annual inspection of minor faults. As an owner, you are responsible for complying with all ADs that apply to your aircraft. If you did your homework before buying your airplane, you should already be aware of the applicable ADs and the compliance schedule.

If your airplane is to be used for IFR flight, your very high frequency omnirange (VOR) equipment must be checked by one of the approved methods listed in the Airmen's Information Manual within the last thirty days and a written notation made in the aircraft log or maintenance record. This notation should include the location of the performance test, the date, the bearing error, and your signature. You should also include the type of VOR check you used (airborne checkpoint, VOT, etc.) and the aircraft tach time when the test was conducted.

If you intend to use your aircraft for commercial purposes (carrying passengers or cargo for hire or giving instruction), you will be required to have a 100-hour inspection performed by a mechanic with an IA, a certificated repair station, or an A&P mechanic. While this encompasses nearly the same items covered in an annual, it cannot be used to meet the requirements of the annual inspection unless it is signed off as such by a mechanic with an IA. It should be noted that use for your own personal business transportation or sharing expenses on business or pleasure trips does not constitute commercial use of your airplane.

Insurance: the expensive enigma

6

Insurance can be one of the most expensive items involved in owning your airplane. It is also an item that has great potential for future bad feelings and sheer frustration. It is certainly one of the least understood areas facing an aircraft owner.

The blame for this, admittedly, must be shared equally among the insurers and the insured. The insurers seem to abhor plain English. Policies always seem to be written by conservative lawyers in gibberish to guarantee that their expensive services will be required any time a sizable claim is filed. And aircraft owners seem determined to remain in the dark by not trying to understand anything but the asking price when they buy insurance and by insisting on their right not to read the policy when they receive it.

Do you really need insurance? As odd as it may seem legally, in many states this is not a requirement. If the state you fly from does not have a financial responsibility law requiring you to prove your ability to pay a minimum amount in the event you crash and cause injury or damage, you may not be required to have liability insurance. However, if you fly into the jurisdiction of a state with such laws (including California, Maryland, Minnesota, New Hampshire, South Carolina, and Virginia), your airplane would be subject to seizure if you would be unlucky enough to be involved in an accident or an incident.

There are more compelling reasons to have aircraft insurance coverage than just those provided by financial responsibility laws. A single lawsuit arising from an aircraft accident or incident could endanger all your assets. Even personal bankruptcy would not be a sufficient shield in some states, where future earnings as well as present assets may be attached to settle claims as a condition of bankruptcy proceedings. Of course, if you have little to lose, it is unlikely that you will face serious, expensive court action.

But let's face it. If you really had that little to lose, you would not have been able to afford the airplane in the first place.

Since it is obviously verging on fiscal insanity not to carry insurance on your airplane, let's look at what kind you should have. There are few "standard" aviation insurance policies. Almost every pilot-owner is a special case, or will become one the moment he or she lends the airplane to a friend, flies it on a business trip, or accepts avgas money from a buddy who wanted to have the kids taken for a ride. You will have to define what coverage you want and need. To do this, you should at least have a minimal understanding of what is and is not readily available in aviation insurance. One major East Coast broker has been quoted as saying that the cost difference between a good policy and a poor policy is not more than 15 percent. A poor insurance policy shot through with loopholes is no bargain. This doesn't mean you should not shop for the best bargain. It does mean you should know what you want in the insurance policy first and then shop for the best deal that contains what you want and need.

Liability coverage

Liability insurance protects your assets against claims arising out of an accident or incident involving your aircraft. This protection may be broken down into separate coverages or may be combined into single-limit liability coverage. Separate-category liability policies generally include bodily injury excluding passengers, covering people injured outside the airplane— $100,000 per person, up to $300,000 maximum per occurrence; bodily injury liability (passengers) —$100,000 per person, up to $300,000 maximum per occurrence; and property damage—$1,000,000.

Single-limit liability coverage combines the three categories into one package, with an upper limit on the total the insurance company would pay for one occurrence. No limit is placed on how much could be paid in any individual category as long as the sum of all liability payments in all categories does not exceed the overall single limit. Some single-limit liability packages are watered down by provisions (usually included in the "endorsements") limiting maximum amounts for bodily injury claims.

How much liability insurance is sufficient? Bodily injury liability should be at least $100,000 per passenger. Bodily injury liability coverage costs are proportional to the number of seats in the aircraft, so four-seaters will cost significantly more than two-seaters. Property damage coverage should also be at least $100,000 and probably more. (If you have problems understanding why it is advisable to carry such high property damage coverage, just check the price of a new Piper Malibu or a Lancair or a Beechcraft Baron. Then think about the kind of claims that would result if your plane should run into one while taxiing or landing and cause it to catch fire.) Ordinarily, it is a good buy to purchase more than the minimum available if you can get it. In the past, the price of doubling or even tripling liability coverage cost only a fraction of the initial amount. Not anymore. With changes in the market around 2001, liability premiums for $5 million liability coverage doubled or even tripled. If you are attempting to move up to a complex single, twin, or a turbine aircraft, you will probably not be able to find the higher liability limits anywhere. One million dollar liability may be all you can get.

A single-limit liability policy is generally considered to be a better buy than coverage with separate category limits. Most reputable brokers recommend single-limit liability coverage of at least $500,000 for any single-engine aircraft. Single-limit liability coverage of $1 million is generally recommended for four-seaters. Again, if you are attempting to move up to a more complex aircraft and have relatively little experience, you may not be able to get a single-limit liability policy and may have to settle for one with sublimits of $100,000 per passenger.

Some less-than-reputable underwriters may be willing to sell you very-low-limit liability coverages, such as $50,000 or $100,000. If an injured party is going to take you to court, the amounts sought will be far, far in excess of such low limits, and you may have to pay the difference if you lose. The amount saved on the insurance premiums seldom is substantial enough to make such risk taking worthwhile.

Medical expense is a separate, relatively minor category in the aircraft insurance policy. Typical coverage is usually $2,500 per passenger. Coverage for the pilot can also be purchased but usually can be obtained from better sources such as company medical benefit plans. (Be sure such plans do not exclude medical expenses "incurred as an aircraft crew member" before you turn down medical benefits on your aircraft insurance policy.)

Hull insurance

Physical damage, or hull insurance, is one area where tailoring your insurance policy can result in immediate savings. Under this part of the policy you are more likely to submit a claim without having destroyed your aircraft or having done grievous harm to yourself or others.

Physical damage coverage is usually provided in three optional levels. The minimum is all-risk, not-in-motion coverage. This protects you from a variety of damages or losses, including vandalism, fire, or theft of the aircraft or internal equipment, provided the plane was not in motion. Generally, this means that if your airplane was parked, hangared, or tied down, you would be covered. In most cases, you are covered if the engine wasn't running. However, if you choose this coverage, you should insist that the term "not in motion" be defined explicitly. For example, would the aircraft be considered in motion if a mechanic towing it into a hangar for maintenance attempts to force your 36-foot Skyhawk's wings through a 33-foot door opening? Most reputable insurance companies will define "in motion" as "the aircraft moving under its own power or the momentum generated therefrom." When limiting yourself to this coverage, you should make sure you are really getting what you think you are.

One small step up the ladder in physical damage insurance is all-risk, not-in-flight coverage, which adds taxiing and other ground operations to the policy. The coverage ordinarily ceases at the start of the takeoff roll and takes effect again at the end of your landing roll. For all practical purposes, you wouldn't be far off to assume that the coverage ends when your plane's wheels are either on the runway or in the air. This coverage may be the best bargain for the average single-engine, fixed-gear owner of an older used aircraft who will be the sole pilot. The cost is usually only a little more than the not-in-motion option and is significantly less expensive than all-risk (full-hull) coverage. As long as Cessnas can be tilted on their wingtips and noses by gusty, quartering tailwinds, or Cherokee Warriors can hit snow banks with their long wingtips, or a small aircraft can come too close behind jets or turboprops and be flipped over by their breakaway thrust, all-risk, not-in-flight coverage will probably be a good buy.

The most extensive and expensive physical damage insurance is all-risk. This starts with the coverage provided in all-risk, not-in-flight, and extends it to cover physical damage caused by an accident or incident during the takeoff, flight, or landing phases of operation (assuming, of course, that the operation of the aircraft was not in gross violation of federal aviation regulations). This type of policy is quite expensive, particularly for new aircraft with hull values approaching or exceeding a quarter of a million dollars. It is not unusual for full all-risk hull coverage to cost more than twice as much as that for all-risk, not-in-flight insurance. For a $40,000 aircraft, opting for in-flight coverage may add over $500 to the annual premium.

Should you carry in-flight hull insurance? If you are the sole owner and operator of an older single-engine, fixed-gear airplane, keep your airplane properly maintained, and fly conservatively and with good judgment, you may decide not to. The risk of serious damage to your airplane is small enough that the money saved from the premiums over several years will probably cover any minor damage you might do in a landing incident or other minor accident. To put it in a more indelicate manner, you could say that if you can walk away from it, you can probably afford it and if you don't walk away from it, you won't be worrying about it anyway. Not carrying all-risk can have an additional advantage, particularly if you are the bashful type when it comes to saying no. If another pilot asks you to use your plane, you can legitimately say, "My insurance doesn't cover you." It's a very handy excuse and one seldom questioned.

If you are one of several partners, if you intend to lend or rent your airplane to other pilots, or if the aircraft is an expensive, late-model airplane, you definitely should carry full all-risk coverage. The possibility that somebody else might not "walk away" from your investment and leave you with nothing should be too great to be acceptable. If the airplane is partly yours and partly the bank's, the decision will have been made for you by the bank officials. They will insist that you buy coverage for their aircraft. And if you have the money to buy a new aircraft, it would be hard to imagine that you would consider risking the loss of such an expensive investment for what you would save by not carrying in-flight hull coverage.

Physical damage coverage is available in "stated-value" or "actual-cash-value" coverage. The stated-value option provides that in the event of total loss or destruction the owner will receive the value of the aircraft as stated in the policy (minus any deductibles). Actual-cash-value coverage would, in theory, repay the owner the market value of the aircraft. The actual cash value, however, may be very difficult to determine. Is it based on the wholesale or retail price of your airplane? How much was that old but functional IFR capability worth? How much time was on the engine? Overall appearance? Because of these variables and the high probability of a misunderstanding in the event of loss with actual-cash-value coverage, most reputable insurers now write physical damage coverage in terms of value placed on the aircraft by the owner. To preclude unscrupulous owners from trying to make a profit by overstating the value of an airplane and then destroying it, most insurers will not accept an unreasonably high stated value. Exceptions will be made if an owner can show that the airplane is uniquely equipped or recently zero-timed or restored, if it is an older aircraft. As a private owner, you should also be sure that your stated value is not too low. This is particularly true of an older airplane whose value is appreciating. If your airplane is totally destroyed, a stated-value policy does not guarantee you will receive enough to replace it. The policy only guarantees that you will receive the stated value. It is up to you to make sure that this accurately reflects the true value of your airplane. Of course, since your insurance premium for physical damage coverage is based on a percentage of the stated value, the higher the stated value the more you pay. Covering your risk by stating a high enough value will always have to be balanced against keeping premiums down by not stating too high a value.

Figure 6.1. Older Beechcraft Debonairs and Bonanzas are actually increasing in value.

The "fine print"

While liability and physical damage coverage is the major concern of aviation insurance, it is not the main determinant of the relative excellence of your policy. Except for differences between single-limit and separate liability coverage, there will be little variation in the major items in any policy written by most reputable aviation insurers. Most variant details will be in the area of exclusions, special terms, and conditions. The "fine print" will determine whether your policy is a comparatively good buy or a blatant rip-off.

Exclusions are the items, areas, and special conditions where your coverage does not apply. They may be explicitly stated as "exclusions," may be implied by expressions like "limits of a company's liabilities" or "conditions," or may implicitly arise from the "definitions." It is absolutely essential to be aware of the exclusions that may exist in an aviation insurance policy. Learning that what occurred was "excluded" after you submit your claim may be expensive education indeed.

Many exclusions are standard within the aviation insurance industry. Some can be eliminated from the policy at your request, possibly at no additional cost. Removal of most exclusions, however, will imply that you are asking for extended coverage beyond the normal basic package. An additional charge should be expected. Standard aviation insurance policies exclude the following:

• Liability assumed contractually by the named insured, except where required by use of military or government facilities. (You cannot agree to terms with a third party that make the insurance company liable for things they didn't agree to. However, use of military facilities, including military aero clubs, may require that you sign waivers protecting the government from a lawsuit if your aircraft is damaged on the base. The insurance company agrees to accept these government waivers.)

- Obligations arising from unemployment insurance, workmen's compensation, etc., and/or liability or bodily injury claims to an employee of the insured arising out of employment by the insured. (You may use your aircraft for your personal business transportation under most aircraft insurance policies, but any other commercial activities are prohibited. Your policy will not cover a paid pilot or any other employee that flies your airplane.)
- Personal property of the insured other than a hangar and its contents. (Your property in the plane, such as cameras, nonaviation radios, etc., is not covered. If your car is in the hangar with the airplane when a fire destroys all three, the car is not covered by the aviation insurance policy.)
- Physical damage to tires other than by fire, theft, vandalism, or malicious mischief. (The insurance company will not pay for your worn-out tires or for tires slashed by broken glass you ran over taxiing at a second-rate airport.)
- Physical damage caused by and confined to wear and tear, deterioration, and mechanical or electrical breakdown. (With a reputable insurance company, this means that the company does not intend to pay for your mechanical or electrical malfunctions. They will pay, however, if you damage the aircraft in a forced landing or crash caused by the malfunction. If you insist on buying bargain-basement insurance, watch out! This exclusion could give a fly-by-night insurance outfit a loophole to avoid paying a claim if anything was wrong with your airplane before you crash-landed.)
- Physical damage or loss due to action of the government or government agencies, or due to war, invasion, civil war, revolution, rebellion, insurrection, or warlike operation, whether declared or not. (If you are flying back from Mexico, don't joke with drug enforcement agents about your Ovaltine or Sweet'N Low. Your insurance company won't reimburse you when the humorless agents seize your airplane. With DEA and Customs seeming not to care about how many innocent pilots or planes are victimized in the name of stopping the drug trade, this one can be downright scary.)
- Coverage ordinarily does not apply to any person, agent, or employee engaged in the manufacture, maintenance, repair, or sale of aircraft, aircraft engines, components, accessories, or in the operation of any airport, hangar, flying school, flight service, or aircraft or piloting service. (Your

policy will not cover mechanics running up your engine after maintenance. You would probably be paid if the aircraft was damaged, but the mechanic could be sued by your insurer. Your instructor's actions as pilot in command while giving you lessons in your aircraft would not be covered either.)

Less reputable companies may expand exclusions to the point of making a policy virtually worthless. The blanket Federal Aviation Regulation (FAR) exclusion is one of the worst you could have in your policy. This exclusion may include a seemingly innocuous statement like "coverage is not provided for any operation not conducted in accordance with applicable Federal Aviation Regulations (FARs)."

Very few reputable insurance companies will write such an exclusion into their policies. While it may sound absolutely reasonable to assume that to be covered an aircraft should be operated in accordance with the FARs, the blanket exclusion was all too often used by disreputable insurance companies to disallow claims in seemingly reasonable circumstances.

Suppose a student pilot loses control of the aircraft on landing at a tower-controlled field after being lost and disoriented in summer haze that reduced visibility to two and one-half miles. He or she didn't request special VFR, so the pilot violated FARs, even though he or she could see the runway throughout the approach. No payment.

Or suppose a Piper Cherokee runs off the runway in strong crosswinds. The fuel selector was on the left tank, and fuel starvation was not a factor. But the fuel gauge for the right tank was inoperative when the pilot flew the plane home. Violation of FARs. No payment.

Legally, the insurance company is totally within their rights in these cases. Common sense would indicate, however, that insurance is probably worthless if the smallest human weakness or ignorance of an obscure regulation will result in a disallowed claim. Fortunately, most reputable insurers are fair, and their policies are not worthless. And most reputable insurers do not see any value in the blanket FAR exclusion.

Some shady insurers may claim that the entire engine was the "defective part" if its failure causes a forced landing. They will pay damage to the airframe caused by the accident but will claim that the engine would be excluded from the coverage.

A reputable insurance company will pay at least part of the cost of engine repair or replacement in the event of an engine failure and forced landing. This does not mean, however, that the insurer will pay for a newly majored engine if an engine past due for major overhaul quit at an inopportune moment. Even the best insurance policy is not going to allow you to profit from an aircraft accident or incident. If your engine was halfway to major overhaul when it quit and an overhaul costs $15,000, you will not be paid that amount for the engine repair. You will instead receive the prorated half-life figure of $7,500.

Other small-print abuses by less than reputable insurance underwriters include exclusions on liability or bodily injury coverage for all "persons acting as crew members." Did the other rated pilot riding with you handle the radio during your emergency? Sorry. That's "acting as a crew member."

If you intend to have a slightly damaged aircraft ferried back to your home field with a onetime special ferry permit, you may not be covered, either, due to a standard policy exclusion.

Tailored policies

Individual policies may often be tailored to your specific needs. If a specific exclusion appears to be a problem in your situation, it may be possible to have it removed for a low additional charge or, in rare cases, no charge at all. Some examples may include personal property riders and additional territorial coverages. A pilot's personal property, such as cameras, luggage, and clothing, is ordinarily excluded from coverage. Insurance for such items may often be added to the policy for a small fee. Many policies will ordinarily limit territorial coverage to the continental United States and Canada. If you are a pilot with a good record and have an airplane that is properly equipped, it may be possible to add territorial coverage for the Bahamas at no extra cost.

There is probably no area of insurance coverage with a wider variation of terms and conditions than in the use of an aircraft by pilots other than the owner. Many policies will allow an owner to lend his or her plane to other pilots, but only so long as no reimbursement is received. And "no reimbursement" means exactly that. The borrower could not even add oil and avgas after a flight. (It is difficult to understand why a pilot would even consider lending an airplane under these conditions.) Other policies will allow the borrower to repay the oil and avgas but will exclude reimbursement of any fixed expenses. The very best policies will allow payment of all aircraft operating expenses as long as the reimbursement does not constitute a profit.

Owners should also be aware that when they lend their aircraft to another pilot, they are not necessarily lending their insurance coverage with it. Ordinarily, a borrower is protected by the owner's liability coverage, but not by the owner's hull insurance. In other words, in the event of a crash, the insurance company would reimburse the owner but could sue the borrower to recover damages. Many pilots who rent aircraft from an FBO fly along blithely unaware that this same situation also applies to them. Most FBOs have liability coverage that extends to renter-pilots, but have physical damage (hull) coverage that covers only the FBO. (Some FBOs offer regular renters the option of buying supplemental coverage to cover this risk. Unlike auto rental collision damage waiver insurance which is purchased each time a car is rented, this supplemental hull coverage is ordinarily purchased for one year. The cost varies with the dollar value of coverage desired by the renter and covers all FBO aircraft the pilot rents. The AOPA Insurance Agency (www.aopaia.com) also offers renter's insurance for any airplane a pilot may rent or borrow; the cost also varies according to the dollar amount of coverage desired. AOPA's insurance is probably a better deal for pilots who fly airplanes from more than one FBO or rent and borrow aircraft.

If you intend to regularly lend your airplane to another pilot or if you have one or more partners flying it, you should be aware that all of the pilots who regularly fly it can be specifically covered by name by asking that a waiver of subrogation be included in the policy. A waiver of subrogation means that the insurance company agrees to waive its rights to sue these named pilots for any damages resulting from an accident or incident involving the aircraft. In other words, pilots other than the owner are now protected from personal loss resulting from damage to the airplane. (Obviously, only the owner or owners will collect on any hull damage claims.) Some companies offer the option of specifying up to five named pilots. This ordinarily indicates that all those named have full coverage under the policy, but it would be wise to insist that the insurer spell out what coverage they have. If there is any uncertainty, it may be best to insist on a waiver (or waivers) of subrogation, particularly if only one or two additional pilots are involved.

If you have an arrangement such as the limited partnership discussed in Chapter 2 (in which you are the sole owner of an aircraft but grant one or more pilots operating rights in exchange for sharing fixed as well as operating expenses), you should be sure to have an insurance policy tailored to your needs. You should insist that your partners be covered by waivers of subrogation, and you should be sure that the policy allows them to reimburse you for all operating expenses and the percentage of fixed costs relating to or incurred by their use of the aircraft.

An additional insurance complication arising from allowing other pilots to use your airplane may be an "experience" clause. This may set limitations on who may be allowed to use your airplane (and still be covered by the insurance policy) in terms of total hours logged and number of hours in your specific type of aircraft as well as specifying requirements for recency of experience. A typical clause would be similar to the following: "Pilot must hold a private or commercial certificate, and have a minimum of 500 total logged flying hours as pilot in command, of which 100 must have been in retractable aircraft and of which not less than 25 shall have been in a Piper Arrow aircraft."

Good risk or bad?

Are you considered a good risk or a bad risk in the eyes of an aviation insurance underwriter? What kind of risk you are can make a significant difference in more ways than just the bottom-line price of your policy. The very best underwriters offer wide-ranging coverage in their policies with relatively few fine-print exclusions to good risks. Tailored insurance policies with specific or unusual terms and conditions are often available to good risks but not to bad risks, who must take what they can get. Bad risks may have to accept lower liability limits and generally higher prices for less coverage. They may also have to settle for coverage from underwriters with a poor record of service and payment of claims.

What will make you a bad risk in the eyes of an aviation insurance underwriter? Obviously, a past history of damage claims is not favorable. And it should be extremely obvious that claims related to proven violations of FARs are not advisable. But what can make you a bad risk in the eyes of an insurer if your record is free of any blatant violations of common sense or the FARs?

Generally, "different" is worse in the eyes of aviation insurance underwriters. And, strangely enough, there are plausible reasons for this situation. Taildraggers, older aircraft, floatplanes, twins, aerobatic aircraft, and warbirds are all considered higher risks than typical single-engine, fixed tricycle gear aircraft. Taildraggers have a history of ground loops and other crosswind landing accidents, and the typical modern pilot trained in Cessna 152s or 172s, Diamond DA-20s, or Piper Warriors is not properly trained to handle such landings without special supplemental training in taildraggers. Floatplanes and amphibians are flown from an environment that is much more variable than any hard-surfaced airport can ever be. The seaplane has the additional disadvantage that a landing or a takeoff incident can be very serious if the aircraft should sink (and all it takes is a hole in a float or in the amphibian hull). Twin-engine aircraft engine failures are potentially deadly, especially on takeoff, to the pilot who hasn't kept current on engine-out procedures. Aerobatic aircraft are intentionally flown near performance and airframe stress limits. It is difficult to find parts for many older aircraft and warbirds if they are damaged; they may even require custom-machined parts.

The airfield you call home could also contribute to your being considered a bad risk. Operation from a rural grass airstrip will generally be considered a high risk compared with operation of the same aircraft from a larger field with a hard-surfaced runway. An airplane that will be flown in IFR conditions may be considered a relatively high risk if it is based at a field with only a single nonprecision approach. Experience is generally considered to be a positive factor in determining risk. Low-time pilots applying for coverage in high-performance aircraft, such as high-powered, single-engine retractables or twins will almost always be looked upon as bad risks and simply may be denied coverage unless special manufacturer's or other aircraft-specific schools are attended as a condition of coverage. The low-time pilot "stepping up" will almost always be required to undergo a stringent checkout with an instructor familiar with the aircraft. Even for high-time pilots, low time-in-type may make them a bad risk in the eyes of the insurance company in that specific make and model. Accident and incident statistics show undisputable evidence that low time-in-type is more important than a pilot's total flight time in determining the risk.

Other miscellaneous factors can also lead to a pilot being considered a bad risk. Despite statistics showing that they are probably safer than younger pilots, pilots over age 60 may have a difficult time obtaining insurance if they have not been previously covered by the insurer. Limitations on a pilot's license, such as "day VFR only," are not looked upon favorably. (It is all too easy to imagine such a pilot being tempted to exceed limitations when he or she is "running late" near sunset with only "a little farther to go.") And obviously, any pilot attempting to insure an airplane for significantly more than its market value will be viewed with suspicion by an underwriter.

What would an aviation underwriter consider to be a good risk? You will probably be between 21 and 60 years old with no loss of license or suspension record and fly a single-engine, fixed tricycle gear aircraft from a field with a hard-surfaced runway at least 3,000 feet long where you have the aircraft hangared. An IFR rating is considered a definite plus. Continuing VFR into IFR conditions is one of the main killers of general aviation pilots. An IFR pilot is expected to be able to handle deteriorating VFR weather and also to have demonstrated a more professional attitude than VFR pilots by having acquired the IFR rating. If you are going to upgrade into a twin or a turbocharged, pressurized single, you may have to have the IFR rating to obtain coverage, particularly if you hit the cyclical insurance market at a time when things are "tight."

If you would like to be considered a "nearly ideal insured" by the underwriters, add a total time of 1,000 hours, of which at least 100 are in the make and model of the airplane you are insuring, 100 are night-flying experience, and 200 are cross-country flight time. You should also fly at least 200 hours a year, take an annual recurrency check such as the three-hour FAA "Wings" program in the aircraft you fly, and live in the East or Midwest where there are fewer mountains to challenge the aircraft's (and your) service ceiling.

One phenomenon which came about in the late 1980s is the aircraft-specific formal training school. These training schools are run by such reputable names as FlightSafety International, which has training courses for the Mooney, Cessna 210, and Bonanzas, as well as larger aircraft, or Simuflite Training International. Manufacturers also offer training programs. While insurance companies do not usually require these courses for light single-engine aircraft, it is not unusual for such a course to be required for coverage in more complex twins or turbocharged, pressurized singles. Taking the courses can result in better rates or better coverage for almost any pilot, however. The tradeoff for the pilot-owner of a light single-engine aircraft comes in deciding if the cost of the school is worth the improved rates and coverage for the insurance (plus, of course, the obvious personal safety benefits). In tight times, of course, the insurance companies may insist you take the courses to even obtain the insurance, which would mean you don't have a tradeoff. On unusual specialty aircraft like the Lake amphibians, for which a company-sponsored training program tied to a special insurance program has been established, taking the program is practically a necessity to obtain coverage at reasonable rates.

One key point to remember if you intend to have partners in your aircraft or lend your aircraft to others: the pilot who is the least experienced and therefore the worst risk will set the rate for the insurance on your aircraft!

Brokers vs. direct underwriters

When you have defined what insurance you need, you still must buy it. The coverage can be obtained from a regular insurance agent, a direct underwriter, or a broker. Which is likely to provide you with the best coverage at the lowest cost?

Buying aviation insurance from an agent who already provides you with homeowner, automobile, or life insurance coverage is foolish at best. Aviation insurance is a very specialized field within the business, and you would probably be severely shortchanging yourself by buying it from an agent who probably knows absolutely nothing about airplanes. It should only be good common sense that an agent who must learn what it is you are seeking will hardly be the person to put together the best possible insurance package. In fact, most reputable general agents will recognize this fact and advise you to buy your aviation insurance elsewhere.

Direct underwriters are representatives of the insurance companies that will be providing your coverage. They consider themselves to be professionals representing their firms. Many direct underwriters are private pilots (some companies require this). A major advantage is that a direct underwriter speaks directly for the company. There is no one in the middle and there are no extra fees.

However, there are several drawbacks to using direct underwriters. While the direct underwriter represents the company when you are buying the insurance, you should not forget that he or she will still represent the company if you ever have to file a claim. If you are the type who likes face-to-face contact in your business arrangements, you will not appreciate dealing with a direct underwriter solely by telephone or e-mail. But perhaps the greatest disadvantage is the lack of direct competition which often results in inflexibility. Direct underwriters are rarely able to tailor a policy to special needs as well as good brokers are. If your insurance needs are relatively straightforward, the direct underwriter may be able to provide low-cost coverage to you without a broker's fee. But if you have any special needs, the relative inflexibility of the direct underwriter will probably mean higher premiums or reduced coverage compared to a tailored policy.

An aviation insurance broker, unlike the direct underwriter, represents you rather than the insurance company. It is the broker's job to obtain the best coverage available. A good broker should have an excellent comprehension of aviation insurance policies and should be able to determine how your special needs can best be met. Larger, reputable brokerage houses also will foster competition between underwriters by seeking from four to six quotes for any insurance package they put together. For performing these services, the broker will receive a 10 to 15 percent commission, which generally will be built into the quote you receive.

If you decide that you need the services of a broker, finding a reputable one will be critical. The only real advantage a broker has compared to a direct underwriter is the ability to provide policies optimized to the needs of the individual pilot. To provide this service, the broker must know the field well. So how do you go about locating a knowledgeable, reputable broker? The best way is far from scientific. Simply ask other pilot-owners as well as FBOs for their recommendations. Who are they satisfied with? Try to find owners who have filed claims. They will be able to tell you whether or not a specific broker stands behind you when the chips are down.

Good brokers should have all the pertinent information you need. They should be willing to discuss your particular situation with you and should ask intelligent questions to determine additional facts. (After all, if you knew how to define all the information needed, you probably wouldn't need the broker.) Do not be surprised if the broker stresses obtaining good coverage over seeking the lowest cost. The cheapest price may buy you just what you paid for—*cheap coverage*. In the final analysis, however, it will probably be your intuition or "gut reaction" that will tell you if the broker is a person you believe and can trust.

What is the best strategy for a private aircraft owner looking for insurance? The first step is to define as precisely as possible what coverage is needed. Second, obtain quotes from one or more direct underwriters. If your needs are relatively simple and straightforward, a broker will probably be unable to match the direct underwriter's deal. The third step should be to contact a broker. With the direct underwriter's quote as a baseline, you will be able to wisely evaluate whether or not the broker can find you a better deal on the coverage you desire. When you have one or more quotes from direct underwriters and one "best" quote from a broker, you should be able to make an intelligent decision regarding the best aviation insurance package for you.

The simplest way might just be to contact the AOPA Insurance Agency (www.aopaia.com). AOPA has become a one-stop service center for private aircraft owners, and the AOPA Insurance Agency is one of their many services. The AOPA Insurance Agency will usually match or beat the quotes available elsewhere.

The best buy

What can you do to save on insurance programs in the long run? Shop around for aviation insurance and let the direct underwriters and brokers know that competition exists. This approach is as old-fashioned American as apple pie and Chevrolet. The kind of person you are looking for should consider competition a challenge, not a threat.

When you are shopping for insurance, try to define all your needs before you buy a policy. A good broker can often include small extras at little or no additional cost before the policy is written. Later add-ons can involve significant expense. If you have found a good broker and underwriter, stick with this person. Accident-free years should be reflected in reduced premiums as time passes. If you are nearing age 60 or looking to upgrade to a more complex aircraft, your long-term loyalty to one good insurer may be returned by their providing you with continued quality coverage that you may not be able to get anywhere else.

Build up your "time-in-type." When it comes to insurability, total time in the make and model you are insuring is far more important than overall total time in a wide variety of aircraft. And make sure that your lowest-time named pilot builds up his or her time-in-type, too.

If you buy a low power, fixed gear four-seat airplane that you intend to use as a two-seater (for example, a Cherokee 140 or Warrior flown from high-altitude fields such as those in Colorado), remove the rear seats and carry only two-seat liability insurance. The same goes for six-seat aircraft which will be used as four-seaters. Since liability coverage for passengers is figured on a per seat basis, the cost will be significantly reduced by carrying it on the basis of the seats actually used. Make sure you physically remove the seats, though. You don't want to be tempted on a long cross-country to the lowlands to fill up the uncovered seats. It could be a very expensive mistake.

Keep the insurance company advised of any changes in your situation, particularly if favorable. Moving your airplane to a better-equipped home field or moving the aircraft from a tie-down to a locked and guarded hangar could result in some reduction of your premium. If you upgrade your license or ratings or take refresher courses, bring these to the attention of your broker or underwriter. Obtaining an instrument rating can be particularly significant. If you can fly IFR, you have reduced the threat of crashes and therefore can probably reduce your insurance premiums.

Maintenance and miscellany

7

When you bought your airplane, you acquired a complex piece of machinery that needs both scheduled and unscheduled maintenance to keep it in top operating condition. You gave some thought to maintenance when you selected a home field. And you sought the services of a mechanic to assist in eliminating the lemons from the gems when you were looking for your very own first airplane. Since you change the oil and even do tune-ups on your Toyota or Ford in the driveway at home, the idea has crossed your mind that there might be a few things you can do on your airplane as well.

The first mechanical problem will probably show up as you preflight your airplane. Maybe it will be a leaking brake line or a deflated oleo strut. It might be a quick-drain on one of your fuel tanks that becomes a constantly dripping "slow drain" when it won't seal completely. Or maybe it will be an excessive mag drop when you do your pretakeoff magneto checks. Even though you knew it had to happen sooner or later, it will come as a nasty surprise. And unless you or your partner is a mechanic, your airplane is on its way to the local maintenance shop.

Shop responsibilities

What should you expect of a maintenance shop? If you base your aircraft at a large field with more than one FBO maintenance facility, which should you choose?

The chief mechanic of a reputable shop should be willing to give you an honest, valid appraisal of the time it will take to do a job. If there are any problems involved, such as difficulties or delays in obtaining specific parts, you should be told before the job begins. If any serious unexpected situations occur or additional malfunctions are found while the job is being done, you should be called by the chief mechanic and consulted before the work proceeds. If the chief mechanic has given you realistic estimates or updated them when additional problems were found, the final bill should be within 10 percent of the quotation you were given. The job should also be finished on the day it was promised unless you were notified there would be a delay.

The work performed by a reputable maintenance shop should be of high quality. Forgetting to reconnect landing light ground wires when reinstalling a cowling, missing items on a checklist, or forgetting some of the screws in an inspection plate are all signs of sloppiness and inattention to detail. A reputable maintenance shop with mechanics who take pride in their work will not tolerate such poor performance.

Work performed coincident with an inspection should not be "doublebilled." Annual or 100-hour inspections ordinarily entail significant effort in removal of inspection plates, cowlings, interior seats and trim, and external fairings and trim items. The cost of the inspection already includes these items. Therefore, maintenance work, modifications, or equipment installations performed during an inspection should reflect a lower additional cost than if such work was performed independently. This applies not only to add-ons that you want but also to the correction of problems located during the annual. Troubleshooting time ordinarily required in localizing a problem is usually a portion of the repair charge. If the problem was located during the annual, this time should not be added to the repair charge.

Even the best mechanic may make a mistake. If a job is done incorrectly, you should be able to expect quick correction of the problem at no additional charge. When the maintenance is completed, everything you specified should have been accomplished or an explanation should be provided. All work should also be properly logged and signed off in the airframe or engine logbooks.

When you receive the bill for maintenance performed, it should be specific enough that you can determine how much you are being charged for each item. Some FBO's billing practices are so poor that it is impossible to determine from the statements whether the charge is for avgas, aircraft rental, or maintenance. On the other hand, some FBOs send out detailed maintenance shop work orders with the billing statements. If the bill you receive is not clear, you should be able to see the itemized work order on request. If a specific order detailing the work performed and related charges does not exist or you are not allowed to see one, this is a solid indication of a less-than-reputable maintenance shop.

All customers should be treated courteously. If you are dealing with a single-person operation at a small out-of-the-way strip, the personality of the mechanic will determine what constitutes "courteous treatment." Even medium to large maintenance shops at larger airports will reflect the personality of the chief mechanic or maintenance supervisor. As a rule, the owner of a small single-engine aircraft is probably better off staying away from very large facilities where clients include corporate accounts with heavy twins, turboprops, and executive jets. You will be better off at a shop where your business isn't "small change."

Reputable maintenance shops do exist. If the first shop you do business with leaves something to be desired, you should change, even if it means moving to a different airport. You will be better off in the long run.

Owner responsibilities

All the responsibility for assuring a smooth working relationship between the aircraft owner and the maintenance shop does not lie on the mechanic's shoulders. Too many pilots cause unnecessary friction by acting like prima donnas whose aircraft ownership entitles them to some kind of special treatment. As an owner, there are many things of which you should be aware to make your plane's maintenance less of a headache to you and the chief mechanic. Some of these items are unique to aircraft, but many are equally applicable to maintaining the family automobile.

When you intend to take your airplane in for maintenance, call ahead to allow the work to be scheduled at a time convenient to the shop if possible. Most chief mechanics will be understanding and very helpful to a transient pilot with a problem. They will be considerably less understanding, however, if a pilot whose airplane is based at the field brings it to the maintenance hangar and, otherwise unannounced, petulantly insists on having the 25-hour oil change done today!

Write out a clear and concise list of everything you want done. If the plane is being taken to the shop for a problem, describe the symptoms as clearly as you can. Do not insist on specific fixes. Leave that to the mechanic. Do try to pinpoint the symptoms, particularly with radio problems. For example, if you have bad audio reception, make a written record of your own preliminary troubleshooting. Does the second radio have the same problem (possible shared antenna, power, or speaker)? Does the problem seem the same with a headset as with the aircraft speaker? Does the nav audio work when the comm audio does not? (Some radios share amplifiers and other stages between comm and nav within the equipment.) Does the problem change if the engine is running (engine interference sources)? By performing such preliminary work and clearly documenting it, you can save yourself money by relieving the mechanic or technician of unnecessary troubleshooting time.

When you take the airplane in, have all the logs and other documentation available and plainly marked, at least with the aircraft tail number. Have similarly tagged keys available. The plane should be free of all extraneous garbage. Leaving your headset, three outdated sectionals, and your portable urinal in the aircraft will do nothing to help the mechanic get the job done. Before you leave, make sure it is understood that you want to be notified if any unusual or unexpected problems arise and leave a phone number where you can be reached.

When arranging for annual inspections, 100-hour inspections, or other extensive projects, go over the work needed with the chief mechanic or service manager. Understand what will and will not be done for the quoted price. Most annual inspections include only the actual inspection and some minor amount of scheduled maintenance in the quoted price. Repairing any troubles that are detected is extra. When problems are found during an annual or other inspection, consult with the service manager or chief mechanic to determine if you could correct any of them yourself to save some of the cost. Be aware, however, that their time is valuable. If you have a 30-minute conference, don't be shocked if you are billed for it.

Many items can affect the cost of maintaining your airplane. Some of these will be at least partly under your control, and some will not. Checking some part which you don't intend to have worked on unless a problem is found, for example, is not a free service. Some owners are appalled when they ask to have an adjustment performed and the bill comes to nearly $100. On some older Cessna 172s, more than 20 screws must be removed just to take off the cowling. It could take an hour just to remove it and put it back. At a shop rate between $50 and $75 per hour, a "minor carburetor adjustment" could be justifiably billed at over $100. It pays to have minor adjustments and checks made when other required maintenance is being done.

Interrupting work in progress can also be expensive. If you own one of those older 172s, you could fly it VFR even without a vacuum pump to feed the directional gyro and artificial horizon. So do you insist that it be buttoned up on Friday if the back-ordered pump won't be in until Monday? Depends on how much that weekend VFR flying means to you. Closing and then removing the cowling again could add an hour of labor charges to your bill.

Reconfiguring an instrument panel is a job entailing far more than the novice aircraft owner may realize. "Let's see ... I'd like that nav head over here, and if I move the oil pressure gauge, I could put the EGT right here." Sound like a thousand dollar job? Don't be fooled; it could be. Relocating instruments in a panel is a lot bigger job than just removing them from their holes and changing them around. That VOR head may require rebuilding the avionics cable harnesses. On a pre-1968 Cherokee 140, it won't even fit in the lower instrument holes between the control wheels without interfering with control wheel travel. The oil pressure gauge is probably fed by a piece of copper tubing that penetrates the firewall. Move it, and you have to have new tubing cut to replace the entire old piece. And so on, and on.... If you have the only old Stinson or Navion on the field, expect to pay more. The mechanic will probably take more time than usual because working on your model is a learning experience. It's not the mechanic's fault if this is a first-time event. And you don't really want a rush job, do you? Since the mechanic doesn't know your aircraft, don't expect realistic time or cost estimates on the job. The mechanic is only being honest when saying there is no way of knowing how long the job will take.

Some shops will add a 5 percent charge for miscellaneous supplies. Before you gripe about this, ask yourself how you would like to calculate how much three screws, three feet of safety wire, and six ounces of grease cost. Sure they were purchased in bulk, but nobody gave the stuff to the shop. And adding this kind of a charge is more honest than burying it in still higher hourly labor charges. Aircraft parts are another huge expense, often shocking. Built in small quantities by a handful of companies to tight FAA restrictions and subject to intensive quality control, aircraft parts often seem unbelievably high priced, particularly in comparison to automobile parts. An excellent and still pertinent article in the June 1974 *Aviation Consumer* comparing similar automobile and aircraft parts concluded that the differences between similar-appearing parts like alternators and starter motors are real, if obscure. The parts expense is one the aircraft maintenance shop is largely powerless to do anything about. As hard as it may be to believe when you get the itemized bill, the truth is that the shop's profit margin on parts is slim indeed.

Most of all, you as the owner should be aware that your expensive hobby is the aircraft mechanic's living. All too many owners seem to feel that shop prices for repair of their recreational aircraft are completely out of line, even though they pay nearly identical rates for automobile repairs and think nothing of it. The mechanics may see very little of what appear to be excessively high rates. At most shops the government levies a seemingly endless burden of taxes and paperwork. Contributions to workmen's compensation insurance, Social Security, and unemployment insurance all take a bite. Then how about heat, lights, phones, and hangar rental? The paperwork has to be done by someone, so throw in a full- or part-time secretary/bookkeeper. And pilots expect a ready supply of parts, so tie up $100,000 or more in inventory. Actually, the labor rate you pay, as stiff as it may seem, may actually allow the FBO maintenance shop very little profit.

You knew when you bought the airplane that flying wasn't free. So don't begrudge the mechanic an honest wage. As a 1970s (and cable channel rerun) TV character used to say, "If you're gonna roll the dice, ya gotta pay the price!"

Doing your own work

Assisting in or performing some of the maintenance on your own airplane is one way to save on costs. It is also excellent experience, making you more aware of your aircraft's capabilities and limitations. It will make you more adept at accurately describing symptoms to a mechanic when problems occur, and it will help you understand what the mechanic is telling you when describing work that must be performed.

Performing your own maintenance on an aircraft is a lot like apartment dwellers' efforts to service their own cars. Work must be performed on property rented from someone else whose policies may or may not allow such activity. Some airports encourage owner-performed maintenance, most tolerate it, and some ban it completely. Before you begin any maintenance on your airplane, you must determine the local policy.

Owner-performed maintenance at the tie-down will be limited not only by regulation but also by weather. While some regular maintenance can be performed outdoors year-round in some areas of the South and West, such work may be realistically limited to six or seven months in more northerly sections. Other restrictions imposed by the nature of the service required may limit outdoor work even if the person intending to perform it is a mechanic. Electricity may be required for the use of drills and other power tools. A source of compressed air may be necessary for pumping up oleo struts, or powering riveting tools, drills, or other air-driven tools. Lack of water may preclude even such menial tasks as washing the airplane.

Some maintenance facilities will permit rental of hangar space for owner-performed maintenance supervised by FBO mechanics. Others may allow an owner to prepare the plane for an annual by doing such activities as removing interior trim and seats, inspection panels, and the cowling and then reinstalling them after the inspection. If you are considering such an arrangement, you should understand what facilities are being made available and what your limitations are. For example, what facility equipment may you use? Will you have access to jacks? If so, how long can you keep them tied up? How long can your aircraft remain in its present location? If your spot in the hangar is only available for several days, it may be necessary to take vacation or other time off from your job to complete the work.

If you will be using or sharing maintenance shop facilities, some common sense rules should be understood and firmly adhered to. The first rule is never to borrow mechanics' tools. These are absolutely essential to their livelihood, and even one missing tool can be a severe handicap. A sure way to alienate a mechanic is to assume that you are free to borrow tools. Second, realize that the aviation mechanic is a proud professional who acquired expertise through dedication and hard work. Don't expect free advice from the mechanic any more than you would expect free legal advice from a lawyer or free medical advice from a doctor. Be willing to pay for assistance when you need it. Third, do your work safely and in accordance with established policies and procedures. The maintenance shop is risking higher insurance rates just by allowing you to use its facilities, so don't ruin a good thing for everybody by your carelessness. And finally, clean up after each day's work. Nobody loves a slob!

If there is a chapter of the Experimental Aircraft Association (EAA) in your area, you can probably pick up many useful tips on how to do your own aircraft maintenance with limited resources by attending their meetings. Be warned, however, that these people are not limited—like you are—by FAR Part 43. They will be talking about doing things to their home-builts that you can do to your certificated production aircraft only with the blessing of a mechanic.

FAR Part 43 authorization

Since a mechanic is responsible for every item he or she signs off in your logbook, the work you can perform under supervision is virtually unlimited. You are limited by federal aviation regulations in the work you can perform solely on your own, however. FAR Part 43 authorizes a pilot-owner to perform certain limited maintenance operations, provided the aircraft is not used for air carrier service. General maintenance items specified in FAR Part 43, which the pilot-owner may legally perform, are listed in Appendix C.

LANDING GEAR. The following owner-performed maintenance for landing gear is permitted by FAR Part 43:

• Removal, installation, and repair of landing gear tires.
• Replacing elastic shock absorber cords on landing gear.
• Servicing landing gear shock struts by adding air, oil, or both.

• Servicing landing gear wheel bearings, such as cleaning and greasing.
• Replacing defective safety wiring or cotter keys.
• Replacing wheels and/or skis where no weight and balance computation is involved.

Servicing of the landing gear by the owner is generally allowed as long as no defective components other than the tires require replacement. While seemingly simple, this is one area that may be more complicated than it looks. Servicing the landing gear will require jacking up the aircraft, which is not as simple as jacking up a car to replace a tire. The recommended procedure for jacking up low-wing aircraft like the Piper Cherokee, for example, is to use hydraulic jacks under the two wing jack points while securing the tail with a heavy weight. Single-engine, fixed-gear Cessnas are slightly easier, and the main wheels can be jacked up one at a time with an automobile bumper jack if a special adapter is fitted against the landing gear above the wheel. (The jack can also be applied to the step, but this is risky and definitely not recommended.) Single-engine Cessnas, like the 150, 172, and 182, have nose gear which can be serviced by tying the tail down with a heavy weight to elevate the nose. Servicing aircraft tires is not necessarily straightforward or easy even after the jacking problem is solved. Aircraft wheels are in two halves bolted together and are usually made of magnesium or aluminum. Unless a special bead-breaker tool is used, it can be very difficult to break the bead between the tube-type tire and the wheel without nicking or denting the wheel halves and pinching the tube.

Elastic shock cords used in a variety of older Piper aircraft, including Cubs, Cruisers, Pacers, and Tri-Pacers, may require replacement because of wear or age. These should be replaced by first removing the shock strut unit after the wheel has been jacked clear of the ground. Taking off the old cord is the easy part. Putting on the new cord unit may require a chain hoist or a special fixture.

Servicing shock struts, such as those used on the Piper Cherokee landing gear and on Cessna nose gear, is complicated by the need for a source of high-pressure air or nitrogen. Owners can help extend the life of oleo struts, however, simply by using a rag soaked in the MIL-H-5606 hydraulic fluid used in the struts to wipe down the exposed portions at regular intervals or any time the struts get particularly dirty.

ELECTRICAL SYSTEM AND AVIONICS. FAR Part 43 permits the following owner-performed maintenance of the aircraft electrical system and avionics:

• Troubleshooting and repairing broken circuits in landing light wiring circuits.

- Replacing bulbs, reflectors, and lenses of position and landing lights.
- Replacing and servicing batteries.
- Removing and replacing self-contained, front instrument panel-mounted navigation and communication devices that employ tray-mounted connectors that connect the unit when the unit is installed into the instrument panel, (excluding automatic flight control systems, transponders, and microwave frequency distance measuring equipment (DME)). The approved unit must be designed to be readily and repeatedly removed and replaced, and pertinent instructions must be provided. Prior to the unit's intended use, an operational check must be performed in accordance with the applicable sections of part 91 of this chapter.
- Updating self-contained, front instrument panel-mounted Air Traffic Control (ATC) navigational software data bases (excluding those of automatic flight control systems, transponders, and microwave frequency distance measuring equipment (DME)) provided no disassembly of the unit is required and pertinent instructions are provided. Prior to the unit's intended use, an operational check must be performed in accordance with applicable sections of part 91 of this chapter.

The items listed are fairly self-explanatory. Note that owner-performed maintenance of aircraft electrical system components is strictly limited to those associated with the landing and nav/position lights and to replacing or servicing the aircraft battery. The last item refers primarily to updating databases in panel-mounted GPS units.

AIRCRAFT INTERIOR. The owner may perform maintenance, allowed by FAR Part 43, on interior components as follows:

- Repairing upholstery and decorative furnishings of the cabin or cockpit interior when the repairing does not require disassembly of any primary structure or operating system or interfere with an operating system or affect primary structure of the aircraft.
- Replacing safety belts.
- Replacing seats or seat parts with replacement parts approved for the aircraft, not involving disassembly of any primary structure or operating system.

The FAA allows the owner a relatively free hand in maintenance of the aircraft interior, as long as no structural changes, changes to operating systems, or changes affecting aircraft weight and balance are made. Replacement seat belts must conform to TSO-C-22, and changes to the seat belt attachment points are forbidden. Replacement seat belts must also have metal-to-metal latches, which have been required by the FAA in all aircraft since December 1980.

LUBRICATION AND HYDRAULIC FLUID. Part 43 also lists permitted owner-performed maintenance associated with lubrication of aircraft components or replenishment of hydraulic fluid:

• Lubrication not requiring disassembly other than removal of nonstructural items such as cover plates, cowlings, and fairings.
• Replenishing hydraulic fluid in the hydraulic reservoir.
• Applying preservative or protective material to components where no disassembly of any primary structure or operating system is involved and where such coating is not prohibited or is not contrary to good practices.

Lubrication of aircraft components will usually be required only at 100-hour or annual inspections and should be accomplished in accordance with the chart provided in the owner's manual or the aircraft service manual. Hydraulic brake fluid for most modern single-engine aircraft can be checked at the reservoir ordinarily found mounted on the firewall in the engine compartment, and it can be replaced as necessary. The last item applies mainly to application of protective coatings to seaplane cables and float attachment hardware.

ENGINE AND FUEL SYSTEM. Part 43 lists the following owner-performed engine and fuel system maintenance permitted by FAR:

• Replacing defective safety wiring or cotter keys.
• Replacing or cleaning spark plugs and setting spark plug gap clearance.
• Replacing any hose connection except hydraulic connections.
• Replacing prefabricated fuel lines.
• Replacing or cleaning fuel and oil strainers or filter elements.
• The installation of antimisfueling devices to reduce the diameter of fuel tank filler openings provided the specific device has been made a part of the aircraft type certificate data by the aircraft manufacturer, the aircraft manufacturer has provided FAA-approved instructions for installation of the specific device, and installation does not involve the disassembly of the existing tank filler opening.

While the owner's latitude in engine maintenance is naturally quite limited, the number and variety of engine maintenance items that can be performed make this a key area for potential savings. While changing the oil is not specifically mentioned, the owner's right to do so is implied in the fifth item above, and Flight Standards District Office (FSDO) interpretations of the FAR tend to support this position. If your airplane has an oil screen, it should be examined for metal particles when removed for cleaning. Metal particles on the screen should be considered a warning sign, and the advice of a mechanic should be sought. (Dark black carbon particles, however, are normal and not necessarily a cause for alarm.) If your airplane has an oil filter, it should be torn open and inspected for metal particles. (This is one distinct advantage of the less-convenient cartridge filter over the spin-on, metal-case type. The spin-on's metal case makes inspection for metal particles in the filter difficult.) Oil changes, oil filter changes, and oil screen cleaning should be done after the engine has been run to normal operating temperatures to assure good oil circulation assist in flushing out contaminants.

Cleaning the screen in the fuel strainer bowl is a relatively simple operation. Caution is advised in removing and cleaning the carburetor fuel filter, because that screen must be removed and reinstalled in precisely the correct manner to prevent damage.

Replacing aircraft spark plugs is a straightforward operation for an owner who has the proper tools and some mechanical experience. Proper cleaning and gapping of the plugs, however, may require a spark plug cleaning and testing machine generally found only in FBO maintenance shops (or well-equipped automobile service stations). Spark plugs removed from the engine for either replacement or cleaning and gapping should be closely inspected to evaluate the condition of the engine. Oily insulators may indicate bad rings or worn valves or valve seats. Plugs that appear too clean may actually be running too hot as the result of an overly rich mixture, indicating a need for more attention to proper leaning procedures.

Engine hoses that may be replaced include the red or black, wire-reinforced, rubberized air hoses known as "scat hoses," used as carb heat and heater hoses. These frequently are subject to wear and chafing and ordinarily can be checked once a year coincident with the annual inspection and replaced if necessary.

Properly replacing safety wiring and cotter keys on drilled bolts and castellated nuts is necessary to preclude essential aircraft components from being vibrated apart in flight. The important thing to remember in performing safety wiring is to ensure that tension applied to the nut or bolt "pulls" in a direction that would cause tightening rather than loosening of the safety wire as the nut or bolt starts to loosen.

Following an unusually large number of accidents due to piston-engine aircraft being misfueled with Jet-A, the aviation and petroleum industries got together to come up with a simple and innovative solution to the problem. Fuel nozzles on the hoses of Jet-A refueling trucks were made larger than the nozzles on the hoses of avgas refueling trucks. Restrictor inserts were developed for the fuel filler necks on piston-engine aircraft fuel tanks. The idea is that if the lineperson tries to refuel your piston-engine airplane with Jet-A, the nozzle won't fit into your fuel tank opening. The inserts are designed to be installed by the owner with a minimum of assistance by a mechanic.

Some aviation insurance companies are so convinced that this is a worthwhile idea that they offer full refunds on the price of the inserts. Having these restrictors installed is a good idea on any piston-engine airplane, but it is a particularly good idea for those aircraft which have both piston and turboprop powered variants, include Aero Commander twins and even Maule taildraggers. (Bob Hoover, one of the world's best pilots, narrowly avoided death by using his superior flying skills to land his powerless Aero Commander twin on the slope of a ravine after his aircraft was misfueled and suffered a double engine failure on takeoff. This was among the more notable incidents which led the FAA to insist that corrective action be taken.)

AIRFRAME. The owner is permitted by FAR Part 43 to perform the following maintenance on the airframe:

• Replacing defective safety wiring or cotter keys.
• Making simple fabric patches not requiring rib stitching or removal of structural parts or control surfaces.
• Refinishing decorative coating of fuselage, wings, tail group surfaces (excluding balanced control surfaces), fairings, cowling, landing gear, cabin, or cockpit interior when removal and disassembly of any primary structure or operating system is not required.
• Applying preservative or protective material to components where no disassembly of any primary structure or operating system is involved and where such coating is not prohibited or is not contrary to good practices.
• Making small simple repairs to fairings, nonstructural cover plates, cowlings, and small patches and reinforcements, not changing the contour so as to interfere with proper airflow.
• Replacing side windows where that work does not interfere with the structure or any operating system such as controls, electrical equipment, etc.
• Replacing any cowling not requiring removal of the propeller or disconnection of the flight controls.
• Replacement or adjustment of nonstructural standard fasteners incidental to operations.

These items deal primarily with preventive maintenance of the aircraft sheet metal or fabric covering, side windows, and paint.

Simple repairs to fabric coverings can be done to mend holes made by gravel or other debris thrown up during landings on rough strips, hangar rash, or other causes of minor fabric punctures. Butyrate dope can generally be used for patching most types of fabric coverings and finishes. Major fabric repairs or repairs that require removal of control surfaces are not allowed.

It is not unusual for used aircraft to develop small fatigue cracks in sheet metal, particularly around the cowling, as well as small cracks in plexiglass side windows. "Stop-drilling," or drilling a hole at the end of the crack to stop its growth, is a generally accepted procedure. Obviously, cracks in structural items should be a cause for alarm. Stop-drilling cracks is only acceptable for nonstructural sheet metal or plexiglass. If the crack continues to grow beyond the hole, it may be necessary to use a riveted patch to reinforce the area. This is not an item every owner will be capable of, however, and most private owners should limit their sheet metal efforts to stop-drilling.

Cracks in fiberglass fairings are readily repairable by owners with little maintenance experience. Fiberglass patch kits are available at most automotive supply stores. Wheel pants—or speed fairings, as some manufacturers prefer to call them—often develop worn spots and cracks. For owners who live in northern areas subject to winter snows, these can be repaired at leisure when the wheel pants are removed for the winter flying season. Fiberglass repair work should be performed in a warm, well-ventilated area, because the fumes from the resins can be irritating; fiberglass patches also will cure better in a warm room.

"Refinishing decorative coating" is not intended to imply that you can strip and repaint your own airplane. Even stripping and repainting seemingly small control surfaces, which could be subject to chips and dings, should be absolutely avoided. Unbalancing a balanced aileron or tail surface might lead to uncontrollable flutter which could be deadly. Most owners should restrain themselves to doing only the most minor touch-up jobs. Of course, beauty is in the eye of the beholder. If you really believe that can of spray paint you bought at Home Depot is close enough to the trim color of your airplane, have at it! Just don't be surprised if your plane gets some odd looks from the line crew.

Replacing side windows is allowed, but replacing front windshields is not, on the rationale that windshields are subject to additional aerodynamic stresses. If the side windows on your aircraft are basically flat, it will probably be cheapest to buy a sheet of plexiglass of the proper thickness and cut your own replacements, using the old window as a pattern. (Using slightly thicker plexiglass than the original can be an improvement in soundproofing, but make sure it fits.) If the side windows have any complex curvature, however, they probably have been molded after being heated in an oven. In this case, you will probably save yourself a lot of time and frustration by ordering a replacement window from a parts company. As an aircraft owner, there is a good chance you will receive aeronautical equivalents of the automotive *Whitney's Catalog* from at least two or three parts suppliers, including Wag-Aero and ACI. If not, replacement parts suppliers can always be found in *Trade-A-Plane*. It may also be advantageous to join a "type club" made up of owners of the make and model of airplane you fly. Their newsletters usually will have advertising from parts suppliers specializing in parts for the club's particular type of aircraft. Their Web sites may also have the information you are looking for, although you may have to be a member to access "member's only" parts of the Web site.

Sources of aircraft maintenance information

There are many sources of information on your aircraft which you should be aware of as a knowledgeable owner or as a pilot-owner who intends to perform or assist in some of the maintenance on his or her own aircraft. Most general aviation aircraft have associations which act as a clearinghouse for information on the care, maintenance, and modification of specific makes and models or families of makes and models of aircraft. Some of the more well-known "type clubs" include the American Bonanza Society, the Cessna Skyhawk Association, and the Cherokee Pilots' Association. Most of these organizations publish a monthly newsletter discussing problems encountered with the aircraft and solutions found by the members. They also may publish a volume of collected wisdom from years of aircraft care and operation. (For an aircraft that has been around for twenty-five years or more, few of the problems will really be all that new.) Membership in these clubs is usually around $25 a year to cover expenses, and it is almost always a real bargain. See Appendix D for a listing of general aviation aircraft clubs and associations.

Cherokee Hints and Tips is a handbook that contains a collection of wisdom for PA-28 and PA-32 Cherokees, Arrows, and Warriors published by the Cherokee Pilots' Association. It is an excellent example of the valuable common sense knowledge available from these organizations. One of the articles in this handbook is a discussion of the many sources of maintenance information available to an aircraft owner. The following information, adapted and updated from *Cherokee Hints and Tips* and intended for the owners of Piper Cherokee-series aircraft, provides an excellent look at the types and sources of maintenance information available to the owners of any aircraft. With the exception of specific references to Piper, most of these tips apply to almost any general aviation aircraft.

1. Start with the Pilot's Operating Handbook (owner's manual on older models) for both the airplane and the engine. Piper may be able to supply these or contact ESSCO, 426 W. Turkeyfoot Lk. Rd., Akron, OH 44319; (330) 644-7724; www.esscoaircraft.com. This firm specializes in reprinting manuals for nearly every airplane in existence. The engine handbook not only contains operating instructions which you should be familiar with, but most also cover a wide variety of maintenance procedures. A very handy source of information.

2. If you are going to tear into your plane you should have a copy of the service and parts manuals for both your plane and your engine. Once again, you may have luck with Piper or Lycoming, but I would bet on ESSCO for these manuals.

3. You should have a complete file of ADs, service bulletins, and service letters. Copies of ADs can be obtained from the FAA Web site (http://www1.faa.gov). Under the heading of Regulation & Policies, click on Airworthiness Directives.

   A comprehensive list of ADs and Service Bulletins for your aircraft can also be obtained from Aerotech Publications (www.adlog.com). Another source of ADs and service bulletins is Aerotech Publications, P.O. Box 1359, Southold, NY 11971-0965, which publishes *AdLog*. They can provide a listing of ADs by serial number and for the accessories on your plane.

4. Check your engine manufacturer's Web site for any publications applicable to your aircraft and engine. They offer a lot of valuable information. Lycoming's Web site (www.lycoming.textron.com) has maintenance publications including *Bulletins, Letters, and Instructions,* and the excellent *Key Reprints from the Lycoming Flyer.* Click on Support Center and Publications.

   For Continental Engines, check the Teledyne Continental Web site (www.tcmlink.com). Under Customer Center, click on Visitor Services and Care & Feeding Library, which includes information on engine operation, engine break-in, engine cooling, and engine lubrication.

5. Likewise, contact New Piper Aircraft, Inc. at www.newpiper.com. A close look at the items under the New Piper Owner FAQs section after clicking on FAQs on this Web site's homepage contains a variety of interesting items for the Piper owner. Piper owners can also get on the

mailing list by mailing or faxing a copy of their registration with their mailing address to The New Piper, Aircraft 2926 Piper Drive, Vero Beach, FL 32960, Attention Technical Publications Dept.

6. Do not forget your propeller manufacturer. (Hartzell Propeller, PO Box 1458, Piqua, OH 43356.) Request any available information on your propeller.

7. The various accessory manufacturers also offer information and catalogs which will take the mystery out of these products. Contact AC, Champion, Bendix, Cleveland Brake Systems, Airborne, Century, etc. Some of the information is really quite extensive, covering complete maintenance procedures for their products.

8. Make sure you have a current crop of applicable FARs. You can purchase a copy from any aviation bookstore or from nearly any mail order house. You can also find FARs on the Internet at the FAA Web site (www2.faa.gov). Click on Regulations and Policies, then on Regulations, then on Current FAA regulations.

9. The government makes a lot of information available to pilots for free. Advisory circulars are available by clicking on http://aea.faa.gov/ aea200/ea01/advisorycirculars.htm.

   One good publication is AC 20-5F, *Plane Sense,* which provides information concerning title, registration, the AD system, maintenance, and reference publications—a good summary of information any owner should have. This is not available from the main FAA Web site, but it is available on the FAA Western–Pacific Region Web site (www.awp. faa.gov/new/info_cd/ASPM%20Info/Plane%20Sense.pdf) or from the private MyPlane Web site (www.myplane.com/BuyingGuide/ PlaneSense.asp).

10. Check with the FAA to make sure your aircraft is properly registered and your correct address is listed. This is the method which will be used to get current AD and service information to you. Contact the FAA Aircraft Registry at AAC-750, Box 25504, Oklahoma City, OK 73125, or by clicking on http://registry.faa.gov/aircraft.asp. This will ensure that you receive all ADs pertaining to your aircraft, but depending on how your plane is coded, it may not ensure that you receive all ADs pertaining to specific accessory equipment on your plane.

11. Various maintenance reference works and publications are available to provide more detail. AC 43.13-1B, *Aircraft Inspection and Repair Acceptable Methods, Techniques, and Practices* is a standard FAA reference. The new edition to the *Acceptable Methods, Techniques, and Practices* (43.13-1B) was published on September 8, 1998. This new

Advisory circular is available for sale by the Superintendent of Documents, U.S. Government Printing Office, Washington, DC 20402 or you may contact the U.S. Government Bookstore at Arco Plaza, Level "C", 505 South Flower Street, Los Angeles, CA 90071. Phone: (213) 239-9844, FAX (213) 239-9848.

Owner's tool kit

The following items should be the minimum required in an owner's tool kit:

- Socket set
  ¼-inch, ⅜-inch socket sets with ³⁄₁₆-inch through ¾-inch sockets, universal joint
  ½-inch female and ⅜-inch male adapter
  ⅜-inch female and ¼-inch male adapter
  ⅜-inch ratchet handle
  ½-inch ratchet handle
  2-inch and 6-inch extensions
  ⅞-inch deep socket, ½-inch drive, 6 point (spark plugs)
  8-inch adjustable-end wrench
- Set of Allen wrenches (avionics, instrument panel work)
- Assorted sizes slot and Phillips-head screwdrivers
- 6-inch diagonal cutting pliers
- Needle-nose pliers
- 6-inch slip-jam pliers
- ¹³⁄₁₆-inch, 1-inch open-end wrench (oil filter removal, installation)
- Soft-face hammer
- Heavy-duty scissors
- Razor-blade knife
- Wire strippers
- Electrical tape
- Masking tape
- Roll of 0.040-inch safety wire
- Miscellaneous sheet metal screws, machine screws, cotter pins, and washers (aircraft-type AN hardware only)

If you perform maintenance on your automobile, there is a good chance you already have three-quarters of the tools on the list.

Care of avionics

Avionics performance is another area that can drive an airplane owner to tears and into bankruptcy if some fundamental precautions are not taken. Some relatively simple and inexpensive modifications and additions to the aircraft may pay for their installation cost in reduced avionics repairs in the first couple of years of ownership.

Heat is the primary enemy of avionics reliability. Excessive heat can cause rapid equipment failures by "cooking" transistors or integrated circuits on a hot summer day or by causing slow deterioration in cables, insulators, and other components, resulting in delayed failures. Even though new, solid-state radios are cooler operating compared to old heat-generating tube-type radios, they are still highly susceptible to problems. Their reduced cross section can allow them to be jammed into tighter spaces than was possible with larger cross-section older units.

TSO'd avionics are designed to operate continuously at 130°F (54°C) and for short periods at up to 160°F (71°C). Amazingly enough, this may not be high enough for use in the average light aircraft parked on a sun baked ramp in the summer. Greenhouse effects of sunlight, passing through an aircraft's plexiglass windshield and striking the black surface of the instrument panel, can cause temperatures within the panel to reach 160°F (71°C) when the outside temperature is only 85°F (29°C). When the radios are turned on, temperatures can soar to a devastating 185°F (85°C).

What is the answer to the heat problem? Fortunately, a couple of partial solutions are relatively inexpensive. External one-piece canopy covers made of soft canvas are available from Airtex Products Inc., Fallsington, Pennsylvania, for about $150. (Airtex also specializes in quality interiors for a wide range of used aircraft which can be installed by ambitious aircraft owners at a fraction of the cost of custom-installed interiors.) Interior heat shields made of fabric coated with a reflective material are available for about half of the cost of the one-piece exterior canopy covers. These heat shields, individually cut to cover each window, are held over the windows with Velcro fasteners. They are available by mail order from catalog order houses like Sporty's Pilot Shop or Aircraft Components, Inc. Both types of covers can keep the temperatures inside the aircraft as low if not lower than the outside air temperature on a hot summer day, which will do wonders for the radios. For low-wing aircraft like the Piper Cherokee series, which are known for water leaks around the cabin door, the one-piece external covers have the additional advantage of keeping the water away from the door seal. One caution: one-piece exterior canopy covers made of soft vinyl plastic with a soft fabric coating on the inside have been reported to cause cracking or crazing of windshields. If you're going to use the one-piece exterior covers, play it safe and stay with the soft canvas versions.

Techniques for attacking other aspects of the avionics heating problem will probably require the assistance of a mechanic. Long-term, in-flight use of avionics requires the removal of heat generated by the radios themselves. If possible, one-quarter inch should be allowed between individual radios for air circulation. Small ram airscoops, available from Narco in relatively inexpensive kits, provide cooling air to be carried to radios via small plastic hoses. (If more than one radio is installed, at least two of these airscoop kits will be required to provide a top-and-bottom flow of cooling air.) An even better arrangement is to use a "piccolo tube," fed from the cabin air or other large intake, to direct multiple streams of air at the entire radio stack. An escape for hot air should also be provided in the top of the instrument panel. A hole covered with a wire mesh screen is best, but even small drilled holes help. (If you drill holes in the top of the panel yourself, take precautions to assure that aluminum shavings don't drop down onto the radios or other instruments.) The best solution to the avionics heating problem definitely requires a mechanic or avionics technician, and that is to install cooling fans.

Antennas are probably the second most crucial component affecting avionics performance. Antenna placement is very important. Communications antennas need a good ground plane, provided by a flat, metal-conductive surface, for optimum performance. The antennas should be mounted at least 4 feet apart, either on the wing of high-wing Maule or Cessna-type aircraft or in tandem on the fuselage centerline of low-wing Piper, Beech, or Grumman-American single- or twin-engine aircraft.

Communication antenna location too near the vertical stabilizer or the windshield does not provide a good ground plane and should be avoided. Navigation antennas should be at least 3 feet from the horizontal stabilizer for best reception.

Figure 7.1. Owner-performed maintenance can sometimes be an "outside job."

The antennas supplied by the aircraft manufacturers are usually properly mounted but are seldom the best available. Simple, thin-rod communications antennas or "cat's whisker" navigation antennas often have low-gain, narrow bandwidth characteristics that cause poor reception at the ends of the dial, and they have poor mechanical strength if icing is ever encountered in IFR conditions. Better communications antennas are fiberglass-wound rod or blade types. The best navigation antenna for light general aviation aircraft is probably the "towel bar" type, available for around $500. If all of your flying will be VFR, the original antennas will probably be more than adequate. But IFR flying, in which icing and other nastiness could cause "pucker factors" at the worst possible moments, will probably make improved antennas a worthwhile investment.

Keeping antennas and connectors clean and free of corrosion can also pay dividends in increased performance and reliability. Wiping down antennas, particularly those belly-mounted transponder antennas, can remove signal-attenuating dirt and oil film. While connectors are usually not easy to get at, they generally can be serviced during annual inspections when the airplane is all torn apart anyway. Disconnect the connectors, clean off dirt and corrosion, and spray the contacts with an electrically conductive spray such as WD-40 (available in RadioShack stores).

Remember that aircraft radios, like any electronic gear, seldom work if they are wet. Be sure to keep the aircraft windshield absolutely watertight by applying new sealer around the base if the existing sealer is cracking or peeling from wear or age. If your aircraft sits out on the line, as most do, check the belly to be sure that water is not collecting and damaging remote-mounted gear. It is not unusual to mount power supplies under rear seats in Cherokees or on doublers or racks on the inside belly between rear bulkheads on almost any type of aircraft. Unfortunately, if drain holes become plugged or were never drilled in the first place, water from small cabin or wing root leaks may also collect in these very same places. The easiest way to solve the problem is to drill small drain holes in the aircraft skin (not in load-bearing components!) to prevent water from collecting.

Modification and installation tips

An airplane won't feel like it is really yours until you have made some modifications. Some you can perform in accordance with FAR Part 43, and some will require the assistance of a mechanic. Two very minor tasks you can do are the installation of small carbon monoxide (CO) detectors and replacement of aircraft screws with stainless steel screws. The CO detectors, with a useful life of about two weeks, cost less than $5 and can be attached to the instrument panel with tape, Velcro, or screws. They could be lifesavers, particularly in the winter. Replacing old, rusting screws with stainless steel hardware can improve the looks of your aircraft and reduce a corrosion problem. Consult your aircraft parts manual to be sure you are using the right replacements.

Among the mods and installations requiring the assistance of a mechanic or an avionics repair station technician (and money) are:

- Oil quick-drain—replaces a threaded crankcase plug with an easy-open valve. Makes doing your own oil changes much easier.
- Oil filter—protects the engine and doubles the recommended time between oil changes in most cases.
- Exhaust gas temperature gauge—allows precise leaning and is critical for maximum fuel economy and avoiding the "100LL blues."
- Ground power plug—a must for cold-weather jump starts.
- Strobe lights—belly strobes are the easiest to install and provide increased safety through increased visibility. They can also act as a backup when the rotating beacon decides to neither rotate nor beacon. Strobes can also be installed to replace unreliable old mechanical motor rotating beacons mounted atop the vertical stabilizer.
- Headset jacks, push-to-talk switches, and intercoms—provide better, clearer communications with hands free when flying IFR.
- Alternator upgrade—low capacity generators and older alternators just don't have it when it comes to carrying an electrical bus loaded with numerous radios, lights, and pitot heat. Upgrading to a high-output alternator can be the answer.
- Second vacuum source—can range from expensive systems with an electric motor driving an independent vacuum pump to a simpler system tapping off the intake manifold or even a trusty old venturi. Good insurance for the IFR flyer.
- Pitot heat—not easy to install with wires to run through the wing, but nice to have when you blunder into light icing while flying IFR.
- Directional gyro, artificial horizon upgrade—these installations are for those who are tired of DGs that "turn the wrong way" and artificial horizons that look like they were B-17 war surplus. If you're blessed with a really fat wallet, you can go for an HSI installation or even a flat panel display!
- Hatrack mod—something for the owners of older Cherokee 140s. Lots of room for coats, purses, and suitcases if you watch the weight and balance.
- Shoulder harnesses—FAA medical studies show that crash landings cause head, face, and upper body injuries if only lap belts are used. Hedge your bets with shoulder harnesses.

• Speed mods—ranging from aileron and flap gap seal kits to wing root and wheel fairings to expensive and exotic end-to-end cleanups, they can make your plane 5 to 15 mph faster than when it came out of the factory. If you have a Comanche, flap gap seals can even tame notoriously recalcitrant landing characteristics.

As an airplane owner you may find the following potpourri of maintenance and operating tips useful:

• Wiping down oleo struts with hydraulic fluid at least once a week will prevent dirt from being ground into the strut seals. Conscientious preventive maintenance can prevent leaking struts.
• Remove wheel pants in the winter. Slush and mud packed in during taxi and takeoff can freeze in the air. Immobilized wheels can be a nasty surprise on landing. Removing wheel pants on the "mains" will be easy. Removing the nosewheel pants will probably require the removal of the nosewheel, and that won't be so easy. But it's better than blowing a tire because of an immobilized wheel, isn't it?
• When moving your aircraft on the ground, use the tow bar if at all possible. If you have to pull or push the aircraft by its prop, do so with your hand on the prop directly beside the spinner. Pulling or pushing on the prop outward toward the tips can cause metal fatigue leading to eventual in-flight prop failure. Be sure not to push on the relatively fragile and often difficult to replace spinner, either.
• In cold weather, starts will be easier if you remove the battery and store it in a warm place when the plane is idle. Replace it only when you go out to fly again. Batteries actually have less power in cold weather, when more power is needed to turn over the engine.
• A clean, waxed airplane is not only prettier but faster as well. But cleaning and waxing an airplane is no easy job. It can be made easier, though, by using a liquid wax such as Turtle Wax to clean the oily belly and underside of the wings. The liquid wax will clean and wax in one step. Use paste wax on the upper surfaces and leading edges, where sunshine and the in-flight impact of rain and bugs requires a more durable surface.
• Carelessness in cleaning plexiglass can result in badly scratched windshields and windows. Carefully clean your windshield and windows by gently washing off dust and dirt with a wet rag, and then apply a plexiglass cleaner like Miracle Glaze or Permatex. Allow the plexiglass cleaner to dry before gently wiping it off with a clean, soft rag. Never use paper towels. Industrial grade paper towels can be abrasive enough to cause small scratches in the plexiglass. And no matter how friendly they may

seem, do not allow the line crew to touch your windshield. If your windshield is scratched once, it will be once too often!

- Keep the prop vertical when you tie down outside during winter months to prevent ice from collecting in the spinner. If ice does collect there, it can result in a severe engine vibration at low RPMs that will disappear at high RPMs but will not affect good mag checks.

- Cowl plugs, generally available from canopy cover manufacturers, are a must to keep birds from building nests in your engine compartment if your aircraft will be tied down outside.

- Pitot covers keep mud dauber wasps and other insects out of your pitot system, and are particularly valuable for low-wing airplanes.

Engine operating practices and overhauls

8

Without a doubt, the engine is the critical component of the aircraft. Failure of the engine to continue functioning in flight means a cold dread, possibly leading to panic, usually followed by a crash landing. Whether it is more crash than landing may be largely a function of luck as much as skill, regardless of what numerous pious FAA, *Flying* magazine, and AOPA Air Safety Foundation writers may tell you. And even slow deterioration of the aircraft engine, with symptoms caught at a 100-hour or annual inspection, can lead to emotional and financial catastrophe for the pilot-owner who fails to comprehend the necessity of careful operation and the possible eventual replacement of the engine.

There are few areas of aircraft ownership where your day-to-day operating habits will have a larger financial impact than in the area of engine operation and maintenance. Poor planning and false economies can be devastating when they lead to premature major overhaul or replacement of your engine.

Time between overhaul (TBO)

The expected life of a small, reciprocating, general aviation engine is measured by a purely statistical figure known as TBO, or "time between overhaul." Table 8.1 shows TBO figures for typical general aviation engines. TBO is defined by AVCO Lycoming, one of the two major U.S. general aviation piston engine manufacturers, in their *Key Reprints from the AVCO Lycoming Flyer* as "a recommended number of use hours by the engine manufacturer." (*Key Reprints* is now available at the Lycoming website at

Table 8.1. TBOs of typical general aviation engines

Lycoming

Engine	TBO (hr)	Octane	Typical Aircraft
O-235	2,400	80	Grumman-American Tr-2/Yankee
O-235	2,400	100	Cessna 152; Beechcraft Skipper; Piper Tomahawk; Grumman-American Lynx
O-320A, E	2,000	80	Piper Super Cub, Cherokee 140, 150, and 151 Warrior; Beech Musketeer/Sport; 1968-1975 Cessna 172; 1968 Cessna Cardinal; Grumman-American Traveler/Cheetah
O-320D, H	2,000	100	Piper Cherokee 160 and 161 Warrior/Cadet; post-1976 Cessna 172
O-360	2,000	100	Piper Cherokee 180 and 181, Seminole Cessna post-1969 Cardinal and Cutlass; Grumman-American Tiger; Beech Sundowner and Duchess; Aerospatiale Tobago
IO-360	2,000	100	Post-1996 Cessna 172 and 172SP, Piper Arrow; Cessna Cardinal RG, Cutlass RG; Beech Sierra; Mooney 201; Rockwell 112; Diamond DA-40
O-540, IO-540	2,000	100	Post-1997 Cessna 182, Piper Comanche, Cherokee 235/236, Cherokee 6, Lance, and Saratoga, Malibu, Aerostar, Aztec, and Navajo; Cessna 182RG; Rockwell 114; Aerospatiale Trinidad
TIO-540	2,000	100	Post-1997 Cessna T182, Piper Turbo Lance, Turbo Saratoga; Aerospatiale Turbo Trinidad; Beech Baron 56TC

Continental

Engine	TBO (hr)	Octane	Typical Aircraft
C75, C85, C90	1,800	80	Luscombe; Cessna 120/140; Ercoupe
O-200	1,800	80	Cessna 150; Taylorcraft F19
IO-240	2,000	100	Diamond DA20-C1
O-300	1,800	80	Cessna 170; 1956-1967 Cessna 172
IO-360K	1,500	100	1977, 1978 Cessna Skyhawk XP
IO-360KB, ES	2,000	100	1979-1985 Cessna Skyhawk XP; Cirrus SR20
TSIO-360	1,800	100	Mooney 231, 252; Piper Turbo Arrow, post-1975 Seneca
O-470, IO-470	1,500	80	Cessna 180; 1956-1976 Cessna 182; 1961-1966 Cessna 185; 1960-1965 Cessna 210; 1957-1963 Beech 35 Bonanza; 33 Debonair
O-470U	2,000	100	1977-1985 Cessna 182
IO-520	1,800	100	Post-1967 Cessna 185, 206, post-1966 210, 310; post-1964 Beech 35 Bonanza, post-1968 E-33, F-33 Bonanza, Beech Baron 55
TSIO-520	1,400	100	Cessna T206, T210, post-1969 310; Beech Baron 58
IO-550	2,000	100	Post-1996 Beech A36 Bonanza; Cirrus SR22; Lancair 350, 400;

http://www.lycoming.textron.com/main.jsp?bodyPage=support/publica-tions/keyReprints/index.html. Teledyne Continental also has service bul-letins and other good information at www.tcmlink.com. The TBO figure usually is derived from manufacturer's data following extensive engineering and reliability tests on a new engine. If field data from actual use of the engine indicate that the original TBO figure was too low, the manufacturer will revise it upward. The manufacturer may also make modifications to improve the weakest parts of an engine to increase its reliability. The Lycoming O-320 and O-360 engines are a classic example of where a major change in one component vastly improved the engine and its TBO figure. The 7/16-inch exhaust valves used in the original engines were known to be susceptible to cracking and breaking around the valve necks, usually when an engine was nearing its 1,200-hour TBO. In 1966 new and remanufac-tured Lycoming O-320 and O-360 engines were fitted with 1/2-inch exhaust valves. The engines, which previously had difficulty reaching the relatively low TBO of 1,200 hours, generally had an excellent reputation for meeting and often exceeding the revised TBO of 2,000 hours. But in the late 1980s, these engines, along with the larger O-540, ran into a problem with sticking and breaking valves which led Lycoming to issue service bulletins calling for more frequent oil changes and 100-hour inspections of the valves. The prob-lems were due in large part to the extra lead in 100LL, which has less lead than old 100-octane avgas but four times the lead in 80/87 avgas. But even with these problems in 80-octane engines using 100LL avgas, the 1/2-inch valves are still far more reliable than the old 7/16-inch valves.

Time between overhaul—or more properly, time between major over-haul—is purely an advisory figure. It has no legal force and it is not spelled out in any FAR that is binding to the pilot-owner. If an engine is running smoothly when it reaches its published TBO figure and has good compres-sion and reasonable oil consumption, the aircraft owner is entirely legitimate in continuing to operate the engine past that time. However, trying to extend the engine utilization beyond the TBO may be false economy. The true cost of a major overhaul usually varies only in the cost of the parts needing replacement. Worn engine parts with loose tolerances may accelerate the wear of other parts, with cumulative effects. An even worse eventuality would be failure of accessories, causing damage to the gear train and effec-tively destroying the engine.

Lycoming, in its excellent *Key Reprints*, emphasizes that the TBO is not a guaranteed figure but is one that an aircraft owner or operator who prac-tices good operation and maintenance should be able to obtain. Use of less careful practices could and probably will decrease your time between over-haul. How you use or abuse your aircraft engine will be crucial in deter-mining its life span and, therefore, its cost to you.

Insufficient use of the aircraft is one of the primary causes of premature engine deterioration that leads to an early overhaul. Normal combustion products, including water vapor and gaseous fumes, combine in the crankcase to form acids. These include sulphuric and nitric acids that can wreak havoc with an engine that is allowed to remain idle for extended periods. Prolonged idle periods have other ill effects. After approximately two weeks without use, the cylinder walls will lose oil protection and be susceptible to rust. Engine gaskets will begin to dry out and crack or shrink, leading eventually to oil leaks. Moisture entering the exhaust stacks and the crankcase breather tube also add to the problem. The ultimate effects can include rusted cylinders, sticking rings, and shorting of magneto breaker points due to condensation.

The only solution is to fly the airplane. Old hangar tales about easy cures like "pulling the prop through" and ground running the engine not only do not help but may actually make matters much worse. Pulling the prop through may make some sense before starting an engine that has been idle, because it will spread the fine layer of oil trapped between the pistons and the cylinder walls to the adjacent areas of the cylinder walls. But if the engine is not actually started, no oil will be pumped out of the engine sump. The residual layer of trapped oil can only be spread just so far. Unless this layer of trapped oil is replenished by running the engine, repeated sessions of pulling the prop through will eventually result in moving unlubricated surfaces against one another.

Ground running an engine to circulate the oil has disastrous long-term side effects. When an engine is cold, the cylinders, pistons, and rings have contracted sufficiently that the "seal" between the combustion chamber and the crankcase does not exist. Until the engine combustion process heats the engine sufficiently to expand the metal parts and re-form the seal, the combustion by-products, including water vapors and gases that form acids when combined with water, condense to form corrosive acid and sludge buildup in the oil. Once in the oil, these corrosive elements are carried throughout the engine.

So what's the answer? The answer, as an oversimplification, is to fly the airplane! If the plane is flown long enough to bring the engine to operating temperatures, the water vapor and combustion by-products will pass out the crankcase breather tube as a steam-acid mixture. (This should also cause any owner who is considering putting an "air-oil separator" condenser system on the breather line to think twice. It won't be just oil vapor that will be returned to the crankcase!)

How long is long enough? How often is often enough? Thirty minutes at or near cruise power should bring the engine up to sufficient temperature to drive out the water vapor and acids. This is probably not much more than three touch-and-gos in the pattern. How often? Once a week is probably sufficient. Expert opinion varies, however. Lycoming experts generally insist that 15 hours per month are necessary to give reasonable expectation of reaching the TBO. Since this works out to 180 hours per year, this is probably an unrealistically high figure for a single owner. It could, of course, add an operational incentive to the financial ones for finding a partner to share the airplane. Another alternative is to consider more frequent oil changes. Recommended oil change intervals are usually every 25 hours if your engine does not have an oil filter and every 50 hours if it does. It is probably advisable to change the oil at least once every 90 days, if this would be more frequent than oil changes based on hours of engine operation.

Operating practices

Pilot technique, or operating procedures, also have a significant effect on the life of an aircraft engine. From the moment you start your engine until the moment you shut it down, you will have a very real impact on its probability of reaching the rated TBO.

Overpriming can accelerate piston and cylinder wear in engines that have fuel injected by the primer into the upper cylinders. Overpriming can wash away any oil that has been retained on the cylinder walls, allowing a detrimental metal-to-metal contact between the piston and the cylinder walls during start-up. If an engine is being started in an ambient temperature environment below 10°F (–12°C), preheat should be used and applied to the entire engine but particularly to the oil pan or lower crankcase area. Without preheat, scored cylinders, scuffed pistons, and broken rings could result from continued engine operation without sufficient oil circulation.

Prolonged ground runs, particularly in the summer, should be avoided. Detrimental effects could include excessive cylinder head temperatures and "baking" of rubber seals and ignition harnesses, leading to oil leaks and ignition harness arcing. Ground runs should be performed into the wind, and whenever possible the aircraft nose should be pointed into the wind while waiting in line for takeoff. After takeoff, climbs at excessively steep angles could also cause overheating effects and should be avoided.

Abrupt throttle changes ("throttle jockeying") can cause severe unbalanced forces on engine components, rapid temperature changes detrimental to engine parts, possible overboosting of turbocharged systems, and a buildup of electrically conductive deposits on spark plugs, leading to preignition. Preignition, or combustion in a cylinder before the timed spark plug firing, is caused by local hot spots in spark plug deposits, high-power operation at excessively leaned mixtures, or broken spark plug insulators. The effects of preignition can be broken rings and "tuliped" intake valves.

Babying an engine is also a bad practice. Light general aviation engines are designed for continuous long-term operation at 75-percent power settings, including full-throttle operation at higher altitudes. Mushing along at a 55 percent power setting does not extend the life of the engine. On a hot summer day, it could easily cause destructive over-heating instead.

Proper leaning will do a great deal to improve the economy and useful life of your engine. Improper leaning could lead to rapid destruction of an engine through detonation, which is usually noticeable as an audible "ping" in automobiles but which cannot be heard above other noises in an aircraft's operating environment. Caused by running with overly lean mixtures at high-power settings, detonation can cause "dished" piston heads; collapsed valve heads; and eroded spots or holes in valves, pistons, and cylinder heads. The long list of possible ill effects due to improper leaning, however, should not be allowed to discourage you from leaning your engine. Proper leaning has many advantages, including better fuel economy and longer range, a smoother-running engine, less spark plug fouling, and cleaner cylinder com-bustion chambers.

Carburetors on normally aspirated general aviation engines are ordi-narily set rich. Contrary to popular belief, engines can be leaned at cruise setting at any altitude. According to Lycoming's *Key Reprints*, "normally aspirated direct drive engines with a manual mixture control should be leaned at cruise powers of 75 percent or less at any altitude while cruising." Many pilots believe that you should wait until reaching 5,000 feet before leaning the engine, but this is the rule-of-thumb altitude where you should begin leaning before takeoff and in climb power, not cruise settings. Leaning should be performed according to aircraft and/or engine manufacturer's rec-ommendations. The following procedures, however, are adequate and safe guidelines for almost all light aircraft:

- Without exhaust-gas temperature (EGT) gauge—lean to maximum RPM or airspeed or to a point just before engine roughness, then enrich slightly.
- With EGT—lean to peak reading, then enrich to 50 degrees on the rich side of peak.

Letdowns prior to landing should be planned in advance and carried out with slow, stepped power reductions. Arriving near your destination "high and hot," and pulling power back to idle for a rapid descent will "tempera-ture shock" your engine, very likely leading to cracked rings, cylinder cracks at spark plug and valve ports, and warped exhaust valves. If you own a sleek retractable like a Mooney or a Bonanza and if you do a lot of high-speed, high-altitude cross-country flying, you should invest in a set of "scissors" type spoilers. These devices will allow you to descend at a high descent rate while still maintaining sufficiently high power settings to keep engine temperatures up during the descent.

Owner-performed maintenance can also affect engine life. Dust and dirt particles in the air are very abrasive on engine components; therefore, air filters should be replaced regularly. Worn air hoses should be replaced when necessary. Using carb heat on the ground should also be avoided except for a short-duration preflight check. Because air for carb heat bypasses the intake filter, unfiltered air is being used. In flight, this is seldom a problem; on the ground it nearly always is. Oil changes should be performed at least as often as recommended to avoid a buildup of corrosive acids. Spark plugs should be rotated between the top and bottom of each cylinder at every oil change, and worn plugs should always be replaced.

100 LOW-LEAD VS. AUTOGAS. Using so-called 100 low-lead avgas in engines designed for 80-octane avgas adds to the severity of many detrimental factors that reduce engine life. Although it contains only half the lead content of regular 100-octane avgas, 100LL still has four times the lead content of 80-octane. In engines designed to use 80-octane avgas, excessive lead salts, which are a by-product of lead antiknock compounds, form a potentially corrosive buildup on valves, rings, and spark plugs. They also enter the crankcase via blow-by. When dry, these lead salts are relatively harmless. When activated by moisture, as they are in any aircraft left idle for extended periods, they become very corrosive. Buildup of lead salts on spark plugs and valves are worse during start-up, taxi, and takeoff. The cold fuel entering the cylinder via the intake valve condenses on the cold metal parts. The carbon in the fuel rapidly burns off, but the lead forms a hard deposit on plugs, valves, and rings. Continental small-displacement engines, including the O-200 and the O-300, seem to be particularly plagued by spark plug and valve problems caused by 100LL. Surprisingly enough, Lycoming O-320 engines designed to use 100LL also experienced a significant number of exhaust valve problems, particularly in the 1980s.

To some extent, 100LL problems can be avoided by following several common sense rules which are good for pilots who fly aircraft with engines originally designed for 90/96-octane and 100-octane avgas and pilots of aircraft with 80-octane burning engines.

- Avoid overpriming when starting up.
- Keep engine RPM at 1,000 or more when idling and taxiing.

- Lean the mixture control while cruising at any altitude and when climbing or taking off above 5,000 feet.
- Perform frequent oil changes to remove accumulated lead salts and other corrosive combustion by-products.
- Use only the correct spark plugs for your aircraft, and don't try to extend their life. A misfiring plug can substantially increase deposits on valves and rings.

A 1977 study conducted by Embry-Riddle Aeronautical University, a major flight training school in Florida, indicated that tricresyl phosphate (TCP) was one cure for the "100LL blues." In 18 Cessna 172s with the 80-octane Lycoming O-320 engine, while burning only 100LL avgas, nine of the planes used TCP and nine did not. Approximately 600 flight hours were accumulated on each aircraft. The results indicated that TCP significantly reduced spark plug fouling; decreased valve sticking; had no adverse effects on the engines; and most surprisingly, appeared to clean out previously accumulated sludge, lead deposits, and other residues. On the basis of this study, the FAA approved the use of TCP, which is marketed by Alcor, Inc.

The Experimental Aircraft Association was responsible for the best solution to the 100LL problems, however. Despite intense opposition to the use of autogas in aircraft by the petroleum industry, aircraft engine manufacturers, and the FAA, the EAA began an autogas flight test program in a Cessna 150 in 1978. After hundreds of hours of flight testing using autogas purchased from a wide range of sources and under a wide range of well-documented temperature, humidity, and altitude conditions, the EAA succeeded in obtaining a Supplemental Type Certificate (STC) from the FAA in August 1982 allowing the use of autogas in Cessna 150s.

The battle to use autogas in most of the 80-octane-engined general aviation fleet took several more years to win. Exxon, Shell, and Mobil continued to bitterly oppose the use of autogas in aircraft after the initial STC was issued. But the door had been opened, and industry red herrings about problems with vapor lock and inconsistent quality of autogas were disproved as EAA tests of other aircraft continued and Cessna 150 owners began piling up hours in the air using autogas without problems. The decision of the normally conservative British Civil Aviation Authority to allow the use of autogas in more than 100 different airplane types also lent credibility to the EAA efforts. In a surprising development, a small Nebraska crop-duster operator began doing his own testing to widen the field of aircraft with STCs allowing the use of autogas. Petersen Aviation, using 150-hour test cell runs similar to aircraft engine certification tests, established itself as an expert in the field of autogas use in aircraft.

Piper Cherokee PA-28-160s and 180s and PA-28-161 Warrior IIs and PA-28-161 Archer IIs with 91-octane rated engines can be converted to 91-octane lead-free autogas use by adding a Petersen-designed kit that replaces the single electric fuel pump with two specially designed pumps and other minor fuel system modifications. Whether most owners would feel that the added complexity of pumps, tanks, and manifolds is worth the money saved by using autogas is debatable. But if economic forces eventually make avgas unavailable or uneconomical, it could be a lifesaver for owners of aircraft with non-80-octane engines.

By the late 1980s, almost every aircraft engine designed to use 80-octane avgas had been STC'd for autogas use. (See Tables 8.2 through 8.5.) Even the FAA belatedly jumped on the bandwagon, and in 1989 FAA Engine/Fuel Safety representatives admitted that tests conducted at the FAA Technical Center in Atlantic City, New Jersey, showed that 80-octane and 91-octane engines actually ran better and with fewer problems using autogas rather than with 100LL avgas.

Table 8.2. EAA Autofuel STCs: Aircraft

Aero Commander
100

Aeronca (including Bellanca and Champion)
Most models including the 7 and 11 series; 7KCAB*

Arctic (including Interstate)
S-1A, S-1B1, S-1B2

Beechcraft
Bonanza 35, A-35, B-35, C-35, D-35, E-35, F-35, G-35, 35R

Cessna
120, 140, 140A; 150, 150A-H, 150J-M, A-150K-M; 152**, A152**, 170, 170A, 170B; 172, 172A-E, 172F (T-41A), 172G, 172H, P172D, 172I, 172K, 172M; 175, 175A-C; 177; 180, 180A-H, 180J; 182, 182A-P; 305A (O1A), 305B, 305E (TO1D, O-1D, O-1F), 305C (O-1E), 305D (O-1G), 305F

Commonwealth (including Skyranger and Rearwin)
175, 180, 185

Ercoupe (including Airco, Forney, Alon, Mooney)
415C, D, E, G, 415CD, F-1, F-1A, A-2, A-2A, M10

Funk
B-85C

Grumman-American
AA-1, AA-1A, AA-1B, AA-1C, AA-5, AA-5A

Luscombe
8 Series, 11A

Maule
M-4, most models

Mooney
M-18C, M-18C55, M-18L, M-18LA

(continued)

Table 8.2. (*continued*)

Piper
E-2, J-2, J-3 (most models), J-4 (most models), J-5 (most models), PA-11 (most models), PA-12 (most models), PA-14, PA-15*, PA-16, PA-17, PA-18 (all models), PA-19 (all models), PA-20 (all models), PA-22 (most models), PA-28-140, PA-28-150, PA-28-151

Porterfield (including Rearwin and Northwest)
305C (O-1E), 305D (0-1G), 305F

Stinson
108 Series*, HW-75, 10

Superior Aircraft (including Culver Cadet)
LCA, LFA

Taylorcraft
A, BC (most models)

Varga 2000C, 2150, 2150A, 2180

NOTE: * Airframe approvals only
** Requires engine modification

Table 8.3. EAA Autofuel STCs: Engines

Teledyne Continental
    A-40, A-40-2, A-40-3, A-40-4, A-40-5
    A-50-1, A-50-2, A-50-3, A-50-4, A-50-5, A-50-6, A-50-7, A-50-8, A-50-9
    A-65-1, A-65-3, A-65-6, A-65-7, A-65-8, A-65-9, A-65-12, A-65-14
    A-75-3, A-75-6, A-75-8, A-75-9
    C-75-8, C-75-12, C-75-15
    C-85-8, C-85-12, C-85-14, C-85-15
    C-90-8, C-90-12, C-90-14, C-90-16
    C-125-1, C-125-2
    E-165-2, E-165-3, E-165-4
    E-185-1, E-185-2, E-185-3, E-185-5, E-185-8, E-185-9, E-185-10, E-185-11
    C-145-2, C-145-2H, C-145-2HP
    O-170-3, O-170-5, O-170-7
    O-200-A, O-200-B, O-200-C
    O-300-A, O-300-B, O-300-C, O-300-D, O-300-E
    GO-300-A, GO-300-B, GO-300-C, GO-300-D, GO-300-E, GO-300-F
    E-225-2, E-225-4, E-225-8, E-225-9
    O-470-A, O-470-E, O-470-J, O-470-K, O-470-L, O-470-R, O-470-S
    O-470-4, O-470-13, O-470-13B

AVCO Lycoming
    O-235-C, O-235-C1, O-235-C1B, O-235-C2, O-235-E1, O-235-E2, O-235-H2
    O-235-L2C, O-235-K2C (modified for 80 octane: engine modification required)
    O-290, O-290-A, O-290-AP, O-290-B, O-290-C, O-290-CP, O-290-D, O-290-D2,
        O-290-D2A, O-290-D2B, O-290-D2C
    O-320-A, O-320-C, O-320-E
    O-540-B1A5, O-540-B1B5, O-540-B1D5, O-540-B2A5, O-540-B2B5, O-540-B2C5,
        O-540-B4A5, O-540-B4B5

Table 8.4. Petersen Aviation Autofuel STCs: Aircraft

Aero Commander
10, 10A, 100, 100A

Aeronca
15AC, S15AC, 65-TC, YO-58, 65-TAC

Beechcraft
35, A35, B35, C35, D35, E35, F35, G35, 35R, 35-33, 35-A33, 35-B33, 35-C33, E33, F33

Bellanca (Champion, Aeronca)
7GCAA, 7GCBC, 7AC, S7AC, 7BCM, 7DC, S7DC, S7CCM, 7EC, S7EC, 7FC, 7GC, 7GCA, 7HC, 7JC, 7GCB, 7KC, 7GCBA, 7ECA, 8GCBC

Cessna
120, 140, 140A; 150, 150A-M, A150K-M, 152, A152, 170A, 170B; 172, 172A-N, 172P, P172D, 175, 175A-C; 177; 180, 180A-H, 180J; 182, 182A-H, 182J-N, 182P, 188, 188A, 188B, 190, 195, 195A, 195B, 305A-F, USAF O-1A, O-1E, TO-1D, O-1D, O-1F

Christen
Husky A-1

Globe (Temco)
GC-1A, GC-1B

Great Lakes
2T-1A-1

Gulfstream American
AA-5, AA-5A

Maule
M-4, M-4C, M-4S, M-4T, M5, M6, M7, MX7, M8

Piper
PA-11, PA-11S, PA-12, PA-12S, PA-14, PA-16, PA-16S, PA-18, PA-18A, PA-18S, PA-18 "105," PA-18A "135," PA-18A "150" restricted category, PA-18S "105," PA-18 "125," PA-18S "125," PA-18 "135," PA-18A "135," PA-18S "135," PA-18AS "135," PA-18 "150," PA-18A "150," PA-18S "150," PA-18AA "150," PA-19, PA-19S, PA-20, PA-20S, PA-20 "115," PA-20S "115," PA-20 "135," PA-20S "135," PA-22, PA-22-108, PA-22-135, PA-22S-135, PA-22-150, PA-22S-150, PA-22-160, PA-22S-160, PA-23-150, PA-23-160, PA-25, PA-25-235 (restricted and normal category), PA-28-140, PA-28-150, PA-28-151, PA-28-160, PA-28-161, PA-28-180, PA-28-181, PA-28-235, PA-36-285, J3C-65, J3C-65S, J4A, J-4A-S

Stinson
108, 108-1, 108-2, 108-3

Taylorcraft
19, F19, BCS-65, BCS12-65, BCS-12D, BCS-12D1, BC-65, BC-12-65, BC-12D, BC-12D1, BC-12D-4-85, DC-65, DCO-65

Varga
2150A

Table 8.5. Petersen Aviation Autofuel STCs: Engines

Teledyne Continental

A-65-1, A-65-3, A-65-6, A-65-6J, A-65-7, A-65-8, (O-170-3, O-170-7), A-65-8F, A-65-8FJ, A-65-8J, A-65-9 (O-170-5), A-65-9F, A-65-FJ, A-65-9J, A-65-12, A-65-12F, A-65-12FJ, A-65-12J, A-65-14, A-65-14F, A-65FJ, A-65-14J

A-75-3, A-75-6, A-75-6CJ, A-75-8, A-75-8F, A-75-8J, A-75-9, A-75-9J,

C-75-8, C-75-8F, C-75-8FH, C-75-8FJ, C-75-8FHJ, C-75-8J, C-75-12, C-75-12F, C-75-12FH, C-75-FHJ, C-75-12FJ, C-75-12J, C-75-12B, C-75-12BF, C-75-BFH, C-75-15, C-75-15F

C-85-8, C-85-8F, C-85-8FJH, C-85-FJ, C-85-8J, C-85-12, C-85-12F, C-85-12FH, C-85-12FHJ, C-85-12FJ, C-85-12J, C-85-14, C-85-14F, C-85-15, C-85-15F

C-90-8F, C-90-8FJ, C-90-12F, C-90-12FH, C-90-12FJ, C-90-12FP, C-90-14F, C-90-14FH, C-90-14FJ, C-90-16F

C-115-1, C-115-2

C-125-1, C-125-2

C-145-2, C-145-2H, C-145-2HP

E-165-2, E-165-3, E-165-4

E-185-1, E-185-2, E-185-3, E-185-5, E-185-8, E-185-9, E-185-10, E-185-11

O-200-A, O-200-B, O-200-C

E-225-2, E-225-4, E-225-8, E-225-9

O-300-A, O-300-B, O-300-C, O-300-D, O-300-E

GO-300-A, GO-300-B, GO-300-C, GO-300-D, GO-300-E, GO-300-F

O-470-A, O-470-E, O-470-J, O-470-K, O-470-L, O-470-R, O-470-S, O-470-4, O-470-7, O-470-7A, O-470-7B, O-470-11, O-470-11B, O-470-C1, O-470-11B-C1, O-470-13, O-470-13A, O-470-15

IO-470-J, IO-470-K

IO-520-A, IO-520-B, IO-520-BA, IO-520-BB, IO-520-C, IO-520-CB, IO-520-D, IO-520-E, IO-520-F, IO-520-J, IO-520-K, IO-520-L, IO-520-M, IO-520-MB, IO-520-NB

W670-6A, (R-670-3, R-670-5), W670-6N, (R-670-4), W670-16, (R-670-8, R670-11, R670-11A), W670-23, W670-24, W670-K, W670-M

Franklin

6A4-150-B3, B4, B31, 6A4-165-B3, B4, B6, $AC-176-B2, B3, BA2, ()-175-1), BA3, C2, C3, D2, D3, F2, F3

AVCO Lycoming

O-145-B1, O-145-B2, O-145-B3, O-145-C1

GO-145-A1, GO-145-A2, GO-145-C1, GO-145-C2, GO-145-C3

O-235-C, O-235-C1, O-235-C1A, O-235-C1B, O-235-C1C, O-235-C2A, O-235-C2B, O-235-E1, O-235-E1B, O-235-E2A, O-235-E2B, O-235-L2A*, O-235-L2C*, O-235-M1*, O-235-M2C*, O-235-M3C*, O-235-N2A*, O-235-N2C*, O-235-P1*, O-235-P2A*, O-235-P2C*, O-235-P3C*

O-290, O-290-A, O-290-AP, O-290-B, O-290-C, O-290-CP, O-290-D, O-290-D2A, O-290-D2B, O-290-D2C, O-290-1, O-290-3, O-290-11

O-320, O-320-A1A, O-320-A1B, O-320-A2A, O-320-A2B, O-320-A2C, O-320-A2D, O-320-A3A, O-320-A3B, O-320-A3C, O-320-B1A*, O-320-B1B*, O-320-B2A*, O-320-B2B*, O-320-B2C*, O-320-B3A*, O-320-B3B*, O-320-B3C*, O-320-C1A, O-320-C1B, O-320-C2A, O-320-C2B, O-320-C2C, 0-320-C3A, O-320-C3B, O-320-C3C, O-320-D1A*, O-320-D1B*, O-320-D1C*, O-320-D1D*, O-320-D1F*, O-320-D2A*, O-320-D2B*, O-320-D2C*, O-320-D2F*, O-320-D2G*, O-320-D2H*, O-320-D2J*, O-320-D3G*, O-320-E1A, O-320-E1B, O-320-E1C, O-320-E1F, O-320-E1J, O-320-E2A, O-320-E2B, O-320-E2C, O-320-E2D, O-320-E2F, O-320-E2G, O-320-E2H, O-320-E3D, O-320-E3H

O-360-A1A*, O-360-A1AD*, O-360-A1D*, O-360-A1F*, O-360-A1F6*, O-360-A1F6D*, O-360-A1G*, O-360-A1G6*, O-360-A1G6D*, O-360-A1H*, O-360-A1H6*, O-360-A1LD*, O-360-A2A*, O-360-A2D*, O-360-A2E*, O-360-A2F*, O-360-A2G*, O-360-A2H*, O-360-A3A*, O-360-A3AD*, O-360-A3D*, O-360-A4A*, O-360-A4AD*, O-360-A4D*, O-360-A4G*, O-360-A4J*, O-360-A4K*, O-360-A4M*, O-360-A4N*, O-360-A5AD*, O-360-B1A, O-360-B1B, O-360-B2A, O-360-B2B, O-360-C1A*, O-360-C1C*, O-360-C1E*, O-360-C1F*, O-360-C1G*, O-360-C2A*, O-360-C2C*, O-360-C2E*, O-360-F1A6*, O-360-G1A6*, O-360-J2A

O-435, O-435 A, P-435C (O-435-1), O-435-C1 (O435-11), O-435-C2 (O-435-13)

O-540-A1A*, O-540-A1A5*, O-540-A1B5*, O-540-A1C5*, O-540-A1D*, O-540-A1D5*, O-540-A2B*, O-540-A3D5*, O-540-A4A5*, O-540-B5*, O-540-A4C5*, O-540-A4D5*, O-540-B1A5, O-540-B1B5, O-540-B1D5, O-540-B2A5, O-540-B2B5, O-540-B2C5, O-540-B4A5, O-540-B4B5, O-540-D1A5*, O-540-E4A5*, O-540-E4B5*, O-540-E4C5*, O-540-G1A5*, O-540-G2A5*, O-540-H1A5*, O-540-H1A5D*, O-540-H1B5D*, O-540-H2A5*, O-540-H2B5D*, O-540-H1B5D*, O-540-F1B5*

Pratt & Whitney
R-985-13, R-985-17, R-985-19, R-985-23, R-985-25, R-985-27, R-985-39, R-985-39A, R-985-48, R-985-50, R-985-AN-1, R-985-1M1, R-985-AN-2, R-985-AN-3, R-985-AN-4, R-985-AN-5, R-985-AN-6, R-985-AN-6B, R-985-AN-8, R-985-AN-10, R-985-AN-12, R-985-AN-12B, R-985-AN-14B, R-985-AN-14MB1, T1B2, T1B3, B-4, B-5, SB, SB-2, SB3

R-1340-E, R1340-19, R1340-22, R1340-29, R1340-36, R1340-40, R1340-47, R1340-49, R1340-49M1, R1340-51, R1340-AN-1, R1340-AN-2, R1340-51M1, R1340-53, R1340-57, R1340-59, R1340-61, S1D1, S3H1, S3H1G, S1H1, S1H2, S1H4, S3H2

*91 octane minimum

So should you use autogas in your airplane? If you own an airplane with an 80-octane burning engine, the answer is almost an unqualified yes. STCs for an 80-octane engined aircraft (and some 91-octane engined aircraft) can be obtained from the EAA Aviation Center at www.eaa.org/education/ fuel/index.html, P.O. Box 3086, Oshkosh, WI, 54903-3086 or 920-426-4800 or from Petersen Aviation, Inc. at http://autofuelstc.com/pa/ petersenaviation.html, 984 K Road, Minden, NE, 68959 or 308-832-2050. STCs from both sources were traditionally priced at approximately $1 per horsepower, which is the aircraft owner's share of the cost of the extensive testing which was required to obtain the STC. (Piper Cherokees and Cessna 210s cost more.) If you buy an 80-octane engined aircraft, you may find that the previous owner has already obtained the STC. If he or she hasn't, you probably should.

The Petersen Web site also notes that several Maule aircraft, including most of those powered by Lycoming 160-hp O-320, 180-hp O-360, and 235-hp O-540 B engines have autogas STCs available from the Maule factory. Modifications are required to the aircraft fuel systems. Contact Maule at 912-985-6197 for information.

The Petersen Web site also notes that Piper Cherokee 160, 161, 180, and 181 series aircraft newer than serial number 28-1761 (which would include most Cherokees) are approved for 91 octane autogas after installation of a Petersen mod kit. The STC requires the removal of the Piper installed electric boost pump and the installation of two redundant electric pumps to allow the planes to pass minimum flow tests. A kit including pumps, fittings, placards, installation instructions, and the STC is available from Petersen for $1,475.

There are several cautions or considerations when using autogas. The first is that commercial or airline operations under FAR Parts 121 or 135 are not allowed. The second, and a major consideration, is that the fuel should be obtained from FBOs that carry autogas or from brand name gas stations or distributors. Not all states have equally stringent laws on the quality and purity of autogas, and unscrupulous cut-rate gas station operators have been known to cut gasoline with low-cost methanol (wood alcohol), which can swell rubber seals and attack other fuel system components (one of the findings of the FAA Technical Center testing). So if you're going to use autogas in your airplane, stick to the good stuff and don't try to squeeze your pennies too tight or you could end up paying a lot more in the end!

Both the EAA and Petersen recommend using auto fuel which conforms to the standards of ASTM Specification D-4814 (formerly D-439). EAA literature, quoting the American Petroleum Institute Digest of State Inspection Laws-Petroleum Products, lists 33 states which require auto fuel to meet the ASTM D-439 standard. (See Table 8.6.) Petersen also recommends using a Hodges fuel volatility tester (which they can provide for about $50) to test for vapor pressure on hot days or when a winter blend is still in the tanks on a warm spring day.

Table 8.6. States where auto fuel meets D-4814 standards

The following states require compliance with D-4814 in whole or in part or require critical specifications values per ASTM D-4814:

Alabama	Florida	Kansas	Nevada	Tennessee
Arizona	Georgia	Louisiana	North Carolina	Utah
Arkansas	Hawaii	Maryland	North Dakota	Virginia
California	Idaho	Minnesota	Oklahoma	Wisconsin
Colorado	Illinois	Mississippi	Rhode Island	Wyoming
Connecticut	Indiana	Montana	South Carolina	
Delaware	Iowa	New Mexico	South Dakota	

Despite all the testing and the years of trouble-free operation by many pilots, there are still skeptics who aren't fully convinced about the safety of using autogas in airplanes. If you're the ultra cautious sort, you can do what other ultra cautious aircraft owners have been known to do—have one tank filled with avgas for takeoff and landing and the other tank filled with high-quality, brand name autogas for a low-cost cruise. The EAA, however, does "not recommend routine and continued mixing with 100LL," citing the undesirable effects of the 100LL's high lead content. Petersen recommends using one tank full of 100LL every 100 hours to replace lead on the valve seats for lubrication. Just remember that an STC is still required if you intend to use any autogas.

Ultimately, the economic forces of the marketplace may force all owners of piston-engined aircraft to convert to autogas use. Shortly after taking over as president of AOPA in 1991, Phil Boyer warned that aviation gasoline constituted such a small percentage of refined petroleum products that fewer and fewer oil companies are likely to continue producing avgas in the future. And as more aircraft owners switch to using autogas, the market for avgas will shrink even more. Eventually, autogas may be the only alternative for owners and operators of piston-engined aircraft.

An article in the July 23, 2001 edition of *Aviation Week & Space Technology* magazine addressed the issue of the eventual demise of 100LL. It noted that Cessna officials said that they expected 100LL to be available until at least 2010. The article also noted that 70 percent of all piston aircraft engines could run on 82 or 91 octane gasolines, meaning that unleaded premium auto gas should be adequate (although for low-wing airplanes, Petersen STC pump installations might be necessary). The engines most likely to have problems if 100LL disappeared would be large turbocharged, nonintercooled engines. One partial solution may be electronic ignition systems which could adjust ignition timing to avoid detonation.

Another solution to the loss of 100LL might be the replacement of large displacement turbocharged aircraft engines with diesel engines. Diesel engines can run on a variety of fuels, including Jet-A, and can offer increased TBOs and lower fuel consumption. In 2003, two European companies had developed diesel engines compatible with at least some general aviation aircraft. SMA, a French company (www.smaengines.com), had developed the six-cylinder, 230 hp SR305. Cirrus and Maule aircraft were being produced with the SR305, and STCs were being developed for airframes including the Cessna 182. German manufacturer Thielart Aircraft Engines had developed a four-cylinder, 135-hp, liquid-cooled FADEC turbo diesel called the Centurion 1.7. The actual thrust level of the Centurion 1.7 was actually nearer to that of a 180-hp engine, and the engine was being flown in Europe on Piper Cherokee and Cessna Skyhawk airframes. Superior Air Parts, once known only for being a PMA parts supplier but now a top-end engine rebuilder and supplier of new cylinders and new engines, had secured rights to the Thielart engine for the North American market (www.centurion-engine.com).

Turbocharging

For the owner who intends to use his or her airplane for serious transportation, the question will arise over whether or not to buy a turbocharged aircraft. Once you step up into the retractables, your options will almost certainly include a turbocharged version of just about any new or used retractable gear aircraft available. Mooney 201s and 205s have turbocharged 231 and 252 counterparts, as do Piper Arrows and Saratogas and Cessna Skylane RGs and 210s. Even upscale fixed-gear airplanes, like the Piper Turbo Dakota, the Cessna Turbo Skylane and Turbo 206, and the Lancair 400, come with turbochargers. Pressurized singles and twins will of course come turbocharged—if you're going to get up high enough to need pressurization, you'll need a turbocharged engine to get you there.

But turbocharging isn't for everyone. The list of negatives for "turbos" is actually longer than the positives. It is definitely an expensive option and not something to have on the airplane just for the status. Generally speaking, if you're going to plan to fly IFR in the western United States on a regular basis, you probably should have a turbocharged airplane. If you're going to do most of your flying between New England and Florida and the Bahamas, you'd probably be better off with a normally aspirated engine swinging your prop.

The turbocharged aircraft's positive points are few, but they are significant. Turbocharging increases the aircraft's performance under high altitude (and density altitude) conditions, allowing a turbocharged aircraft to climb to altitudes a normally aspirated aircraft can't reach and to maintain a high rate of climb getting there. Top speed at the higher altitudes will be greater than the normally aspirated aircraft will be capable of, and the turbocharged aircraft will be able to ride high altitude winds. This allows the aircraft, on rare occasions, to achieve groundspeeds nearly doubling those of their lower-flying nonturbocharged brethren. Turbocharged twins will have a higher single-engine ceiling and generally will have a better single-engine rate of climb.

But there is a price to be paid for these benefits. The initial purchase price of a turbocharged aircraft will be higher, and the maintenance costs may be significantly higher. Turbocharging increases the stress on an engine, and most turbocharged engines will have a lower TBO than nonturbocharged versions of the same engines. Cylinders of turbocharged aircraft are more likely to require a top overhaul. The turbochargers themselves will probably have to be replaced more than once before the engine reaches its time for major overhaul.

Turbocharged engines are also likely to be more difficult and expensive to convert to autogas if market conditions eventually do lead to elimination of reasonably priced aviation gasoline. As already noted, large displacement turbocharged engines are the least tolerant to fuels with less than 100 octane.

The turbocharger glows red hot in operation. Minor fuel and oil leaks that would be an annoyance in a normally aspirated engine can be deadly in the vicinity of the operating turbocharger. Rubber hoses and seals near the turbocharger dry out and age more quickly. The higher speed also comes at the cost of a higher fuel burn. The turbocharger brings more air to the engine and allows more fuel to mix with it to provide normal full-rated power at higher altitudes. It is generally not more fuel efficient, just faster. And one consideration that many pilots may not even think of is the need for oxygen. If you are going to fly high enough to make the turbocharger useful, you're going to be up in oxygen mask country (unless you have the investment portfolio necessary to step up into a pressurized cabin).

Are there any special considerations for operating a turbocharged engine? First, be especially rigorous about doing all the good things you should be doing with any engine. Regular usage. Slow, smooth power changes. No extended descents with the power pulled all the way back, shock-cooling the engine. (And in a turbo, you'll have to plan your descents farther ahead because you'll have more altitude to lose.)

In a turbocharged aircraft, takeoffs are more complicated than just firewalling the throttle. The throttle will have to be advanced slowly and carefully to avoid overboosting the engine. Automatic wastegates are supposed to take care of those kinds of things in theory, but if you rely on the wastegate to prevent overboosting you'll be a prime candidate for lots of serious engine maintenance earlier than scheduled. And if you want to make your turbocharger have as long a life as possible, you'll have to get used to patiently running your engine at idle for a few minutes before shutting off the engine. The turbocharger takes several minutes to "spool down," and its bearings are lubricated from the engine's oil supply.

If you are going to spend the money for a turbocharged aircraft, there are several modifications and additions which will add significantly to the life of your aircraft's engine, reduce your maintenance costs, and even add to your aircraft's capabilities. These are the intercooler, speedbrakes, and pressurized magnetos.

One of the main reasons that most factory-installed turbocharged engines do not last as long as normally aspirated engines in similar airframes is that the process of compressing air, which is the turbocharger's only reason for existence, heats the air. So an air-cooled engine is receiving preheated air. If the airframe manufacturer is not a near genius in engine cooling design, problems result which reduce engine life or performance or both. The Cessna P210 was a classic case of an aircraft which did not live up to its performance claims, due to overheating. Cessna's original answer was in part to increase the fuel flow for increased engine cooling at the cost of fuel efficiency. The Continental TSIO-360 engines used on the Piper Turbo Arrow and Seneca and on the Mooney 231 were likewise plagued by heat-caused detonation, which brought about serious engine problems—unless richer fuel mixtures were used. Intercoolers solve the air compression heat problem by effectively mounting a radiator between the turbocharger and the engine. The air stays compressed, but is much cooler when it gets to the engine.

Some new turbocharged aircraft, like the Piper Malibu and Malibu Mirage and the Beechcraft Turbo Barons, come with intercoolers. Mooney, learning their lesson with the 231, equipped the 252 with an intercooler. But for most of the others, an add-on installation by TurboPlus, Inc., of Gig Harbor, Washington, for Mooneys or Pipers or by Riley SuperSkyrocket, of Carlsbad, California for 200 and 300 series Cessnas, should be considered a must. TurboPlus installations are available for many turbocharged aircraft, including the Piper Turbo Arrows, Turbo Dakotas, Seneca twins, and Mooney 231s. Riley installations are available for turbocharged 200- and 300-series Cessnas. The price will be less than $10,000 (per engine) and worth the money in the long run.

If the turbocharged engine runs too hot climbing and cruising, it is susceptible to being shock-cooled coming back down. Precise Flight of Bend, Oregon, offers the answer to this problem, which applies not only to turbocharged aircraft but to any fast, slick airplane. Precise Flight speedbrakes allow a rapid but fully controlled descent rate with the engine developing enough power to maintain proper operating temperatures. Performance-wise, the speedbrakes allow you the option of being able to comply with a controller's request for a rapid descent from turbo altitudes with no problem.

The system on single-engine aircraft looks like a pair of blades popping up in a scissor-like motion out of the top of the wing to act as a spoiler. On twins, the two sets of blades come down out of a metal channel which extends sideways from the rear of each engine cowling. Mooney liked the system so much that it is offered as a factory option on the slick and fast singles. It is also an option on the equally slick and fast fixed-gear Lancairs. In addition to Mooneys and Lancairs, Precise Flight speedbrakes can be installed on Beechcraft 33, 35, and 36 Bonanzas; Cessna 180s and 182s; all 200-series Cessna singles; most 300- and 400-series Cessna twins; and Piper Arrows, Lances, Saratogas, and Senecas. Precise Flight speedbrake prices have actually dropped since they were originally introduced. For $3,995 for most singles and twins, and less than $5,000 for any aircraft, it is another feature that anyone who is serious enough about aerial transportation to buy a turbocharged aircraft should definitely have on their aircraft.

Another problem common on early TSIO-360-engined and other turbocharged aircraft was that standard magnetos were beset by internal arcing at high altitudes, causing engines to misfire and run rough. A solution—going back to Army Air Force high-altitude, piston-engine operations in World War II—was pressurized magnetos. If you are going to own a turbocharged aircraft, pressurized mags are another item that should be on your "must-have" list.

Are you getting the impression that owning a turbocharged aircraft can be an expensive proposition? If you are, you're right!

What is a major overhaul?

Eventually, every aircraft engine must undergo a major overhaul. With proper operation, good maintenance, and a little luck, the engine will reach its rated TBO figure. Typical symptoms of a "tired engine" due for major overhaul are low compression on one or more cylinders and high oil consumption. Compression checks are ordinarily performed by applying 80 pounds of air pressure to a cylinder and checking to see how much it can retain. New or reconditioned cylinders ordinarily read between 75 and 79 pounds. Over the life of the engine, worn rings or valves cause losses in the capability of the cylinder to retain the necessary tightness for proper compression. When the differential compression check shows a loss of 25 percent of the applied pressure (a reading of less than 60 pounds) a top or major overhaul is required. High oil consumption is ordinarily defined as consumption of one quart per hour or more in a typical, light general aviation engine.

Other more critical reasons for major overhaul of an engine, often before reaching its TBO, include broken rings, pistons, or valves; accessory failure causing contamination of the crankcase with metal fragments; and an accident causing prop stoppage.

What is a major overhaul? In general, it is the return of a worn or damaged engine to serviceable condition by disassembly and replacement of worn-out parts. Specific work performed as a part of the major overhaul includes removal and limited inspection of engine accessories, removal and reconditioning of the cylinders, splitting the crankcase, inspection of all parts for wear, replacement or reconditioning of worn parts, and reassembly and retest of the engine. As an option, a rework or overhaul of accessories may also be done during a major overhaul not only because it makes good economic sense but also because it contributes to an owner's peace of mind to know that "everything up there is in good shape." It is not unusual for an owner to be faced with a situation where the engine is only halfway to its rated TBO and has low compression or high oil consumption, with the problems localized to the cylinders. Or perhaps a single cylinder has low compression due to hairline cracks, valve seat erosion, or lead buildup on valves and seats. In these cases, it may be possible to correct the problems for less expense by having a top overhaul performed.

Key Reprints from the AVCO Lycoming Flyer provides a good definition of a top overhaul and how it differs from a major overhaul:

> "AVCO Lycoming Williamsport defines a top overhaul as the repair or overhaul of those parts on the outside of the crankcase without completely disassembling the entire engine. It includes removal of the cylinders and deglazing the cylinder walls; inspection of the pistons, valve operating mechanism, and valve guides; and replacing piston rings. A major overhaul consists of the complete disassembly of an engine, its repair, reassembly, and testing to assure proper operation."

There are several prevalent misconceptions concerning top overhauls. The first is that most general aviation engines require at least one top overhaul to reach the rated TBO. The August 1977 edition of the *AVCO Lycoming Flyer* emphatically stated that, "with proper operation, good maintenance, and fairly frequent flight (15 hours per month minimum), today's engines should reach their expected TBO without a top overhaul along the way."

A top overhaul will probably be required on engines left idle for long periods, with corrosive effects eroding cylinder walls and valves and causing rings to seize. Use of 100LL avgas in 80-octane engines is also a frequent cause for complete or partial (such as a single cylinder) top overhauls. A second misconception is that a top overhaul will extend the TBO. Since the TBO was established based on wear rates of the entire engine, a top overhaul affecting only the cylinders obviously does nothing to slow the wear on the components inside the crankcase and therefore does not extend the TBO. Another misconception is that a top overhaul will overstress components within the crankcase. Cylinders and their "innards" are more vulnerable to abuse and neglect than other engine components. A top overhaul that returns the cylinders to their proper operating tolerances will not overstress other engine components.

The decision to top an engine or major it when low compression or high oil consumption are found is almost completely economic. The price of a top overhaul of all cylinders is usually approximately half the price of a major. If an engine is only halfway to its TBO and has a history of infrequent use and no other serious symptoms, a top overhaul would probably be a wise investment. If the engine is 90 percent of the way to its TBO, a top overhaul is probably a waste of money. The real problem comes when an engine has between 300 and 600 hours left to the TBO. Top or major? The decision is up to you the aircraft owner, and there are no easy rules to guide you.

Cylinder reconditioning

The critical item in any overhaul is the method used to bring the cylinders back to a serviceable condition. The replacement of the cylinders with new cylinders is now the preferred alternative. Because many used aircraft are powered by engines with reconditioned cylinders, and because some shops still do top and major overhauls using reconditioned cylinders, the prospective aircraft owner should understand cylinder reconditioning.

The cheapest and least desirable way to recondition a cylinder is to grind down the walls to the next largest standard dimension and to replace the rings and sometimes the pistons with oversize parts. This method has serious drawbacks. Although the cylinder walls must still meet service (not new) limits, the grinding makes the walls thinner and therefore weaker. It would be foolish to assume that the thinner walls will be able to take the wear that could reasonably be expected over a full TBO span. The oversize units could also create a parts availability problem if difficulties are encountered with either the pistons or rings at a later time.

The most popular and possibly the best method for reconditioning worn cylinders is to have the barrels replated with chrome and then reground to new tolerances. This process, performed by a relative handful of specialty shops, is more expensive than grinding but less so than using new cylinders or those with new barrels. Chrome cylinders are not as strong as the all-steel ones they replace, but they are strong enough for most nonturbocharged general aviation engines. Using the chrome-plating process generally allows the overhauler to save cylinders that otherwise might be worn beyond serviceability; it can even allow some cracked and welded cylinders to be restored. The average owner, particularly if the plane is not used as often as recommended for best engine life, benefits from the hard, corrosion-resistant properties of chrome plating.

Chrome cylinders are not without their disadvantages, however. Their use may require a longer time for rings to seat and may even require the use of matched pistons, rings, and valves in extreme cases. Chrome cylinders also use more oil than steel cylinders because of the high porosity of the chrome plating. Poor quality control in the application of the chrome plating and in the regrinding process can increase the severity of ring-seating and oil consumption problems.

Generally, however, the average buyer of a nonturbocharged aircraft can consider an aircraft equipped with chrome cylinders to be a good value. Chrome cylinders can be identified by an orange band around the base or by an orange-painted area on the top of cylinder head fins between the valve pushrod tubes.

Cylinders can also be reconditioned by having the steel barrels replaced with either plain steel or nitrided steel barrels. Plain steel barrels are cheaper, but they are far more vulnerable to rust and corrosion than chrome cylinders. Nitrided steel barrels have had nitrogen added to the surface of alloy steel to produce a hardened, wear-resistant surface, which wears very well, has great fatigue strength, is resistant to softening if subjected to overheating, and has excellent oil consumption characteristics. However, these cylinders, designated by azure blue markings, are extremely susceptible to pitting and damage due to rust and other corrosive effects. Their strength makes them an excellent choice on a turbocharged business aircraft seeing regular use, but their susceptibility to corrosion probably makes them a poor choice for the average pilot-owner who flies only occasionally.

The very best cylinders available are "choke bored." This process, generally performed on nitrided or chrome cylinders, improves the straightness of cylinder walls at operating temperatures by flaring the upper end of the inside of the cylinder inward. However, ring seating is crucial and can be a problem with choke-bored cylinders. It is questionable whether the advantages of choke-boring are worth the added cost for the type of aircraft flown by the average private pilot.

Cylinder work performed as a part of either a top or major overhaul will also include removal, inspection, and replacement of the valves; regrinding of valve seats and replacement of valve guides; and the installation of new rings. New pistons will be installed if the overhaul is to new limits, or they may be inspected and reused if the overhaul is being done to service limits.

Cylinder replacement with new cylinders

When factory replacement cylinders were the only source of new cylinders, even many quality top and major overhauls were performed using reconditioned cylinders. Superior Air Parts (www.superiorairparts.com) turned the market upside down in the 1990s. Superior had been the best known parts manufacturer authorization (PMA) supplier of engine piece parts such as valves, rings, bearings, and pistons for many years. But in 1992, they offered PMA'd cylinders for the Continental O-200 engines used in Cessna 150s. In 1994, they revolutionized the market when they offered the Millennium line of new cylinders for a wide range of general aviation engines, which they improved with the new Millennium II line in 2002. Another manufacturer, Engine Components, Inc. (www.eci2fly.com), also offered a competing line of high quality cylinders. Both Superior and ECI cylinders offer a quality equivalent to factory cylinders at a lower price—one low enough to be competitive with reconditioned cylinders. The price of Superior Millenium and ECI cylinders is low enough that any quality top or major overhaul should probably be done with new cylinders, and anything less is probably a cut-rate job.

Overhaul alternatives

Your decision to have a major overhaul on the engine of your airplane will probably not be completely voluntary. If you are lucky, low compression readings may confirm what you really knew, since the bird had seemed a little "sick" lately. If you are not so lucky, maybe it's a scary in-flight engine failure that makes the need inescapable. Since the engine's nearing the TBO, there's no sense considering a top overhaul. Time to major.

Your decisions are just beginning, though, and you had better decide wisely. Will you have a custom overhaul on your present engine, and give up four to six weeks of flying and maybe more? Or will you swap at a large regional FAA-certified repair station? How about installing a factory reman-ufactured engine or even a new (!) engine? If you have an overhaul, will it be to service limits or new limits? And how do you sort out the confusing jumble of price estimates from various shops? Can they live up to them? Will they? And are you comparing apples and apples or apples and maybe a sour lemon? No, the decision to major is easy compared to the decisions of "how." The overhaul will cost you several thousand dollars no matter what your choices are. And if you make the wrong choices, it could cost you thousands more correcting your mistakes. A new engine will also be the most expensive choice. There are good reasons why most aircraft engines are overhauled and reused rather than discarded and replaced. And at the top of the list is the price tag of a new engine.

With the purchase of a new engine, you are assured of having one that has all new parts and accessories built to factory production specifications, has received standard factory quality control inspections, and has been test-ed to FAR standards. The engine will have a zero-time log, and you will receive the standard factory warranty. And the warranty may well be the best available. In October 1988, Lycoming announced that its new and remanufactured engines had a full one-year warranty, with an additional warranty prorated against engine time for an additional year or until the engine TBO was reached.

The next most costly alternative is to trade for a factory remanufactured engine. AVCO Lycoming, in *Key Reprints*, defines a factory remanufactured engine as an aircraft engine originally designed and manufactured by AVCO Lycoming, having been disassembled, repaired, or altered and inspected in accordance with Lycoming Service Bulletins and/or Instructions, incorporat-ing applicable mandatory engineering changes and any Airworthiness Directives, and all work being done at the Lycoming Factory. Tolerances and limits established and published by Lycoming, and those approved applica-ble rework applications, are used during the manufacture of the engine and the engine brought to zero time. Such engines retain their original serial number but will add the "R" preceding the letter "L" on the data plate which designates remanufactured by Lycoming.

The factory remanufactured engine, as defined, will be "brought to zero time." Lycoming defines zero-time engines as those using parts that "have been completely inspected and found to meet Lycoming's specifications. This allows the same amount of time between overhauls as a new engine, and the factory remanufactured powerplant (to) be considered capable of being overhauled by another agency and attaining at least one additional time between overhaul runs."

It should be noted that the definition does not state that all parts used will meet new tolerances. Major parts reused in a factory remanufactured engine include the crankcase, crankshafts, gears, and gearshafts, provided those parts meet factory tolerances. Most of the engine parts will meet new tolerances; some may be slightly outside new limits but well within service limits. A crankshaft, for example, could be reused even though it was slight-ly below new limits, if oversize bearings and bushings are used. Other parts more vulnerable to wear and corrosion will be to new limits, however.

SERVICE LIMITS. Whether or not parts reused in a major overhaul meet new or service limits is the critical question if you choose to replace your present engine with one overhauled by a mechanic, an FBO, or even a FAA-certified repair station.

What are "service limits," and why is this issue so crucial? Service limits are tolerances specified by the manufacturer for engine parts beyond which they are no longer considered usable. Continental and Lycoming do build in a margin for these limits. A part will not automatically break as soon as the service limit is reached, but it certainly has to be "nearer the edge."

It is unrealistic to assume that a majored engine full of parts at or approaching their service limits will be able to reach TBO. Not only will specific parts in such an engine wear out faster but the less-strict service limit tolerances of all the parts mean the engine has more "slop," more looseness, leading to an overall acceleration of engine wear. Spending money on a major overhaul to service limits is at best a gamble and at worst an outright waste of money. Neither of the largest engine manufacturers, Continental nor Lycoming, will major an engine to service limit tolerances, nor will Superior Air Parts shops doing Millennium overhauls. Most FAA-approved certified repair stations overhaul only to new tolerances. So why should you assume that a small FBO that overhauls engines as a sideline, or even a free-lance mechanic, knows better than the experts when that FBO or mechanic advises you to have a major overhaul done to service tolerances? Will the engine majored to service limits make TBO? Almost certainly not. Could it have a serious breakdown within 500 hours, or even 50? Possibly. After all, when does the wear to critical parts go from serviceable to critical? Even if you save $2,500 on the job, is it really a bargain?

CERTIFIED REPAIR STATION. The best buy for the money in engine overhauls is probably one to new limits performed by an FAA-approved certified repair station. These repair stations must establish and maintain certain minimum standards to obtain and hold this designation. Such a shop must set up and adhere to an FAA-approved Inspection Procedures Manual. The shop must also demonstrate that it has certain minimum capabilities, including proper tooling, floor space, and testing procedures. Strict record-keeping standards must be met on all engines the shop has repaired, overhauled, or altered.

The designation "certified" can become a badge of honor. Several of the best known overhaul shops in the United States, like Mattituck Aviation on Long Island, New York (now owned by Teledyne Continental), Penn Yan Aero Service in upstate New York, Zephyr Aircraft Engines in Florida, Western Skyways in Colorado, and Air West Aircraft Engines in California, are in this category. All have well-deserved good reputations. Mattituck's facilities, for example, include a staff of 30 mechanics who have specialized in rebuilding engines, a Cherokee 6 to pick up and deliver engines, and a 2,200-foot airstrip to service fly-in business. An owner who has made prior arrangements can fly into Mattituck, stay overnight at a nearby motel recommended by the shop, and fly out as soon as 24 hours later with an over-hauled replacement engine.

Superior Air Parts has also set up their own "Certified Millennium Pre-Owned Engine Program," with more than two dozen highly rated engine overhaul facilities all over the country doing major overhauls to Superior's high standards. Obviously, you are going to get new Millennium cylinders with a Superior Air Parts Millennium overhaul. But keep in mind that most of the shops doing Millennium overhauls are probably also willing to do their own high quality but less expensive overhauls. A shop certified by both the FAA and Superior Air Parts will probably be a good bet for an overhaul whether or not the overhaul carries the Millennium tag.

Although the engines overhauled by a certified repair station may be to the same limits as a factory remanufactured engine, the term remanufactured is usually not used to describe them. It is interesting to note that the term remanufacture is not officially defined by the FAA, nor is overhaul. The FAA uses the term rebuild, which is almost totally overlooked in general aviation industry literature. Another term, overhauled and certified (OHC), is occasionally used to describe engines overhauled by a certified repair station.

As an owner, you must decide whether you want to exchange for a different overhauled engine or whether you want the present engine in your aircraft custom overhauled. Choosing a new or factory remanufactured engine means that you have chosen the exchange route. While most certified repair stations specialize in an exchange engine trade, they will generally provide a custom overhaul if the owner wants it badly enough to pay extra for it. The overwhelming advantage to exchanging the engine is the dramatic reduction of downtime for your airplane. To have your present engine removed and replaced with an overhauled one of the same type can take as little as 24 hours and seldom more than 72. A custom overhaul on your own engine, by comparison, will take anywhere from two weeks to six weeks or even longer, depending on shop workload, parts availability, and other factors. The primary advantage of a custom overhaul is the ability to retain an engine that has a good overall reliability record. If you have flown your airplane for a significant period prior to major overhaul, you are aware of the history of the engine. Most certified repair shops do not overhaul specific engines— they are stripped down and lose their identity. Serviceable parts from several engines may be used, along with new parts, to put together the overhauled engines in an assembly-line type of operation. Factory manufactured zero-time engines are delivered with zero-time logbooks, effectively obliterating the history of any specific engine. So the custom overhaul remains the only way for an owner to retain an engine with a known history.

FBO SHOP. The riskiest, although usually the least expensive, major overhaul is one performed by an FBO maintenance facility or even by a free-lance

A&P mechanic in his or her own shop. There are several potentially severe problems with having your overhaul performed in a small shop. Price constraints often lead the mechanic to overhaul the engine to service limits only. Another problem is that small shops may not be up on the many service bulletins or even the ADs put out by the engine manufacturer or the FAA. Large shops have personnel hired to keep up with the ever-changing deluge of paperwork. By contrast, paperwork, although critical, may be "put off to another day" in a small one-person shop.

Another problem with small shops is the high probability that they will lack the clean, well-equipped facilities available in certified repair stations. An open crankcase left sitting around for weeks during the overhaul may pick up dirt that will adversely affect the engine's future operation when it is reassembled. Large certified repair stations generally overhaul engines in scrupulously clean facilities, and parts may even be cleaned in large ultrasonic cleaners prior to reassembly. The large shops also have stands to test-run the reassembled engines, eliminating the bothersome need to do an on-the-aircraft run-up, test, and break-in. The biggest problem with having an overhaul done by a small FBO shop or a free-lance A&P mechanic is the total lack of consistency in the quality of such operations. Since the engine manufacturer and the certified repair stations must meet self-imposed and FAA minimum standards, their output can generally be assumed to be of high quality. But the small shops are not required to meet the same standards. One small shop could have a wise old mechanic who is a true engine expert with high personal standards, while another apparently similar shop could be a fly-by-night operation with no standards except a desire to take your money. If you decide to go to a small shop for your overhaul, it's your gamble.

COST EVALUATION. Like almost everything else concerning major overhauls, there are many ifs, ands, and maybes regarding the price. If you are looking for an easy answer to "what's the best buy for my money?" forget it. Straightforward it isn't.

However, take heart because some basic premises do not change. The first is that airplane engines are just too expensive to throw away, as are the airframes in which they are mounted. If this seems so obvious that it's silly to even mention it, think about the American automobile. In many areas of the country, where inclement seasonal weather is not a factor, it would certainly be possible to keep cars running 20 years or more if airplane-style maintenance and overhaul practices were used. But Detroit (and now Tokyo) have built an industry around the fact that the American driver believes a car is "dead" at 100,000 miles or 10 years, or maybe even less.

In truth, any piece of machinery can last almost indefinitely. The critical question is whether or not the replacement of key parts is worth the cost involved. And this, more than anything else, is the factor that determines how many overhauls an engine can undergo before it must be junked. Two or three overhauls is the generally accepted number. Even this number may not really be as low as it seems at first glance. Assume for a moment that the average first-time owner buys a used airplane with 2,500 hours on the airframe and with a 2,000-hour TBO engine with 500 hours since its first overhaul. With proper maintenance, the owner can expect 1,500 hours from the engine before it needs a second major overhaul. Even if the engine cannot economically be majored a third time, this owner could have 3,500 hours and pay for only one major overhaul. If the plane is flown 200 hours per year, this will represent 17.5 years of use. And that is with only two major overhauls. Not everyone agrees an engine or any piece of equipment can be economically majored only two or three times. Large radial engines, which are no longer produced in the United States and have been widely used in agricultural applications, often were majored a half dozen or even a dozen times.

Economic pressures force some unreliable FBOs and independents to cut their prices to the bone, and sometimes beyond, to appear to be offering a competitive price. You should be very wary of unrealistically low advertised prices. The basic job to be performed in a major overhaul requires engine disassembly, inspection of parts, and reassembly. Unless a shop has a very low labor rate, there is no room for margin in the basics. So where is the difference coming from? You won't get "something for nothing." The usual way to shave prices is to major to service limits instead of new limits, meaning fewer parts to be replaced. Drastically lower reliability and probably a reduced TBO will be the results, but you won't be told that! You will almost certainly get reconditioned cylinders, possibly even poorly reconditioned ones, rather than Superior Millennium II or ECI new cylinders. Another area for price shaving is in optional items. Certified repair shops may include overhauled mags and new cable harnesses in the deal. The "bargain" probably won't.

Key questions

There are certainly key questions that will allow you to determine what you are getting for your overhaul dollar. Some of these apply only to specific types of overhaul shops, whereas some will apply to the whole spectrum of alternatives, from installing a factory-new engine right down to having a major overhaul done by a free-lance mechanic. But taken together, the questions will give you a good basis for comparing what you are being offered when faced with a major overhaul.

What is the engine deposit policy when you trade in your old engine? The trade-in price for a new engine, a factory remanufactured engine, or a swap at a certified repair station assumes that your trade-in has serviceable major components. You may have to pay a deposit that will be refunded when your old engine has been dismantled, inspected, and major components found serviceable; or you may be subject to an additional charge later in lieu of a deposit. Major problems that could result in such large additional expenses include crankcase cracks, a crankshaft worn beyond limits, or serious cylinder cracks that would preclude the cylinders being brought back to serviceability by welding and chroming. The price impact of such problems depends on the individual components but could easily be in excess of $5,000.

Is the major overhaul performed to new or service limits? Engines majored to service limits are unlikely to reach a full TBO to the next major. Having your engine majored to service limits may seem cheaper today, but unless you are going to sell the airplane to some other "sucker," you will pay more in the long run.

What parts will be automatically replaced? Some parts, like cylinders and main bearings, are ordinarily replaced by reputable overhaulers, regardless of condition. The length of this list is one indication of how much you are getting for your money and is one basis for comparison with what different overhaulers are offering.

Will replacement parts be new or reconditioned? New parts are superior to reconditioned ones, but reconditioned parts can be a good buy if up to new standards. After all, a majored engine is "reconditioned" rather than new. New parts can be either factory manufactured or produced by a parts manufacturer authorization (PMA) supplier. PMA suppliers, the chief of which is Superior Air Parts, must meet rigid FAA standards. This is one area where factory-authorized service centers, which are under coercion to use only the more expensive factory parts, can be legitimately undercut by independent overhaul shops (including certified repair stations) using cheaper but equally reliable PMA parts. And as noted above, in today's market a quality overhaul should include new, not reconditioned cylinders.

Which accessories are and are not included in the basic price? This is another area where one shop's "bargain" may not be a bargain at all. A major overhaul usually (but not always) includes overhaul or replacement of the magnetos, ignition harness, and engine-driven fuel pump in the basic price. Overhauling the starter, alternator/generator, or carburetor may or may not be included. You should also make sure engine removal and installation is included in the basic price.

What additional charges should you expect? You should probably allow 10 to 15 percent above the cost of the basic overhaul for optional items that should be taken care of but are not included in the basic overhaul price. Such items include overhauling or replacing accessories such as the vacuum pump and auxiliary fuel pump; replacing engine mounts, cracked exhaust stacks or mufflers, worn wiring, and fuel, oil, and air hoses; and even cleaning the engine compartment with solvent. While the total of such extra charges may seem like a "heavy hit" on top of the basic overhaul cost, it will almost certainly be cheaper in the long run than piecemeal replacement. (Remember how long it takes to remove some aircraft cowlings? Time is money in airplane maintenance.) Another extra charge you should be prepared for is the cost of packaging and shipping items sent to specialty shops for repair, including alternators or generators and accessories.

What kind of warranty does the shop offer? The standard warranty is usually between 500 and 1,000 hours and is prorated based on the number of hours on the engine since the overhaul. For example, if you had problems requiring major engine work after 250 hours of flying since the overhaul and the warranty was prorated against a base figure of 500 hours, you would have to pay 50 percent of the cost of repairs. A better warranty, offered by some shops, is one in which a 100 percent warranty is offered over a shorter period. An example may be a warranty good for 100 percent if any problems develop in the first 6 months or 100 hours. Major individual engine components such as crankcases and crankshafts may have separate warranty clauses if the engine is factory new or remanufactured. The separate clause may prorate use hours on these parts against a life figure of between 2,000 and 3,000 hours. When comparing warranties, seemingly minor items such as troubleshooting costs, engine removal, and transportation to the overhaul facility may make a big difference in the potential coverage provided. Check the fine print closely. And above all, be sure you will receive a written warranty. For factory and certified repair station overhauls, this is nearly automatic. But the local free-lance mechanic may need some prodding to "put it in writing."

How do you decide?

So which course of action is best for you? For most aircraft owners, the best trade off is an engine overhauled to new limits by a certified repair station.

Reputable certified repair stations such as Mattituck provide engines comparable to factory remanufactured ones at a significantly lower price. Having an overhaul done by a local maintenance shop should not be ruled out if the shop is willing to do a new-limits overhaul with the same accessories and warranty terms as a certified repair station, if you know other satisfied customers of the shop, and if a check with the local FAA General Aviation District Office (GADO) or Flight Standards District Office (FSDO) shows that the shop does not have any significant record of complaints.

The crucial thing to remember when making the big decisions associated with a major overhaul is that this is not the time nor the place to cut corners or pinch pennies. Reputation of the overhaul shop, the quality of the work, and the shop's willingness to back it up should come first; and the price should come second. In the long run, you will fly longer, safer, and even cheaper if you put quality first at major time.

Good aircraft for the first-time owner

9

Basic modern-design, two-seat and four-seat aircraft such as the Cessna 150/152, and 172; the Piper Cherokee and Warrior series; the Piper Tomahawk; the Beechcraft Musketeer/Sport; the Beechcraft Skipper; and the Grumman-American Tr-2 and its Traveler, Cheetah, and Tiger descendants offer excellent choices for the first-time buyer. These tricycle gear, fixed-pitch prop aircraft all offer the assurance of relatively simple, low-maintenance ownership. When maintenance is required, parts should be available and finding knowledgeable, experienced mechanics should be no problem.

The aircraft described in this chapter are the Cessna 150 and 152, Cessna 172 Skyhawk, Cessna 177 Cardinal, Piper Cherokee 140, Piper Warrior 161, Piper Cherokee 180/181, Piper Tomahawk, Beechcraft Musketeer/Sport, Beechcraft Sundowner, Beechcraft Skipper, Grumman-American Tr-2/Yankee, Grumman-American Traveler/Cheetah, Grumman-American (now Tiger Aircraft) Tiger, and the Dimona/Diamond Katana/Evolution/Eclipse. For the first-time owner, the two-seat 150/152, Tomahawk, Tr-2/Yankee, Skipper, and even Rotax-engined Katanas offer good buys and economical operation, as do the four-seat 140s, older 172s, Sports, Travelers, and Cheetahs. Aircraft powered by the 180-hp Lycoming engine, such as the 180/181, the Sundowner, the Tiger, and most Cardinals, will probably be a bit steep for the first-time owner, as will later model 160-hp Skyhawks and Warriors. These simple, low-maintenance aircraft will not be a heavy burden to own if you can afford the initial purchase price.

When the FAA finally brings out the final version of the Sport Pilot Certificate, a whole new class of affordable aircraft could become available. The Sport Pilot Certificate proposes to allow pilots with less than Private Pilot qualifications to fly VFR daytime-only flights including Class B, C, and D airspace. A U.S. driver's license from any state would meet the minimum medical standard, with no FAA medical exam required. But most important, there would be simplified certification requirements for Light Sport Aircraft certified to carry a maximum of two persons, have a maximum takeoff weight of 1,232 pounds, a 39-knot stall speed, and a 115-knot maximum operating speed. The limitations on the aircraft are slightly more stringent than those for the Recreational Pilot's license, which the Sport Pilot License will replace. But most people would agree that the Recreational Pilot's license has pretty much been a failure in attracting large numbers of new pilots. The Sport Pilot License will probably mean a Renaissance for some very old aircraft like the 65-hp Taylorcraft, the Aeronca Champ, and the J-3 Piper Cub.

New modern two-seaters are also very likely to go into production in response to the Sport Pilot License rules, including the cute Zenith 601, a low-wing tricycle gear plane with a bubble canopy. Maule announced at the 2003 EAA AirVenture in Oshkosh that a prototype Light Sport Aircraft was flying at the Maule Aircraft factory. Called the M-4-100, the 1,000-pound empty weight tailwheel aircraft is powered by a Rotax 912S 100-hp engine and was expected to be priced at $80,000. Also at the AirVenture, Mooney announced their intention to manufacture and market a racy looking two-seat Toxo low-wing sportplane originally developed by CASA in Spain. The new aircraft could revitalize the lower end of aviation, assuming, of course, that the Light Sport Aircraft manufacturers can keep their prices well below $100,000.

Even if you are one of those rare individuals who can afford a brand new airplane, you will probably be better off buying a very well-maintained, late-model, relatively simple used airplane for your first airplane. Buy a simple and straightforward four-seater, learn what aircraft ownership is all about, and then trade up in a year or two to a more complex new aircraft. An excellent used airplane will have almost the same performance as most of the new ones on the market, and if it has received top-notch maintenance, it probably shouldn't have many more problems.

Short summaries of the history of each aircraft are provided as an interesting sidelight. Comments on overall appearance, handling, and performance are of course opinionated and subjective and should not be considered to be the last word on the subject. Reading between the lines may be necessary to provide objective truth. Comments on the specific problems of each aircraft come from experience, actual observed failures, and descriptions of problems by real-life mechanics. The problems described may not occur on all or even most aircraft of the type being described, but each has happened on at least one. Knowing this can help make sure you don't buy the second plane with that specific problem!

The data sheets on individual aircraft are taken from owner's manual listings and statements. The figures should not be taken as gospel truth. After all, owner's manual figures were derived from performance data from new airplanes flown by test pilots under optimum conditions. Empty-weight figures are for stripped airplanes, so subtract 50 to 150 pounds from the useful load for radios, wheel pants, and the hand-brushed aluminum ashtray. Cruise speeds are accurate for some aircraft but not for others. It is common knowledge, for example, that a Tr-2 is fast. A Beech Musketeer, though, will seldom if ever keep up with a Cherokee, let alone the Tr-2, even though the numbers do look nearly equal on the charts. Take heart, Beech fans! At least it really is faster than a Cessna 150! Service ceiling figures may likewise be reasonably true for a Skyhawk, but for a Cherokee 140 at gross weight to make it to 14,300 feet even on a very cold day would be a momentous undertaking indeed. Range with a 45-minute reserve hopefully takes into account the fuel used to taxi out, wait in line, and climb to altitude in an airplane that the line crew didn't really top off when asked to do so! But don't assume that you have that 45 minutes unless you want to find out the scrap value of your aircraft. And last but not least ... taking off or landing a fully loaded airplane over that 50-foot obstacle may be a good way to take a "crash course in trees of the world" if you insist on using the minimum runway length listed.

Cessna 150 and 152

Nearly half of all general aviation pilots trained in the United States in the '60s, '70s, and '80s learned to fly in a Cessna 150 or 152. It was the rare general aviation pilot who did not have at least one hour in this seemingly omnipresent little bird.

The Cessna 150 is a tricycle gear aircraft derived from the Cessna 140 taildragger. Cessna, having produced the ragwing 120 and the metal-wing 140 two-seaters from the introduction of the prototype 120 in 1946 until the end of 140 production in 1953, reentered the two-seat trainer market with the 150 in 1959. Numerous changes and improvements followed. In 1961 the main landing gear was moved back 2 inches from the original modified-140 location, after early models demonstrated a disquieting tendency to squat back on their tails on the ground when carrying a light fuel load. In 1964 an omnivision rear window added rear baggage space but knocked off about 3 mph, which was not recovered until 1975. In 1965 the rakish, swept vertical tail was added. Another dubious improvement that year was the replacement of manual flaps with the interminably slow electric flaps that seem to be a Cessna trademark. In 1970 droop wing tips were added, contributing a small amount of low-speed controllability and a lot of Detroit styling. The year 1971 brought wider-stance, tubular-style main landing gear to replace the original spring steel, and 1975 brought several major changes that returned the 3 mph lost in 1964 to the omnivision window. These changes included a more aerodynamic cowling, more aerodynamic wheel pants with wheel-brake fairings, and a larger rudder for added controllability in spins and other maneuvers. In late 1977 the Cessna 150 technically "died," replaced by the 152 with a Lycoming 108-hp engine. The airframe remained, but the Continental engine was gone. The 152 also had flaps limited to 30 degrees of travel compared to 40 degrees in the Cessna 150, probably because the 150 wouldn't climb on a go-around until flaps were reduced to 30 degrees and more than one student had crashed trying go-arounds with full flaps.

The line died out with Cessna being gobbled up by monster conglomerate General Dynamics and the cessation of single-engine aircraft production and the delivery of the last 152 in 1985. When production finally ceased, 31,340 of the 150/152 line had been produced, a number exceeded only by the "big brother" Skyhawk/172. Cessna did not resume production of the 152 when production of the Skyhawk and Skylane was restarted in 1997. With Cessna now touting the 172 as a trainer, it is unlikely that Cessna will ever build another 152. And with the sleek and responsive new generation Diamond DA20 available as very tough competition in the two-seat trainer class, in the new aircraft market it really won't be missed.

Throughout its life, the 150 has been known by a variety of model names and designations. The four designations of the late 1960s and early 1970s (Standard, Trainer, Commuter, and Aerobat) are most often seen in the used plane market, however, if any model delineation is made. The Standard was a stripped, bare-bones airplane, with single controls and little else but basic VFR instruments. Few were built, and if any remain in their unmodified state, they are probably museum-worthy curiosity pieces. The Trainer added the basics for VFR training, including dual controls, a sensitive altimeter, an electric clock, sun visors, a turn-and-bank indicator, and a 90-channel nav/comm radio. The Commuter went still further, adding a basic gyro system, including a vacuum system and suction gauge, a directional gyro, and an artificial horizon as well as other niceties like a rotating beacon and wheel pants (speed fairings). The Aerobat is basically a Trainer beefed up structurally and fitted with quick-release doors, qualifying it for basic aerobatic flight.

The Cessna 150, as most pilots know, is basically a light-handling, moderately stable aircraft with just enough quirks to make sure you pay attention. It is forgiving, but not too much so. Mistreat it in a departure stall, and it just might drop a wing violently enough to put you in a spin (a characteristic that makes it a better trainer than the too-docile Piper Cadet and other Cherokee derivatives). With its light wing loading, it can give you a bouncy ride in turbulence. Against a headwind its real, used-airplane cruise speed of 110 to 115 mph may seem quite slow indeed. Properly used, the flaps make the 150 an excellent short-field airplane. But improperly used, the electric flaps can be irritatingly and even dangerously slow in a go-around situation. The 150 is no great weight carrier, either. When the plane's fuel tanks are topped, two full-size all-American males will very likely exceed allowable gross weight. Why Cessna even provided the option of a child's seat for the large cargo area behind the two regular seats is a question only some past Cessna designer can answer. With 26-gallon (22.5 usable) standard fuel tanks, the 150 is also no rangemaster.

The 150 cabin is graciously called "cozy," or not so politely called "cramped." Interestingly enough, older models may seem more comfortable, because Cessna seemed to think that nobody would notice if they removed some of the padding from the seats to pretend the cabin is bigger in the newer models. The 150's high wings are not good for visibility, particularly in a crowded pattern. Even the skylight windows in the Aerobat don't improve visibility very much. Cabin ventilation through the wing root air vents is quite good, if noisy, in the summer. Unfortunately, the vents don't seal very tightly when closed, and ventilation is also quite good in the winter. Cabin heat, unfortunately, is not so satisfactory, and the 150 can be a moving icebox in a cold climate. One plus for the 150 is a simple, on-off,

Table 9.1. Cessna 150 Commuter (1969)

Specifications	
Wingspan	32 ft 8 in
Length	23 ft 9 in
Gross weight, normal category	1,600 lb
Empty weight	1,060 lb
Useful load	540 lb
Useful load, full fuel	384 lb
Fuel capacity, standard tanks	26 gal (22.5 usable)
Performance	
Cruise speed, 75% power, best altitude	117 mph
Fuel consumption, 75% power	5.5 gph
Range 45-min reserve, 75% power	390 mi
Sea level rate of climb	670 fpm
Service ceiling	12,650 ft
Stall, clean	55 mph
Stall, full flaps	48 mph
Takeoff over a 50-foot obstacle	1,385 ft
Landing over a 50-foot obstacle	1,075 ft

gravity-feed fuel system, feeding the economical 100-hp engine which uses 5.5 gph at cruise speed. Another minus, however, is its ground-handling characteristics. Cessna 150s are easily tipped onto the nose and a wingtip, or even flipped over, by gusty quartering tailwinds.

Some articles on the Cessna 150 make it sound like an amazingly durable airplane. Considering the abuse to which training aircraft like the 150 were subjected, it has held up well. It is, however, relatively lightly built. It can and does develop an assortment of minor and major problems with long use or abuse. Major difficulties with the airplane after 3,000 to 4,000 hours (not unusual for most 150s and even 152s) can include fuselage cracks near the vertical stabilizer attach point and engine mount cracks that can result in failure of the mount and nosewheel structure. The FAA issued a warning in late 2003 concerning cracks in vertical fin attachments on Cessna 150 and 152 aircraft. The FAA expected to order mandatory inspections of all models made from 1966 to 1980. Only four cracks were reported in the 1970s, then six in the 1980s, and 12 in the 1990s. But another 12 cases of fin attachment cracks were found between 2000 and 2003. The FAA recommended that owners would have to get the tail inspected in the next 100 hours and then every 1,000 hours thereafter.

The Continental O-200 engine seems particularly susceptible to valve problems with the regular use of 100LL avgas. Even before the advent of 100LL, the O-200 engine had a reputation for needing a top overhaul on one or more cylinders before reaching a major overhaul. With 100LL, it is not unusual for an O-200 engine to need a cylinder pulled due to valve problems with as little as 250 hours between incidents. Fortunately, the Cessna 150 was the first aircraft in the United States to be certified to use no-lead autogas, which does wonders to alleviate most of the problems that 100LL can cause. Every Cessna 150 owner should obtain the EAA or Petersen autogas STC.

There can be other problems, however, that autogas won't cure. With a regular regimen of student touch-and-go training giving the engine a good dose of heat cycling, crankcase cracks as well as cylinder cracks around the spark plugs are not unusual. More problems with 150s include a nosewheel prone to shimmy between 30 and 50 mph, nose spinner cracks (minor, but not cheap for a replacement), and a fuel vent that perpetually drips after topping off the fuel tanks unless the left wheel is elevated on a ramp or block.

Cessna 152s have nearly identical flying characteristics as their older kin, but the 100LL-rated Lycoming is a better engine in several ways than the Cessna 150's Continental O-200. The Continental's 100LL spark plug and valve problems are alleviated. (The Continental O-200 won't have many spark plug or valve problems if autogas is used, as it should be.) One real advantage of the Lycoming engine is an honest 2,000-hour TBO compared

Figure 9.1. People often assume that a Cessna 150 pilot must be a student.

to the Continental O-200's seldom attained TBO figure of 1,800 hours. But Cessna did the average cold-weather pilot a real disservice with the 28-volt ignition system on the 152. Forget the ground power plug. Automobiles run on a 12-volt electrical system, so the good old days of pulling your car alongside your balky cold airplane for a jump start won't be repeated on 152s.

All in all, the Cessna 150 and 152 are inexpensive, readily available, well-known light trainers. They are basically reliable and interesting, but not exciting. It will not be an ego booster, because it often seems anyone flying into any airport in a 150 or 152 is automatically assumed to be a student or someone who couldn't afford something bigger and better. Aerobat versions of the airplane offer a credible, if unexciting, aerobatic fun ship.

The Continental O-200 engine was a real problem before the advent of the autogas STC, but any owner using autogas shouldn't have any unusual reliability problems.

If you like Cessnas and are short on money and long on the desire to own an airplane, don't overlook the friendly little 150s and 152s.

Cessna 172 Skyhawk, Skyhawk XP, Cutlass, Skyhawk SP

The Cessna 172, or Skyhawk, is the most commercially successful aircraft flying today in terms of sheer numbers. The May 1989 edition of *Flying* magazine stated that 33,629 172s/Skyhawks were built in the United States, and another 2,144 built by Reims in France for a grand total of 35,773. And this number doesn't include variants like the Skyhawk XP or the Cutlass! Only Russian World War II fighters beat it out for the honor of the most heavily produced aircraft in the history of aviation.

It is an airplane that has changed by evolution rather than revolution. A pilot familiar with a 1965 Skyhawk will notice little difference in the handling of a 1970 or even a 1981 model. And contrary to what many people believe, the 172 preceded the Cessna 150. The Cessna 172 prototype appeared in 1955 as a tricycle gear version of the popular Cessna 170. It quickly outdistanced the 170 in popularity, resulting in the end of 170 production. In 1960 extensive model changes were made, including the addition of a swept tail, a lower landing gear mounted farther back on the fuselage, an exterior baggage door, a wider cabin, and a revised instrument panel. The cowling was drooped to provide a lower silhouette, and the newly revised aircraft was designated the 1961 Skyhawk. In 1963 a one-piece windshield was added, as well as the omnivision wraparound rear window. In 1965 the Skyhawks received the curse of slow electric flaps. The 1968 model brought the biggest change of all. The 6-cylinder Continental O-300, 145-hp engine was replaced by the longer-lived, more reliable, 40-pound lighter, 4-cylinder Lycoming O-320 150-hp engine. The year 1970 brought droop tips for styling, and supposedly, added controllability. In 1971 a wider-based tubular steel main landing gear was introduced, and the landing light was moved from the left wing to a position under the nose spinner. In 1973 a camber-lift airfoil was added, along with cleaner wheel pants and an improved cowling, bringing the 172's speed claim up to 138-mph cruise.

In 1977 Cessna replaced the 150-hp, 80-octane O-320E with a brand-new version of the O-320—the 160-hp, 100LL-rated O-320H. The O-320H was plagued by cam spalling and other major problems, and this switch was to be a minor disaster for Cessna. In April 1978 Cessna, in an unprecedented move, recalled all the 1977 and 1978 Skyhawks produced up to that time. All 3,700 aircraft were fitted with new, redesigned valve tappets and oil pump gears, and 287 were also fitted with new crankshaft accessory gears. An oil additive, a variant of TCP (tricresyl phosphate) was also recommended. But nothing totally solved the problem, and in 1981, Cessna dropped the O-320H for the older style 160-hp, 100LL-rated O-320D Lycoming. This engine would be the power plant of the 172P until production temporarily ceased in 1986.

The year 1978 brought the "Big Iron" 28-volt electrical system, and the handy days of cold-weather jumpstarts from the pilot's car (and reasonably priced batteries and electrical system components) were gone forever from Skyhawk country. The durable O-320D engine was not the only change for 1981, which also saw gross weight increased to 2,400 pounds, and fuel tank options, including a standard 43 gallons in addition to 54- and 68-gallon tanks available. No really major changes were made as production declined through the early 1980s through 1986, although minor improvements continued year by year. Following changes to liability laws, Cessna resumed production of the Skyhawk and other single engine, fixed gear Cessnas in 1997 in a brand new factory in Independence, Kansas (www.se.cessna.com). The new 172R is powered by a fuel-injected (no more carb heat) Lycoming IO-360 derated to produce 160-hp at 2,400 rpm. In addition to the new engine, the 172R has 53 gallons of usable fuel and a rate of climb of 720 fpm. The max speed of around 140 mph was not much improved over the last 172 built in 1986.

One striking difference is the price. Well-equipped IFR 1997 172Rs cost just under $150,000. Despite 1997 to 2003 being a period of low inflation, the price of a well-equipped IFR 2003 172R climbed to nearly $200,000. *Flying* magazine of course has run articles trying to justify such prices. But post-2000 prices of new aircraft are totally out of line if one takes 1970s or even 1980s prices and adjusts those prices for inflation, often by as much as 50 percent.

The Skyhawk, never an aircraft described as overpowered, was the basis for a couple of more powerful although less successful variants as well as a reasonably successful retractable. Due in large part to the low sales of the excellent but unfortunately maligned 180-hp Cardinal, in 1977 the Skyhawk received a 195-hp, 6-cylinder Continental engine driving a variable-pitch prop, to become the Skyhawk XP. Hundreds of Hawk pilots bought the XP in 1977 and 1978, probably feeling that the right step up was at hand, undeterred by the fact that the XP's fuel consumption is markedly higher and its engine TBO markedly lower than that of the largely ignored Cardinal.

The Continental IO-360K engine was the weak link in the XP. The original version of the engine, which appeared in the 1977 and 1978 XPs, was plagued by crankshaft and connecting rod failures and had only a 1,500-hour TBO. Continental beefed up the crankshaft in 1979, and raised the TBO to 2,000 hours. Since more than half of the XPs were produced with the less reliable engine, anyone purchasing an XP should be sure that it received the beefed-up crankshaft at major overhaul. The engine continued to have a reputation for cylinder, piston, ring, and other top end problems, remaining less reliable than Lycoming-powered Skyhawks.

With optional 66-gallon fuel tanks introduced in 1979, the XP can be a good long-range airplane. The 195-hp engine also gives it good climb characteristics that the standard Hawks were never known for, and its takeoff and climb performance makes it a popular airplane on floats.

In 1979, the Skyhawk airframe was given a 180-hp Lycoming O-360 engine, a variable-pitch propeller, retractable gear, and a new name, the Cutlass RG. The Cutlass RG was an essentially good, successful, economical, basic four-seat retractable. (See Chapter 11.)

In 1983, at the request of the Embry-Riddle flight school, Cessna introduced another variant of the Skyhawk, again without the Skyhawk name.
Like its retractable namesake, the Cutlass used the basic four-seat Skyhawk
airframe with a different variant of the trusty 180-hp Lycoming O-360
engine. This aircraft was not to be a great success. Priced $8,000 more than
the 160-hp Skyhawk, it offered only a couple of knots greater airspeed and
about 100 pounds greater payload. With identical payloads, the Cutlass
could outperform the Skyhawk, but carrying the extra 100 pounds, its takeoff and landing distance figures were inferior to the Hawk. Cutlasses were
introduced as Cessna began to act like it didn't even want to be in the light
plane market any longer. And because the general aviation market became
depressed, few Cutlasses were built.

In 1998, again partly due to prodding by Embry-Riddle, Cessna brought
back the 180-hp Cessna 172. Not bothering with silly names, they just called
this one the 172S Skyhawk SP. This one also has the Lycoming IO-360
engine, but not derated. Performance is only slightly better than the 172R,
at a price differential of $16,000 when the plane first was introduced. By
2003 Cessna had reduced the price differential to $10,000. The differential
was even less if you wanted leather seats, standard in the SP but a $2,900
option in the basic 172S.

After-market modification shops have actually produced a better 180-hp
Lycoming-engined Skyhawk than the Cessna factory, and have offered one
reasonable answer to the problem of what to do with the awful O-360H-
engined models. Penn Yan Aero Service's (www.pennyanaero.com)
Superhawk conversion offers conversions to the O-360 engine with a fixed-
pitch prop for any Lycoming-engined Cessna 172 (1968 or newer). The
Superhawk outperforms the Cutlass, proving that Cessna did not have a
monopoly on intelligent engineering applied to the Skyhawk. For a price of
$20,000 to $25,000 for the engine kit, plus installation, the modifications
also offer a much more reasonably priced alternative for a more powerful
Hawk than the overpriced Cutlass or 172S.

The Skyhawk is very stable and more resistant to stalls than the 150.
And the addition of droop tips makes it just a little more stable. Of course,
stable can be another word for "slow to respond" or even "a little dull."
Aileron response on the Skyhawk will never be confused with an aerobatic
aircraft. It's more like a flying four-seat family station wagon. Rear-seat passengers (often family members) appreciate the excellent view of the ground
provided by the high wing. Unfortunately, pilot visibility to the sides and
above, as in the 150, is lacking—as is apparent in a crowded airport pattern.
The huge, slow electric flaps are very effective, and the use of some flaps is
usually necessary to stop the aircraft from floating a long way down the runway. The flaps can even be used in crosswind landings, which are accom-

Figure 9.2. The ever-popular Skyhawk has been built in greater numbers than any other single general aviation aircraft.

plished with surprising ease in the 172. Pilots should be warned, however, that the 172 can be trickier on the ground than in the air on a windy, gusty day. Like the 150, the 172 is susceptible to being tipped on its nose and a wingtip by gusty, quartering tailwinds, if anything but correct aileron-elevator combination is used when taxiing.

The Skyhawk/172 line is relatively free of AD notes, and *Aviation Consumer* magazine reports that it is a safe and strong aircraft that has one of the lowest in-flight airframe failure rates of any aircraft flying. It is not without its problems, however. Like the 150, the nosewheel on the 172 is prone to an irritating shimmy. Make sure the seat tracks are in good shape and the seat locking pins on the front seats engage securely, too. Cessna lost a major lawsuit as a result of a crash caused by the pilot's seat slipping as the aircraft took off. The pilot, of course, held onto the yoke and the airplane went up until it stalled and crashed.

Another serious problem reported in *Aviation Consumer* is a problem with corrosion under improperly prepared and applied paint on 1977-1981 Skyhawks (yes, the ones with that wonderful O-320H engine!). Because Cessna did not follow DuPont's recommendations for application of usually-superior Imron paint, aircraft produced during these years were cursed with higher-than-average rates of filiform corrosion under the paint. Many of these aircraft will have been repainted by now, but even new paint jobs on aircraft in this year group should be given extra scrutiny.

The biggest drawback, however, is in the engine compartment of two different year groups of 172s. The Lycoming O-320Hs in 1977 to 1980 Cessnas, as discussed earlier, make them models to avoid completely unless you find one with a great, uncorroded airframe and a superior radio stack for a 180-hp conversion job. Older 172s with the Continental O-300 engine can be troublesome, too, although using autogas can cut down on problems. The O-300 shares the problems of its O-200 "little brother," which has the same cylinders. Both engines are very susceptible to valve problems and spark plug problems if they are run on any 100LL avgas. "Soft" cylinders can be a common malady on these engines. Fortunately, autogas STCs are available for aircraft with these engines, and it is probably not even a good idea to buy one of these aircraft if the present owner hasn't already obtained the STC and has been regularly using unleaded or low-lead autogas.

Unfortunately, the O-300's problems aren't all solved with autogas. Oil leaks seem to plague the engine. It is a rare Continental-engined 172 (discernable by the two exhaust stacks) that does not have oil dripping on its nosewheel after a flight. The engine was not well designed for maintainability, either. If there are oil leaks around the boots where the pushrod housings enter the crankcase, it is necessary to pull the cylinders to make the fix. The Lycoming O-320 and O-360 engines, by comparison, use O-rings that can be changed without cylinder removal. Leaks around the O-300 oil pan gasket are even worse. The oil pan is bolted not only to the bottom of the crankcase but also to the accessory section, which, of course, has a one-piece gasket which is also shared with the back of the crankcase. To make a long story short, if you want to replace the oil pan gasket, you must also remove the entire accessory section to replace its gasket if you really intend to do the job correctly. And to add insult to injury, Cessna fastened the two-piece cowling of O-300 equipped 172s with nearly two dozen machine screws. If a few are corroded (and they probably will be), you could pay for two hours of labor before the mechanic ever touches your sick O-300!

Cessna, in their zeal to standardize the electrical systems of their entire line, "blessed" 1978 and later Skyhawks with the 28-volt electrical system used in everything from the 152 to the Citation. The new system is not an advantage to the average owner. Batteries are nonstandard, expensive, top-of-the-line items. Parts cannot be obtained from supplemental suppliers as easily or from used or reconditioned parts sources because the 28-volt system is not common to other manufacturers' lines or even to the multitude of older 172s. Nonessential light bulbs, like dome lights and courtesy lights, can no longer be replaced at the local auto supply store. And jump starts from an automobile battery are no longer possible for the cold-weather pilot.

Whatever Cessna did in producing the Skyhawk must have been right because it is still one of the most popular airplanes flying today (and still in production). It is conservative in design and performance, has a much better-than-average safety record, and is an excellent family airplane. Even older models are not cheap. Used Skyhawk prices are traditionally higher than those of Cherokee 140s, Musketeers, or even Warriors of the same vintage. In the late 1980s, many were sold for export to Europe and other overseas locations when the dollar lost its value on the world market and made

Table 9.2. Cessna 172 Skyhawk

	1966 (Continental O-300)	1969 (Lycoming O-320)
Specifications		
Wingspan	36 ft	36 ft
Length	26 ft 11 in	26 ft 11 in
Gross weight, normal category	2,300 lb	2,300 lb
Empty weight	1,300 lb	1,315 lb
Useful load	970 lb	985 lb
Useful load, full fuel	742 lb	757 lb
Fuel capacity, standard tanks	42 gal (38 usable)	42 gal (38 usable)
Performance		
Cruise speed, 75% power, best altitude	131 mph	132 mph
Fuel consumption, 75% power	8.5 gph	8.1 gph
Range 45-min reserve, 75% power	487 mi	521 mi
Sea level rate of climb	645 fpm	645 fpm
Service ceiling	13,100 ft	13,100 ft
Stall, clean	57 mph	57 mph
Stall, full flaps	49 mph	49 mph
Takeoff over a 50-foot obstacle	1,525 ft	1,525 ft
Landing over a 50-foot obstacle	1,250 ft	1,250 ft

used aircraft prices cheaper for citizens of other countries, further raising the prices of those that remained in the United States.

The airframe cannot be faulted, except for 1977 to 1981 models plagued with corrosion and paint problems, which should also be avoided because of the O-320H engine. Skyhawks powered by the 150-hp Lycoming engine (1968 to 1976) are probably the best of the older Skyhawks, and probably the best value. Still older models powered by the Continental O-300 engine can be a good buy if one is prepared to run them only on autogas. The last of Skyhawks built with the more reliable older design 160-hp Lycomings after 1981 before production was terminated are also excellent (although expensive) aircraft. Best of all, but a bit on the expensive side, are those with the Lycoming O-360 180-horsepower conversions.

Of course, for those with money to spare, the best Skyhawks are new Skyhawks.

Cessna 177 Cardinal

Looking for a sleek, sexy-looking, sweet-flying, reasonably fast fixed-gear airplane? Do you think a Skyhawk is just a little dull, but you still want a high-wing airplane that will carry four and come at a reasonable price? Try Cessna's beautiful—but neglected—stepchild, the aircraft Cessna got wrong the first time and made only a half-hearted attempt to sell once they got it right. Try a Cardinal!

The Model 177 Cardinal was supposed to be the successor to the Skyhawk when it came out in late 1967, Detroit automotive style, as a 1968 model. But its 150-hp Lycoming was just not up to lifting a sturdy airframe that was 100 pounds heavier than the Skyhawk's, and one that had larger fuel tanks and a bigger baggage compartment as well. Big and roomy, it just begged to be overloaded. To make matters worse, Cessna gave all 1,158 models of 1968 a high-performance airfoil with poor low-speed handling traits. The stabilator was culture shock to the Skyhawk drivers, and the ones on the first-year model were overly sensitive and could be stalled in the landing flare. The result was an underpowered airplane with lousy climb characteristics when the big cabin and fuel tanks were full, with twitchy pitch characteristics and the tendency to act weird when the Skyhawk driver tried to land it. (Hell, it flew like a damn Cherokee! Only worse!)

In mid-1968, all Cardinals were recalled to undergo the "Cardinal Rule" change, which modified the stabilators with slots to alleviate the landing stall problem and which also changed balance weights to dampen the pitch sensitivity. In 1969, the 177A came out with a 180-hp Lycoming engine with a fixed-pitch propeller. In 1970, the 177B brought the biggest changes. A constant-speed prop was added, and a more docile wing with better low-speed characteristics was introduced. The year 1971 brought a retractable gear version, the 177RG (see Chapter 11). Sixty-gallon fuel tanks were a 1973 option, and the last Cardinals produced in 1978 got the blessing of a 28-volt electrical system.

Table 9.3. Cessna 177B Cardinal

Specifications	
Wingspan	35 ft 6 in
Length	26 ft 11.5 in
Gross weight, normal category	2,500 lb
Empty weight	1,475 lb
Useful load	1,025 lb
Useful load, full fuel	731 lb
Fuel capacity, standard tanks	49 gal
Performance	
Cruise speed, 75% power, best altitude	139 mph
Fuel consumption, 75% power	10.1 gph
Range 45-min reserve, 75% power	560 mi
Sea level rate of climb	840 fpm
Service ceiling	14,600 ft
Stall, clean	63 mph
Stall, full flaps	53 mph
Takeoff over a 50-foot obstacle	1,400 ft
Landing over a 50-foot obstacle	1,220 ft

Figure 9.3. The Cessna Cardinal is one sleek and beautiful aircraft.

Cardinals are sleek, rakish, and beautiful. Long, wide, and low-slung, with big cabin doors on both sides, they are easy to get into and out of, and leg room is excellent. Visibility from the pilot's seat is amazingly good for a high-winger, with the leading edge just slightly behind the pilot's head and no struts to obscure the view (or the photography). They even have crank-open side vent windows!

In the air, this is a sweet airplane. Controls are smooth, beautifully coordinated, precise, and relatively quick. If the Skyhawk is a big station wagon, then this is a sports sedan! While the controls are a pleasure, performance figures for rate of climb, airspeed, and useful load are only average compared with other 180-hp Lycoming-powered aircraft, however.

Problems are few but can be bothersome. The big doors are notorious for leaking water, and the door latches aren't the best. In a gale force wind with the plane tied down, it is possible for the doors to violently pop open and damage their hinges as well as the forward fuselage. The Bendix dual magneto, with two magnetos on one shaft and known for less than sterling reliability, was used on 1975 to 1978 models. Some owners have been known to swap for an earlier model engine with conventional mags at overhaul time.

This is a beautiful airplane with nice flying characteristics. Most Cardinals available will be 177B models, although many of these are modified A models. It's too bad Cessna gave up on this one so easily. This could have been a very worthy complement to the dull Skyhawk, but Cessna lost its nerve and never really tried to sell the 180-hp version. And it was a real shame that Cessna chose to replace the Cardinal with the unreliable and inferior Skyhawk XP. If you want a high-wing airplane without a "trucky" feel, give this one a try!

Piper PA-28 Cherokee 140, 180, Warrior, Archer, and Cadet

The Piper Cherokee series is the only real competition Cessna had for many years, and there is a certain irony in the fact that "Number 2" was producing planes in the late 1980s when "Number 1" was gone from the new aircraft marketplace. The *Piper Owners Magazine* notes that 44,179 PA-28 series aircraft, ranging from Cherokee 140s up to Cherokee 235s and Arrows, had been produced by late 1991—less than the number of aircraft produced by Cessna, but an impressive number. But regardless of the vagaries of the market, Cherokees have always been different from their high-wing brethren!

The early history of the Cherokee series is rather strange, with engines and models being added to and subtracted from the lineup. Despite having similar performance capabilities to early 172s, the Cherokee 140 never fared well in direct competition with early models of the Skyhawk. Perhaps it was because Piper never seemed to be able to decide whether it wanted the public to consider the 140 to be a big two-seater or a little four-seater. And if Piper couldn't make up its mind, the flying public could hardly be faulted for not being sure, either!

The Cherokee was introduced in 1961 as a 160-hp four-seater followed closely by a 150-hp four-seater. Both included the large baggage compartments with exterior baggage doors (identical to those found on Warriors and larger single-engine Pipers nearly 30 years later) as standard. The Cherokee 180 first appeared in 1963 with the snub nose more commonly identified with all Cherokee 140s and Warriors. (The 180 would achieve its sleek, racy, tightly cowled look two years later with advent of the Cherokee 180C.) In 1964, the Cherokee 140 appeared as a two-seater with a climb prop, a 150-hp engine derated on paper to 140 hp, and a load limitation of 1,950 pounds gross weight. (An engine can be "derated" on paper when the owner's manual limits the operating range by restricting the top-end RPM to a lower number than the engine is actually rated for. It is a questionable procedure that some people claim adds to the life of the engine, although Lycoming literature says *their* engines can operate continuously at a *full-rated* 75-percent power for a full TBO. Cessna also played this game with the Skyhawk XP, partly as a device to meet some threatened EPA noise standards.) Derating the Cherokee 140 to 140 hp did not last long, however; an option soon appeared providing two add-on rear seats and allowing a "high gross" back up to 2,150 pounds with the engine operating at its full-rated power of 150 hp. It was effectively a Cherokee 150 without the baggage compartment or baggage door, even though it would always be called a Cherokee 140.

By 1966 all Cherokee 140s were 150-hp models, most of which were equipped with optional rear seats. The year 1968 saw one of the largest changes in this lower end of the Cherokee line. The 150 and 160 models, which had been slipping badly alongside the 180 as well as the Cessna 172, were dropped. The 140 and the rest of the Cherokee line received a major revamp of the interior, with a striking new panel providing for improved instrument placement and much greater radio space, addition of a "T-stick" throttle quadrant, replacement of the ceiling-mounted trim handle with a floor-mounted trim wheel (not a popular move with "real" Cherokee buffs who said that Piper had knuckled under to Cessna drivers), and the addition of the 140's rear hat shelf in the place of the old flat bulkhead—a change which made the airplane seem significantly roomier. The 180C became a 180D with the new panel, throttle quadrant, and two new small side windows above the baggage compartment at the rear of the cabin.

In 1973, the 180 got an 8-inch fuselage extension, a 2-foot wingspan extension, and a new name: Challenger. The name would be dropped in favor of Archer in 1974. The year 1974 also saw the start of the biggest change to hit the PA-28 and PA-32 line, with the "Hershey-bar" wing in the bottom line 140 Cruiser finally giving way to a new, longer wing in the PA-28-151 Warrior. The Warrior also had the stretched fuselage and baggage compartment introduced in the 1973 Challenger, making it a big step up over the 140. In 1976 the Warrior wing appeared on the Cherokee 180, which became the PA-28-181 Archer II. The year 1977 saw the basic Warrior given the original 160-hp engine to become the PA-28-161 Warrior II. The 1978 model year sealed the fate of the Hershey-bar wing on the lower end of the line, with the two-seat Tomahawk finally nailing the coffin shut on the lowly Cherokee 140. Also in 1978, large, ungainly looking and difficult-to-remove wheel fairings were added to the Warrior II and Archer II which increased the speed of the aircraft.

There were few substantial changes to the lower end of the Cherokee line between 1978 and the 1990s, and Piper was to see a severe period of trial along with the rest of the general aviation industry. Struck by the malaise of rising prices, incredible liability lawsuit judgments, and declining production rates plaguing all of general aviation in the early 1980s, Piper appeared headed for oblivion. In 1984 Piper was sold to the huge conglomerate Lear-Siegler, and in 1986 production of all models except the top-of-the-line single Malibu and turboprop Cheyenne IIIA and 400LS was halted. But Piper, historically the handiwork of one man (who originally made his money elsewhere but who loved aviation), was to be saved by another such man. In 1987, independent businessman and aviation enthusiast M. Stuart Millar bought Piper and a year later had a complete line of general aviation aircraft back in production, with PA-28 Cherokee descendants predominating. Deciding that a trainer was needed by the flying community, in 1988 Millar decided to bring out a stripped-down, no-frills Warrior. Much as Piper had done in developing the Cherokee 140 from the fancier Cherokee 150 and 160, the Cadet was developed from the Warrior II with no third window, no wheel pants, and no baggage compartment. The March 1992 issue of The *Piper Owner's Magazine* reported that 44,179 PA-28 series aircraft (including the larger and faster 235s, 236s, and Arrows but not counting PA-32 Sixes and Saratogas) had been built up to that time, with more still coming off the line.

But the PA-28 Cadets, Warriors, Archers, and Arrows built in early 1990 were nearly the end of the line. Facing cash-flow problems due in part to an overly ambitious attempt to do too much too soon and to sell too many airplanes at too low a price, and beset by serious in-flight airframe failures bedeviling the top-of-the-line Malibu, Piper declared bankruptcy in 1991. Production was reduced to barely a trickle until CEO Chuck Suma and other employees acquired the company in 1995. To avoid legal hassles over control of the Piper name, the company took the somewhat "tacky" name of "The New Piper Aircraft, Inc." The good news was production of the Warrior, Archer, and Arrow would resume. The bad news was New Piper prices would be even more outrageous than those of the new Cessnas.

New Piper (www.newpiper.com) brought out the Archer III in 1995. The main change was to the engine cowling, which now had the small circular air inlets which originated in LoPresti's speed shop mods. Piper finally went to the 28V electrical system, which had become the new industry standard. There was also a new instrument panel. In a dumb move, most of the switches which had resided below the panel were moved to above the windshield on the Archer III. Not only is the effective windshield area significantly reduced, but the switches are up where older guys with bifocals (the ones with enough money to pay the outrageous prices in excess of $200,000 for a well-equipped new Archer III) will have to look at the ceiling to read the writing on the switches. The Archer III does have Garmin avionics in its standard stack and IFR option packages, a marked advantage over the Bendix/King line avionics in the new Cessnas. Curiously enough, the 2003 Warrior IIIs and Arrows have nearly identical new panels, but with the switches neatly beneath the Garmin 430s and the nice big older-style windshields!

The post-2000 pricing for new Warrior IIIs and Archer IIIs has to lead one to question New Piper's commitment to selling these aircraft in the personal aircraft market. In the '60s, '70s, and '80s, Cherokees, Warriors, and Archers were priced very competitively with Cessna Skyhawks and even Skylanes. But 2003 list prices (see Appendix E) for Warrior IIIs are $20,000 more than Skyhawks, and Archer III list prices are $40,000 more than the

180-hp Skyhawk SPs. An IFR-equipped Archer III is significantly more expensive than the newer and faster Diamond DA40 Diamond Star and slightly more expensive than even a Cirrus SR20. Other than the college flight schools New Piper seems to target (and who probably get discounted prices), it is hard to understand who they think would pay these new prices for these aircraft. In 2003, New Piper was purchased and recapitalized by American Capital Strategies, who left the existing management in place. New model development was promised, and it will be interesting to see what the future holds for the Cherokee line.

The Cherokee 140, beset by the identity crisis imposed by its makers, never acquired the reputation for excellence it deserved. If you compare the performance of the mid-1960 Cherokee 140s with the mid-1960 Cessna 172s, it is readily apparent that the 140 is a near match for the early Continental-engined 172 and clearly outclasses the 150. Part of the 140's problem was that pilots growing up on Cessnas checked the Cherokee's load-carrying figures with full fuel, not taking into account that the plane carried a full 10 usable gallons more fuel than standard 172s of the same vintage. With nearly identical speeds, the Cherokee 140 could stay in the air an hour longer. And Piper even conveniently provided tabs in the low-wing-mounted fuel tanks of the 140s (as well as in the fuel tanks of all of the Cherokee-series aircraft, including modern Warriors and Cadets), permitting easy fueling to a total of 36 rather than 50 gallons on all Cherokee-series air-craft with standard tanks. The Cherokee 140 offers an easy trade-off between using a plane as a very long-legged two-seater with ample baggage and full fuel or as a four-seat pleasure flyer with little or no baggage or fuel "to the tabs." Yes, the early Skyhawks could carry more as a four-seater. But the high-wing advocates couldn't add more fuel to the Skyhawks to make them long-range IFR two-seaters, a capability inherent in a properly equipped PA-28-140.

In the air, the Cherokees and Warriors are a pleasure to fly. They are nearly as stable as Skyhawks, but they have a much quicker response to aileron control pressures. Visibility from the two front seats is excellent in all directions except down and behind, but rear-seat passengers may be less than thrilled to have to lean forward to look down behind the wing. Cherokees seem spacious and solid inside, with plenty of leg room for the rear-seat passengers who sit on the massive main spar carrythrough box.

Cherokee/Warrior/Cadet stalls are almost a joke. A Cherokee stall from almost any attitude will ultimately result in the plane being slightly nose down with wings level. Hold the wheel back in a power-off configuration, and the Cherokee will gradually head earthward with the nose bobbing up and down as the plane alternately stalls and regains flying speed and stalls and ... Not the best characteristic for teaching stalls to pilots who may make the transition to aircraft with far less benign stall manners, but you would have to work to kill yourself in a stall-spin accident in any of the Cherokee-series aircraft.

Flaps are manually operated like a sports car parking brake and have four positions (0, 10, 25, and 40). The flaps are not tremendously effective, but the older Hershey-bar wing Cherokees can be brought in at a surprisingly steep angle by a pilot who knows how to hold the aircraft just above stall speed with full flaps. (A slight miscalculation will not kill you, considering the Cherokee's stall characteristics.) Don't try this with the Warrior-winged versions, though. The longer, slimmer wing will just result in a long, floating glide. Short-field takeoffs in older Cherokees are also surprisingly effective, if the pilot is gutsy enough to hold the nose down until takeoff speed is obtained, as the owner's manual says you should. Bring the nose up too soon, and the older Cherokee will mush along into the trees. This is where the Warrior-winged PA-28s shine—the long wing gets off the ground quickly and provides excellent takeoff and climb characteristics.

Crosswind landings in a Cherokee are seldom a problem. On the ground, Cherokees are rock solid in anything short of a hurricane, sitting low with the mains a full 10 feet apart. It is only 10 more feet to each wing tip on older Cherokees, and not much more than that on newer models, and that's not much! Nosewheel steering is tied directly to the rudders and feels very stiff. But once you get the knack, it is surprisingly quick. Many early Cherokee 140s had no toe brakes; many more have toe brakes only on the

Table 9.4. Piper Cherokee PA-28-140 (1967) and PA-28-161 Warrior II (1983)

	Cherokee 140	Warrior II
Specifications		
Wingspan	30 ft	35 ft
Length	23.3 ft	23.8 ft
Gross weight, normal category	2,150 lb	2,440 lb
Empty weight	1,201 lb	1,350 lb
Useful load	949 lb	1,090 lb
Useful load, full fuel	649 lb	790 lb
Fuel capacity, standard tanks	50 gal (48 usable)	50 gal (48 usable)
Performance		
Cruise speed, 75% power, best altitude	133 mph	139 mph
Fuel consumption, 75% power	8.4 gph	8.5 gph
Range 45-min reserve, 75% power	660 mi	681 mi
Sea level rate of climb	660 fpm	650 fpm
Service ceiling	14,300 ft	14,000 ft
Stall, clean	63 mph	57.5 mph
Stall, full flaps	54 mph	50.5 mph
Takeoff over a 50-foot obstacle	1,700 ft	1,625 ft
Landing over a 50-foot obstacle	1,700 ft	1,125 ft

left side, because the stiff nosewheel steering and the parking brake handle mounted below the left center of the instrument panel are more than adequate for ground operation.

Cabin ventilation was not a Cherokee strong point until the Warrior and Archer models brought excellent large floor vents and airline-style ceiling vents. Older Cherokees have only one vent by the pilot's left foot, and one small vent at chest level by each of the front seats. Life can be miserable for rear-seat passengers on a hot day. You soon learn why Cherokees are sometimes known as "the airplane that taxis with its door open." There is a redeeming virtue for all Cherokees, however. They are not drafty in the winter, and their cabin heaters are excellent.

Cabin entry and exit through the line's standard single door is not a virtue, however. Getting in to or out of a Cherokee must be a coordinated operation. Add rain, and it's really challenging!

Another plus for Cherokee 140s, older 160s and 180s, all 151 and 161 Warriors and the Cadet is the cowling design. Hinged like an old Model A Ford, the open cowling cover allows a thorough preflight. Access to the engine is so good that oil and even spark plug changes can be made without removing a single screw from the cowling. This is also a real advantage for good student instruction in the 140, the Warrior, and the Cadet. The two-piece fiberglass cowls used on the 180s, 181s, 235s, and 236s, as well as on the big Sixes and the retractable Arrows and Saratogas are not as good for access as the hinged cowlings on the smaller Cherokees. Even the one-piece fiberglass top cowl, however, can be removed for minor maintenance after merely releasing four hold-down clips. Clearly, Piper engineers were thinking about ease of maintenance when they designed the Cherokee-series cowlings.

Figure 9.4. The Cherokee 140 is an excellent airplane with an undeserved lackluster reputation.

Cherokees are beset by many minor ADs, including fuel gauge sender unit problems, leaking underwing fuel drain sumps, fuel selector handle problems, muffler cracks, and control wheel cracks. All these will already have been taken care of by a conscientious owner or can be handled with relatively little cost at an annual. Considering the nature of most of the minor ADs, you have to wonder if Piper's problem was one of bad relations with FAA personnel rather than bad airplanes.

In 1987 and 1988, a wing spar AD controversy arose which showed just how far the FAA would go. When one 181 Archer with nearly 7,500 hours (which had been used in low-altitude, pipeline-patrol work) lost a wing and crashed, an AD was issued requiring all Cherokees with more than 5,000 hours to have their wings pulled for inspections! To put this in perspective, more than 200 Model 35 Beechcraft Bonanzas broke up in the air over a 20-year period before the FAA decided to issue an AD to strengthen supports in the Bonanza's V-tail. When hundreds of inspections of high-time Cherokees showed only three more with cracks, all in very-high-time aircraft which had been operated under severe conditions, the FAA was finally convinced to rescind the AD. Piper researched the problem and brought out a realistic and responsible "mandatory" service bulletin to replace the AD. Piper Service Bulletin No. 886 recommended the wing removal inspection only for high-time, "severe service experience" aircraft or aircraft with a significant damage history, but effectively eliminated aircraft with a normal use history from the inspection.

Should anyone considering buying a Cherokee worry about this problem? The answer is that you probably should. Damage history can be very important. The service bulletin defines "Extreme usage, Class C" as including aircraft with damage "which required major repair or replacement of wings or the engine mount." For these aircraft, and for aircraft rated "extreme usage" such as low-altitude pipeline patrol, wing removal inspections are required within 50 hours and every 1,600 hours thereafter. Aircraft with an unknown service history are tagged with a recommendation for the wing removal within 50 hours, and repetitive inspections as recommended by the mechanic doing the initial inspection. While the service bulletin is not an AD and therefore not really "mandatory," it is possible that conservative insurance companies could require that the service bulletin be complied with. So if you're buying a Cherokee, you'd probably better check the logs very closely to assure that they are complete and that they don't show any significant damage history that would put the aircraft in "Class C." For an aircraft with no damage and a fully documented normal-usage history, don't worry about it at all. An aircraft in this category will be removed from a museum by your great-great grandchildren and have its wings pulled after it has flown the recommended 62,900 hours. Some DC-3s have that much time in service, but it's doubtful that any general aviation airplane has that long a service history.

Early model Cherokees also had two other problem areas. If a Cherokee is well-maintained, both of the situations will have been corrected, and the Cherokee is probably a good buy. If any of the problems still exist, you should stay away from the aircraft entirely.

The first problem with older Cherokees was their main landing gear. AD 70-18-5 required inspection and replacement of landing gear torque link bolts on 1962 to 1970 models and AD 72-8-6 required replacement of landing gear torque links on 1962 to 1972 models. Pre-1968 model Cherokees were prone to pitting on chromed surfaces of their oleo struts, causing the rubber seals in the oleos to wear away and leak. Cherokee 140s, because of their heavy use as trainers, as well as any other Cherokees subject to heavy use, could develop fatigue cracks in the main gear castings where the torque links attach to the heavy aluminum casting. All these potential problems should be checked closely by a mechanic before you buy a high-time Cherokee.

The second problem with older Cherokees was fuel tank leaks. Tank sealant used by Piper prior to 1968 had a history of becoming brittle and cracking, leading to leaks. Such leaking manifested itself as a discoloration, often accompanied by corrosion, around the screws holding the fuel tanks to the front of the wings. The only reliable way to stop the leaks permanently is to remove the tank and have it completely disassembled, cleaned to

Table 9.5. Piper Cherokee PA-28-180C (1966) and PA-28-181 Archer II

	Cherokee 180C	Archer II
Specifications		
Wingspan	30 ft	35 ft
Length	23 ft 6 in	23 ft 10 in
Gross weight, normal category	2,400 lb	2,550 lb
Empty weight	1,230 lb	1,137 lb
Useful load	1,170 lb	985 lb
Useful load, full fuel	870 lb	849 lb
Fuel capacity, standard tanks	50 gal (48 usable)	50 gal (48 usable)
Performance		
Cruise speed, 75% power, best altitude	143 mph	150 mph
Fuel consumption, 75% power	10 gph	10.5 gph
Range 45-min reserve, 75% power	579 mi	573 mi
Sea level rate of climb	750 fpm	735 fpm
Service ceiling	16,400 ft	13,650 ft
Stall, clean	66 mph	62.5 mph
Stall, full flaps	57 mph	56 mph
Takeoff over a 50-foot obstacle	1,625 ft	1,625 ft
Landing over a 50-foot obstacle	1,750 ft	1,390 ft

bare metal, and resealed with a new, improved sealing compound. A repair shop called Skycraft Corporation at the Hampton Airfield in North Hampton, New Hampshire, specializes in this repair. Skycraft charges approximately $1,100 for both tanks, or $600 for one tank, plus shipping. It is advisable to replace the fuel sender gauge assembly at this time as well, because it will probably be worn and it is sealed to the rear of the tank. Replacing the unit at a later time will necessitate removal of the tank a second time and will compromise the tank seal. Also have the rubber connections in the fuel lines from the tank to the engine and overflow vent lines checked while the tank is off the front of the wing. Aromatics in some avgas mixtures can cause cracking and other problems with these rubber parts in the fuel system, leading to frustrating leaks which will show up as a strong gasoline smell, usually as the plane makes a turn while taxiing on the ground. (Even newer Cherokees and Warriors, and those that have had their tanks done by Skycraft, may have problems with deteriorating fuel lines.) Piper service manuals indicate that the tanks can be "sloshed" with new compound without disassembly. This cheaper fix has proved to be inadequate. Applying new sealer over dried-out old sealer is prone to failure if the older sealer continues to crack and chip away. The Skycraft solution appears to be the only one in which the repaired tank ends up "better than new."

PA-28 series aircraft are comfortable planes to fly. They are definitely not the same as the mass-produced Cessnas, which many people learned to fly in. Their low-wing characteristics take "getting used to," particularly for pilots making the transition from Cessnas. Flown improperly, the Cherokee (particularly the older Hershey-bar wing model) can seem to be a real dog. Flown with the right touch, it is a really fine airplane. The stiff nosewheel steering on the ground seems irritating until you realize that you can turn without toe brakes in a tighter circle than you can swing a Skyhawk with toe brakes. In the air, the ceiling crank found on pre-1968 Cherokees is an annoyance until the day comes when it is second nature and you reach up and turn it without looking. Then it is "unique," "different," and a sign that you are flying, not driving, and you secretly regret that Piper eventually bowed to the Cessna-trained types and put the trim on the floor, hidden down between the seats.

While almost any one of the fixed-gear PA-28s are a good choice for a private owner, well-kept older Cherokee 180s and rare Cherokee 160Cs with the modern fiberglass cowlings can be especially good buys on the used plane market. If you can find a good one, it may be a rare find, so grab it if the airframe and engine times are not excessive. They are both good, honest airplanes in terms of load carrying and speed, and they come with cavernous baggage compartments and comfortable seats and price tags comparable to

Figure 9.5. Older Cherokee 180s provide excellent performance at a reasonable price.

Skyhawks of the same vintage. Anyone considering owning a Cherokee, or anyone who already owns one, should consider joining the Cherokee Pilots Association (www.piperowner.com). Especially valuable is the approximately 360-page *Cherokee Hints and Tips* sold by the CPA for $29.95 plus postage.

The Cherokee 180 and the 181 Archer IIs and Archer IIIs are second only to the Tiger Aircraft Tiger in providing maximum performance for a minimum of maintenance expense. Of all the fixed-gear aircraft using the highly reliable 100LL-rated Lycoming O-360 engine, only the Cherokee 180 (and its direct successors, the 181 Archer/Archer II/Archer III) has been produced in sufficient quantities for a long enough time to assure ready availability at a reasonable price (by used aircraft market standards). The 180's 143-mph cruise, and the Archer II's 150-mph cruise, is exceeded only by the much rarer Tigers or DA40s or by aircraft with variable-pitch props and retractable landing gear that are more expensive to maintain. Cherokee 180s and Archers do not come cheap, however, and should probably not be considered by first-time buyers with tight budgets. If you are a prospective first-time owner of modest means, try looking for a good Cherokee 140 or an early model Warrior. Use it to build up your time and experience and your bank account, and then step up to a 180 or a late-model Warrior, or even an Archer. For those who love the low-wing Pipers and have enough money to consider buying a new aircraft, buying an early 1980s vintage 181 Archer II and giving it an AOPA-style makeover may be one way to have a "better than new" late model Cherokee and still save a significant amount of money. You'll have better visibility out the windshield, and you'll probably save at least $50,000.

PA-38 Tomahawk

Introduced in 1978 as an aircraft designed with the inputs of instructors in mind, the Tomahawk ultimately failed in the marketplace due to poor quality control destroying its reputation before it got a fair trial. Its major drawback is a T-tail that probably never should have been part of the design. But even though it was not the revolutionary success as a trainer that it was intended to be, an individual Tomahawk with its problems corrected can be a good, two-seat personal airplane.

Setting up a new production line with new workers on a new airplane, Piper turned out 2,000 Tomahawks in 1978 and 1979. Needless to say, quality control suffered, and the Tomahawk was one Piper that deserved most if not all of the numerous ADs it got. Faulty magnetos grounded the Tomahawk fleet for two weeks in late 1978. Cracked and weakened engine mounting bolts were also a problem. The tail was a major weak point, with ADs to correct cracked rudder hinge brackets, cracked vertical fin spar attachment plates, and cracked stabilizer pulley mounting brackets. There were more ADs to correct loose attach bolts and to provide more clearance between the front of the rudder and the fin trailing edge. Control wheels jammed in flight. Incorrect main landing gear bolts and washers had to be corrected. Missing rivets in the rear-wing spar to fuselage attach fitting had to be repaired. In short, the early history of the Tomahawk was a classic bad example of poor quality control.

The poor quality control also affected the handling qualities of the aircraft. Designed to be spinnable for spin training, the Tomahawk had an early problem with nasty and unpredictable stall-spin characteristics that led to a poor record for stall-spin accidents. Making the problem worse, particularly for a training airplane, was that different Tomahawks would behave differently in the same maneuvers.

Prodded by the FAA and perhaps by corporate embarrassment, Piper tightened up the quality control, provided some support for fixing airplanes in the field, and made minor changes to improve the airplane. Stall strips were added to the front of the wings, raising the stall speed of the aircraft but making the stall-spin characteristics more predictable and benign. In 1981, a Tomahawk II was brought out with the stall strips on the wings, larger 6.006 tires on all three wheels replacing the smaller and relatively toy like ones on the early models, and better door latches and other beefed up components.

Unfortunately, not many of the II models were built before production ended in 1982. In all, a total of 2,513 Tomahawks were built. In 1988, Piper owner and aviation enthusiast Millar decided to build the Cadet—a stripped-down Warrior—as the Piper trainer, sealing the fate of the Tomahawk within Piper. With the far more modern and better handling Diamond DA20 available to flight schools, it is unlikely that a new Tomahawk will ever come down the line again. Or that anyone would buy it if it did.

What kind of a plane is the Tomahawk and how does it fly? For a trainer, it has some very nice features. The 42-inch-wide cabin is a full 5 inches wider than the comparatively claustrophobic Cessna 150/152, and it does make for a comfortable cabin. The panel is nicely configured, if Spartan. The fuel selector and gauges (a good idea stolen from Grumman-American) are mounted in plain sight on the lower center of the instrument panel, with the selector pointer indicating the tank in use, and the fuel-off position plainly marked. Cockpit visibility is excellent, with nearly 360-degree visibility and slim wings which do little to block the view below. The cowling has Cherokee 140/Warrior large, hinged access doors that allow a really good look in the engine compartment before each flight. And the spring-steel main landing gear should be relatively problem free (if the AD assuring that they are properly bolted on has been complied with).

The T-tail is not a positive feature. It makes it damn near impossible to do a real short- or soft-field takeoff or landing, because propwash does absolutely nothing to help you raise the nose or keep it off the ground at speeds below about 40 knots. On takeoff, one must be careful not to over-rotate and stall as the elevators go from useless to extremely sensitive very quickly. In the air, the Tomahawk is relatively pleasant to fly, with a quick

Table 9.6. PA-38-112 Tomahawk (1979)

Specifications	
Wingspan	34 ft
Length	22 ft
Gross weight, normal category	1,670 lb
Empty weight	1,109 lb
Useful load	561 lb
Useful load, full fuel	381 lb
Fuel capacity, standard tanks	32 gal (30 usable)
Performance	
Cruise speed, 75% power, best altitude	117 mph
Fuel consumption, 75% power	5.6 gph
Range 45-min reserve, 75% power	538 mi
Sea level rate of climb	718 fpm
Service ceiling	13,000 ft
Stall, clean	60 mph
Stall, full flaps	56 mph
Takeoff over a 50-foot obstacle	1,460 f
Landing over a 50-foot obstacle	1,540 ft

rudder and elevator. Ailerons are less sensitive and don't seem well balanced with the rudder and elevator. Unlike Cherokees, stalls in a Tomahawk can be very abrupt. This is not an airplane to stall close to the ground! And don't look at the T-tail as you enter stall buffet. Seeing it shake violently back and forth will not do wonders for your confidence in the aircraft. (Its post-AD record has not been a problem, however.) Like the Tr-2, trim and the small flaps are relatively worthless.

A good Tomahawk could be the modern-design, inexpensive sport aircraft for you, the first-time owner. But make sure you have a mechanic check the plane and its AD record very closely before you buy it!

Grumman-American AA-1 Yankee, AA-1A and AA-1B Tr-2/Trainer, AA-1C T-Cat/Lynx, AA-5 Traveler, AA-5A Cheetah, Tiger Aircraft AG-5B Tiger

Grumman-American airplanes were sleek and modern, and today's Tiger Aircraft Tigers still look it. Fast and sporty, their large canopies bring to mind visions of World War II fighters, an image that Grumman-American tried to nurture among general aviation pilots.

The Tiger Aircraft/Grumman-American story started with Jim Bede, the flamboyant aircraft designer who, despite apparent good intentions, always seemed to promise just a little more than he could deliver. Bede originally designed the BD-1 as a light personal aircraft with a 65-hp engine. In the early 1960s, the Bede Aircraft Corporation was set up in Cleveland, Ohio, to manufacture the BD-1. When the venture ran into difficulties, financial backers "asked" Bede to step aside. The reorganized company became American Aviation in 1966. In April 1968 the BD-1, redesigned to better suit large-scale manufacturing techniques, emerged as the American Aviation AA-1 Yankee.

In 1970 the original BD-1 wing section was replaced with a modified airfoil to give the Yankee more docile traits, after the aircraft's relatively high stall speed and somewhat tricky handling characteristics gave it a reputation of being an airplane "too hot to handle" for the average student. With its new wing, the Yankee became the AA-1A and received not one but two new names. Sporting a cruise prop, the ship became the Tr-2; with a climb prop for better in-the-pattern performance, it became the Trainer. The company also took a major step forward in 1971. By lengthening the fuselage of the AA-1, extending its wingspan by 7 feet, and replacing the 108-hp Lycoming O-235 with the well-known and reliable 150-hp Lycoming O-320 engine, the two-seat AA-1 Yankee grew into the four-seat AA-5 Traveler. Then in 1973, gross weight in the Tr-2/Trainer was increased to 1,560 lb, and the aircraft became the AA-1B.

Also in 1973, impressed with the unprecedented market penetration American Aviation had achieved in less than five years, Grumman Aviation Corporation bought controlling interest in the company. Overnight, by adding the Yankee and the Traveler to its Ag-Cat and prestigious Gulfstream II, Grumman became the fourth largest general aviation manufacturer in the United States. The new Grumman-American division did not stand still for long, either. Use of extensive Grumman wind tunnel facilities by aerodynamics genius Roy LoPresti led to an improved cowling for the Traveler in 1975, which improved its speed by more than 5 mph. And in 1975 the revolutionary 180-hp Tiger was introduced, with airspeeds matching and even exceeding some 200-hp retractables. In 1976 the enlarged rear stabilizer of the Tiger was added to the Traveler, which also lost its ventral fin and acquired slightly more effective flaps. This Traveler, renamed the Cheetah, was now a 150-hp nearly identical twin to the Tiger. The year 1977 brought an enlarged rear stabilizer and a 115-hp, 100LL-burning version of the Lycoming O-235 to the Tr-2/Trainer, which now became the AA-1C T-Cat/Lynx. And in early 1978 Grumman-American brought out its long-awaited light twin, the Cougar, to round out its potent "kitty litter."

In a very surprising development, described by one aviation magazine as "Jonah swallowing the whale," American Jet Industries in late 1978 bought

Table 9.7. Grumman-American AA-1B Tr-2 (cruise prop)

Specifications	
Wingspan	24.5 ft
Length	19 ft
Gross weight, normal category	1,560 lb
Empty weight	980 lb
Useful load	580 lb
Useful load, full fuel	436 lb
Fuel capacity, standard tanks	24 gal (22 usable)
Performance	
Cruise speed, 75% power, best altitude	133 mph
Fuel consumption, 75% power	6.3 gph
Range 45-min reserve, 75% power	364 mi
Sea level rate of climb	660 fpm
Service ceiling	11,500 ft
Stall, clean	63 mph
Stall, full flaps	60 mph
Takeoff over a 50-foot obstacle	1,590 ft
Landing over a 50-foot obstacle	1,100 ft

the entire Grumman-American line of general aviation aircraft. American Jet Industries, which had previously been known primarily for modifying and updating old airliners into cargo carriers, was in the process of attempting—though unsuccessfully—to certify a radical new turbojet/turboprop executive aircraft known as the Hustler. It seemed to be a case of buying an entire line to fit around one aircraft, with the Hustler fitting nicely between the Cougar and the prestigious Gulfstream.

It was too good to be true. In late 1978 Gulfstream-American, as the new company was called, announced that the T-Cat/Lynx would be dropped from their 1979 lineup. In mid-1979, the twin-engine Cougar was dropped, and by the end of 1979 the Cheetah and Tiger were finished, too. It was apparent that all American Jet Industries had really wanted was the prestigious Gulfstream executive jet and the Georgia production facilities. The much-admired light aviation line was put up for sale, but with the general aviation industry headed for a near depression in the 1980s, the remarkable lineup seemed doomed.

The rights to this outstanding line of aircraft were finally purchased from Chrysler-owned Gulfstream near the end of the 1980s, and the new American General produced its first reborn Tigers in 1990. The new Tiger, dubbed the AG-5B, had minor improvements like a throttle quadrant and wingtip-mounted landing lights. Lack of suppliers for 12-volt electrical systems also forced them to bring out the new Tiger with the now nearly standard 24-volt electrical system. Perhaps the most significant change was the replacement of the troublesome McCauley propeller with a Sensenich. This change eliminated "yellow arc" restrictions on operation between 1,850 and 2,200 rpm and repetitive inspections every 200 hours which plagued owners of McCauley-equipped Tigers. American General produced slightly more than 100 of the new and improved Tigers before going out of business in 1993.

The Tiger is apparently too good an airplane to die, and in 2001 it was back in production in a factory in West Virginia. The new Tiger Aircraft was funded with a large infusion of Taiwanese investment money. The main differences from earlier versions were minimal, including leather seats and a radio stack with two Garmin 430 color GPS mapcomms for a price around $220,000. The Tiger is up against stiff competition with a similarly equipped, faster, and more modern Cirrus SR-20 only $10,000 more expensive, so keeping the breed going will be an uphill battle. But the Tiger is a much nicer flying aircraft than the Cirrus, so maybe there is hope that "real pilots" will buy enough of them to keep the line going.

The little two-seater AA-1s will not be coming back. Their inability to recover from a spin was deemed too much of a liability, and neither American General nor Tiger Aircraft put them back in production.

Figure 9.6. The Yankee and its descendants are fast, fun, and just a bit challenging.

The Yankee/Tr-2/Trainer seems surprisingly roomy and comfortable inside, considering how tiny and almost toy like it seems from the outside. It is a fun ship to fly, with lively, crisp response. It can be a handful for the unsuspecting pilot, however. The rivetless, bonded aluminum sheet and honeycomb construction make it a very fast little airplane on little more than 100 hp. The relatively high, clean stall speed of 63 mph, which drops to a still fast 60 mph with full flaps, can catch an unwary pilot making the transition from a slower Cessna 150 or a docile Piper Warrior by surprise. Stalls can be brisk, with a wing dropping toward the fullest fuel tank. The Tr-2/Trainer has milder manners than the Yankee, which had the reputation of a "killer" in a spin, but the Tr-2/Trainer can still be a challenge (and it was never cleared for spins, either). The aircraft has a fairly high wing loading for a trainer, which gives it a smooth ride through bumpy air but which can cause a steep approach angle on final if speed is not maintained.

Special features make the Yankee/Tr-2/Trainer a really "different" airplane. The large bubble canopy gives the plane a fighter-plane aura, which is further enhanced by the fact that the canopy can be left partially open in flight. In the summer this can be handy, because the canopy can create an uncomfortable greenhouse effect. A semitransparent, dark sunshade is available (and advisable), but it significantly reduces the airplane's unexcelled visibility. (Unfortunately, Grumman-American promoted the "fighter-pilot" image by painting some of its Tr-2s and Trainers with camouflage paint schemes, a dumb idea still carried on by some G-A airplane owners. Camouflage colors were designed to make the airplane blend into the background and reduce its visibility. Just what one needs in a crowded airport pattern where you're a mid-air collision waiting to happen!) One adverse side effect of the canopy is that the airplane seems very noisy at a 75 percent cruise power setting. But on the ground the canopy allows simultaneous entry from both sides. Even getting into a G-A airplane is different. Before you step into the airplane, you kick back the seat cushion and step down onto the metal seat bottom, then onto the floor, finally remembering to replace the seat cushion before settling in.

Fuel tank gauges on a Yankee/Tr-2/Trainer are unusual, too. There aren't any. Plastic sight tubes on either side of the cockpit indicate your fuel quantity, if you can see them around your own knee and that of your passenger. Nosewheel steering is also notable by its absence. The airplane has a free-castering nosewheel, and steering is performed by differential braking. The airplane can almost literally turn on a dime on the ground, which is impressive. Not so impressive, though, is the tendency of the Yankee/Tr-2/Trainer to weathervane into strong crosswinds while taxiing or before reaching the rudder-effective speed of 40 mph on the initial takeoff roll.

Like the Tr-2, the Traveler, Cheetah, and Tiger have a very responsive control feel. They have a canopy that can be left partially open up to about 130 mph, and they share the same ground entry and exit problems as the Tr-2. They also share the free-castering nosewheel and toe brake steering of the older and smaller plane, although the added size of the bigger aircraft seem to make weathervaning into crosswinds less of a problem on takeoff than in the smaller Yankee/Tr-2/Trainer.

The Traveler, Cheetah, and Tiger do have some differences, though. Unlike the smaller Tr-2, the larger aircraft have a long, low landing approach which makes them less-than-super short-field aircraft. They have a decided tendency to float with any excess airspeed, and their flaps are just not effective enough to really slow down the airplanes or steepen the approach without resorting to a sideslip. Not surprisingly, these three airplanes have a high incidence of landing accidents.

However, the Traveler, Cheetah, and Tiger share some nifty innovations. The fuel selector and fuel gauges in these aircraft are combined as an integrated unit located between the center console and the instrument panel. The pointer of the fuel selector points to the gauge for the tank you are selecting. You really have to be an idiot to switch to an empty tank with this setup. Another good idea put into these aircraft is a pair of metal-backed rear seats that fold forward to make a spacious cargo area. This could also serve as a sleeping area for two in a pinch (like during an aerial pilgrimage to Oshkosh), although the two had better be on intimate terms! The location of the seats relative to the wing spar is not so nifty, however. Unlike the Cherokees, which have the rear-seat passengers sitting over the main spar, the Traveler, Cheetah, and Tiger have their front seats over the tubular main spar. Rear-seat leg room is not overly generous.

Grumman-Americans seem to be relatively trouble-free aircraft. It may be because of the use of reliable Lycomings in a simple airframe or it may be just luck, but problems of Grumman-American planes are relatively minor, with two major exceptions. *Aviation Consumer* magazine reported that AA-1s and Tigers built between April 1974 and December 1975 were constructed with a bad batch of bonding compound and suffered delamination problems, leading to an AD in 1976 requiring rivets along some seams. The second major potential trouble spot is due to the G-A's otherwise nearly ideal aerodynamic design. All of the Grumman-Americans are tightly cowled, and the engines can run hot. Top overhauls between majors are not unusual, and the prospective G-A buyer should definitely have a compression check done before paying full price for a used AA-1, Cheetah, or Tiger.

A minor problem is a canopy seal that has a tendency to leak in a heavy rain, often creating a problem with the electric flap switch mounted on the console between the seats. A one-piece canopy cover might be a wise investment for G-A owners. Early-model Yankees and Travelers also had problems with canopies that would not slide smoothly in their tracks. Another potential long-term disadvantage of the canopy is its ultimate replacement cost when cracking or crazing of the plexiglass eventually takes its toll. Paying to replace half a Cherokee windshield is one thing. Paying for a whole new G-A canopy is in a different league altogether.

The tubular-steel nose gear, according to one aviation insurance agent, is susceptible to collapsing during landing or takeoff on grass strips or in other rough-field operation. One claim was even filed by a Traveler owner whose nose gear collapsed while he was taxiing in grass (1976 and later Cheetahs and Tigers have beefed-up, shock-mounted nose gear). Steering by differential braking also can cause accelerated brake wear, but this is no big problem for any G-A owner who learns the relatively simple procedure for replacing the brake pads. The free-castering nosewheel can develop the bad habit of shimmying at certain speeds (which can be annoying), if it is not kept properly adjusted.

While relatively few problems have been reported with the bonded metal wing structure of G-A aircraft in normal operation (except for the 1974-1975 models), it could present a problem if the wings suffer damage. Most aircraft mechanics specializing in sheet metal repair are adept at riveted skins, but use of special glues and other unique processes used in bonded metal construction may be beyond the capability of the average FBO repair shop. Care should be exercised if a bonded metal wing is being prepared for repainting, because some paint removers can act as a solvent to glues used in the bonding process.

Early Tigers with the standard McCauley prop are cursed with a repetitive AD that requires inspections every 200 hours for hub cracks; there are also "yellow arc" restrictions on the tach limiting operation between 1,850 and 2,200 RPM. A Sensenich prop, used on new AG-5B Tigers, can be installed on older Tigers to eliminate the inspections and the restrictions and

Table 9.8. Grumman-American AA-5A Cheetah and American-General AA-5B Tiger

	AA-5A Cheetah	AA-5B Tiger
Specifications		
Wingspan	31.5 ft	31.5 ft
Length	22 ft	22 ft
Gross weight, normal category	2,200 lb	2,400 lb
Empty weight	1,262 lb	1,285 lb
Useful load	938 lb	1,115 lb
Useful load, full fuel	710 lb/622 lb	800 lb
Fuel capacity, standard tanks	38 gal (37 usable)	52.6 gal (51 usable)
optional tanks	52.6 gal (51 usable)	
Performance		
Cruise speed, 75% power, best altitude	147 mph	160 mph
Fuel consumption, 75% power	8.75 gph	10.5 gph
Range 45-min reserve, 75% power	746 mi	630 mi
Sea level rate of climb	660 fpm	850 fpm
Service ceiling	12,650 ft	14,600 ft
Stall, clean	62 mph	65 mph
Stall, full flaps	58 mph	61 mph
Takeoff over a 50-foot obstacle	1,600 ft	1,550 ft
Landing over a 50-foot obstacle	1,100 ft	1,100 ft

even add a couple of knots of cruise speed. The price, however, is over $2,000.

The Tr-2 may be just the right choice for the accomplished private pilot looking for a sporty, inexpensive, economical first airplane. Its flight and ground-handling characteristics are challenging, but they are nothing a reasonably good pilot could not easily master after a thorough checkout by an instructor familiar with the breed. By buying a cruise prop and a climb prop, the Tr-2/Trainer owner can have virtually two airplanes in one. If rate of climb is valued for short-field or higher-altitude performance, a climb prop will provide a 705 fpm rate of climb, but at a 75-percent-power cruise speed of only 124 mph. A cruise prop will provide a 75-percent-power cruise speed of 133 mph, but sea level rate of climb will drop to 660 fpm. Watch out for early Yankees, though, unless you already have a lot of time in the AA-1 family. They are fast, but have a high stall speed and can be unforgiving enough to kill a pilot who gets sloppy with his or her turns in the landing pattern.

The Traveler and the Cheetah provide an interesting, sporty, and speedy alternative to the Skyhawks and Cherokees. The Tiger, more than any other single-engine, general aviation aircraft produced, epitomized the state-of-the-art of production light aircraft in the 1970s. No other production airplane could match its blending of simplicity, reliability, economy, and speed, and it retains its edge over other production airplanes into the new millennium. For the private owner, the Tiger is the ultimate simple, fixed-gear air-

Figure 9.7. The Tiger may be the nicest handling, fixed-gear single in production today.

plane. Prices on used Grumman-Americans can be surprisingly reasonable considering the excellence of the aircraft.

For someone who can afford a new aircraft, a new Tiger Aircraft Tiger can offer the speed of a retrac without the maintenance headaches of the retractable gear or the constant-speed prop. It is definitely worth a look, especially if you aren't wild about the feel of the sidestick controllers in the Cirruses and Lancairs.

Beechcraft B19 Sport and C23 Sundowner

The Beechcraft Model 23 Musketeer and its derivatives, the B19 Sport and the C23 Sundowner, are reasonably good airplanes that historically have had poor sales records. Their limited success was originally due to only grudging sales support by their maker. Unlike Piper, which traditionally considered itself a builder of airplanes for the common person, Beechcraft has traditionally aimed for the top of the market, coming down to light general aviation aircraft only with reluctance. Since they are Beechcraft, the Musketeers (Sports, Customs, Supers, Sundowners, and Sierras) have been well built, perhaps overbuilt. Park a Sport next to a Cherokee 140, which has the same size engine, and it looks large. It is bigger and heavier, and the penalty for size and weight is paid in performance. Another penalty of Beech quality for those who bought them new was the price. Beechcraft aircraft are never inexpensive, let alone cheap! So, the Musketeer/Sport/Sundowner line has suffered—from price, performance, and a reluctance on the part of the manufacturer to push such an "ordinary" airplane.

The first Model 23 Musketeer was produced in 1962. Powered by the 160-hp version of the Lycoming O-320, the four-seater was met with overwhelming buyer apathy. Perhaps because of its disappointing sales or because of the then-low TBO of the O-320, in June 1964 Beech brought out the Musketeer II, powered by a 6-cylinder, fuel-injected, 165-hp Continental engine. In late 1965 the Musketeer III line was quite naturally expanded to "three Musketeers"—the Sport, powered by a 150-hp Lycoming O-320; the Custom, powered by a 165-hp Continental; and the Super, powered by a 200-hp Lycoming. In 1968 the entire line of Musketeer IIIs "went Lycoming," with the Custom III receiving the excellent 180-hp O-360.

In 1970 the fuselage was redesigned to be wider and more rounded, providing more front-seat roominess. Windows were reshaped and enlarged, and rear windows were added to the Custom and Super. A retractable was finally added to the line and was known as the Super R, a development of the 200-hp Super.

In 1972 the Musketeer name was dropped, and the Beech lower-end line was renumbered and renamed. The Sport became the A19 Sport. The Custom III became the Model C23 Sundowner. The fixed-gear Super was dropped, and the Super R became the A24R Sierra. The only other really significant change was that the entire line now had at least two cabin doors as

Table 9.9. Beechcraft Model B19 Sport and Model C23 Sundowner

	B19 Sport	C23 Sundowner
Specifications		
Wingspan	32 ft 10.8 in	32 ft 9 in
Length	25 ft 9.6 in	25 ft 9 in
Gross weight, normal category	2,150 lb	2,450 lb
Empty weight	1,274 lb	1,450 lb
Useful load	776 lb	1,000 lb
Useful load, full fuel	423 lb	652 lb
Fuel capacity, standard tanks	58.8 gal (56 usable)	58 gal (57 usable)
Performance		
Cruise speed, 75% power, best altitude	131 mph	136 mph
Fuel consumption, 75% power	7.8 gph	10.8 gph
Range 45-min reserve, 75% power	889 mi	615 mi
Sea level rate of climb	700 fpm	820 fpm
Service ceiling	10,700 ft	13,650 ft
Stall, clean	61 mph	68 mph
Stall, full flaps	56 mph	60 mph
Takeoff over a 50-foot obstacle	1,626 ft	1,380 ft
Landing over a 50-foot obstacle	1,257 ft	1,275 ft

Figure 9.8. The Musketeer/Sport line emphasizes solidity and comfort rather than speed.

standard equipment, locking in a popular option. Little was changed in the lineup after 1972 (other than the A19 becoming the B19 and the A24R becoming the B24R). The introduction of the T-tailed two-seat Skipper in 1979 as Beechcraft's trainer marked the end of the production run for the Sport, and the Sundowner was phased out in 1984.

The Beech Sports and Sundowners are pleasing to fly, with fairly responsive controls for such relatively big aircraft. They feel very solid, even in turbulence. In-flight visibility is excellent, with long thin wings (compared to Cherokees) aiding visibility downward and to the side. Visibility over the nose is also excellent, the airplanes seeming to fly nose low by Cessna or Piper standards. Stall response is also quite good. The airplanes are difficult to stall, even on purpose. They provide plenty of buffeting to warn of impending stalls and retain good aileron control even through the stall break.

Performance figures are less than impressive, however. True airspeeds are in the neighborhood of 115 mph for the Sport and 125 to 135 mph for the Sundowner, even at best altitude. Actual rate of climb and load-carrying capabilities are also deficient compared to Cherokees equipped with the same Lycoming engines. Although the Sport comes with a back seat, it is best considered a two-seater unless the two in the back seat are small children. Musketeers, Sports, and Sundowners have large fuel tanks which can make them good long-duration aircraft. With their modest speeds, however, this doesn't necessarily translate to long range compared to other aircraft in their class.

Some aerobatic Sports are available and could add an extra "fun" dimension to an otherwise conservative airplane. The Beechcraft structure is so strong that only minor modifications, including extra bonded skin on the leading edge, cowling strakes, a ventral fin, and quick-release doors are required to make the Sport/Musketeer aerobatic.

The Beechcraft Sports and Sundowners are roomy, comfortable aircraft with a relatively quiet cabin for their class. Ground-handling characteristics are excellent with an 11-foot, 10-inch wide main gear and very effective nosewheel steering. Landing characteristics, however, have been a serious problem. The Sport and Sundowner series have a reputation for landing damage. Unless a pilot is very careful with speed control, an overshoot or a porpoise following a bounce from landing too hard on the unforgiving, hard-rubber donut shock absorbers in the landing gear can lead to disaster. An all-too-common scenario is porpoising, nose gear collapse, and prop strikes—or worse—with the aircraft flipping over!

Despite the vaunted Beechcraft reputation for quality, the Musketeer/ Sport/Sundowner series has not been problem free. Cracks and breaks in forward-wing attachment fittings on some Musketeer/Sport/ Sundowner aircraft were the subject of one expensive AD note and should be checked on an aircraft being considered for purchase. Still another AD called for the inspection of fuel lines in the wings, and yet another called for a fuel selector stop and a decal to be installed on the selector valve. And of course, the landing gear should be closely inspected for cracks and other damage resulting from lousy but not quite catastrophic landings. If you intend to have your aircraft serviced in a Beechcraft shop, be prepared for a nasty financial surprise. Beechcraft dealers and distributors, reflecting the longtime corporate philosophy and bias, are almost without exception large, expensive operations geared more to King Air or Bonanza owners than they are to helping a small-time private owner get his troublesome Sundowner running again. The "little guy" may find that everything seems to be very expensive at the sign of the Beechcraft.

Being solid and comfortable airplanes with a reputation for lackluster performance, the Beechcraft Musketeer/Sport/Sundowner series can provide some real bargains in the marketplace. They will almost always be less expensive, model for model, than Pipers, Cessnas, or even Grumman-Americans. Unless you get a really good deal, stay away from the 165-hp Continental engine versions, though. That engine had a reputation for running hot in the Musketeer. It also was a relatively rare engine that could lead to parts availability and other service problems.

Beechcraft Model 77 Skipper

The Beechcraft Model 77 Skipper, look-alike to the Piper Tomahawk, was a project initiated by Beechcraft in 1973, which did not result in a publicly available aircraft until 1979. Unlike Piper's Tomahawk, the Skipper was a well-designed aircraft with excellent quality control. By being more slow and deliberate, Beechcraft got it right the first time, unlike the Piper organization of the late 1970s. But unfortunately, the delay meant that the Skipper hit the market just as it was going into an industry depression. Just over 300 were built in only three years of production.

The Skipper is a solid, well-built, comfortable two-seat trainer aircraft. The panel is clean, neat, and spacious; it has enough space to make the Skipper an IFR trainer (although its slow speed and small fuel tanks do not make it particularly well suited to that role). Unusual for Beech single-engine airplanes is the modern-design throttle quadrant, similar to those found on present-day Pipers. Unlike the Pipers, the Skipper's throttle quadrant looks a bit large and ungainly, though. One surprising touch found in the Skipper's cabin is large, spacious, and very comfortable high-backed bucket seats. Many of the Skippers even came with seats finished with crushed velour. It may not be fast, but it definitely is comfortable. It's too bad Beech didn't keep building this one, because wealthy BMW and Saab drivers would feel right at home learning to fly in this airplane.

In the air, the Skipper is a good, honest trainer. Surprisingly, despite its T-tail, the Skipper has much better low-speed controllability than the Tomahawk. It is possible to lift the nosewheel before lift-off speed on take-off and to keep it off the ground for short- or soft-field landings. Control feel in the air is nice, with controls light but well coordinated. Flaps are marginal, though, and they wouldn't teach a student much about what real flaps would do on an airplane. Stall speed with full flaps is only 2 mph less than the stall speed with no flaps, and it would be a very astute student who would really notice that difference.

Visibility is excellent. You can't see directly out the back though, so if the Skipper's tail surfaces shake as violently in a stall as a Tomahawk's (they are built more solidly so they probably don't), you'll never know it.

The Skipper's flaws are relatively minor. The door closing and latching system isn't all that good, and can be difficult if the doors become misaligned by even a little bit. The Lycoming O-235 engine can be hard starting in the Skipper. The starter motor will swing the prop really fast, but the engine won't always catch early. The engine also has had problems with lead fouling causing spark plug fouling and stuck valves, and since it's a 100-octane-rated engine, autogas isn't a solution.

Generally though, this may very well be the nicest two-seat trainer ever built. It is solidly built, it has easy-to-maintain, simple landing gear, it has nice flying characteristics with few or no surprises, and it is far more spacious and comfortable than anything else in its class (remember the velour

Figure 9.9. How about high-back velour bucket seats in a trainer! (Courtesy Beech Aircraft Corporation)

Table 9.10. Beechcraft Model 77 Skipper

Specifications	
Wingspan	30 ft
Length	24 ft
Gross weight, normal category	1,680 lb
Empty weight	1,100 lb
Useful load	580 lb
Useful load, full fuel	406 lb
Fuel capacity, standard tanks	30 gal (29 usable)
Performance	
Cruise speed, 75% power, best altitude	121 mph
Fuel consumption, 75% power	5.6 gph
Range 45-min reserve, 75% power	535 mi
Sea level rate of climb	720 fpm
Service ceiling	12,900 ft
Stall, clean	56 mph
Stall, full flaps	54 mph
Takeoff over a 50-foot obstacle	1,280 ft
Landing over a 50-foot obstacle	1,313 ft

buckets!). If you can locate one, it's probably a real find if you want to start with a modern two-seater. Too bad Beechcraft only built them for three years!

Diamond DA20 Katana/Evolution/Eclipse

A new design family of trainers and light sport aircraft evolved from an Austrian motorglider has the potential capability of filling the production niche once filled by the Cessna 150 and 152. It's the Austrian designed and Canadian-built Diamond (formerly Dimona) DA20 Katana and DA20-C1 Evolution and Eclipse. While not perfect, once you've flown a DA20 you'll probably agree that it's okay if Cessna never builds another 150 or 152 again, or Piper another Tomahawk.

The company, then called Hoffman Flugzeugbau-Friesach, began building gliders and motorgliders in Austria in 1981. The first Dimona Katana was built in Austria in 1993. Production was shifted to London, Ontario, nearer the prime U.S. market, in 1994. In 1996, the company name was officially changed to Diamond Aircraft Industries. The original Austrian-built, as well as the Canadian-built, DA20-A1 Katanas came with an 80-hp Bombardier Rotax with electronic ignition and gear reduction driving a constant-speed Hoffman prop.

The Rotax engine is more than adequate, but it has some distinct disadvantages. It has only a 1,500-hour TBO, and with a starter spinning the geared prop drive at more than 100 rpm for the engine to start, hand-propping is out of the question. Typical cruise power settings are 2,200 rpm and 26 inches manifold pressure, "over square" and not recommended for many older and more complex aircraft by normal standards. The Rotax-engined Katanas also have no carb heat or mixture control, so a student can't learn the standard drill of "carb heat on, mixture rich, check fuel, check mags" in a Katana.

In 1998 Diamond switched to the 125-hp Continental IO-240B engine with a fixed pitch prop and a 2,000 hour TBO to make the DA20-C1 version of the Katana. Fifty-seven pounds was also added to the gross weight, providing a 379-pound payload with full fuel. In 1999, the DA20-C1s were split into two separate aircraft, an Evolution basic trainer and a fancier Eclipse sport plane. The Evolution came with basic Bendix/King avionics, whereas the Eclipse added leather seats, rear windows, wheel fairings, a Garmin 430 color GPS/com, and options such as a horizontal situation indicator (HSI) and an autopilot. The line got a big boost in its credibility and stability when the U.S. Air Force declared the modified "Falcon" version of the Eclipse the winner of the Air Force basic trainer competition. Diamond also got a $14.5 million, five-year contract from the Air Force. While Diamond no longer builds new Rotax-engined DA20-A1s, it does offer DA20-A1s rebuilt at the factory into Katana 100s with a 100-hp Rotax 912S replacing the 80-hp engine.

The DA20's modern, sleekly clean lines, with wings and fuselage free of rivet lines, make an impression as you do your first preflight. Except for the narrow tube of a rear fuselage, the plane looks small but not markedly smaller than a 150 or 152. When you open the rearward hinged bubble canopy and see the slightly reclined seats and sticks rather than control wheels, a hint of F-16 comes to mind. The seats don't move, but the rudder pedals are easily adjustable. One nice touch is the built-in intercom system, with headset jacks above and behind the seats to markedly reduce the typical "rats-nest" of wiring cluttering many cockpits.

Figure 9.10. The Diamond DA20-C1 Eclipse: Choice of the U.S. Air Force Academy. (Courtesy of Diamond Aircraft)

The sleek glass-reinforced plastic and carbon fiber-reinforced plastic construction is not without drawbacks. If you review the manual as you should before your first flight, you'll note one slightly disquieting difference from aging aluminum designs. There is a temperature gauge in the cabin, and if the temperature of the aircraft is over 131°F (55°C), it's not safe to fly. And that's not all that hot for a sun-baked ramp in the summer in many parts of the country. One nice touch is the clear inspection ports under the wings that allow viewing the bellcranks as the ailerons are moved—good for checking the free movement and security of the cables, and also good for showing students how the ailerons really work.

Another significant weakness of the DA20s is that they are VFR only. Diamond estimates that they would have to add 35 pounds of wire mesh to the aircraft to meet lightning tolerance requirements needed for IFR certification. While not a particularly limiting factor for a two-seat basic trainer, it is a significant limitation for a high-end sport plane like the Eclipse with a base price of $139,900 and a fully equipped price at least $20,000 higher. (The Evolution starts at $125,900 and comes better equipped for around $10,000 to $15,000 more.) A four-seat growth version, the DA40 discussed in Chapter 11, is IFR capable.

The nosegear is free-swiveling, so differential braking is required for taxiing, much like Grumman-American Tr-2s and Tigers. It isn't all that hard to get used to, however. Even though the Rotax 912F engine used in the Katanas is a four cylinder, four stroke design, the sound of the engine at full power for takeoff is more of a buzz than a roar. (An instructor said the first

Table 9.11. Diamond DA20-C1 Evolution

Specifications	
Wingspan	35 ft 8 in
Length	23 ft 6 in
Gross weight, normal category	1,764 lb
Empty weight	1,166 lb
Useful load	598 lb
Useful load, full fuel	454 lb
Fuel capacity, standard tanks	24 gal
Performance	
Cruise speed, 75% power, best altitude	150 mph
Fuel consumption, 75% power	7 gph
Range, 45 min reserve, 75% power	402 mi
Sea level rate of climb	1,000 fpm
Service ceiling	13,000 ft
Stall, clean	48 mph
Stall, full flaps	39 mph
Takeoff over a 50 foot obstacle	1,470 ft
Landing over a 50 foot obstacle	1,280 ft

time he saw one taxiing by on the ramp he thought somebody was using a weedwhacker!) Although the aircraft has a T-tail, it doesn't exhibit any of the Tomahawk's difficult pitch control tendencies on rotation for takeoff. Rate of climb for the Rotax-engined Katana is not exceptional, with about a 500 fpm rate of climb showing on most of our takeoffs on a hot and humid summer afternoon.

The airplane is nicely responsive in the air. Visibility through the canopy is excellent. There is an opaque area on the top of the canopy which reduces some of the sun's heat and glare. Approach stalls are a nonevent, with the stall horn sounding but the plane barely shuddering and definitely not dropping noticeably. Departure stalls are another matter. The nose drops sharply, as does one wing, usually the right. Recovery is relatively easy, but only with proper technique emphasizing rudder over ailerons. The stall characteristics are excellent for a trainer: departure stalls are nasty enough to make a student pay attention and learn proper recovery technique without being nasty enough to also scare the instructor.

Full flaps are amazingly effective for an aircraft that is so clean and which has such an excellent glide ratio. Flaps are two-position electric flaps, with one position for takeoff and one for landing. With full (landing) flaps selected and the nose pointed down, the aircraft descends amazingly well, picking up little excess airspeed and having surprisingly little tendency to float. Rounding out to landing, even after a steep descent, is easy. The spring-steel main gear looks built to take the kind of punishment students can dish out, although the nose gear doesn't look quite so solid.

Taildraggers and other traditional airplanes

Two-seat taildraggers like the Cub, the Champ, and the Cessna 120/140 offer the prospective first-time owner an interesting alternative to more modern airplanes. Other old tricycle gear airplanes like the Ercoupe and the Tri-Pacer also offer unique selections. Some four-seat taildraggers like the Stinson 108 and the Cessna 170 provide a still wider range of interesting older aircraft.

Some older two-seaters can be the lowest-price aircraft on the market. A well-chosen old taildragger can give its owner years of very economical flying and can be sold for as much, if not more, than it cost, if it is maintained with tender loving care. The picture is not all rosy, however. Parts may not be readily available at the average FBO. Patience will be rewarded, however, with parts from specialty sources like Univair (www.univair.com) in Colorado and Wag-Aero (www.wagaero.com) in Wisconsin. Care and replacement of fabric is often a lost art at most large metropolitan airports. The prospective taildragger buyer would be well advised to find a smaller field where similar aircraft are present in significant numbers, giving promise at least of mechanics who know and love the old beauties, or of EAA aficionados who have revived the arts embodied in older aircraft.

Most older aircraft, by Skyhawk and Cherokee Warrior standards, are noisy, cramped, and cursed with poor visibility and odd crosswind handling traits. To the person who knows and loves taildraggers, they are the very essence of fun flying. The Cub pilot, flying low and slow over sunny pastures with the side panel doors open to the wind, doesn't miss a 150-mph cruising speed. The Champ pilot flying from the small grass strip really doesn't miss the IFR panel made to serve demanding FAA masters of the dreaded terminal control area. It's fun flying—and freedom.

Ten older aircraft or their descendants are described in this chapter: the Piper Cub, Aeronca Champ and Citabria, Taylorcraft, Cessna 120/140,

Cessna 170, Luscombe Model 8, Ercoupe, Stinson 108/Station Wagon, and Piper Tri-Pacer. Bigger and pricier taildraggers like the Cessna 180 and 185, Maules, Aviat Husky and Pitts, and the Waco YMF-5 are included in Chapter 11.

Performance figures presented in this chapter should be taken as ballpark, not gospel. Most of the aircraft discussed have seen such a wide range of engine choices and other adaptations that presenting firm figures on any specific airplane is nearly impossible. The Piper Cub, for example, has seen nearly a dozen different engines ranging from 20 hp in the E-2 prototype to 150 hp in the 1989 Super Cub.

Piper Cub and Super Cub

The Piper Cub, the venerable and still active grandparent of all general aviation airplanes, began life as a 1930 design by C. Gilbert Taylor. The grossly underpowered Taylor Cub prototype had all of 20 hp up front and was soon succeeded by the 40-hp Continental-powered E-2 Cub. An oilman named W. T. Piper, Sr., took over as a senior business partner as part of a bankruptcy reorganization during the Depression years, and the legendary name of Piper Cub was sealed when Taylor left the company several years later.

Figure 10.1. The J-3 Cub is the forerunner of today's general aviation fleet.

In 1936 the Cub, with the more rounded lines developed by design engineer Walter Jamoneau, became the J-2. The famous J-3 followed in 1937 with upholstered seats, brakes, and a tailwheel. In addition to the 40-hp Continental, available engine options included a 65-hp Continental or Lycoming, or a 60-hp Franklin. Black trim on yellow became the rule for Cubs, replacing old red, green, or blue paint. The J-3 and the L-4 were the basic flight trainers and artillery spotters of World War II. It was to remain the predominant basic trainer in the United States until the late 1950s, when the ascension of the Cessna 150 signaled the start of a new era. Nearly 20,000 J-3s were built, including more than 6,000 in a seemingly mad frenzy of postwar activity in the single year of 1946.

After a painful reorganization of the Piper company, a modernized PA-11 Cub Special appeared in 1947, powered by a 90-hp Continental engine. In 1949 the first PA-18 Super Cub appeared. Powered by a 108-hp Lycoming, it was the first of a small but steady stream of modernized Super Cubs. In 1950, a 125-hp Lycoming version appeared, followed in 1952 by a 135-hp version and finally in 1955 the ultimate 150-hp Super Cub. Production of the Super Cub tapered down in the early 1980s, and production ceased in 1984, with 10,224 Super Cubs having been built since 1949. Piper owner Millar brought back the Super Cub in 1988 at a price of $42,595. 102 more Super Cubs would be built before production terminated in 1992.

The Cub has always been a simple, rugged, relatively easy to maintain design. The basic J-3 had a simple steel-tube fuselage and wood-spar wings, all covered by grade A cotton fabric. The interior had slab seats and a plywood floor. The split side door, opening top half upward and the lower half downward, leaked sufficient air to make winter flying a cold experience in the heaterless cabin. Fuel gauges were sight tubes in the wing roots (an "innovation" later appearing in the G-A Tr-2).

The Super Cub is exactly what its name implies. It is definitely a Cub, but with aluminum-spar wings, a Lycoming engine of 108, 125, 135, or 150 horsepower. It also has an electrical system to do away with the death-defying J-3 trait of hand prop starting. A few tradition-destroying Super Cubs can even be found with IFR capability, a far cry from the really basic J-3 panel.

Getting into the Cub can be a real gymnastic exercise, and getting out is even more challenging. The Cub's upright tandem seats are not designed for lay-back comfort once you are in either. Vision of the instruments is barely adequate from the rear seat, from which the J-3 must be soloed. Of course, any good J-3 pilot considers even the few instruments provided as a wasteful extravagance anyway! The heel brakes below the rudder pedals are challenging to an experienced Cub pilot and damned near impossible to a visit-

ing nosewheel driver. Ground handling on takeoff, landing, or taxiing in a
high wind is tricky. A novice pilot, particularly a Cessna 150/152 or
Warrior/Cadet graduate, may find "life down the runway" a series of
swerves, skids, and impending disasters. Seasoned taildragger types, of
course, know about the apparent lag in the rudder and tailwheel cables and
proceed with dignity.

The J-3 Cub is slow in flight. Visibility is excellent compared to other
vintage taildraggers and may even be better than some modern Cessnas. All
Cubs are very good short-field airplanes, able to clear 50-foot obstacles in
less than 1,000 feet. The landing gear can take a lot of rough-field handling.
Large tires and bungee-cord shock absorbers provide a landing gear that can
take a lot of hard punishment.

Table 10.1. Piper J-3 Cub (65-hp Continental)

Specifications	
Wingspan	35 ft 2 in
Length	22 ft 4½ in
Gross weight, normal category	1,220 lb
Empty weight	730 lb
Useful load	490 lb
Useful load, full fuel	418 lb
Fuel capacity, standard tanks	12 gal
Performance	
Cruise speed, 75% power, best altitude	75 mph
Fuel consumption, 75% power	4.3 gph
Range 45-min reserve, 75% power	150 mi
Sea level rate of climb	450 fpm
Service ceiling	12,000 ft
Stall, clean	38 mph
Stall, full flaps	N/A
Takeoff over a 50-foot obstacle	700 ft
Landing over a 50-foot obstacle	800 ft

Flight characteristics have been described as both docile and responsive.
The aircraft, unlike the modern Cherokees, must be flown. Aileron and rudder coordination must be learned and practiced because the airplane won't
provide coordination for the pilot. Spins are legal, and spin recovery is relatively easy.

Cubs are not really cross-country airplanes, though. The seats are hard,
and leaks in the door will make even Super Cub heaters seem totally inadequate. The light wing loading of the large wing makes for a rough ride in
turbulence. This is not to imply that Cubs can't be flown cross-country, however. W. T. Piper, Sr., and his sons flew them on cross-country trips before
World War II, and people have been flying them long distances ever since. If
cross-country is your primary flying requirement, however, you really should
be able to find something more appropriate.

Table 10.2. Piper PA-18-150 Super Cub

Specifications	
Wingspan	35 ft 2 in
Length	22 ft 7 in
Gross weight, normal category	1,750 lb
Empty weight	930 lb
Useful load	820 lb
Useful load, full fuel	604 lb
Fuel capacity, standard tanks	36 gal
Performance	
Cruise speed, 75% power, best altitude	115 mph
Fuel consumption, 75% power	9 gph
Range 45-min reserve, 75% power	374 mi
Sea level rate of climb	960 fpm
Service ceiling	19,000 ft
Stall, clean	47 mph
Stall, full flaps	43 mph
Takeoff over a 50-foot obstacle	500 ft
Landing over a 50-foot obstacle	725 ft

The newer 150-hp Super Cub not only survives but thrives as a workhorse, a recreational aircraft, and, with a revitalized interest in old style basic flying, as a trainer. Its workhorse roles include air taxi, glider and banner tow, fish spotting, crop dusting, border and pipeline patrol, and all-around light delivery vehicle for bush flying and other places where a short-field capability is required. It's most appealing use, however, is just as one hell of a fun airplane on wheels, floats, or even skis.

Cubs are not problem free. As fabric-covered airplanes, they can cost the owner a sizable amount of money if re-covering is needed. Any prospective buyer should have a punch test done on wings, fuselage, and control surfaces before buying a Cub. Modern fibers like Ceconite and Stits Polyfiber are much more desirable than grade A cotton, except possibly to purists who insist on everything genuine.

Rear fuselage steel tubing, wing struts, and older style, steel fuel tanks are all susceptible to rust and should be checked carefully. AD 77-03-08 was issued on a wing strut corrosion problem in 1977 calling for internal preservative treatment to prevent corrosion and for five-year inspections. But in late 1989, the NTSB claimed that the problem still existed, and called for replacement of unsealed struts with sealed units. Piper also recommended replacement of the unsealed struts with new sealed ones.

Since the engines in the Cub series were all designed for 80-octane gas, and since autogas STCs are available, use of autogas is advised. Older Continental engines in J-3s are more likely to be susceptible to problems caused by the use of 100LL avgas than the more modern Lycomings used in the Super Cubs, which are more tolerant to the use of 100LL.

While parts for older J-3 models may not be readily available at the average big city airport, the Cub parts supply is not limited. Wag-Aero, in Lyons, Wisconsin, specializes in J-3 parts. The company even provides parts for a kit called the Cuby, which is a virtual copy of the J-3 Cub. You can literally build your own nonauthentic J-3 replica from Wag-Aero parts. Univair in Colorado also stocks a significant number of parts.

A company in Yakima, Washington, called Cub Crafters, Inc. (www.cubcrafters.com), specializes in rebuilding Piper Cubs and also builds limited numbers of 180-hp STC'd versions of new Super Cubs or at least an essentially identical aircraft. Cub Crafters claims the aircraft they build meet the original Piper Type Certificate information, and that the copyright on the name "Cub" expired in 1977. The Cub Crafters, Inc. 2002 price for a standard equipped 2002 "Top Cub" was $135,975. Cub Crafters claims, of course, that their plane will outperform the Husky despite not having the Husky's constant speed prop.

The Cub is not for everyone. It is slow, uncomfortable, and not a good cross-country airplane. On the other hand, it is also a fun short-field and soft-field airplane that can leisurely circle over treetops on a warm summer day with the hinged door panels open in flight. It is a wonderful old airplane with the 3-axis responsiveness and coordination that only real stick and rudder (not control wheels) can provide. The airplane has become a classic. Prices for J-3s get higher, not lower, every year. Cessna 150s offer greater performance, often at lower prices. But that's not really the point. ... If you are a Cub lover, maybe nothing else will do!

Aeronca Champion and American Champion Aircraft Citabria, Scout, and Decathlon

The Aeronca Champion evolved from the Model T Aeronca, which first appeared in 1940. It was the successor to several other noteworthy designs of the Cincinnati-based Aeronautical Corporation of America. Aeronca's first airplane, the 30-hp C-2, evolved into the low-slung Bathtub Aeronca C-3, which was followed by the side-by-side seating Aeronca Chief in 1939. The Model T was known as the 65-TC, 65-TF, or 65-TL, depending on whether the engine was the 65-hp Continental, Franklin, or Lycoming. The T was a conventional, steel-tube and fabric airplane with wooden wing spars and ribs. Unlike the Chief, it had tandem seating.

With larger windows, the T became the O-58A. With aluminum ribs and a different airfoil, it became the Defender civil trainer. After World War II more slight modifications produced the classic model 7AC Champion. The

Champ became the 7DC with an 85-hp Continental. With 90-hp it was the 7EC, forerunner of the Citabria. Before the Aeronautical Corporation of America finally ceased production in 1950, more than 10,000 of the various Champion models had been built, including more than 7,200 of the 65-hp 7AC model alone.

Champion Aircraft Corporation of Minneapolis, Minnesota, took over the Champion line in 1951 and marketed the 7EC as the Traveler. In 1957 the Champ got three legs, becoming the 7FC Tri-Traveler. The modern era arrived in 1964, when a beefed-up aerobatic version of the Champ was presented with the name Citabria—airbatic in reverse. Bellanca of Alexandria, Minnesota, merged with Champion Aircraft in 1970 and made a valiant attempt to turn back the clock in the early 1970s with a very basic 60-hp Franklin-engined 7AC Champ. Doomed by a variety of factors including a factory fire, sharp price increases for the engine, and severe competition from its 115-hp larger counterpart, the new 7AC "died" after only about 100 were produced.

In the hands of Bellanca, the Champion sired a small line of Lycoming-powered tandem two-seaters with a bewildering array of model numbers. These ranged from the basic 115-hp 7ECA Citabrias to the workhorse utility 180-hp 8GCBC-CS Scout to the beefed-up, top of the aerobatic line 8KCAB-180 Super Decathlon. Perennial best-sellers, however, were probably the 150-hp Citabrias in the middle of the lineup. Production of the line ceased in 1979. American Champion Aircraft (ACA) of Rochester, Wisconsin, (www.amerchampionaircraft.com) purchased the rights to the line in 1989 and began building the 8KCAB Super Decathlon aerobatic aircraft again in 1990. The first of the new aircraft had an all-metal wing, new for the Decathlon. ACA's Web site claimed they had built 500 aircraft by the end of 2002, including "almost 100" produced in 1999.

In 2003, American Champion Aircraft produced what may be the only reasonably priced line of aircraft, if reasonable is defined as what prices would be if one took prices from the 1960s, 1970s, and 1980s and adjusted them for inflation. The ACA lineup in 2003 included five different models, all taildraggers. The most humble is the 7ECA Citabria Aurora, with a 118-hp Lycoming engine, a fixed pitch prop, no flaps, and a modest (by 2003 standards) base price of $73,900. The 7GCAA Citabria Adventure has a 160-hp engine, fixed pitch prop, no flaps, and an $84,900 base price. For $3,000 more than the 7GCAA, the 7GCBC Citabria Explorer adds flaps to the 160-hp package. ACA describes the 8GCBC Scout as the "Work Horse" of their line. It comes with a 180-hp engine, flaps, a constant speed prop, and a 2003 base price of $106,900. At the top of the line is the 8KCAB Super Decathlon, offering fully aerobatic performance in a package with a 180-hp engine, flaps, a constant speed prop, and a 2003 base price of

Figure 10.2. The aerobatic Super Decathlon is one fun airplane!

$113,900. It should be noted that like the Luscombe and the Taylorcraft, these prices do not include even VFR radios.

American Champion also inherited a serious problem with older 8KCABs. In 1989, a Decathlon lost a wing during an aerobatics lesson, and the NTSB investigation showed that fatigue cracking in a strut-to-spar attachment had caused the accident. An emergency Airworthiness Directive was issued for all 8KCABs, and American Champion produced fitting replacement kits for all older Decathlons. Metal spar wing retrofits remained a major line of work for ACA through the 1990s and into the 2000s. Another option offered by American Champion is to replace wood spar wings with complete metal spar wings, at a price ranging from $12,500 for unpainted wings to just under twice as much for painted ones. The company claims the wing replacement will also provide slight improvements in climb and roll rates.

The original Champ was, like the J-3 Cub, a very basic airplane. It had no electrical system, no starter, no flaps, and a wooden prop. The 13-gallon fuel tank nestled between the firewall and the instrument panel contained a float with a wire protruding from the cowling to provide a rudimentary but effective fuel gauge.

Like the tandem Cub, the Champ is relatively hard to get into and out of. Some pilots consider it more spacious and comfortable than the Cub once they get settled, however. Visibility on the ground is relatively good for

Table 10.3. Aeronca Champ (65 hp)

Specifications	
Wingspan	35 ft 2 in
Length	21 ft 6 in
Gross weight, normal category	1,250 lb
Empty weight	750 lb
Useful load	500 lb
Useful load, full fuel	422 lb
Fuel capacity, standard tanks	13 gal
Performance	
Cruise speed, 75% power, best altitude	90 mph
Fuel consumption, 75% power	4.4 gph
Range 45-min reserve, 75% power	202 mi
Sea level rate of climb	500 fpm
Service ceiling	12,500 ft
Stall, clean	44 mph
Stall, full flaps	N/A
Takeoff over a 50-foot obstacle	650 ft
Landing over a 50-foot obstacle	885 ft

a taildragger. Tailwheel steering on the Champ is slightly more responsive than the Cub, and the ride on the ground also seems softer. With those infernal heel brakes positioned slightly inboard of the rudder pedals, smooth coordinated braking is a mystery to most tricycle gear pilots who are making the transition.

The Champ is a slow-flying, slow-climbing, docile airplane. Like the Cub, it requires good rudder coordination. Its stalls are docile, with power-off stalls being more mush than stall. If cross-controlled, it can be put into a spin. It has relatively good in-flight visibility. Its large, lightly loaded wings can make it very bouncy in turbulence. Slips must be mastered to conquer short fields, since no flaps are provided.

The modern Citabria retains the basic Champ lineage in a beefed-up, high-power, dressy package. The Citabria has a full electrical system, nav lights, and a starter. Some rare examples are even IFR equipped. Spring-steel landing gear can make landings a bouncy challenge if proper technique is not used. The Citabria is probably a better all-around package than the old Champ, combining reasonable speed with short-field capability while adding a touch of excitement by having a limited capacity for aerobatics. The aerobatic Decathlons are the top of the line, with the 8KCABs with 180-hp Lycoming engines and constant-speed props being the best of all. Decathlons are respectable aerobatic airplanes and excellent aerobatic trainers, and they are considered much better in this role than Cessna 150 and 152 Aerobats. The Scout is a good bush plane, offering Husky-like performance at a new aircraft savings of $50,000 or more.

Table 10.4. ACA Citabria 7ECA (115 hp)

Specifications

Wingspan	33 ft 5 in
Length	22 ft 8 in
Gross weight, normal category	1,650 lb
Empty weight	1,030 lb
Useful load	620 lb
Useful load, full fuel	464 lb
Fuel capacity, standard tanks	26 gal

Performance

Cruise speed, 75% power, best altitude	117 mph
Fuel consumption, 75% power	6.5 gph
Range 45-min reserve, 75% power	380 mi
Sea level rate of climb	725 fpm
Service ceiling	12,000 ft
Stall, clean	51 mph
Stall, full flaps	N/A
Takeoff over a 50-foot obstacle	890 ft
Landing over a 50-foot obstacle	775 ft

Like all steel-tube and fabric airplanes, older Champs and even early Citabrias should be checked carefully for rust in the tubes. Fabric should be tested to assure it is in good condition. Decathlons, subject to the stresses of regular aerobatic use, should be carefully checked to assure that all ADs have been complied with and that there is no hidden serious wear or damage. Parts for Champs and Citabrias, Scouts, and Decathlons are available from American Champion Aircraft. Univair and Wag-Aero can also be relied on for Champ, Citabria, and Decathlon parts.

If you want a new aircraft but you don't want to pay a quarter of a million dollars or more, and if you are willing and capable of flying a taildragger, an American Champion Aircraft Citabria, Decathlon, or Scout may be just the plane for you. ACA is one of the very few, if not only, manufacturers who will sell you a brand new real airplane for under one hundred thousand dollars.

Taylorcraft

The original Taylorcraft was designed by C. Gilbert Taylor (who also designed the Piper Cub) after Taylor left the Piper organization and started the Taylorcraft Company in Alliance, Ohio. The original A model gave way to the B-12 in 1939, and the Continental-powered 65-hp BC-12D postwar evolution of the B-12 became the classic Taylorcraft. Nearly 2,800 of the BC-12D models were produced in 1946 before the company slipped into receivership in 1947, with Taylor again being pushed out of the aircraft-building picture.

Charlie Ferris, a Taylorcraft aficionado and onetime T-craft distributor, reopened the Alliance, Ohio, Taylorcraft factory in 1973. The F-19 (F for Ferris), with larger windows, a 100-hp Continental O-200 engine, and greater fuel capacity, was produced until 1980, when the F-21B was introduced with the 118-hp Lycoming O-235 engine. Dorothy Ferris kept the T-craft in production following her husband's death in 1976 until she sold the plant to George Ruckle in 1985. Ruckle moved T-craft production to the old Piper facilities in Lock Haven, Pennsylvania, hiring workers who had spent most of their lives building Piper Cubs. Unfortunately, Ruckle's dreams of a tricycle gear F-22 Taylorcraft and an even more powerful 160-hp Taylorcraft ended when the company went bankrupt and production ceased in 1988.

In 1990, amid a swirling tangle of investment deals, buyouts, and take-overs, a revived Taylorcraft Aircraft Corporation began building modern-ized 118-hp Taylorcraft taildraggers now designated the Classic 118 (offi-cially called the F22). In 1991, the company received FAA certification of the 118-hp tricycle gear F22A. The new F22s were a significant improvement over earlier models, with a 5-inch-wider cabin, wing flaps, adjustable seats, an all-metal panel, and a standard intercom, communications radio, and Mode C transponder. In an odd twist of fate, the T-craft were produced at

Table 10.5. Taylorcraft

	BC-12D (65 hp)	F-21B (118 hp)
Specifications		
Wingspan	36 ft	36 ft
Length	22 ft	22 ft 1 in
Gross weight, normal category	1,200 lb	1,750 lb
Empty weight	750 lb	1,025 lb
Useful load	450 lb	725 lb
Useful load, full fuel	378 lb	485 lb
Fuel capacity, standard tanks	12 gal	42 gal (40 usable)
Performance		
Cruise speed, 75% power, best altitude	95 mph	122 mph
Fuel consumption, 75% power	4.5 gph	6 gph
Range 45-min reserve, 75% power	182 mi	722 mi
Sea level rate of climb	900 fpm	750 fpm
Service ceiling	15,000 ft	18,000 ft
Stall, clean	38 mph	48 mph
Stall, full flaps	N/A	N/A
Takeoff over a 50-foot obstacle	400 ft	1,140 ft
Landing over a 50-foot obstacle	400 ft	400 ft

the Lock Haven, Pennsylvania, facilities where thousands of Piper Cubs were once assembled. Unfortunately, only a few F22s were built before production ceased in October 1992.

The T-craft is apparently another airplane that refuses to die. In 2003, Taylorcraft Aviation Web sites (www.taylorcraft.org and www. taylorcraft.com) announced that the "parts, tools, jigs, and machinery" had been moved to a 55,000 square foot manufacturing facility in LaGrange, Texas. Company president Harry Ingram said that parts were the first priority "to service 4,500 Taylorcrafts flying today." But new F22 Taylorcraft aircraft with a 118-hp Lycoming O-235 were offered for sale at a 2003 base price of $59,995, which would make it one of the lowest cost new aircraft on the market. The tricycle gear F22A was offered at $63,995. Two models were also offered with the 180-hp Lycoming O-360 engine, the taildragger F22B at $69,995 and the tricycle gear F22C at $73,995. (It should be noted, however, that these base prices are for planes with no radios and no gyro panel.)

The T-craft is a steel-tube and fabric airplane. Early models had wood spars and ribs, whereas the "modern" T-craft have wood spars and aluminum ribs. Like the Cub, the Taylorcraft uses heel brakes. Unlike the Cub, the T-craft has side-by-side seating and control wheels rather than sticks. Ground handling of the T-craft, like other light taildraggers, can be tricky. Heel brakes seem to ignore the physiology of the foot, and the light weight makes it susceptible to weathercocking into any kind of a crosswind.

The 1970s vintage T-craft have one somewhat strange feature. The fuel system has a 12-gallon tank between the firewall and the instrument panel, which is where older T-craft had a similar-sized tank. There are also single 6-gallon tanks in each wing. The odd feature is that the wing tanks drain into the main tank by gravity feed. Normal technique is to burn off fuel from the main tank and refuel from the wing tanks by operating the wing tank valves. Problems can arise if the wing tanks have more fuel than the main tank has empty space. Kiss the excess goodbye, because it is going out the filler cap overflow vent. The same thing occurs, of course, if the wing tank valves are not closed during refueling.

In the air the T-craft is a typical old taildragger with excellent short-field capabilities and relatively docile traits. It has surprisingly quick elevator control and sluggish ailerons. Stalls are docile, and spins are casual compared to other taildraggers. With no flaps to depend on (except for the newest 1990 and later versions), slips are necessary to get the most out of the airplane's short-field capabilities. The old BC-12D T-craft, at 95 mph, is also quicker than its 65-hp Cub and Aeronca counterparts.

The T-craft is noisy to fly, and visibility from the older models is very poor by modern standards. Even the 122-mph cruise speed of the F-21 makes for a long day on cross-country flights. Like the Champ, its light wing loading makes it a rough rider on a bumpy day.

Like the Cub and the Champ, T-craft are steel-tube and fabric construction. Watch for rusty tubes and bad fabric when buying one. The F-19 has the Continental O-200 engine that also powers scores of Cessnas. The O-200 engine is susceptible to 100LL lead-fouling problems, and autofuel should be used in the F-19 and earlier BC-12D T-craft. Whether the new Taylorcraft Aviation is a success or not, parts should remain readily available. Companies like Wag-Aero and Univair will probably have parts for T-craft and other old aircraft for years to come.

Cessna 120, 140, and 170

In many ways, the Cessna 120, 140, and 170 aircraft are the first of a new breed. Unlike the Cub, Champ, Taylorcraft, and Ercoupe, the 120/140/170 series are all post-World War II designs. Production of the 120 and 140 models began approximately five months after the end of World War II on Cessna production lines that had produced no light single-engine aircraft during the war years.

More than 7,000 of the 120 and 140 models were produced from 1946 to early 1949, with all-metal fuselages, fabric wings, and 85-hp Continental engines. More than 500 of the metal-wing 140A models, powered by 90-hp Continentals, were produced between 1949 and the end of production in 1953. The Cessna 170A was first produced with fabric wings and single tubular wing struts. Nearly 750 of the 170As were produced with fabric-

Table 10.6. Cessna 120 (85 hp)

Specifications	
Wingspan	33 ft
Length	21 ft
Gross weight, normal category	1,450 lb
Empty weight	800 lb
Useful load	650 lb
Useful load, full fuel	500 lb
Fuel capacity, standard tanks	25 gal
Performance	
Cruise speed, 75% power, best altitude	110 mph
Fuel consumption, 75% power	5.5 gph
Range 45-min reserve, 75% power	418 mi
Sea level rate of climb	600 fpm
Service ceiling	15,500 ft
Stall, clean	41 mph
Stall, full flaps	N/A
Takeoff over a 50-foot obstacle	1,400 ft
Landing over a 50-foot obstacle	1,100 ft

Table 10.7. Cessna 170

Specifications	
Wingspan	36 ft
Length	25 ft
Gross weight, normal category	2,200 lb
Empty weight	1,200 lb
Useful load	1,000 lb
Useful load, full fuel	784 lb
Fuel capacity, standard tanks	36 gal
Performance	
Cruise speed, 75% power, best altitude	120 mph
Fuel consumption, 75% power	8.5 gph
Range 45-min reserve, 75% power	418 mi
Sea level rate of climb	650 fpm
Service ceiling	15,500 ft
Stall, clean	57 mph
Stall, full flaps	53 mph
Takeoff over a 50-foot obstacle	1,750 ft
Landing over a 50-foot obstacle	1,150 ft

covered wings in 1948. More than 1,500 metal-winged 170As and an additional 2,900 of the 170Bs were produced between 1949 and 1956. Production of the 170B was ended in 1956 when the newly introduced tricycle gear 172 outsold its taildragger predecessor by nearly seven to one.

The 120 had fabric wings with no flaps. The 140 had flaps that were comparatively ineffective and made the 140 slightly slower than the cleaner-winged 120. The 140 also added such refinements as skylight windows, an electrical system, and an additional small, rear-fuselage window on each side of the aircraft. (Many surviving 120s have been modified to incorporate these refinements, so it is not always easy to differentiate between ragwing 120s and 140s.) The metal-winged 140A stepped up to a 90-hp Continental

Figure 10.3. Cessna 120s and 140s originally came only in bare-metal silver.

engine, but the extra 5 mph did not markedly change the aircraft's performance. (See Table 10.6 for data.)

In the air, the 120 and 140 fly as one might expect—in other words, like old 150s. On landing, of course, they are taildraggers and must be treated accordingly. Visibility by modern 150 and 152 standards is poor, and the noise level can be tiring if extra soundproofing has not been added by some proud owner over the life of the aircraft.

The 170 is very much like an early 172, but with the ability to handle rough gravel or grass strips better than its more modern three-legged counterpart. The 170 has developed an enthusiastic following among collectors of modern classic aircraft, and prices for good 170s are likely to exceed those of early 172s, often by a fairly substantial margin.

The 120/140/170 Cessnas are, like the more modern Cessnas, relatively reliable aircraft. Fabric coverings should be inspected closely on the ragwing versions, of course. The 120s and 140s, like the later 150s, may have seen some heavy student training use. The main landing gear attachment points should be inspected closely for cracks.

The Continental engines in these aircraft are all susceptible to 100LL spark plug and valve fouling problems. The 145-hp engine used in the 170 is also particularly susceptible. Use of autogas will be necessary to prevent 100LL problems, and owners of most of these aircraft are likely to have already acquired the necessary autogas STCs.

Many parts from these aircraft are identical to those used in the Cessna 150, 152, and 172, and Cessna parts are likely to remain accessible even if new single-engine aircraft production is not resumed. Other aircraft suppliers of parts for older aircraft, like Univair and Wag-Aero, are also likely to assure that parts availability for these aircraft will not be a serious problem.

Luscombe Model 8 Silvaire and Model 11A/11E

The strong, fast, tricky-to-land Luscombe is a direct descendant of the other inventions of Don Luscombe, designer of the Monocoupe and the Luscombe Phantom. (The Phantom was claimed to have been so tricky to land that even its designer once flipped one over on landing.)

The Luscombe Model 8 Silvaire was introduced in 1937, with a choice of 50-hp, 65-hp, or 75-hp engines. Nearly 1,200 were built prior to World War II. Production resumed in 1946 with the 65-hp 8A, the 85-hp 8E, and the 90-hp 8F. Production by the Luscombe Aircraft Company ceased in 1949 when the company went bankrupt. Fifty Silvaires were later built by Temco, and 80 of the 8F models were built in Fort Collins, Colorado, by the

Silvaire Aircraft Company between 1955 and 1960. In all, close to 2,500 Luscombe Silvaires were built.

The situation surrounding the Luscombe Model post-2000 was somewhat bizarre. The Don Luscombe Aviation Historical Foundation (www.luscombe.org), based in Chandler, Arizona, claimed on their Web site to own "the FAA Type Certificate #694 for the Luscombe Silvaire 8 series." The DLAHF Web site claimed that the foundation had saved the Luscombe series by purchasing the Type Certificate from a prior owner who had intended to destroy all Luscombe papers to create a tax loss and to reduce personal liability. The DLAHF offered restored, improved, like-new Luscombes for $40,000 to $50,000. But in October 2003, a visit to www.luscombe.org would see the statement, "Oops, it's not the DLAHF anymore ..." and "DLAHF has filed for bankruptcy."

Another organization, Renaissance Aircraft (www.renaissanceaircraft.com) in Cape Girardeau, Missouri, claims to be building and selling an updated version of the classic Luscombe 8F they call the Renaissance 8F. Unlike early 8Fs, Renaissance 8Fs are powered by 150-hp Lycoming O-320 engines. The Renaissance 8F has a large spinner and a large cowling, giving the plane a racier and more powerful look, like a classic Silvaire on steroids. As might be expected from what is basically a small two-seater with a relatively big engine, performance is impressive. Cruise speed at 75% power is 140 mph, and sea-level rate of climb at gross weight is 1,500 feet per minute.

The advertised 2003 base price for the Renaissance 8F, without any radios, is $77,500. Add $8,500 for a King Silver Crown VFR avionics pack-

Table 10.8. Luscombe 8F (90 hp)

Specifications	
Wingspan	35 ft
Length	20 ft
Gross weight, normal category	1,300 lb
Empty weight	770 lb
Useful load	530 lb
Useful load, full fuel	380 lb
Fuel capacity, standard tanks	25 gal
Performance	
Cruise speed, 75% power, best altitude	118 mph
Fuel consumption, 75% power	4.5 gph
Range 45-min reserve, 75% power	562 mi
Sea level rate of climb	900 fpm
Service ceiling	16,000 ft
Stall, clean	45 mph
Stall, full flaps	N/A
Takeoff over a 50-foot obstacle	1,850 ft
Landing over a 50-foot obstacle	1,540 ft

Figure 10.4. The Silvaire has a reputation for speed in the air and elusiveness on the ground.

age, or $4,600 for a full gyro package, and an additional $19,500 for a King IFR avionics package.

The Luscombe Silvaire design sacrificed comfort and good ground handling for speed. Among its 65-hp two-seat peers, it was a very fast bird indeed, topping 100-mph cruise speed. To put this in perspective, one needs only to consider that the Mooney 201 and the Grumman-American {now Tiger Aircraft} Tiger received high praise for merely approaching 1 mph per horsepower. (The Renaissance 8F, with a 150-hp engine and a 142 mph cruise speed, falls just short of the old classic Luscombe standard.) The stick-controlled, side-by-side two-seater has good handling traits in the air, with a sensitive rudder and relatively slow ailerons requiring concentration to perform "ball-in-the-center" coordinated turns. It stalls abruptly and can be spun readily.

The Silvaire is notoriously tricky when landing or even taxiing in anything but mild winds. The airplane has a small cabin with near-claustrophobic visibility. It is also a very noisy bird. Landings are an interesting experience to hear as well as feel. When the tailwheel touches the runway, the long, empty metal tailcone transmits enough bangs and rattles that tricycle gear pilots could be tempted to check for nonexistent damage. Most Luscombe Silvaire parts are available from Univair in Colorado. Many Luscombe Silvaires do suffer corrosion problems, and anyone seriously looking at purchasing an old used Silvaire should have the aircraft carefully checked for corrosion.

Luscombe also produced a small number of lesser-known four-seater taildraggers known as the Model 11A Sedan. Ninety-two were built by the Luscombe Aircraft Company in 1948 before the company went bankrupt a year later. The 11A Sedan was powered by a Continental E-165 engine. Amazingly enough, in late 2002 a new Luscombe Aircraft Corporation (www.luscombeaircraft.com) was awarded an Amended Type Certificate for the Luscombe Model 11E. The 11E is a modern-looking tricycle gear airplane with an IO-360-ES 185-hp fuel-injected engine. Looking like a sexier Skyhawk with a big angular tail, the 11E in 2003 was advertised with a VFR base price of $155,900, compared to the $155,000 VFR base price for the 160-hp Skyhawk and a base price of $165,000 for the 180-hp Skyhawk SP. (Of course, you will have to spend at least another $15,000 to $20,000 for typical IFR avionics in any of them.)

Ercoupe/Aircoupe

The once controversial, now much-loved Ercoupe was originally designed as the Model 415 in the late 1930s. Designed by Fred Weick (who would later have a hand in designing another drivable airplane—the Cherokee), the Ercoupe was intended to be simple, safe, unspinnable, and stall resistant. The aircraft was rendered unstallable by a collar on the control wheel, limiting elevator travel. This was combined with the Engineering Research Corporation (ERCO) Simplomatic aileron-rudder interconnect system to produce an aircraft that was nearly impossible to cross-control, stall, or spin.

The Ercoupe was first produced in 1939 by ERCO as the 65-hp Continental-engined 415A or 415B. More than 100 were produced before production was halted by World War II. Production hit a peak when it was resumed in 1946; more than 4,000 of the 415C models were produced with a 75-hp Continental engine. Thereafter, production tapered off sharply, with a combined total of just over 600 of the 415D, 415E, and 415G models being produced before production by ERCO ceased in 1950.

Between 1950 and 1958 the rights to the Ercoupe were held by Universal Aircraft (now known as Univair). Univair produced Ercoupe parts but did not resume production of any complete aircraft. In 1958 Forney Aircraft Corporation obtained the rights to the Ercoupe. Forney produced nearly 150 of the F-1 model, which was powered by the 90-hp Continental engine. The Forney Aircoupe differed from the original Ercoupes mainly in its use of metal-covered wings instead of the original fabric covering. Alon, Inc. produced nearly 200 additional A-2 Aircoupes. These aircraft had metal wings, rudder pedals, a sliding bubble canopy, and spring-steel main landing gear.

Mooney acquired the rights to the design in 1968, when they produced nearly 50 of the A-2 models. The aircraft was then given a classic Mooney-style tail, making it the M-10 Cadet. Many consider the M-10 to have emas-

Table 10.9. Ercoupe 415E (85 hp)

Specifications	
Wingspan	30 ft
Length	20 ft 2 in
Gross weight, normal category	1,400 lb
Empty weight	830 lb
Useful load	570 lb
Useful load, full fuel	426 lb
Fuel capacity, standard tanks	24 gal
Performance	
Cruise speed, 75% power, best altitude	97 mph
Fuel consumption, 75% power	4.8 gph
Range 45-min reserve, 75% power	412 mi
Sea level rate of climb	600 fpm
Service ceiling	17,300 ft
Stall, clean	40 mph
Stall, full flaps	N/A
Takeoff over a 50-foot obstacle	1,150 ft
Landing over a 50-foot obstacle	1,100 ft

culated the Ercoupe's superior traits, with the Ercoupe's nonspinnable characteristics disappearing along with the twin vertical tails. More than 50 of the M-10 Cadets were produced in 1969 and 1970. Univair again acquired the Ercoupe/Aircoupe in 1973 for parts production rights, ending the long line of Ercoupes.

The Ercoupe's most notable feature was its lack of rudder pedals. Ground steering was done by turning the control wheel like a steering wheel on a car, in keeping with ERCO's intent to build an airplane anyone could fly. The only foot controls in original Ercoupes were brakes, just as in an automobile. Such features made it an object of disdain by taildragger pilots. Apparently the comments hit their mark, because ERCO made rudder pedals an option on the 1949 model 415G.

Figure 10.5. Aren't most things that are ahead of their time laughed at? But the Ercoupe is now beloved.

In the air the Ercoupe/Aircoupe airplane is easy to fly. Visibility is excellent, which is rare for a prewar-designed airplane. The nearly full-span ailerons give the Ercoupe a rapid roll rate. The quick aileron response, low wings, and slide-down windows that can be opened in flight give the Ercoupe a minifighter feel similar to the much newer Yankee/Tr-2.

Even though early vintage Ercoupes have no capability for cross-control, crosswind landings are not a problem. The time-tested technique for landing an Ercoupe in a crosswind has always been to crab the aircraft right onto the ground. Once the main wheels touch down, the trailing beam landing gear automatically straightens out the aircraft. Later Alon Aircoupes replaced the original landing gear with a spring-steel type. These versions are equipped with rudder pedals to allow conventional cross-controlled crosswind landings.

The Ercoupe has always had one problem that could "reach up and bite" unsuspecting first-time pilots who tried to drive their airplanes. The rate of descent in an Ercoupe can rapidly become substantial in power-off landings. Without the prompt application of power, the Ercoupe can develop a sink rate that can lead to a very hard landing. (The rate of climb is nothing to brag about, either.)

While most Ercoupes today are owned by dedicated, careful owners who keep them in good shape, some are owned by pilots trying to get by with a minimum of expense. Remember when you are buying an Ercoupe that this is at least a 40-year-old airplane, and have it inspected carefully. The generally rugged Ercoupes have not been problem free. AD notes were issued against early models, and one of the most significant of these was for cracks in the rear wing spars. Wing spars should also be carefully inspected for corrosion, since most Ercoupes are tied down outside where years of moisture can take a toll. In the 1980s, a number of Ercoupes had catastrophic in-flight airframe failures due to failures of the spar attach points where the wings join the fuselage. So take an extra hard look for evidence of corrosion there.

The aircraft's potential for developing a high sink rate could also take its toll on the landing gear. The nose gear should be given a careful inspection before an Ercoupe is purchased. Nosewheel problems may also show up as shimmying on the takeoff or landing roll. A strengthened dual-fork nose gear modification has been installed on many Ercoupes and is desirable.

Original Ercoupes had, and many still have, fabric wings. These should be tested for fabric strength before the aircraft is purchased. Many original Ercoupes have been modified with metal-covered wings and rudder pedals. The metal-covered wings reduce long-range maintenance and upkeep expenses but reduce the useful load of the aircraft by 30 to 40 pounds. The rudder pedal modification is of doubtful value. The usual modification has

only one of the two rudders deflecting when a turn is made, and the result-
ant rudder effectiveness is marginal. Ercoupe parts may be hard to find at
the local FBO but are readily available from Univair and other specialty suppliers.

Stinson 108 Voyager and Station Wagon

The Stinson 108 series is just about the only four-seater designed before
World War II that was produced in large enough quantities to still be a
viable candidate in the used-plane market. The Stinson 108, a direct descendant of the prewar Model 90, was produced from 1946 to 1948 by the
Stinson Aircraft Corporation. Piper bought the rights to the 108 in late 1948
and built a handful before halting production in 1949.

The first Stinson 108 models were produced with a 150-hp Franklin
engine. The large aircraft was relatively underpowered with 150 horsepower, so the 108-2 and 108-3 models were produced with 165-hp Franklins.

The Voyager differed from the Station Wagon principally in interior
refinements. Both tended to be plush, roomy, and comfortable by aircraft
standards. The Voyager had vinyl interior furnishings. The Station Wagon
bore a resemblance to the highly treasured "woody" automobile station
wagons of the late 1940s, with a strengthened, polished-mahogany veneer
interior and easily removable rear seats.

The Stinson 108 is a ruggedly constructed aircraft, with steel-tube fuselage construction, two metal spars in the wings, and metal wing ribs. The
aircraft were originally fabric covered, although many surviving models are
all or partly metallized. It is large and comfortable, with rotund rather than
trim lines. The 108 models feel very stable in the air, and control response is
good. The Stinson wing has leading-edge slots forward of the ailerons for
improved low-speed control. The 108 also has elevator-flap interconnects
that limit elevator travel unless flaps are extended. This makes it difficult to
get a real stall break in a Stinson. Stalls are generally forward mushes, much
like Cherokee power-off stalls. The limited elevator travel can limit a pilot's
options in climb-out and landing flare phases of flight.

Landing characteristics are fairly standard for taildraggers. The oversize
tail on the 108-3, which gives added in-flight stability, can act as a huge sail
and create problems on crosswind landings.

Stinson 108s powered by the 165-hp Franklin engines with a light
crankcase experienced crankcase cracking problems. Later "heavy-case"
Franklins cured this trouble. Most if not all surviving Stinson Voyagers and
Station Wagons which have not been converted to Lycomings have the

Table 10.10. Stinson 108 (165 hp)

Specifications	
Wingspan	34 ft
Length	25 ft 2 in
Gross weight, normal category	2,400 lb
Empty weight	1,300 lb
Useful load	1,100 lb
Useful load, full fuel	800 lb
Fuel capacity, standard tanks	50 gal
Performance	
Cruise speed, 75% power, best altitude	125 mph
Fuel consumption, 75% power	9.5 gph
Range 45-min reserve, 75% power	556 mi
Sea level rate of climb	600 fpm
Service ceiling	15,000 ft
Stall, clean	65 mph
Stall, full flaps	62 mph
Takeoff over a 50-foot obstacle	1,400 ft
Landing over a 50-foot obstacle	1,500 ft

heavy-case Franklins. Some crankshaft problems were also a recurring difficulty, and retrofitting the engine at major overhaul with a crankshaft certificated for the 225-hp version of the Franklin engine was the standard solution to the problem. If you are considering buying a Stinson, also check for corrosion and note the condition of the fabric carefully, as you would with any older (and some not-so-old) aircraft.

Parts availability may not be as good as for other makes, since the Franklin engine was not as widely produced as many older Lycomings and Continentals. Suspended production of Franklin engines in the United States and the sale of production rights and tooling to Poland cannot really be considered positive notes, either. Little Red Aero (308-234-1635) and Franklin Aircraft Engines (www.franklinengincs.com, 970-224-4404) are American sources for Franklin engine service and parts. Although Franklin engine and Stinson airframe parts will not be readily available at most FBOs, the situation is probably not hopeless for patient Stinson owners willing to closely scrutinize *Trade-A-Plane*. Stinson airframe parts are readily available from that Old Faithful for old-airplane owners, Univair.

The Stinson can offer a good buy in the older four-seater market for the prospective owner who is willing to be patient while the airplane is grounded waiting for parts, or for the pilot who can find one that has been converted to a Lycoming engine or who is willing to go to the trouble to have the conversion done. The Stinson has performance equal to or better than older 172s and can often be found in a reasonable price range.

Piper PA-22 Tri-Pacer

The Piper Tri-Pacer is a transitional airplane in design, with its fabric covering over steel framework being a throwback to earlier years and its tricycle gear giving visions of things to come. The Piper Tri-Pacer can offer an excellent buy for the first-time owner and should not be passed by without serious consideration. With its high stance, short stubby wings, and nosewheel that looks like (and in some ways was) an afterthought, the Tri-Pacer never was and never will be a winner in airplane beauty contests. But the "flying milk-stool," as some have snidely called it, can deliver "four-place" performance matching or exceeding that of older Cherokees, Cessna 172s, and Musketeers and Sports but at a price often several thousand dollars cheaper.

The Tri-Pacer was developed the same way as the Cessna 172 but four years sooner. In 1951 the four-seat, 125-hp Piper Pacer, a taildragger that had a tendency to be tricky in crosswing landings, was given a nosewheel to make it the Tri-Pacer. In 1953 the 125-hp Lycoming was replaced by a 135-hp variant of the same engine. In 1955 the Tri-Pacer received the 150-hp Lycoming O-320, making it a true four-seater for the first time. 1956 models were the first to have a more modern panel, with radios moved to the center of the panel and a larger gyro panel provided in front of the pilot. In 1958 the 160-hp version of the O-320 was added as an option.

In 1960, in a less-than-successful effort to counter the already popular Cessna 150, the Tri-Pacer was trimmed down to a two-seat trainer powered by a 108-hp Lycoming engine. Although manufacturing of the Tri-Pacer ceased at the end of 1960 to make way for the 1961 introduction of the Cherokee, production of the two-seater known as the Colt continued until 1963. In all, nearly 6,000 Tri-Pacers were produced in its ten-year existence, as well as an additional 1,700 Colts.

The rugged, compact Tri-Pacer is a good four-seat airplane with the larger engines. It is also an "old" airplane in design, with many quirks and oddities that only a dedicated owner could love. Originally produced as a fabric-covered airplane, it has often been modified with full or partial metal covering. Some fully metallized Tri-Pacers can be found, as well as some with metal wings and fabric fuselages and still others with fabric wings and metal fuselages.

The airplane has two doors. The one on the left provides entry only to the rear seats, while the smaller one on the right provides a jungle-gym style of access to the front seats. With all four seats full, the pilot can be sure he or she will not be the first one out of the plane. (Why does Piper do that? Do they think the pilot might go for a walk when the passengers aren't looking?) Baggage, limited to 100 pounds, is loaded through a small hatch behind the rear seats. Starting the engine can be a confusing game for pilots trained in more conventional aircraft, because the master switch and starter button are located under the seat.

Ground steering and braking will seem strange, too, except for pilots familiar with older Cherokees. The nosewheel is hard-tied to the rudder pedals for hard but responsive steering, while both main brakes are controlled by a single brake handle located under the throttle. The nosewheel is as large as the main gear and very rugged. (It is claimed that the nosewheel was once tested by taxiing the Tri-Pacer factory prototype over more than 3,000 miles of rutted roads at speeds up to 70 mph. Nothing broke, so the story claims.) On the ground, the high stance of the main gear can create a problem on windy days, particularly when making turns from downwind taxiing.

Modifications are available to add dual toe brakes to the Tri-Pacer, although only Cessna lovers are likely to feel it is essential. A more popular modification is the Univair brake STC to replace old drum-type brakes with disk brakes.

In the air, cross-connects between the aileron and rudder controls make it difficult to execute a poorly coordinated turn. Unfortunately, this also seems to fight against cross-control pressures needed in a crosswind landing. This can be annoying, even though it is easy to override the cross-connects. The Tri-Pacer's visibility leaves a lot to be desired by modern standards, and the steep climb angle makes over-the-nose visibility particularly poor in a climb. The Tri-Pacer is also noisy by modern standards, although the latest

Table 10.11. Piper PA-22-150 Tri-Pacer Caribbean

Specifications	
Wingspan	29 ft 4 in
Length	20 ft 7 in
Gross weight, normal category	2,000 lb
Empty weight	1,104 lb
Useful load	896 lb
Useful load, full fuel	680 lb
Fuel capacity, standard tanks	36 gal
Performance	
Cruise speed, 75% power, best altitude	132 mph
Fuel consumption, 75% power	9 gph
Range 45-min reserve, 75% power	421 mi
Sea level rate of climb	725 fpm
Service ceiling	15,000 ft
Stall, clean	55 mph
Stall, full flaps	49 mph
Takeoff over a 50-foot obstacle	1,600 ft
Landing over a 50-foot obstacle	1,280 ft

models (and many others retrofitted by their owners) are quieter due to added soundproofing.

Generally, the Tri-Pacer is safe and easy to fly. Its stalls are similar to those of a Cherokee, with the aircraft tending to mush downward rather than breaking sharply, seldom dropping a wing. It is not a very good short-field airplane, even though its book rate of climb is better than that of Cherokees, Skyhawks, and Musketeers. The Tri-Pacer is also notorious for its rocklike descent path if it is allowed to get too slow with power off.

The main problems with Tri-Pacers are forward of the firewall. All Lycoming engines used in the Tri-Pacer series were produced with the problem-plagued 7/16-inch valves. Any Tri-Pacer still around with the original engine is not even likely to be airworthy, and is likely to be a "basket case" in need of restoration and a newly majored engine. A close check should be made of aircraft with engines majored more than ten years ago to assure that the 1/2-inch valves were installed as they should have been. Cracked and broken engine mounts are another standard Tri-Pacer problem. Engine mounts should be carefully inspected for cracks, particularly at weld points.

Another potential problem for Tri-Pacers is the main landing gear shock cords. It may be difficult to find replacements at most FBOs, so it would probably be a wise move to carry a spare set. (Wag-Aero, in Lyons, Wisconsin, specializes in replacement parts for older Piper aircraft.) Check the wing struts for corrosion on these airplanes, too. Note that the Pacer and Tri-Pacer are covered by the wing strut corrosion AD 77-03-08 (see Super Cub section) and the 1989 NTSB and Piper recommendation to replace unsealed wing struts with sealed units. In the 1990s, ADs 93-10-6 and 99-01-05 also called for annual inspections of the wing struts as well as treatment with rust inhibitors. Sealed struts which will eliminate the annual inspections are available from Univair. AD 99-01-05 also covers the lift-strut forks, which are prone to fatigue cracking. Improved rolled-thread forks are available from Piper and should be installed on any Tri-Pacer worth buying (or accounted for in the purchase price).

A metallized Tri-Pacer with a 150-hp or 160-hp Lycoming engine can be an excellent buy. Cherokee or Skyhawk performance can be obtained for several thousand dollars less than either of those two more modern aircraft would cost. Anyone considering buying a Tri-Pacer should check the Web site for the Short Wing Piper Club (www.shortwing.org) for valuable information on the plane. If you are really serious about buying one, you probably should join the SWPC.

One modification to the Tri-Pacer, which seems to be much more effective on the stubby-winged Tri-Pacer than on other longer-winged aircraft like the Cessna 172, is Plane Booster "drooped" wingtips. The tips, which add nearly 10 square feet to the effective wing area, seem to make a notice-

Figure 10.6. The Tri-Pacer can provide modern four-place performance at old airplane prices.

able improvement in the short-field takeoff performance and low-speed controllability of the Tri-Pacer. They also seem to reduce its excessive low-speed sink rate.

Another surprisingly popular modification which may make it increasingly more difficult as years go by to find a standard Tri-Pacer is the modification to remove the nose gear, move the main gear, and make Pacers out of Tri-Pacers. A new appreciation for taildraggers in the 1970s, 1980s, and 1990s has been reversing the process by which the Tri-Pacer was born, resulting in higher prices for Tri-Pacers.

High-performance singles: fulfilling the dream 11

If you're like most aircraft owners, your first airplane will be something you'll be proud of all your life. You'll look back on it with pleasant memories ... look back because sooner or later you're likely to decide that the wonderful little bird is too small, too slow, too old, or not powerful enough. And there are any of a dozen other reasons to move up. Maybe you've moved up once already, from a 100-hp two-seater to a 150-hp or even a 180-hp four-seater. But now it's time for the big step up to a high-performance single. With a constant-speed prop and an engine of 200, 250, or even 300 or more horsepower, it'll carry four and maybe even six adults and do from 165 to nearly 250 miles per hour. And unless you opt for a cargo hauler like the Cessna 182 or the Cherokee 6 or 235, or unless you have the money for a new Cirrus or Lancair, it might be a retractable.

If you're strapped for cash but doing it for the love of flying, you're probably going to have to find a partner now. These airplanes are going to start at over $50,000 and probably cost more than $100,000 for a really good used one. If you've been very successful in your business and financial dealings and can afford to buy a new bird from Piper, Mooney, Beechcraft, or even Cirrus or Lancair, plan on spending a quarter of a million dollars on up.

Despite articles in *Flying* and *AOPA Pilot* magazines asserting that the prices of today's new airplanes are reasonable, they are in fact unconscionably, outrageously overpriced by any reasonable standard. In the early 1980s, Cessna and Piper and other aircraft manufacturers claimed that the prices of their aircraft were overly expensive and inflated to reflect the very high costs of protecting themselves against liability claims. As noted on the AOPA Web site, "After a decade of lobbying by the industry and AOPA, President Clinton signed the General Aviation Revitalization Act in August 1994. It limited airframe manufacturers' liability to 18 years." So a reasonable person would expect that today's aircraft should be less expensive than the mid-1980s aircraft, after adjusting for inflation.

But in fact, after adjusting for inflation, one finds that the prices of new aircraft are at least twice what they should be based on presumably inflated 1980s prices. The following calculations were done using the Inflation Calculator at the U.S. Bureau of Labor Statistics Web site. The base price (bare-bones VFR) of a Piper Archer III in 1982 was $44,470. Plugging that into the Inflation Calculator, the inflation-adjusted price for 2003 would be $99,625. But the base price of a 1994 Archer III was $144,900, and the base price of a 2003 Archer III was an incredible $205,500! Cessna prices are only slightly less outrageous. A 1983 Skyhawk had a base price of $44,500, which means the 2003 inflation-adjusted price should have been $82,475. But Cessna's Web site listed a 2003 Skyhawk base price of $155,000. A 1983 Cessna Cutlass II, equivalent to a Skyhawk SP, was priced at $52,450. The 2003 inflation-adjusted price would be $97,215, but the 2003 base price for a Skyhawk SP was $165,000. The manufacturers claim that their aircraft are much better than they used to be. But anyone who has flown both the new and old versions know the new aircraft certainly don't justify prices one-and-one-half to twice what the inflated adjusted prices should be. And those inflation adjusted prices are based on 1980s prices the manufacturers claimed included excessively high liability costs which should have been reduced by the 1994 legislation.

Whether you are going to buy a new aircraft or a more reasonably priced good used one, before you sell your trusty old Skyhawk or Warrior, be sure that you and your partners are going to be able to handle the insurance. If times are tight in the insurance market, you and your partners may not be able to get coverage in a fast retractable without an instrument rating. Expect to be required to have up to twenty-five hours of dual time in your new dream airplane before you take the family on that big vacation. You may even have to go to a manufacturer's school or one set up by outfits like FlightSafety.

And if you are going to buy a new aircraft, be sure to get a good demo flight if you have never flown the aircraft before, especially if it has features or characteristics you have never experienced. For example, the Cirrus and Lancair both have sidesticks, and not everyone who has flown them thinks sidesticks are an improvement. Cirrus and Lancair landing characteristics are different from those of most other aircraft as well, and you will have to decide if you like it after you have flown it.

If you can afford a new aircraft but don't want to pay the absurdly high prices, AOPA has demonstrated an alternative for someone wanting a like-new or even better-than-new aircraft. You buy a good late model used aircraft, invest money in new avionics, a new engine, new paint, and new interior, and you will have a like-new aircraft at only a little more than half the price. If you don't like some of the new design features, like the overhead switches, small windshield, and reduced payload of a Piper Archer III, for example, an upgraded to like-new early 1980s vintage Archer II will outperform the new Archer III.

Let's take a look at the numbers. New Garmin avionics should go for about $35,000. Allow $15,000 for a new or high quality overhauled Lycoming O-360. Figure about $10,000 for new paint, and $5,000 for a new interior. Add it all up and it comes to $65,000. A look at *Trade-A-Plane* in late 2003 showed low-time early 1980s vintage Archer IIs with asking prices around $65,000 to $70,000. That means your "better-than-new" Archer II+ will cost less than $135,000 for a fully IFR-equipped bird equivalent to Piper's 2003 Archer III which has an IFR asking price of over $230,000. You could even step up to a late model used retractable Arrow, which in late 2003 had *Trade-A-Plane* asking prices around $100,000 or less. Upgrade your Arrow, and you have a hell of a lot better and faster airplane than the Archer III for a price at least $60,000 less than a new Archer III. Cessna Skyhawk numbers for a 1981 are similar to those of the Archer II—just under $65,000. Add the mods and the price goes to $130,000. A new IFR 172 goes for a not quite as outrageous $165,000 to $175,000, so the numbers aren't quite as dramatic for Cessnas.

One drawback to this approach, of course, is that it usually takes AOPA months to do their upgrades. Of course, if you live in the northern states, it would be ideal to buy your plane in late fall, plan the work for the winter, and have your "better-than-new" aircraft flying in the spring. If you aren't up to managing the job, budget a couple thousand more dollars and hire an aviation consultant or even a mechanic to make the arrangements and keep everything on track.

High-performance aircraft covered in this chapter include fixed-gear load haulers like the Cessna 180, 182, and 185; the Cherokee 6/Saratoga and 235/236 Dakota; and the utilitarian and independent Maules. Fast four-seaters include Cessna's Cutlass RG (sneaking in, as is the fixed-gear Aerospatiale TB10 Tobago, with only 180 hp), Cardinal RG, and Skylane RG; Piper's Arrows; the (not-so-fast) Beechcraft Sierra and Model 33 and 35 Bonanzas; and the early Mooneys plus the 201, 231, 252, PFM, TLS, Ovation, and Bravo. (If you're interested in 160-mph-plus speed and performance without the cost, complication, and status of retractable gear and a constant-speed prop, be sure to check into Tiger Aircraft's reborn Tiger discussed in Chapter 9.) In the bigger, six-seat category are the Cessna 210 Centurion line; the Piper Cherokee Lance and Saratoga SP; the Beechcraft A36 and B36TC; and for a touch of foreign spice, the Aerospatiale TB20 Trinidad and TB21 Trinidad TC. Three really new "clean sheet of paper" singles, the Lancair, the Cirrus, and the Diamond DA40, are introduced. Among the exotic, the Lake Buccaneer, Renegade, and Seafury are included, as well as the Waco YMF-5 Classic and the Pitts aerobatic biplanes. The less exotic but only slightly less expensive Husky, the upgraded SuperCub clone built by Aviat, is also included. If this list doesn't fulfill your wildest flying dreams, you'll have to move up to a twin or maybe join the military!

Cessna 180 and 185 Skywagon

Cessna had produced big high-wing singles before, starting with the Airmasters in the late 1930s and the 190 and 195 after World War II. These were big, tough, cantilever (strutless), radial engine birds, and the modern Cessna 140s and 170s introduced in 1946 and 1947 looked like toys alongside them. The first modern Cessna workhorse, the 180, was introduced in 1953. Powered by the highly reliable O-470 Continental engine, the 180 saw only relatively minor changes throughout its lifetime. The O-470 started out rated at 225 hp, and in 1957 the O-470 became a 230-hp engine and the 180's gross weight went up 100 pounds. In 1964, fuel tank capacity was raised from 55 to 65 gallons in the standard tanks and an 84-gallon option was offered. In 1978, the 180 got the 100-octane-rated O-470-U.

In 1961, Cessna introduced a more powerful model of the 180 powered by the 260-hp IO-470-F and called it the 185. It had 84-gallon fuel tanks and it was a real load hauler, with a gross weight of 3,200 pounds compared to the 180's 2,650. The 300-hp Continental O-520 was offered in 1966, and it quickly became the standard engine for the 185.

The year 1973 brought the camber-lift wing with its revised leading edge for improved low-speed controllability to both the 180 and the 185, and in 1974 visibility-improving lower door side windows and wing "skylight" windows were offered as options. In 1978, a three-blade prop was a 185 option which became standard on 1980 185s. In a strange move which shows the odd nature of the bush-flying market, Cessna made 88-gallon "wet" wing tanks standard in 1979, but continued to offer 40-gallon bladder tanks as an option to backwoods operators who considered them more rugged. Production of the 180 was terminated in 1981, while production of the 185 tapered down until all Cessna piston singles died in 1985. Production of the 180 and 185 was not restarted when the Skyhawk, Skylane, and Stationair were brought back in the late 1990s.

Like its better-known and sleeker younger brother, the Cessna Skywagon is a heavy, solid, fairly fast load hauler. This is a taildragging

Table 11.1. 1974 Cessna 180 Skywagon and 1983 A185F Skywagon

	180	185
Specifications		
Wingspan	36 ft	36 ft
Length	25 ft 8 in	25 ft 8 in
Gross weight, normal category	2,800 lb	3,350 lb
Empty weight	1,598 lb	1,708 lb
Useful load	1,202 lb	1,642 lb
Useful load, full fuel	812 lb	1,138 lb
Fuel capacity, standard tanks	65 gal	88 gal (84 usable)
Performance		
Cruise speed, 75% power, best altitude	162 mph	169 mph
Fuel consumption, 75% power	14.2 gph	15.8 gph
Range 45-min reserve, 75% power	620 mi	771 mi
Sea level rate of climb	1,090 fpm	1,075 fpm
Service ceiling	19,600 ft	17,900 ft
Stall, clean	63 mph	64.5 mph
Stall, full flaps	55 mph	56 mph
Takeoff over a 50-foot obstacle	1,205 ft	1,430 ft
Landing over a 50-foot obstacle	1,360 ft	1,400 ft

workhorse, not a racehorse. It is powerful enough to get off the ground in a hurry, even with a full load, and the rate of climb is good up to and through 10,000 feet. Both 180s and 185s are built for short, rough-field operation, and both are very good at it. While not a true STOL airplane, it has near-STOL characteristics. One New England Yankee aircraft broker routinely used a Skywagon to commute from an 850-foot island runway to his office at a suburban Boston airport, using aircraft capabilities that also make these planes one of the aircraft of choice by bush pilots in Canada, Alaska, and Maine. Unlike the "modern" tricycle gear Cessnas and their incredibly slow electric flaps, Skywagons come with quick-reacting manual flaps. The manual flaps take muscle, but they give you a range of tricks to use in short-field takeoffs and landings not available to pilots with electrics.

In the air, the Skywagon, like the Skylane, is heavy on the controls but not ponderous. Elevators are particularly heavy and trim is needed unless you want to try a course in advanced bodybuilding.

Landings are another story. Landing these big taildraggers, particularly in a tailwind, deserves your full attention, from the final approach until you are tying the tie-down ropes. *Aviation Safety* magazine reported that groundloops on takeoff or landing accounted for nearly half of all Skywagon accidents. The spring-steel landing gear can make wheel landings tricky, and some experienced 180/185 pilots recommend sticking to full-stall, three-point landings. But if you have the trim rolled back and the flaps set for a three-pointer, be damn careful on the go-around. Hit full power without dumping some of the flaps and trim and you'll find the nose heading skyward quicker than you want!

The Skywagons are spacious cargo haulers for four people or a wide range of cargo with the rear seats removed, but a third-row child seat is pretty much useless except for really small children. Late-model 185s can be well appointed, but generally Skywagons will look rather Spartan alongside Skylanes. And be sure to bring your noise-blocking headsets ... these birds have a minimum of insulation and are noisy!

Problems with these birds are relatively few, as one should be able to expect of a family of aircraft built for more than 20 years with only minor changes. The main landing gear fittings should be closely checked for cracks and damage. It is likely that a Skywagon has been the victim of a ground-loop accident, so make sure the landing gear is in good condition and that any repairs have been done correctly. Check the pitch trim jackscrew to the adjustable stabilizer. It can be worn, loose, or subject to binding. The main thing to remember about a Skywagon is that it is an aircraft that may have seen some rough operation in out-of-the-way strips or on floats. An especially careful inspection for hidden damage or corrosion is in order.

If you're looking for a tough, powerful single-engine airplane to carry four people and baggage to dirt strips or on floats at a respectable speed, the Cessna Skywagon is almost sure to be your first choice. (Unless a newer Maule would better serve your needs.) The most reliable and economical Skywagon is a good pre-1977 180 with an 80-octane-rated O-470 engine which is STC'd for autogas use. If you need the capability to carry heavy loads or are considering putting the plane on amphibious floats, you'll probably want to move up to the 185. You can hardly go wrong in any case. The Skywagon, like the DC-3, has become an aerial legend in places like Alaska where planes and not roads provide a lifeline.

Cessna 182 Skylane

A momentous year for Cessna was 1956. It was a year that two of their best-selling taildraggers would be modified into two of the most heavily produced tricycle-gear airplanes in the world. The 170 with a nosewheel became the 172, and the 180 became the 182. Unlike the 172, which would see four different engines with three different horsepower ratings in the basic 172 alone, and more variations in offshoots like the XP and the Cutlass, the 182 would have only the 230-hp Continental O-470 as its powerplant for more than 20 years.

The 182/Skylane is the airplane for the pilot who likes a high-wing airplane but who is just a little dissatisfied with the 172, which often seems to be a bit underpowered, a little too light, and a little too little all around. There's nothing too little or underpowered about the Skylane. This is a big, solid, powerful handful of an airplane, as any pilot who tries to pull back and flare this airplane without trim will soon find out. You'd better either learn to use your elevator trim early and often or take up Olympic bodybuilding if you intend to fly this bird. This is a big, strong, powerful, and honest airplane.

The Skylane did see slow evolutionary changes, and the Skylanes from the early 80s and later look like they've been on steroids if you see them alongside one of the first-year models. Gross weight for the 1956 182 was 2,550 pounds, while gross weight for the Skylane built in 1985 was 3,100 pounds. The Skylane name was introduced to a fully painted, deluxe model of the 182 in 1958. The sweptback tail first appeared in 1960, when fuel capacity was also increased from 55 to 65 gallons. The biggest changes came in 1962, when the cabin was widened and lengthened, a rear window was added, electric trim became standard, gross weight increased to 2,800 pounds, and optional 84-gallon fuel tanks were offered. The camber-lift wing, with a constant radius, leading-edge droop to improve low-speed handling, appeared in 1971.

More significant changes occurred in 1978, when 88-gallon integral wet-wing fuel tanks replaced the problem-plagued bladder tanks that all earlier models had, and when the O-470-U 100-octane-burning engine replaced 80-octane-rated versions of the engine. That same year also saw the production of a retractable Skylane, the Skylane RG. Amazingly enough, considering the excellent reliability of the O-470 series engines, the Skylane RG was powered by a 235-hp Lycoming O-540. The following year, the Skylane Turbo RG was introduced with a turbocharged version of the big Lycoming. And in 1981, a fixed-gear version of the Turbo RG was introduced, again with the Lycoming O-540 to round out the family. Production of the Skylane line ceased in 1985 but was restarted in 1997, with the new 182T models powered by a 230-hp fuel-injected Lycoming IO-540. Also introduced was a turbo T182T powered by a 235-hp TIO-540. RGs were not brought back into production. Post-1997 models finally got rid of the old Royalite plastic on the instrument panel; newer panels are made of a solid and respectable gray metal. Bendix/King radios replaced the notorious Cessna avionics (although Bendix/King radios in the post-2000 era seemed a bit dated compared to fancy Garmin color map units). New 182Ts also have an impressive three-blade prop. Top-of-the-line Garmin G1000 primary flight displays and integrated multifunction displays became available in new 182s and turbo 182s in early 2004, with the announced price being the same price as for other Nav II avionics packages previously offered.

The Skylane is an airplane that feels solid and stable in the air, not quick and responsive. The elevators are very heavy, and ailerons are firm and deliberate in their response. Cessna has worked some aeronautical engineering magic on the newer post-1997 182Ts. The elevators on the latest ones don't feel quite as heavy. The big, powerful engine does require a lot of right rudder pedal on takeoff, which can be neutralized with rudder trim on some models. The 182/Skylane is an excellent instrument airplane. It is a fast airplane compared to the Skyhawk, with a cruise airspeed in the same range as 200-hp retractables, but its six-cylinder 230-hp engine is a gas hog compared to the four-cylinder Lycomings in the retracs. The airplane is a good load hauler, and at anything but maximum gross weight it will have a sea-level rate of climb near 1,000 feet per minute.

Its stall characteristics are very "honest." A full-power departure stall is almost impossible to accomplish—the 182 will hang on its prop in an extreme nose-high attitude. (One instructor, during an attempted demonstration of a full-power departure stall, pointed out the loud roar, the buffeting and shaking, and the extreme nose-high attitude of the not-yet-stalled 182 to a pilot he was checking out in the aircraft. "Never mind trying to get it to stall," he told the student. "If you don't know that this is not normal, there's nothing more I can do for you!") Surprisingly, the newer 182Ts will drop their noses with a departure stall break. The 182Ts also feel lighter on the controls than earlier models.

The 182's heavy elevator on landing is also legendary, and few pilots can pull the wheel back with one hand to flare without using a lot of elevator trim. It's not unusual for a hard landing to slam the nose gear down violently if the pilot forgets to use enough nose-up trim on final approach. Check any 182/Skylane you intend to buy for damaged nose gear mounts and for a damaged firewall. Making good landings in a 182 is not difficult, however. Use a generous amount of trim for a slightly nose high attitude on final, and the airplane will come down as if it were riding tracks, with just a slight tug on the wheel to flare for a really nice landing.

Inside, the Skylane's cabin is wide, spacious, and comfortable. Entry to the cabin is easy through two wide doors, one on either side of the aircraft. Seating is high, wide, and comfortable. While a late-model Skylane with the big fuel tanks can't take an unlimited load, there should be few weight and balance problems with most anything you can stuff in this bird. If you load it lightly and have most of the weight up front, though, make sure to give yourself lots of nose-up trim to help you get the nose up on the landing flare.

The biggest problem affecting most Skylanes (all models built prior to 1978) is AD 84-10-1, dealing with trapped water in the bladder tanks. If

Table 11.2. 1979 Cessna 182 Skylane

Specifications	
Wingspan	36 ft
Length	28 ft
Gross weight, normal category	2,950 lb
Empty weight	1,700 lb
Useful load	1,250 lb
Useful load, full fuel	722 lb
Fuel capacity, standard tanks	92 gal (88 usable)
Performance	
Cruise speed, 75% power, best altitude	163 mph
Fuel consumption, 75% power	13 gph
Range 45-min reserve, 75% power	981 mi
Sea level rate of climb	1,010 fpm
Service ceiling	16,500 ft
Stall, clean	64.5 mph
Stall, full flaps	57.5 mph
Takeoff over a 50-foot obstacle	1,100 ft
Landing over a 50-foot obstacle	1,350 ft

water is trapped in wrinkles in the rubber bladders, it cannot be removed by normal preflight sump draining, and it will end up in the fuel lines following pitch-up on takeoff. A high incidence of engine failures was attributed to this problem. The AD called for a "smoothing and blending" of any wrinkles found in an inspection of the tanks and moving tank drains. If a test showed that more than 3 ounces of trapped fluid (the gascolator capacity) could still be trapped after the smoothing, a 182 pilot is supposed to do a "rock 'n' roll preflight" procedure. This procedure calls for holding down the tail and simultaneously rocking the wings up and down a dozen times, 10 inches up and 10 inches down, and repeating the procedure until no water is found with the sumps drained. In addition to this wonderful procedure, you're also supposed to put a sizable placard on your panel describing the whole damn maneuver just in case you may have forgotten how or left your copy of the Cessna service bulletin at home.

The new production 182Ts solve the water problem with an irritating solution probably devised by ultraconservative liability lawyers. The 182Ts have five fuel drains under each wing fuel tank plus three more drains under the fuselage!

If you're looking at buying a Skylane that still traps water, or any other pre-1978 Skylane, consider eliminating the problem forever by factoring in the $2,695 price of a set of plastic fuel tanks from Monarch Air & Development, Inc. (P.O. Box 419, Oakland, OR 97462 or www.monarch-air.com) into the price of the aircraft. (The development of the tanks and the fight by the developer, William J. Barton, are stories in themselves. Barton's efforts to develop a tank that would increase the safety of big Cessna singles were blocked for more than two years by the FAA Seattle Region. Barton, with the assistance and advice of a former Cessna chief test pilot, finally secured the STC from the FAA Wichita Region.) Monarch also sells a greatly improved fuel tank cap to replace the recessed Cessna ones that seem to specialize in trapping water in the first place, and these Monarch caps are also a good idea for all Skylanes.

Buying a 1978 or newer Skylane with the big, integral wet-wing tanks would solve the trapped water problem. But *Aviation Consumer* reported that 1977 to 1981 Skylanes, like their smaller Skyhawk kin, had problems with corrosion under improperly prepared and applied paint. Cessna did not follow DuPont's recommendations for applying the usually superior Imron paint, and Cessna aircraft produced during these years were cursed with higher-than-average rates of filiform corrosion under the paint. If you're looking at one produced during these years, check closely for paint quality and corrosion.

Although Skylanes are not particularly high-maintenance aircraft, they are not low-cost aircraft, either. Little things, like the cowl flap pushrod that has to be disconnected to remove the lower cowling, can up the labor rates. Newer models have 20 camlock screws per side on the top of the cowling, 7 screws on each lower cowling, and 12 screws on the lower nosebowl, which have to be removed before your mechanic can start any serious engine maintenance. And you will have a constant-speed prop that will require overhaul and occasional service.

Figure 11.1. The Cessna 182 is an honest four-seat and lots-of-baggage airplane. (Courtesy Cessna Aircraft Company)

If you want a big, solid, reliable, reasonably fast, and modern Cessna, the Skylane is the airplane for you. What's the best Skylane? If money is no object, buy a post-1997 182T or even a new one for around $300,000 in 2003 vintage dollars. Other good ones to look for include the few hundred 182Rs built between 1982 and 1985. The 182R has the big 88-gallon wet-wing tanks and the 100-octane-burning O-470-U engine with a 2,000 hour TBO. If your initial purchase and operating budget is more limited, look for a good mid-1960s to mid-1970s model. Get a copy of AD 84-10-1, and make sure the one you buy has all the wrinkles nicely smoothed out or a set of Monarch plastic tanks installed so you won't have a gymnastic exercise every time you preflight the bird. The O-470-R engines in this year group have a 1,500 hour TBO, but this is offset by the availability of autogas STCs for this 80-octane engine. Because the 182 can be a thirsty bird, the reduced price of autogas can add up to some significant savings over the years.

Cessna Cardinal RG, Skylane RG, and Cutlass RG

Beginning in 1971, Cessna brought out three different retractables based, like Piper's Cherokee Arrow, on fixed-gear aircraft already in the corporate lineup. The landing gear, however, was based on the landing gear first used in the Cessna 210 in 1959 and in the twin-engine 337 Skymaster in 1965. It was a gear adapted with varying degrees of success to the three different retracs. Early Cardinal RGs had a very troubled history, whereas the later-model Cardinal RGs, the Cutlass RG, and the 182 RG have had fewer problems. But the motion required to retract the gear up and back into the fuselage is naturally much more complex than the simple hinge action used in almost all low-wing retractables. And that means that the Cessna gear will inevitably have more problems and be less reliable than those used by the low-wing competition. Watching the gear retract doesn't add to your confidence in it, either. The initial motion looks like a cross between a wounded seagull and a broken airplane as the gear first flops down and seems to dangle before finally deciding to shift back and upward into the fuselage. It's also a landing gear that doesn't do great things for unimpeded access to a spacious baggage compartment.

These single-engined Cessna retractables provide only one green light on the panel to show all three gear down and locked. Having only one light for all three landing gear up and another light for all three landing gear down does not give you the confidence that checking for "three green" does, though. Of course, it's not that hard to see the main gear, but a well-placed mirror on the wing strut might be required for real assurance that the nose gear is really down. (Lakes put a mirror on the wing float.) For a line of retractables with a history of gear problems, the lack of "three green" is particularly annoying.

The gear doesn't have the solid feel of the spring-steel or later steel-tube gear of the fixed-gear Cessnas, either, when you taxi along the ramp and taxiways. The RG-series birds seem to wiggle and squirm their way over bumps. Nothing serious, but it does take some getting used to, particularly compared to the rock-solid ground handling of more conventional low-wing retractables. And Cessna's failure to put any RGs back into production post-1997 certainly didn't give the strange retractable gear a vote of confidence.

But if you like a high-wing airplane and you want modern speed and performance and all you need are four seats, these might be the birds for you.

CARDINAL RG. After improving the sleek and beautiful fixed-gear Cardinal and then nearly abandoning it (see Chapter 9), Cessna came out with a more powerful retractable gear version in 1971. Other than the retractable gear, the only real difference was the replacement of the carbureted 180-hp Lycoming with the fuel-injected 200-hp Lycoming IO-360. The wide cabin, big doors, roominess, and excellent visibility are shared by the fixed and retractable Cardinals.

The only real changes in the Cardinal RG over its short seven-year production history were improvements to the landing gear. The 1971 and 1972 Cardinal RGs had a real mixed electrical and hydraulic kludge, with the gear handle sending electrical signals to a control unit which sent electrical signals to the hydraulic actuators and which then relied on electrical downlock switches sending signals to electrical solenoids to engage locking pins. In 1973, the hydraulics were used to engage the downlock actuators, replacing the electrical solenoids. A third improved system was used in the 1974 to 1977 models, simplifying the system by making the selector a hydraulic valve, which reduced some electrical wiring. The last year's model, the 1978, got the Cessna standard 28-volt electrical system. In the Cardinal RG, it was an improvement, and Cessna designed a new higher-voltage power pack for the gear retraction system. The gear was much more reliable than earlier models, but Cessna dropped the entire Cardinal line with only about 100 1978 models being built with the new gear.

In the air, the Cardinal RG shares the crisp, smooth flying characteristics of its fixed-gear brethren. Its ailerons are quick, responsive, and nicely balanced. It is easily the most pleasant Cessna in the air. In the 200-hp retrac class, it is faster than either the Piper Arrow or the Beechcraft Sierra. Sixty-gallon fuel tanks give it good endurance and range.

Table 11.3. Cessna Cardinal RG

Specifications	
Wingspan	35 ft 6 in
Length	27 ft 3 in
Gross weight, normal category	2,800 lb
Empty weight	1,765 lb
Useful load	1,035 lb
Useful load, full fuel	675 lb
Fuel capacity, standard tanks	60 gal
Performance	
Cruise speed, 75% power, best altitude	165 mph
Fuel consumption, 75% power	10.4 gph
Range 45-min reserve, 75% power	828 mi
Sea level rate of climb	925 fpm
Service ceiling	17,100 ft
Stall, clean	65.5 mph
Stall, full flaps	57.5 mph
Takeoff over a 50-foot obstacle	1,585 ft
Landing over a 50-foot obstacle	1,350 ft

The Cardinal RG is one sweet airplane to fly, but if you own one you'll always have to worry about whether your gear will come down for every landing.

SKYLANE RG. The Skylane RG developed by Cessna in 1977 wasn't really a new idea. It was an idea that Cessna had tried with great success back in 1960, when it took a 182 and put retractable gear on it. Only back then, they added 30 hp and the airplane grew from a four-seater to the six-seat 210/Centurion. This time around, only 5 hp would be added, but it would still be a tremendous success. In only eight years of production, from 1978 to 1985, more than 2,000 Skylane RGs and Turbo Skylane RGs would be built.

The Skylane RG, unlike the 230-hp Continental-engined Skylane, used a 235-hp Lycoming O-540. A Turbo Skylane RG, introduced in 1979, also used a 235-hp Lycoming O-540 with a turbocharger for improved high-altitude performance. Changes over the short life of the Skylane RG were relatively modest, including improvements to avionics fans, door latches, air vents, muffler shrouds for better heating, and fuel valve detent upgrades. The most significant change in 1979 was to go from the troublesome, water-retaining bladder tanks with 61-gallon capacity (80 gallons optional) to integral tanks with 92-gallon capacity.

There are some things Cessna apparently never learned, like easy access to the engine. The opening to check the oil and drain the gascolator is barely 4 inches across. Each upper cowling half is fastened with 21 half-turn release screws, with still more to remove the bottom cowling. Compared to similar Piper and Beechcraft aircraft, engine access in this one is a bad joke.

Even though the design is typical single-engine Cessna, the Skylane RG and Turbo Skylane RG can come with "Big Iron" touches shared with the bigger 210 line. A three-bladed prop can give the plane a nice, smooth-running feel. Other options available in a "loaded" aircraft include radar in a pod on the right wing leading edge; built-in oxygen outlets in the ceiling; slaved HSI; a ton of radios; and a myriad of lights, including underwing courtesy lights, an icing light shining from the upper cowling to the left wing leading edge, instrument "eyebrow" lights, map lights, and other cabin lights. The suction gauge, however, is still the super-cheap-looking, tiny, "Crackerjack Box" prize kind.

Like the Skylane, the cabin is large and roomy, and the entry doors on both sides are large, making boarding easy. Like most big Cessnas, the 182RG instrument panel is quite high, but the pilots' seats can be raised and lowered with cranks. There is no problem seeing over the panel in all phases of flight, including approach to landing. Front-seat headroom is generous,

Figure 11.2. The Skylane RG is a big, comfortable, and fast cargo hauler. (Courtesy Cessna Aircraft Company)

Table 11.4. 1983 Cessna R182 Skylane RG

Specifications	
Wingspan	36 ft
Length	28 ft 7.5 in
Gross weight, normal category	3,100 lb
Empty weight	1,767 lb
Useful load	1,333 lb
Useful load, full fuel	805 lb
Fuel capacity, standard tanks	92 gal (88 usable)
Performance	
Cruise speed, 75% power, best altitude	179 mph
Fuel consumption, 75% power	14.1 gph
Range 45-min reserve, 75% power	983 mi
Sea level rate of climb	1,140 fpm
Service ceiling	14,300 ft
Stall, clean	47 mph
Stall, full flaps	45 mph
Takeoff over a 50-foot obstacle	1,320 ft
Landing over a 50-foot obstacle	1,320 ft

but rear-seat headroom is not. And like the other Cessna RGs, the main gear exacts a price in the size and shape of the baggage compartment compared to the fixed-gear models.

The 182RG and T182RG are surprisingly light and responsive on the ailerons for such big airplanes. While this type is no acro bird, it is seemingly faster on aileron response than the Skyhawk and much more so than the "straight-legged" 182. It is a big and powerful airplane, and it feels solid in the air. Like all Skylanes, the Skylane RGs will carry a heavy load a long distance but with a high fuel consumption.

Slow flight controllability is good, and approach stalls are easily recognizable and easy to recover from. The aircraft is easy to set up for landing, and it is easy to land if you roll back the trim as you set up for the approach. Having to control the throttle, prop, landing gear, wing flaps, and cowl flaps can make the pattern a bit busy. One danger is that you might lower the cowl flaps and "in a pinch," forget to lower the landing gear!

First-year models with the bladder tanks should probably be avoided. ADs on the Skylane RGs called for inspections and modifications to both Bendix and Slick magnetos, and for inspection of fuel tank caps for leakage. And as with almost all Cessna RGs, Service Difficulty Reports for Skylane RGs show a litany of problems covering almost all parts of the landing gear retraction mechanism.

But if you love the Skylane and want more speed, this is probably your bird. Unless, of course, you're willing to settle for a fixed-gear model with speed mods.

CUTLASS RG. Like the Cherokee Arrow, the evolution of the Cutlass RG is so obvious that one can only ask why Cessna waited so long. Of course, the apparent answer appears to be that they didn't really want to completely kill off the Cardinal, so they kept the RG version alive until 1978. But the Cutlass RG appeared in late 1979 as a 1980 model, so it didn't take Cessna long after the final demise of the Cardinal line to come up with retractable gear versions of both the highly popular Skylane and Skyhawk. One also has to wonder, though, whether playing cutesy name games didn't hurt, rather than help, the airplane.

This one just begged to be called the Skyhawk RG. The Skyhawk went through four engine changes without a name change, and the 182 retractable was simply called the Skylane RG, so why "Cutlass" instead of just "Skyhawk RG"? The Cutlass name was another of Cessna's dumb moves on the way to the eventual mid-1980s demise of their light single-engine line. Cessna also seemed to have a lackadaisical attitude toward quality control when the Cutlass RG came out. Factory-demo Cutlass RGs were flown by Cessna marketing representatives to special showings at dealers all over the country in 1980. Unfortunately, they had obvious defects, including peeling paint, noisy and defective avionics cooling fans, and ailerons out of alignment. And if you asked the Cessna reps about the obvious flaws, they would insult your intelligence by telling you, "It's supposed to be that way."

Nothing dumb about the design of this airplane, though. If you love Skyhawks but want more speed, this is the one you want. It looks like the sleek Skyhawk, and flies like a fast and more responsive Skyhawk. The cabin is pure Skyhawk, too. But performance-wise, this is a damn good airplane. With the super-reliable, carbureted 180-hp Lycoming O-360 engine under the cowling, this bird is faster than the Beechcraft Sierra and only slightly slower than the Piper Arrow, both of which have 200-hp fuel-injected engines. (Of course, the Grumman-American/Tiger Aircraft Tiger matches the Cutlass RG's speed with the same engine, fixed gear, and a fixed-pitch prop!) With a fuel capacity of 62 gallons usable, this bird has the capability to fly for more than six hours in VFR conditions.

One nice design feature is the ability to drop the gear at cruise speed, which can help you slow down quickly in the pattern or on final, if you have to do a high-speed descent with faster traffic on your tail. Cessna engineers left the troublesome main gear doors off this airplane, camouflaging the fuselage wheel holes with a novel paint scheme. Without main gear doors on the fuselage, there's less to go wrong, and the gear can operate at a higher airspeed without worrying about extraneous parts coming off. And the need for cowl flaps to properly cool the engine also adds to the pilot's workload in the pattern. Just don't get confused and think you put the gear down when you opened the cowl flaps, or you could be in for a nasty surprise on short final.

Table 11.5. Cessna Cutlass RG

Specifications	
Wingspan	36 ft
Length	27 ft 5 in
Gross weight, normal category	2,650 lb
Empty weight	1,558 lb
Useful load	1,092 lb
Useful load, full fuel	720 lb
Fuel capacity, standard tanks	66 gal (62 usable)
Performance	
Cruise speed, 75% power, best altitude	161 mph
Fuel consumption, 75% power	10 gph
Range 45-min reserve, 75% power	877 mi
Sea level rate of climb	800 fpm
Service ceiling	16,800 ft
Stall, clean	62 mph
Stall, full flaps	57.5 mph
Takeoff over a 50-foot obstacle	1,675 ft
Landing over a 50-foot obstacle	1,350 ft

Like all retractable gear Cessnas, the condition of the landing gear needs to be closely checked before buying one of these airplanes. One of the few design changes that Cessna made in the short life of the aircraft was to improve a troublesome hydraulic landing gear power pack and add it to the 1982 models. Most of the Cutlass RGs are 1980 and 1981 models, so it would be wise to check before buying one and make sure that the newer model power pack has been retrofitted into the aircraft.

But if you're a Skyhawk lover who just wants a little more speed, a good Cutlass RG is the airplane for you. And go ahead, call it a Skyhawk RG if you want. Cessna doesn't care anymore anyway!

Figure 11.3. The Cutlass RG is really a faster and nicer Skyhawk!

Cessna 210 Centurion, T210 Turbo Centurion, and P210 Pressurized Centurion

The Cessna 210 Centurion is fast, long-legged, and capable of carrying heavy loads—the ultimate in single-engine, high-wing airplanes. The 210s are more like a family of big, fast retractables than just one kind of airplane, with progressively greater capabilities and progressively greater demands on the pilot (and the maintenance budget) as you move up the line. This is a line of pioneering aircraft with a lot of single-engine firsts for production single-engine aircraft: first high-wing retractable, first pressurized single built in large numbers (the Mooney Mustang was the first produced and the P210 fuselage came right from the Pressurized Skymaster), first with deicing and approval for flight in icing conditions, and first to be outfitted with weather radar. Owners of early 210s and P210s discovered some more unpleasant firsts: first to have serious problems with the weird "dying seagull" landing gear and first to find that Cessna hadn't done a very good job of engineering in the P210's engine compartment.

The first 210, which flew in 1959, was a strut-braced, 260-hp four-seater with a gross weight of 2,900 pounds. If you were to compare it to the 1985 Cessna line, you might think it was the forerunner of the Skylane RG rather than of the massive 3,900 pound P210R. The first big change came in 1964, when the 260-hp Continental IO-470 was replaced with the 285-hp Continental IO-520, gross weight increased, and kiddie seats were added. The Turbo 210 appeared in 1966. The most visible change was made in 1967, when a fully cantilevered wing replaced the draggy strut-braced version. In 1970 the basic 210 grew up, with the cabin being enlarged to accommodate six real adult seats and more baggage in an aircraft with a gross weight of 3,800 pounds. Takeoff rating of the new IO-520-L engine was increased to 300 horsepower. In 1972, an electrohydraulic system replaced the troublesome engine-driven hydraulic system. In 1979, Cessna decided that gear doors over the main gear were more trouble than they were worth, and removed them permanently.

The Pressurized Centurion was introduced in 1978. It was an airplane introduced too soon with too little testing, coupled with the fact that it was not really the great technological advance that Cessna claimed. It was merely a T210 engine overtaxed trying to handle pressurization in a Pressurized Skymaster fuselage. Running too hot and too lean, detonation problems and engine failures led to an AD in 1980 requiring economy and range destroying rich mixtures. A new turbocharger introduced in 1981 in a "Performance Plus" package was a bad joke. It was really "Performance Minus," and P210 owners found the modified airplane too weak to hold manifold pressure and cabin pressure much above 18,000 feet. And if that wasn't enough, the P210 shared a vapor lock problem with other 210 models.

A much-improved 1982 version had a new induction system, a new turbo controller, a new fuel system, and engine improvements. Dual vacuum pumps and alternators were also offered, solving a potentially dangerous problem with a high rate of failure in single vacuum pumps that couldn't handle a full gyro panel plus deicing boots (and would likely fail in IFR icing conditions). To Cessna's credit, the corporation offered to retrofit the induction system mod and the fuel system improvements into earlier P210s, and most are likely to have the mods. But even the improved 1982 and 1983 models seemed bedeviled by quality control problems, and they couldn't match the performance of the then new Piper Malibu. Cessna brought out a much-modified and even more improved P-210R in 1985 with a 325-hp version of the Continental TSIO-520 equipped for the first time with an intercooler to cool the turbocharged air into the engine. The P-210R also had a big new horizontal tail, making the big airplane reasonably pleasant to handle for the first time in its short and troubled history. But all for naught .... After production of only 38 "R"s, Cessna gave up and ended production. In the late 1990s, Cessna brought back the fixed-gear 206 Stationair, but did not bring back the retractable 210s.

The long suit of the Centurion is performance. Any of its variants carry 1,000 pounds of payload over 1,000 miles at a speed of nearly 200 mph. That makes it about equal to a Beechcraft A-36 in speed and quite a bit faster than the Piper Saratoga.

This is a fast cargo hauler, not a sweet-handling machine. Although the basic 210 has been described by some as reasonably good at the controls, even it is very heavy in pitch, particularly if empty seats in the back move the c.g. forward. For no apparent reason, the T210 is not even as pleasant in control response as the 210. With controls passing through the pressure vessel, the P210 is downright stiff to handle and truck-like on the ground and in the air. A fully loaded 210 is one heavy airplane and should be treated with respect, particularly on landing, where accident reports show undershoots and hard landings as not uncommon. Also watch it when taxiing a 210 on anything but level pavement. The plane sits with a level attitude—its prop tips close to the ground—and uneven grass fields with dips and ridges could lead to a prop strike.

One disquieting note is that the cantilever-winged post-1967 210s have a relatively high rate of reported in-flight airframe failures. Unlike the V-tail Bonanzas, there does not appear to be any single structural weak point involved. The message here is that the airplane is not an invulnerable tank in nasty instrument conditions, and slowing up in severe turbulence may be

Table 11.6. Cessna 210 Centurion, T210 Turbo Centurion, and P210 Pressurized Centurion

	210 Centurion	T210 Turbo Centurion	P210 Pressurized Centurion
Specifications			
Wingspan	36 ft 9 in	36 ft 9 in	36 ft 10 in
Length	28 ft 2 in	28 ft 2 in	28 ft 3 in
Gross weight, normal category	3,812 lb	4,016 lb	4,016 lb
Empty weight	2,133 lb	2,133 lb	2,490 lb
Useful load	1,679 lb	1,833 lb	1,526 lb
Useful load, full fuel	1,145 lb	1,299 lb	765 lb
Fuel capacity, standard tanks	90 gal (89 usable)	90 gal (89 usable)	90 gal (89 usable)
Performance			
Cruise speed, 75% power, best altitude	197 mph	222 mph	222 mph
Fuel consumption, 75% power	15.9 gph	16.3 gph	17.5 gph
Range 45-min reserve, 75% power	955 mi	1,045 mi	962 mi
Sea level rate of climb	950 fpm	1,120 fpm	930 fpm
Service ceiling	17,300 ft	27,000 ft	23,000 ft
Stall, clean	75 mph	75 mph	77 mph
Stall, full flaps	63 mph	67 mph	67 mph
Takeoff over a 50-foot obstacle	2,030 ft	2,160 ft	2,160 ft
Landing over a 50-foot obstacle	1,500 ft	1,500 ft	1,500 ft

Figure 11.4. The Cessna 210 Centurion: Once at the top of Cessna's single-engine line. (Courtesy Cessna Aircraft Company)

necessary for survival. A dual or backup vacuum pump should probably be considered a mandatory item if you intend to buy a 210 for reliable transportation, too.

The 210 cabin is wider than that of the A-36 but not as wide as the Piper Six/Saratoga's cabin. Cabin appointments in the 210 and T210 include Cessna's crummy, crack-prone Royalite plastic trim, which seems more appropriate in a 150 than in a top-of-the-singles 210. Cabin seating for four in all models is comfortable, but rear-seat headroom in the last seat leaves something to be desired, particularly in the tighter confines of the P210. This is a big bird with a high instrument panel, and pilots who have to crank their seats up to see over it properly may have problems seeing out the side as their line of vision gets closer to the bottom of the wing and makes the view a little narrow. The P210's "porthole" side windows may restrict the view, too. Definitely not good for claustrophobics!

The problems in getting the engine and turbocharger right aren't the only problems you need to watch for if you're looking at a P210. This was the first Cessna to use the weird Cessna retractable gear, and the 210 gear has had a lot of problems, particularly on earlier models. Pre-1972 models have an engine-driven hydraulic system that is failure-prone and expensive to maintain. Models from 1960 to 1969 had problems with cracks in landing gear saddles, resulting in a 1976 AD requiring saddle replacement. Unfortunately, some replacement saddles only lasted slightly longer before they also needed replacing. The landing gear doors on 1978 and earlier models also add to complexity and maintenance cost, and some owners have had them removed.

The fuel system of early 210s was prone to vapor lock, causing fuel starvation and power loss. Post-1982 210s had an improved fuel system, and

Cessna service letter SE 81-42 addressed a vapor return line fix available as a mod. But even the improvements may not be enough to solve significant fuel system problems. In December 1990, the FAA issued a notice of proposed rulemaking inviting comments on fuel loss or problems in fueling 210 series aircraft. The FAA cited the involvement of 100 of the aircraft in a five-year period in fuel starvation accidents as the reason for its action.

One theory was that the 210 has fuel tanks that are extremely difficult to fill completely. Magazines ranging from the January 1981 *AOPA Pilot* to the July 1989 *Aviation Safety* noted that extreme care had to be taken to refuel a 210 slowly and at a level attitude in strict accordance with the owner's manual. FAA sources reported that in-flight siphoning or constraints to fuel flow by some filler caps are also suspect. In any case, if you are going to fly a 210, you should be aware that you may have a full hour's less flying time available than the gauges and the owner's manual indicate. Plan accordingly.

Despite problems, the Cessna 210 Centurion may be just the plane for you if you love high wings and want a fast airplane with more than four seats. Make sure you have the gear checked very carefully, buy one with the improved vapor return fuel system, and check that your plane has a backup vacuum pump if you're going to fly "hard IFR." Unless you can find a rare "R" model, P210s should probably be avoided, or you should plan to invest the time and money to have an intercooler and other worthwhile mods done that correct the problems resulting from engineering that Cessna didn't bother to do right the first time.

Piper Cherokee 235, 236, Dakota; Six, Lance, Saratoga; Arrow

From its humble beginnings as a 160-hp four-seater, the Cherokee was to grow to an entire line of aircraft ranging from the original Cherokee 140 two-seat trainer all the way up to the six-passenger twin-engine Seneca. Sharing the same modern instrument panel from 1968 to the early 1990s, all of these Cherokee descendants have a similar look and feel inside, which makes it possible to move easily up the Piper line.

Unlike the Cessna line, where the Cessna 182 and 210 series aircraft feel much bigger and heavier than the 150s and 172s even when empty, the Cherokee line shares its look and even aerodynamic feel almost all the way up the line. A lightly loaded Cherokee 236 or even a Saratoga will feel familiar to the accomplished Warrior pilot—heavier, more powerful during the takeoff roll, but familiar. The Arrow is more complex and seems a lot quieter and faster, but it will still seem familiar. But danger can come from complacency. The "big brothers," when fully loaded, are a severe challenge to the unprepared Warrior pilot. The Saratoga will be more than a thousand pounds heavier fully loaded! And everything will be happening faster in these bigger and more powerful Cherokee siblings. A challenge? Yes. But the similarities in the look and feel of the entire line make them good candidates for the individual, partnership, or club that started small with a Cherokee 140 or Warrior and is ready to move up to the "big time."

CHEROKEE 235, 236, AND DAKOTA. The Cherokee 235 was the first of the "big Cherokees," appearing in 1964 with a 235-hp, six-cylinder, 80-octane-rated O-540 Lycoming engine and a variable-pitch propeller. Like the other Cherokees, it was certified in the Utility category as well as in the Normal category. It was touted as an airplane which could carry its own weight in useful load. It has the reputation, like the Cessna 182, of being an airplane which can carry four passengers, all of their baggage, and full fuel and still not exceed weight or balance limitations. The original 235 came with the same standard 50-gallon fuel tanks as the rest of the Cherokee line, but optional wing tip tanks were available which provided a total of 84 gallons of fuel (82 usable).

In 1968, the 235C made the 84-gallon tanks standard. In 1973, more changes came along with the start of name games. In 1973 the 5-inch longer fuselage and the larger stabilator that had originated with the Arrow were added to the 235, which for one year would be called the "Charger." In 1974, the 235—which had always been a noisy airplane—got a one-quarter-

Table 11.7. Piper PA-28-236 Dakota (1979)

Specifications	
Wingspan	35 ft
Length	24.67 ft
Gross weight, normal category	3,000 lb
Empty weight	1,634 lb
Useful load	1,366 lb
Useful load, full fuel	934 lb
Fuel capacity, standard tanks	77 gal (72 usable)
Performance	
Cruise speed, 75% power, best altitude	166 mph
Fuel consumption, 75% power	12 gph
Range 45-min reserve, 75% power	872 mi
Sea level rate of climb	965 fpm
Service ceiling	19,000 ft
Stall, clean	72.5 mph
Stall, full flaps	64.5 mph
Takeoff over a 50-foot obstacle	1,300 ft
Landing over a 50-foot obstacle	1,740 ft

inch thick windshield (up from one-eighth-inch) and right side toe brakes became standard. In 1974 the airplane was given the name "Pathfinder."

The year 1979 brought not only another name change (Dakota), but the biggest changes to the aircraft since it had been brought out 15 years earlier. The aircraft received the tapered Warrior wings, a 100-octane version of the O-540 engine, aerodynamic boot-type wheel fairings, and smaller capacity but simpler 77-gallon fuel tanks (72 usable), with one large tank located in the usual Cherokee position in each wing. Piper also tried a one-year experiment in 1979, giving the Dakota the same 200-hp turbocharged Continental TSIO-360 engine used in the Turbo Arrow IV. Although production of the Dakota ceased in the mid-1980s, the Lycoming-engined version was brought back as part of the full Piper line when M. Stuart Millar bought and revived the company in 1987. However, Piper would declare bankruptcy and cease production in 1991, and when "New Piper" restarted production in 1995 the Dakota was no longer in the lineup.

If you like Cherokees and have the need for a four-seater that will carry a full load even in high-density altitude conditions, the 235s and Dakotas are good airplanes. The Lycoming O-540 engine, like other Lycoming engines used in the Cherokee line, is a reliable engine with a 2,000 hour TBO. And 1964-1978 models can be STC'd for autogas usage, partly offsetting the expense of the high fuel consumption of the six-banger. But stay away from the turbocharged Continental. The TSIO-360 was a problem-plagued engine with a very high failure rate, including a high rate of in-flight failures. It is probably no accident that the Turbo Dakota was produced for only one year. And it is a shame that New Piper doesn't build the strong and reliable Lycoming-powered Dakota anymore.

CHEROKEE SIX, LANCE, AND SARATOGA. The first of the really big long-nose "Sixes" made its appearance in 1965 with a carbureted 260-hp Lycoming O-540, followed a year later by the fuel-injected 300-hp Lycoming IO-540 version. Other changes came a couple of years after they appeared in the smaller Cherokees: 1/2-inch valves instead of 7/16-inch valves in the 260-hp version in 1968, and the modern panel and throttle quadrant in 1970. An extra rear window was added in 1974.

In late 1975, a retractable Six was introduced as the Lance. In one of their better moves, club seating was introduced as an option in 1977. Later that year, in a less brilliant move, Piper moved the tail up, making the T-tailed Lance II, and also provided a turbocharged T-tailed Turbo Lance II. With the Lance rapidly (and deservedly) gaining the reputation of a nose-heavy ground-lover on takeoff and landing, Piper put the tail back down where it belonged in early 1980.

Three years later, 1980 brought a very big change to the whole line, with a beefed-up Warrior wing added to the entire Six/Lance line, which now became the Saratoga, Turbo Saratoga, Saratoga SP (retractable), and Turbo Saratoga SP. Production of the Saratoga series sagged with the rest of the general aviation market, dying out in 1986. The Saratoga and Saratoga SP were brought back in late 1988 as a part of M. Stuart Millar's revitalization of Piper. Production would again cease when Piper went bankrupt in 1991. New Piper would resume production of the retractables, beginning with the Saratoga II HP in 1994.

The Saratoga II HP had a new cowling with the round inlets developed by LoPresti and a three-blade propeller. There was a new and more professional looking flat gray metal panel, with the engine instruments now in a vertical column rather than low on the panel. The electrical system was now a 28V, 90 amp system, and the maximum takeoff weight was up 200 pounds to 3,600 pounds.

New Piper brought back the turbocharged retractable Saratoga II TC in 1998. One unique option was an "entertainment/executive console" to replace one of the aft-facing club seats, with a beverage cooler, AM/FM/CD player, laptop computer station, and multimedia entertainment system. In 1999, Garmin 430s and an advanced S-Tec autopilot would become standard in both the HP and the TC.

July 17, 1999 was a black day for the Saratoga line. John F. Kennedy, Jr. died flying one into the ocean. Spatial disorientation on a dark hazy night, not a problem with the airplane, was the NTSB probable cause. But it was still a black mark on the otherwise excellent record of the big sleek Piper.

In July 2003, New Piper was bought out and recapitalized by American Capital Strategies, claiming that the move would bring new resources to the company. About the same time, New Piper announced they were bringing back fixed-gear versions of the Saratoga. Surprisingly, they weren't called Saratogas, but rather simply the "6" and "6X" for the turbocharged version. The Cherokee 6 had finally returned, but without the "Cherokee" name. Another surprise were the announced prices. Unlike the Warrior III and the Archer III, which were priced tens of thousands higher than the Cessna Skyhawk and Skyhawk SP, the 6 and 6X were actually priced less than the Cessna Stationair and Turbo Stationair.

All of the Cherokee Sixes, Lances, and Saratogas are big and reasonably comfortable cargo haulers. The planes have voluminous cargo space, with a 7-square-foot compartment in the nose and an 18-square-foot area behind the seats if all of the seats are in use. The cabin is 48.75 inches wide, one of the widest in its class. The big nose is so long that you feel like you are taxiing a taildragger, particularly in the old fixed-gear models that sat nose high

Table 11.8. Piper PA-32-300 Cherokee 6 and PA-32R-301 Saratoga SP

	Cherokee 6	Saratoga SP
Specifications		
Wingspan	32 ft 10 in	36 ft 2 in
Length	27 ft 8 in	28 ft 2 in
Gross weight, normal category	3,400 lb	3,600 lb
Empty weight	1,846 lb	2,045 lb
Useful load	1,554 lb	1,555 lb
Useful load, full fuel	1,052 lb	943 lb
Fuel capacity, standard tanks	84 gal (83.6 usable)	107 gal (102 usable)
Performance		
Cruise speed, 75% power, best altitude	168 mph	180 mph
Fuel consumption, 75% power	16 gph	16 gph
Range 45-min reserve, 75% power	752 mi	1,012 mi
Sea level rate of climb	1,050 fpm	990 fpm
Service ceiling	16,250 ft	16,700 ft
Stall, clean	71.5 mph	69 mph
Stall, full flaps	63 mph	65.5 mph
Takeoff over a 50-foot obstacle	1,350 ft	1,575 ft
Landing over a 50-foot obstacle	1,000 ft	1,015 ft

and tail low. The nose on the older models is so high and long you can't see over it to see ahead of you on the ground. Retractable Lances and Saratogas sit flatter on their gear so it isn't a problem. Many of the aircraft have the huge double cargo door behind the left wing, allowing oil drums, caskets, or even upright pianos to be carried if the seats are removed. Center of gravity range is good, with the only problem being that the c.g. may be too far forward with only two up front in the airplane. The cabin is roomy and relatively comfortable, with considerably more headroom for rear-seat passengers than a Cessna 206 or 210.

Sixes, Lances, and Saratogas are not particularly fast and they do burn a lot of fuel, with normal fuel burns in the 14-to 16-gph range. The Sixes and Lances, with their Hershey-Bar wings, are known for having a "trucky" feel when heavily loaded. But at lower gross weights, Sixes and Lances just feel like the big overgrown Dakota and Arrows that they are. Watch the sink rate on landing, though.

The Saratogas, with their longer, sleeker wings and nicely balanced ailerons, have a better feel in the air as well as during takeoff and landing. The T-tail Lances, of course, are known for their long takeoff runs and the tendency of the tail to quickly go from being totally ineffective to too effective, in turn leading to a tendency to overrotate. For the pilot who will not be tempted to try short strips and who is willing to get used to the unusual characteristics on takeoff and landing, the T-tail Lance could be a good buy.

Sixes, Lances, and Saratogas are relatively reliable and trouble-free, with trusty Lycoming O-540s with 2,000 hour TBOs (1,800 in the turbocharged models) giving generally good service. Turbocharged models have a reputa-

Figure 11.5. The Piper Saratoga: A big flying station wagon. (Courtesy Piper Aircraft Corporation)

tion for running hot, and intercooler and induction system modifications and top cowl louvers are recommended for these aircraft, or a retrofit with the LoPresti cowls.

Just as with the PA-28 Cherokees, Piper Service Bulletin 886 applies to the PA-32 series. If you're in the market for one, make sure that it has complete logbooks showing "normal" service and no significant damage to wings or engines mounts, or you may have to have the wings pulled for inspections within 50 hours of the time you buy it and every 800 hours thereafter. (The service bulletin mandates only one-half the number of hours between recurrent inspections for retractables like the Arrow, Lance, and Saratoga SP compared to the fixed-wing PA-28s.)

CHEROKEE ARROW. In 1967 the highly successful Cherokee 180 became retractable and was named the PA-28R-180 Arrow, giving the Cherokee line more speed and carrying capability. But the Arrow was more than just a swing-gear 180 with a fuel-injected 180-hp engine and a variable-pitch propeller added to the new retrac. The Arrow was also the first of the Piper line to use the now traditional T-throttle power quadrant and the modern Cherokee instrument panel. Two years later, the Arrow got a higher compression 200-hp version of the Lycoming IO-360, which was plagued by early AD problems. Even so, by 1971 production of the basic 180 came to a halt. The Arrow II, perhaps the "classic" Arrow, came with a longer fuselage, longer wings, and a larger stabilator. The Florida-built Arrow II also saw the introduction of air conditioning as an option in the Cherokee line, then a rarity in lower-cost singles.

Figure 11.6. The Piper Arrow: "Everyone's single-engine retrac."

In 1977 the longer, tapered Warrior wing appeared on the Arrow, which became the PA-28R-201 Arrow III. In addition to the debatable advantages of the longer tapered wing, the Arrow III had fuel tanks holding 77 gallons of avgas (72 usable). And heresy of heresies for Piper, which originated in the same Pennsylvania river valley and shared a long history with Lycoming, 1977 also saw the Arrow get a Continental engine option. With the turbocharged 200-hp Continental TSIO-360-T, the Arrow became the PA-28R-201T Turbo Arrow III. In 1979 dubious Detroit-styling advantages of the Tomahawk and Lance T-tail were added to the PA-28RT-201 Arrow IV and the PA-28RT-201T Turbo Arrow IV.

Piper, hit with the twin curses of a depression in the general aviation industry and conglomerate ownership, inexplicably dropped the highly reliable Lycoming-engined Arrow IV in 1982, and kept the less reliable Turbo Arrow IV in limited production. Manufacturing of the Cherokee line had all but ceased by 1986. But in 1988, Piper's eventually ill-fated shining knight, M. Stuart Millar, brought back the Arrow in his revitalized line. Being a man who listened to his customers rather than telling them what they'll take or else, Millar junked the T-tail and brought back what had been called the Arrow III and the Turbo Arrow III. With his innate common sense, he now just called them the Arrow and the Turbo Arrow. The new Arrows had an improved instrument panel with the engine instruments brought up from low on the panel where they had resided for years to a spot just to the left of the radios. Another big plus was a standard backup electric vacuum pump. Arrow and Turbo Arrow production ceased with the bankruptcy of Piper in 1991.

New Piper would put the Arrow, but not the Turbo Arrow, back into production in the late 1990s. New Piper's Web site listed the Arrow as a "Trainer," not a "Personal" aircraft, indicating that their emphasis for the Arrow was on large flight schools and not on private owners. Surprisingly, post-2000 era New Piper Arrows did not have the round intake LoPresti cowls which had been applied to the Archer III, the Saratoga IIs, and the Seneca V twins. It also was not cursed with the Archer III and Saratoga II windshield-shrinking overhead switch panel. With Cessna not producing any single engine retractables, and with the sleek new Cirrus, Diamond, and Lancair aircraft all being fixed-gear singles, the Arrow was just about the last affordable single left. (If one could call any of the absurdly high new aircraft prices of the post-2000 era "affordable.") But oddly enough, given the lack of competition from Cessna, in the post-2000 era New Piper seemingly was downplaying the Arrow and not marketing it as a personal aircraft. Piper's "Step-Up" program advertised the Archer III as the entry level personal aircraft, and then showed the new 6X as the next step up to the Saratoga, the Seneca V, the Mirage, and the Meridian. The Arrow and the Warrior were nowhere to be seen in advertising appearing in magazines like *Flying* and *AOPA Pilot*.

If the Cessna Skyhawk is "everyone's fixed-gear four-seater," the Arrow has to be "everyone's single-engine retrac." An easy step upward from the Cherokee 180/181 or even from the Warrior, the Arrow introduced an automatic landing extension mechanism which vastly reduces the possibility of gear-up landings. Using an auxiliary pitot tube mounted on the left fuselage just behind the pilot and a switch on the throttle, the typical older Arrow would automatically lower the gear on any aircraft going slower than about 105 mph with power reduced or 85 mph with power being applied. There is an override switch to allow immediate retracting of the gear for short-field takeoffs and to allow the glide to be extended in case of engine failure. In case of engine failure, you have to be quick to override the gear, or it will drop and vastly reduce your gliding distance. In late 1987, conglomerate Piper's lawyers sent out letters to all Arrow owners insisting that this magnificent safety system be disabled because of the liabilities resulting from this eventuality. Fortunately, Millar ended this foolishness for owners of existing Arrows when he bought Piper, and threw out the unpopular service letter. But strangely enough, new Arrows available in 1990, or the ones reintroduced by New Piper in the late 1990s, did not come with the excellent automatic gear extension mechanism. If you want to be saved from extravagant insurance premiums as well as from the embarrassment of a gear-up landing, you'll have to buy an Arrow built before the mid-1980s.

The Arrows fly like what they are—slightly bigger and heavier and definitely faster Cherokees and Warriors. Their overall characteristics definitely show their family background, but the Cherokee pilot making the transition should be prepared for a faster sink rate and approach speed and a nose-heavy feel compared to fixed-gear Cherokee-series aircraft. The constant-speed prop helps provide a smoothness that is missing in the lesser brethren. The Arrow II is probably the nicest of the Arrows, larger and more comfortable than the earlier models, and seemingly a little faster and just a little more solid feeling than the Warrior-winged IIIs and IVs. The IV's T-tail is nice in the air, but definitely nose heavy on takeoff and landing.

The Arrow is one of the most reliable retractables around, but it has had some problems. Piper Service Bulletin 886 applies, so be sure your dream Arrow has no damage and a documented normal service history, or your insurance company may insist that you have the wings pulled for inspections within 50 hours of the time you buy it and every 800 hours thereafter. Engines have also been a problem in the Arrow, although most engine problems should have been fixed by now for any well-maintained Arrow. A 1971 AD called for inspection of the Lycoming IO-360 for shifting crankcase bearings, and it took longer bearing dowels added in 1971 and a redesigned camshaft in 1973 to bring the TBO up from 1,200 hours to its present value of 1,800 hours. Be sure the engine of any 1969-to-1973 200-hp Arrow you're looking at has all the latest upgrades.

The TSIO-360 Continental has had a history of even more serious problems. Early models had crankshaft failure problems, resulting in a modification by Continental in 1979 to strengthen the crankshaft. Other problems included a higher-than-normal incidence of connecting rod failures, turbocharger housing cracks, and problems with misfiring and detonation, particularly at higher altitudes. Pressurized magnetos and an intercooler are definitely desirable add-ons to the Turbo Arrows. With an intercooler, pressurized mags, and a newly majored engine incorporating all of the Continental

Table 11.9. PA-28R-201 Arrow III

Specifications	
Wingspan	35 ft 5 in
Length	24 ft 8 in
Gross weight, normal category	2,750 lb
Empty weight	1,585 lb
Useful load	1,165 lb
Useful load, full fuel	733 lb
Fuel capacity, standard tanks	77 gal (72 usable)
Performance	
Cruise speed, 75% power, best altitude	164.5 mph
Fuel consumption, 75% power	10 gph
Range 45-min reserve, 75% power	1,061 mi
Sea level rate of climb	831 fpm
Service ceiling	16,200 ft
Stall, clean	72.5 mph
Stall, full flaps	65.5 mph
Takeoff over a 50-foot obstacle	1,600 ft
Landing over a 50-foot obstacle	1,525 ft

beef-ups, the Turbo Arrows can be good airplanes. Just stay away from unmodified early models.

Like the rest of their Cherokee and Warrior kin, the Arrows are nice, solid, respectable airplanes. Not necessarily the best in their class in any individual category, but one of the nicest all-around packages available.

Beechcraft 33, 35, and 36 Bonanzas

Bonanza. The very name calls to mind an image of aerial elegance and performance. The Cadillac of airplanes, choice of doctors and lawyers. No general aviation airplane was so far ahead of its time. None ever spawned such a large and successful family (although the more modest Cherokee comes close). But no other general aviation airplane has a history so full of intrigue, with the alleged cover-up of a fatal flaw that eventually marked the end of the line for the V-tail beauty that started it all, leaving its straight-tailed siblings to carry on a line that has surpassed 50 years of uninterrupted production.

With a tail reportedly inspired by a Polish aviation magazine, the sleek V-tail Model 35 first flew on December 22, 1945, and was first made available to the public in 1947. It offered a performance break-through at a time when the standard light airplane was a ragwing taildragger. Only the relatively slow and ponderous Navion could claim to offer similar advances in postwar technology. Beech Aircraft Corporation had produced a line that rewrote general aviation history, generating a whole family of high-performance singles and twins, as well as military trainers. The not-so-lowly 165-hp Bonanza would ultimately become a 285-hp airplane itself, and would lead to the large six-place Model 36. A Twin Bonanza would evolve into a sleeker Baron which would grow all the way up to a pressurized, turbocharged Model 58P. With a tandem cockpit, it would become the Air Force and Navy T-34 basic trainer, ultimately acquiring a turboprop engine to become the T-34C for training Navy cadets into the late 1990s.

The 1947 Bonanza came with polished aluminum, a 165-hp Continental engine, and 175-mph speed. It also came with serious weaknesses in the wings, and 16 structural failures in two years caused Beech to beef up the wing structure in the 1949 Model A35. The A35 also offered a steerable nosewheel and an exterior paint option. The C35, introduced in 1951, came with a 185-hp engine. In a much more critical change, it was also the first V-tail Bonanza with a larger tail intended to enhance stability. The growth was all forward of the main spar, which would result in a serious weakness for all succeeding V-Bonanzas. The E35 offered a 225-hp engine in 1954, with the engine becoming standard with the G35 two years later. The 1957 H35 came with a further beef-up to wing, tail, and fuselage structures, as well as an optional 240-hp O-470-G engine. The 1958 J35 was the first with a fuel-injected IO-470. The 1959 K35 had larger 50-gallon standard, 70-gallon optional fuel tanks. The 1961 N35 came with a 260-hp engine and optional 80-gallon fuel tanks, and introduced the signature "Ram's horn" control wheel. The 1964 S35 brought maturity to the line. It came with a longer cabin, moving the aft bulkhead back 19 inches, adding a third side window, and allowing fifth and sixth seats. To move the bigger bird came a big IO-520 285-hp Continental engine. A turbocharged engine was available from 1968 to 1970, and 79 V35TCs were built during that period. The last significant change came with the last-of-the-line V35B, which offered baffled antislosh fuel tanks to combat unporting problems which occurred during slips, skids, or takeoffs after rapid turns onto the runway.

The V35B was discontinued after the V-tail's 35th birthday in 1982. In all, 10,403 had been built. Though Beech never admitted it, an article in *Aviation Consumer* magazine blew the lid off of an apparent 20-year cover-up of a fatal flaw in the plane's V-tail. It is likely that this is what led to the aircraft's termination. In February 1980, *Aviation Consumer* published a detailed 12-page article describing how weaknesses in the Bonanza's tail had probably contributed to more than 200 in-flight fatal airframe failure crashes.

The article claimed that the CAA and its successor, the FAA, knew of the problem and had not pressured Beech to fix it. Even after the publication of the article, Beech continued to insist that the crashes were due to pilots flying the aircraft beyond its design limits, and not due to an aircraft flaw. Much to their discredit, *Flying* and the *AOPA Pilot* magazines generally supported Beech in its defense of the airplane's integrity. (*Flying*'s May 1980 issue included a 7-page testimonial to the aircraft, and the *AOPA Pilot* in a January 1981 issue concluded that the *Aviation Consumer* claims were "much ado about nothing"!)

The problem as described by *Aviation Consumer* in the 1980 article and in later articles was one in which the unsupported stabilizer leading edge, in severe turbulence, would begin to twist, leading to a complete failure of the tail. *Aviation Consumer* supported its position with photographs, quotes from accident investigators' reports, and even computer-generated drawings of what a typical failure would look like. Perhaps most telling, though, was a comparison of Model 35 statistics with those of the Model 33. Despite being identical from the tail forward, the Model 33 had almost no in-flight airframe failure accidents attributed to it, compared with more than 200 for the Model 35. More V-tails had been built than straight-tails, but the comparison was still undeniably striking.

Figure 11.7. The Model 35 Bonanza: A wonderful airplane—after they fixed the tail! (Courtesy Beech Aircraft Corporation)

Despite Beech's denials, the article had its impact. The value of the V-tails compared to the 33s plummeted, and in 1982 Beech terminated production of the line. Mike Smith, a Bonanza specialist, began offering tail-strengthening kits over Beech's objections that they weren't necessary, and cautious V-tail owners quickly started installing them.

But the story wasn't over. *Aviation Consumer*'s embattled reputation was supported by a 1983 incident. A Bonanza pilot approaching Tucson in VFR conditions hit wake turbulence from a 727, and nearly crashed before regaining control of his plane and landing safely. Investigation of the aircraft on the ground showed the first stages of tail failure nearly identical to that described in the 1980 *Aviation Consumer* article. Amazingly, the FAA was prepared to turn over the tail of the aircraft to Beech for "destructive testing" following investigation of the incident by the NTSB! Fortunately for truth, justice, and the American way, a slipup between the NTSB and the FAA resulted in the bent tail pieces being returned to the owner. The owner promptly turned them over to Mike Smith, who safeguarded them as further evidence that his mod was necessary.

The issue was finally laid to rest in 1984 and 1985. A reasonable and impartial new FAA Administrator, Donald Engen, commissioned a Department of Transportation study to settle the issue. The exhaustive study identified possible airframe failure modes which could occur without warning within the normally permissible airspeed envelope with severe gust encounters or unusual control movements. Beech came out with a service bulletin and a tail strengthening fix, and the FAA issued an AD. In what was probably an act of spite, Beech refused to accept the Mike Smith mod as equal to its own, forcing some owners to add the Beech mod to the Smith mod.

It is a shame that Beech hasn't resumed production of this otherwise excellent airplane. Apparently they never learned to gracefully admit that they were wrong.

The Model 33 straight-tail Bonanza was introduced in 1960 as the Debonair. It was a cut-rate version (225-hp compared to the 1960 Bonanza's 250 and paint as an added cost option only) intended to offer a lower-cost alternative as Beech's answer to the cheaper and very competitive Piper Comanches and Cessna 210s. It was not a great success, and Beech began adding "real Bonanza" features. The 1961 A33 got paint, a small third fuselage window, and a 100-pound increase in gross weight. The 1962 B33 got 74-gallon Bonanza fuel tanks replacing smaller 63-gallon ones. The 1965 C33 brought a larger third window and other small changes. The year 1966 brought a big change: the C33A with the optional IO-520 285-hp engine. In 1968, Beech decided the gap was closed, and the E33, E33A, and the aerobatic E33C were now "straight-tail Bonanzas." The F33, introduced in 1969, brought full commonality with the V35 (forward of the tail, of course). In 1971, the 225-hp engine disappeared, leaving the F33A. One last attempt was made in 1972 and 1973 to bring out a cut-rate model, the 260-hp G33. With the demise of the V-tail, ironically enough, the former poor little brother Debonair had become the surviving high-status F33A Bonanza. According to the American Bonanza Society, the last new F33As were built in 1994, although some remaining unsold after 1994 were sold as 1995 models.

The big-brother Model 36, another straight-tail variant, was added to the line in 1968. It had the same 285-hp engine as the V35, but it had a 10-inch fuselage extension which not only made it an honest 6-seater but also improved the V35's problems with the aft c.g. limit when fully loaded and double rear doors to make full loading easy. Changes were few. The A36 in 1970 brought the popular club seating option, which provides more-than-ample leg room but allows little room for baggage if all six seats are filled. A 300-hp turbocharged A36TC was introduced in 1979. In 1982, the B36TC brought longer wings with their weird leading edge vortex generators, and larger fuel tanks, for greatly improved high-altitude performance. In 1984, the A36 got an increase to 300 horsepower with the Continental IO-550 engine. Both the A36 and B36TC got new-world instrument panels (which the F33A still didn't have entering the 1990s) with individual control wheels replacing the massive "throw-over" or even more massive two-wheels-on-a-huge-bar control system on all older and smaller Bonanzas. Another important change was standardizing throttle, prop, and mixture controls as well as flap and gear switches to the same arrangement used by everybody else. (Again, the F33A did not share in the change.)

In 1989, Teledyne Continental Motors announced a retrofit program for Model 36 Bonanzas, offering a liquid-cooled, turbocharged T-550 Voyager engine. Benefits claimed for the 350-hp engine modification include a 20-knot increase in airspeed and a 2,000 hour TBO.

Beechcraft was bought by Raytheon in 1980. In the succeeding years, Raytheon executives in their arrogance and shortsightedness began phasing out the legendary Beechcraft name, effectively throwing away decades of hard-earned goodwill. At least when you go to the Raytheon Aircraft Web site (www.raytheonaircraft.com) you have to click on "Beechcraft" for information on the A36. Unlike Cessna and New Piper and Cirrus, Raytheon Aircraft won't quote prices on the Web site, but a search of dealers on the Internet showed a price of $650,000 for a 2003 A36.

In September 2003 the CEO of the parent Raytheon Company announced that "Raytheon Aircraft" (notice he didn't say "Beechcraft") was for sale. Time will tell whether this will mean a new beginning for Beechcraft or its demise.

In the 1990s, a company named General Aviation Modifications, Inc. (www.gami.com) came out with a small but significant improvement to that Bonanza owners should be sure to have on their IO-520s and IO-550s. GAMI produces precision calibrated fuel injectors (GAMIjectors) that are engineered to provide a uniform fuel/air ratio to all engine cylinders. Reported results are outstanding and include reduced cylinder head temperatures, reduced fuel consumption, and smoother engine operation.

The flight characteristics of the V-tail 35s and the straight-tail 33s are some of the sweetest of any airplane in the air. This is the Mercedes of light airplanes—smooth, well coordinated, silkily responsive, an airplane that

Figure 11.8. The F33A: One of the sweetest flying and most comfortable airplanes around. (Courtesy Beech Aircraft Corporation)

seems to respond almost to the pilot's thoughts. It is spacious, comfortable, and has almost 200-mph cruising speeds adding to the top-of-the-line reputation. (For years, Beechcraft used to claim that the F33 had a 200-mph top speed and claimed that the V35 had a 203-mph top speed, a 3-mph "advertising advantage" that disappeared just before they quit building the V35. By 1980 they were claiming 170 knots for both!) Takeoff and landing characteristics are some of the nicest and most predictable in any airplane flying.

The delightful characteristics come with a price, though. This is not a dynamically stable airplane, and if you don't pay attention the plane will smoothly roll into a bank that could become a spiral. Its slickness can also make it pick up speed almost too quickly in any kind of a nose-down attitude, and pilot inattention is what Beech used to try to blame Bonanza crashes on before the truth came out about the V-tail. For instrument work, a reliable autopilot is a good companion in this airplane. Stalls are relatively sharp breaking, but readily recoverable with proper technique. In rough air, the short-body Bonanzas have a characteristic tail-wagging tendency which can make rear-seat passengers look for the sick sacks. For some reason, the V-tails seem to be a little worse than the straight tails for this characteristic. (Yaw dampers are an available and worthwhile option.) The V-tails also have to be watched more carefully for weight and balance problems. It is very easy to exceed aft c.g. limits in a V-tail, making the sensitive birds even more sensitive in pitch (another excuse Beech used to give for pilots losing it).

You also sit high in the Bonanzas, so if you like the sports car-like feel of Mooneys or Pipers you may not like the Bonanzas. The massive throw-over or "two-wheels-on-a-huge-bar" control system also blocks the pilot's view of some instruments and gauges. By the standards of airplanes built after 2000, the instrument panels of 33 and 35 series Bonanzas look almost ancient.

While the big-brother 36 is still a nice smooth-flying airplane, nobody confuses it for an aerial sports car like the smaller Bonanzas. It's fast and very comfortable, particularly with the club seating for the passengers, but it is a big and heavy airplane. Because of its greater size, it is a better and more stable instrument platform with or without an autopilot. For high-speed, high-altitude cruising, the long-wing B36TC tends to be a better choice than the shorter-winged A36 or A36TC.

All Bonanzas except for post-1984 36s have one version or another of the strange and different Bonanza instrument panel and control wheel. A nice-feeling control wheel is mounted on an incredibly massive "throw-over" beam mounted to the center of the panel in standard Bonanzas. Since it is a bit dicey to show your other half how to fly the airplane with only one control wheel, and since the FAA tends to frown on checkrides with the only

controls on your side, many Bonanza owners have opted for a doubly massive center-mounted beam with two nice-feeling control wheels on it. A fine
touch, but it adds to the number of right side knobs, dials, and switches the
pilot can't see all that well anyway. Another problem with most Bonanzas is
that engine controls and gear and flap controls are not arranged according
to "industry standard." Bonanzas have a higher-than-average incidence of
gear-up landings, possibly due to pilots retracting the gear when they
thought they were retracting the flaps. Early Model 33 and A33 Debonairs
with optional fuel tanks also had a tricky fuel gauge system which only read
one tank at a time.

The hinged upper cowling doors are another nice touch on all Bonanzas,
particularly appreciated during preflight or oil changes—just like Cherokee
140s and Warriors, only with that strong solid feel of a Beechcraft.

Being Beech (Raytheon) airplanes, the Bonanzas are rugged and solid
and will be straightforward to maintain. Expect genuine Beechcraft
(Raytheon) parts to be very expensive, even by general aviation's normally
inflated standards. Older Bonanzas and Debonairs with the IO-470, 225-hp
engines are probably the most reliable if properly maintained and if the STC
to use autogas has been maintained. The Continental IO-520 engine with
the front-mounted alternator used in Bonanzas has long had a reputation for
developing crankcase cracks. Switching to heavy case versions of the
crankcase lessened but did not fully eliminate the problem. Factory-reman-
ufactured engines are popular with late-model Bonanza owners, because the
Continental factory has a good warranty policy if your engine develops
cracks. In the mid-1980s, there was also a rash of problems with cylinder
cracks on IO-520 engines.

Other unusual problem areas to look for, primarily in older Bonanzas
and Debonairs, are Goodyear fuel cells and Goodyear brakes. Goodyear
tanks in older airplanes are more susceptible to cracking than Uniroyal bladders, and replacement is expensive. Goodyear brakes are a maintenance hassle, and replacement with Clevelands is recommended. Fortunately, the pas-
sage of time will tend to cull out airplanes still cursed with Goodyear fuel
tanks and brakes.

Interested in a Bonanza? It's legendary as one of the fastest, sweetest-fly-
ing, and most comfortable airplanes around. Except for the earliest Model
35s with the weak wings and the problems with unmodified pre-AD V-tails,
the Bonanza's safety record is actually very good. Don't expect a Bonanza to
be a bargain, though, particularly if you buy one any newer than 25 years
old. The Continental IO-520 engine is a nice, powerful, smooth-running
engine, but if you want an engine that will make it to a long TBO, you'll
probably have to buy a Lycoming-powered Mooney or Piper. If you're willing to sacrifice a little speed for economy and better reliability, an older

Table 11.10. 1981 Beechcraft V35B Bonanza, 1985 F33A Bonanza, and 1989 A36 Bonanza (300 hp)

	V35B Bonanza	F33A Bonanza	A36 Bonanza (300 hp)
Specifications			
Wingspan	33 ft 6 in	33 ft 6 in	33 ft 6 in
Length	26 ft 5 in	26 ft 8 in	27 ft 6 in
Gross weight, normal category	3,412 lb	3,412 lb	3,663 lb
Empty weight	2,117 lb	2,125 lb	2,247 lb
Useful load	1,295 lb	1,287 lb	1,416 lb
Useful load, full fuel	815 lb	807 lb	936 lb
Fuel capacity, standard tanks	80 gal (74 usable)	80 gal (74 usable)	80 gal (74 usable)
Performance			
Cruise speed, 75% power, best altitude	197 mph	197 mph	204 mph
Fuel consumption, 75% power	14.4 gph	14.4 gph	17 gph
Range 45-min reserve, 75% power	864 mi	864 mi	753 mi
Sea level rate of climb	1,167 fpm	1,167 fpm	1,208 fpm
Service ceiling	17,858 ft	17,858 ft	18,500 ft
Stall, clean	74 mph	74 mph	79 mph
Stall, full flaps	59 mph	59 mph	68 mph
Takeoff over a 50-foot obstacle	1,769 ft	1,769 ft	2,100 ft
Landing over a 50-foot obstacle	1,324 ft	1,324 ft	1,450 ft

Figure 11.9. The A36 is like flying a big high-flying Mercedes station wagon. (Courtesy Beech Aircraft Corporation)

Bonanza or Debonair with the 225-hp engine burning autogas might also be the answer.

V-tails with the tail AD complied with were a good deal in the 1980s, when *Aviation Consumer* let the truth be known about their checkered past. Keep an eye out for a good Model 35. You might still find a bargain in a V-tail Bonanza that you won't be able to find in a straight-tail. Just make sure the AD has been done right and watch your weight and balance.

And unless you want to buy a new A36, you don't have to call them "Raytheons."

Mooney

The long history of the Mooney really is best told as two separate tales: Pre-201 and Post-201. The Pre-201 story is one of a good and fast but out-of-the-mainstream and often cramped retractable single produced by a marginally successful company owned by a string of owners. The Post-201 story is one of the odd cult airplane being modified by a general aviation hero, built by a company with a policy of integrity, and becoming a much-desired industry standard for blazing single-engine speed and reliability at a time when the old giants of the industry were giving up and leaving the playing field. Unfortunately, in the 1990s and into the new millennium, Mooney again became a marginally successful company owned by a string of owners.

The Mooney story begins in 1948 with expert aircraft designer Al Mooney first introducing his trademark vertical tail with the forward-swept rudder on an odd little retractable single-seater with wooden wings and tail called the M18 Mooney Mite. The first four-seat M20, also a retractable with wooden wings and tail and powered by a 145-hp Continental engine, was certificated in 1953. The M20 entered production in 1955 with a 150-hp Lycoming engine. (All production Mooneys were Lycoming powered until the introduction of the 231 in 1979.) Al Mooney exited the picture early in 1957, and the new owners put a 180-hp Lycoming in the M20A in 1958.

The year 1960 saw the introduction of the first all-metal Mooney, the M20B, and a dizzying array of models, names, and numbers would appear and disappear through the '60s, early '70s, and on into the new millennium. The M20C, known as the Mark 21 and the Ranger, was an M20B with an increase in gross weight and with electric, instead of manual, flaps. The M20D Master was an oddity, a fixed-gear Mooney intended as a trainer. Mooney offered a retrofit kit to convert the M20D back (up?) to an M20C, and any existing fixed-gear M20Ds are almost museum-piece rarities.

The Pre-201-era speedster, the 200-hp M20E, was introduced in 1964. Short-bodied and the fastest of the Pre-201 Mooneys, it was in and out of production until 1975, and bore the names Super 21 and Chaparral. In 1965, Mooney added the Brittain "Positive Control" wing leveler to enhance spiral stability. Electric landing gear to replace the manual gear handle was first offered in 1966 and became standard in 1969.

Mooney finally got tired of its reputation for building airplanes you wore in 1967 when it brought out the M20F Executive with a cabin 10 inches longer than earlier Mooneys. The Executive stayed in production until 1977, when it was replaced by the 201. A 180-hp long-cabin M20G Statesman came out in 1968, but it was a slow slug by Mooney standards and only stayed in production three years.

The years 1969 to 1973 were trying times for Mooney. An attempt "ahead of its time" to develop a pressurized single resulted in the overly large, overly heavy, and overly expensive M22. Only 28 were ever built, and a bankrupt Mooney soon sold out to American Electronics Laboratories, who then sold the line to Butler Aviation. Butler Aviation intended to integrate the fast Mooneys into a line with the even faster Aerostar twins. It didn't work out, but Butler produced Mooneys with strange "beak" or "bullet" protuberances sticking forward from the top of the vertical stabilizer, and odd names like 200, 201, and 220 Aerostars for the Ranger, Chaparral, and Executive. Production ceased in 1971, and did not resume until late 1973 when Republic Steel bought the line.

Oddly enough for a company with no aviation experience, Republic's ownership resulted in a total revitalization of Mooney and its aircraft line. Republic not only restarted production of the Mooney line, they also hired

Table 11.11. Mooney M20C Ranger, M20J 201 (MSE), M20K 252 (TSE), M20L PFM, M20M TLS

	M20C Ranger (180-hp Lycoming O-360-A1D)	M20J 201 (MSE) (200-hp Lycoming IO-360-A3B6D)	M20K 252 (TSE) (210-hp Continental ISIO-360-MB1)	M20L PFM (217-hp Porsche PFM 3200-NO3)	M20M TLS (270-hp Lycoming TIO-540-AF1A)
Specifications					
Wingspan	35 ft	36 ft 1 in	36 ft 1 in	36 ft 1 in	36 ft 1 in
Length	23 ft 3 in	24 ft 8 in	25 ft 5 in	26 ft 9 in	24 ft 10 in
Gross weight, normal category	2,575 lb	2,740 lb	2,900 lb	2,900 lb	3,200 lb
Empty weight	1,525 lb	1,671 lb	1,830 lb	2,033 lb	2,012 lb
Useful load	1,050 lb	1,069 lb	1,070 lb	867 lb	1,188 lb
Useful load, full fuel	738 lb	685 lb	614 lb	504 lb	648 lb
Fuel capacity, standard tanks	52 gal	66.5 gal (64 usable)	79 gal (76 usable)	66.5 gal (60.5 usable)	96 gal (90 usable)
Performance					
Cruise speed, 75% power, best altitude	190 mph	195 mph	234 mph	186 mph	259 mph
Fuel consumption, 75% power	10 gph	10.8 gph	12.7 gph	11.1 gph	11.1 gph
Range 45-min reserve, 75% power	845 mi	1,010 mi	1,225 mi	874 mi	921 mi
Sea level rate of climb	800 fpm	1,025 fpm	1,080 fpm	1,050 fpm	1,230 fpm
Service ceiling	17,500 ft	18,800 ft	28,000 ft	19,300 ft	25,000 ft
Stall, clean	N/A	73 mph	71 mph	74 mph	75.5 mph
Stall, full flaps	57 mph	64 mph	65 mph	66 mph	70 mph
Takeoff over a 50-foot obstacle	1,250 ft	1,770 ft	2,000 ft	2,510	N/A
Landing over a 50-foot obstacle	1,550 ft	1,990 ft	2,280 ft	1,900 ft	N/A

the sharpest general aviation design genius alive to make the fast airplanes even faster. Roy LoPresti had taken the mediocre American Aviation four-seat Traveler and turned it into the blazingly fast Tiger and Cheetah. The Mooney Executive was about to undergo an equally amazing transformation at his hands and emerge as the 201 and then the turbocharged 231.

The M20J emerged in 1976 with a comprehensive drag reduction program including a tighter and sleeker cowl covering a 200-hp Lycoming IO-360, a new windshield, improved landing gear doors, and a laundry list of small items that added up. Twenty-one mph faster than the Executive, it had a top speed of 201 mph that would give it its name. In 1978, an even bigger and faster Mooney would emerge with a 210-hp turbocharged Continental TSIO-360 engine. It had a top speed of 231 mph. The 201 was a total and unqualified success. The 231 was not, with a hot-running engine having detonation problems at high altitude.

Republic Steel and parent conglomerate LTV ran into severe financial problems in the mid-1980s, and Mooney ended up being sold to a Frenchman, Alexandre Couvelaire. Fortunately, Monsieur Couvelaire recognized the quality of the flying gems he had purchased, and continued to improve the line. The production line remained in Kerrville, Texas. Mooney corrected a mistake it had made in not giving the 231 an intercooler for its turbocharger. In late 1985 the improved 252 came out with an intercooler and a variable wastegate on its improved Continental TSIO-360-MB1, as well as a 28-volt electrical system with a 70-amp alternator and a standby vacuum system standard. In 1986, the 201 was upgraded to the 205 with a 28-volt electrical system, improved landing gear doors for even more speed, and 252-style curved windows. Somehow it disappeared, though. In 1989 Mooney ads showed a 205 look-alike but called it the 201.

For an airplane which had always been hard to slow down for fast descents from altitude or when entering the pattern, an excellent option was first offered in the mid-1980s. This was a scissorlike set of wing-mounted speedbrakes developed by Precise Flight. With a touch of a button, it was now possible to descend from altitude at a descent rate of 2,000 fpm and still keep engine power up enough to avoid shock-cooling the engine.

Late 1987 saw the introduction of a really different Mooney. The Mooney PFM was a foot longer and had a Porsche variant of sports car engines. It was a work of art with a spacious custom cabin designed by Porsche designers, with exterior paint matching the interior trim. The engine and its controls were "the wave of the future." Many have complained that the old individual throttle, prop, and mixture controls are archaic in an age of computerized electronic ignitions in cars. Mooney and Porsche did something about it. This plane came with a single power quadrant which took the place of throttle, prop, and mixture controls in a "normal" airplane. It also was cooled with a continuously running, dual belt-driven fan running at speeds proportional to engine RPM. This means that if you needed to make a rapid descent, you did not have to worry about shock-cooling the engine.

Unfortunately, despite the engine's rating of 217 horsepower, the aircraft was not as fast as the Mooney 201. It also came with a very high price. Mooney hoped to attract the rich yuppies who would think nothing of paying $60,000 for a true state-of-the-art performance automobile. Mooney's marketing strategy also offered a guarantee that unscheduled engine maintenance would be limited to $2,500 and a guaranteed $14,500 overhaul exchange price. But it was asking a lot to think that you'd elect to take the PFM at nearly $200,000 when the same money might buy a nice, new (and slightly faster) 201 and the Porsche Targa! The experiment with sexy but slow Mooneys came to an end in early 1991.

Mooney remedied the big PFM's lack of speed with yet another variant: the 1989 M20M TLS. TLS, by the way, stood for "Turbo Lycoming Sabre"! In a real departure for a company known for getting lots of speed from small fuselages and modest engines, this one had the PFM's long fuselage and a 270-hp, six-cylinder, turbocharged, intercooled brute of a Lycoming TIO-540 up front driving a three-blade McCauley propeller. And this sucker was fast! Its max cruise airspeed was over 250 mph. It also came with speed-brakes as standard equipment to allow rapid descents from cruising altitude without destroying the traditionally aircooled engine.

In late 1989, Mooney also took a short-lived step into the training aircraft market, introducing a simplified 201 as the AT advanced instrument training aircraft. The AT came with a basic but fully capable King avionics package, a four-seat intercom system to allow students in the back seats to learn by observing when they aren't flying, and other small modifications. In 1990, Mooney decided it liked three-letter initials. The big change that year

Figure 11.10. The Mooney 201: Transformed by LoPresti's genius. (Courtesy Mooney Aircraft Corporation)

was to switch the designation of the 201 to MSE, the 252 to TSE, and the advanced trainer (AT) to ATS.

In 1994, Mooney apparently gave up on the three-letter initials, bringing out the new M20R Ovation using the PFM and TLS long fuselage. It was a 220-mph airplane powered by a non-turbocharged 280-hp Continental IO-550 driving a three-blade prop. In 1997 the Encore was introduced, a 252 upgrade with 10 additional horsepower and 230 pounds more useful load. And the 201 then MSE became the Allegro.

In what would turn out to be a financial disaster, in 1997 Paul Dopp and AVAQ Partners bought Mooney. In 1998 Dopp named his son company president. They decided to phase out the short-fuselage Allegro (201) and Encore (252). A 244-hp version of the IO-550 was installed in the long fuselage to create the 200-mph "entry level" Eagle as a replacement for the Allegro, at a not-so-entry-level price of nearly $325,000.

With the Dopps trying to sell their planes at outrageously high prices even in the excessively priced late 1990s market, Mooney was in deep trouble in 2001 and went into bankruptcy and ceased production. Production resumed under new management at the Mooney Airplane Company when the company exited bankruptcy in 2003. The 2003 line consisted of a stripped-down Ovation selling for around $300,000, an Ovation II DX with a full line of Garmin avionics for $385,000, and the Bravo DX for $435,000. (These are "reduced" prices. Pre-bankruptcy prices had been $445,000 for the Ovation II and $505,000 for the TLS Bravo, which may be why they didn't sell very many.) TKS deicing is offered as a $40,000 option. Future success is not assured with competitors like the baseline IFR Cirrus SR22 selling for around $315,000 and the Lancair 350 selling for $370,000. Further complicating matters was shabby treatment in the bankruptcy courts of pre-2001 owners, with warranty claims being dismissed. Would you buy an airplane costing well over a quarter of a million dollars from a shaky company that had shrugged off serious warranty problems encountered by prior Mooney buyers who had paid similarly obscene amounts of money?

The Mooneys are known as very fast and very efficient transportation machines. Mooney owners brag about how fast they got there and how few gallons of gas it took to get there. There's nothing wrong with the way a Mooney flies, but its handling doesn't inspire Bonanza-like raves. The yoke connects with the ailerons through pushrods, so response is crisp. Even so, the roll rate is nothing to write home about. The long, narrow Mooney wing and marginally effective flaps make steep short-field takeoffs difficult. The long wing gives the Mooney a reputation as a floater for any pilot who brings one in carrying a little extra airspeed. The long wing also makes the

Figure 11.11. The Mooney PFM is indisputably "the Porsche of light aircraft"! (Courtesy Mooney Aircraft Corporation)

airplanes difficult to slow down, and rapid descents from altitude are not easy to accomplish without shock-cooling the engine. Later models with speedbrakes are a good investment for the serious traveler, both for controlled descents from high altitude and for adding to landing controllability.

Make sure you check your weight and balance charts in a Mooney. None of the Mooneys are "fill the tanks and all of the seats" airplanes, and most (even the 252/TSE and the PFM) can handle only the pilot and one passenger on a long-distance, full-tanks flight. Loading the baggage can be a chore due to an oddity common to the whole Mooney line, including the big-bodied PFMs, TLSs, and Ovations. The baggage door is on the top half of the fuselage, meaning bags have to be hefted up to get them in and out.

Early Mooneys had some interesting quirks. The 1965-to-1975 vintage Mooneys with the PC wing-leveler were very difficult to turn unless one held down the button on the yoke and disengaged the wing leveler. Pilots often flew with big rubber bands holding the button down. Many pilots liked the manual landing gear for its simplicity, reliability, and sure feel. But it took either technique or a weightlifter's right arm to retract the gear. Retracting the gear before the airspeed built up following takeoff helped. By 1969, however, the manual landing gear was phased out.

On the ground, the rubber discs that act as shock absorbers in the landing gear can give a bumpy ride. Watch those long wings, too, while taxiing down narrow rows of parked planes or near snow banks. And be careful of the prop. The low-slung Mooney is a fabulous transportation machine operating off of paved surfaces, but anyone who looks at the minimal prop clearance and tries a true soft-field landing in a Mooney is a little soft up top already.

With the exception of the newer long-body PFMs, TLSs, and Ovations, most Mooneys range from compact to downright claustrophobic. The early short fuselage Mark 21s, Rangers, Super 21s, and Chaparrals had almost no rear seat legroom unless the front seats were all the way forward on their tracks. You sort of wore early Mooneys, sitting with your legs under the panel. The Executive brought a reasonably sized fuselage, and 201s (MSEs/Allegros), 231s, and 252s (TSEs/Encores) all have a reasonable amount of space. The PFMs, TLSs, and Ovations, of course, are downright spacious by Mooney standards.

Lycoming-engined Mooneys have some of the most reliable engines of any line of airplanes flying. If you're buying an early '60s Mooney, make sure the engine has been overhauled with all the modern touches like half-inch valves and improved connecting rods and main bearing dowel pins in the 200-hp versions. With a recent major overhaul or a new engine, you're probably looking at a 2,000 hour TBO, much more than the big Continentals on the Bonanzas and some of the big Cessna singles. Stay away from the 231s and their troublesome Continentals, though, unless the engine has been swapped for the LB model or modified with a Turboplus intercooler.

Don't expect to be popular with any mechanic if you own a Mooney, unless your mechanic is a Mooney specialist. These are tight airplanes allowing precious little room to work behind the instrument panel, in the wings, or under the cowling. Other problems to watch for include leaky fuel tanks in older Mooneys; tube-frame corrosion in 201s, 231s, and 252s; and the curse of the Hartzell prop AD mandating an expensive inspection (and probably repairs) every five years or 1,500 hours.

If you're looking for fast, reliable aerial transportation between civilized fields, and if you're not too much over 6 feet tall, there's probably no better retractable in the air than a Mooney. The best buys of the used Mooneys are undoubtedly the 201s/MSEs, with the 252s/TSEs a good choice for Western flyers looking to tackle the Rockies. You'll be buying an airplane tweaked to as near perfection as anything general aviation produces. If you're over 6 feet and have some extra money, take a look at the PFM, the TLS, and the Ovation. The rare PFM may particularly interest you if you are the type who likes to be unique. With its smooth Porsche engine and single control throttle, this is one of the classiest, smoothest flying airplanes ever built, even if it's not the fastest thing in the air.

Maule MX-7-180 Star Rocket, M-7-235 Super STOL Rocket, and a whole lot more

Interested in a surprisingly good airplane that was originally developed as a home-built, that has great STOL characteristics but a terrible pilot's/owner's handbook, and that has some of the most atrocious names ever hung on a steel-tube and fabric taildragger? If so, you may be in the market for a Maule. Built by a small family-run business in Georgia, these chunky but still sleek, utilitarian airplanes provide an excellent buy for the dollar and can match performance figures with many better known aircraft.

Developed from the 1957 EAA Fly-In prizewinner, four-seat high-performance Bee Dee M-4 (for Belford D. Maule, not Jim Bede), the first production Maule M-4 was sold in 1960. Powered by the same Continental O-300 engine used in Cessna 172s of the same vintage, it was to be the precursor to a confusing line of aircraft with a wide range of engines and some of the oddest names ever to be appended to taildraggers. The odd engines and names of early Maules included 180-hp and 220-hp Franklins and 210-hp Continentals in airplanes with names like Jetasen, Lunar Rocket, Astro Rocket, and Strata Rocket.

Modern 1980s vintage Maules settled on reliable Lycoming 235-hp O-540s and 180-hp O-360s, although even a 420-hp Allison turboprop version called the Starcraft could be had for the right price.

One reason Maule (www.mauleairinc.com) stayed in business, other than sheer spunk and orneriness on the part of old B. D. Maule, was that he priced his aircraft at just slightly over what it cost him to build them. The 1980s Maules were a bargain compared to what few conglomerate-built Cessnas and Pipers were available, and they still were in 2003. At one point in the mid-1980s it was actually possible to buy a 180-hp Maule for less than what Cessna was asking for a 152 trainer! By 2003, more than 2,000 Maules had been built, at the modest production rate of 60 to 70 per year.

A typical late-model Maule airplane is a steel-tube and fabric taildragger airplane with metal wings and a reliable Lycoming engine. The M-5-235C was introduced with a carbureted 235-hp Lycoming in 1977. A M-5-180C with a 180-hp Lycoming was introduced in 1979, and a fuel-injected version of the 235C came in 1981. In 1981, the M-5 was superseded by the M-6, which had a longer wingspan and which introduced flaps with a negative 7 degree (up) setting that was claimed to provide a higher cruise speed.

In late 1983 the M-7 was introduced, with improved ailerons and a stretched cabin with an additional seat. In 1985, the MX-7-180 and MX-7-235 came out with the shorter M-5 wing, M-7 ailerons and fuselage, and the M-6 four-position flaps.

The year 1990 brought a tradition-defying Maule innovation: a tricycle gear MXT-7 version. The tricycle gear Maule is a surprisingly attractive airplane. Most taildragger–to–tricycle gear conversions, like the Tri-Pacer, tend to look a bit weird and ungainly, but the Maule MXT-7 comes with a sleek cowling and a stylish paint scheme that makes it look very nice indeed.

In 2003, one could choose from 20 different models of Maules. One could order an MX or an MT, with the "T"s being 3 inches higher and having a 5-inch longer cargo area. Engine choices included 160-, 180-, 235-, or 260-hp Lycomings, or even the incredible 420-hp Allison turboprop. The M-9-230 was introduced at the EAA AirVenture 2003 with an SMA SR305 230-hp diesel and a price around $200,000 (a price about $55,000 more than a similar gasoline-engined model). Three landing gear choices were available as well. There was the original oleo strut tailwheel gear, aluminum spring steel tailwheel gear, and the tricycle gear model with spring steel main gear and a hydraulic strut nosegear. Standard-equipped new 2003 MX-7-160s cost $105,000. The MT-7-260 Super Rocket cost $171,000, not cheap but a lot less than other new aircraft with similar horsepower.

Maules come with four doors—one for the pilot on the left side and three doors on the right side. Access is excellent, although this doesn't translate into making it easy to get into or out of the Maule's seats. Like a big

Table 11.12. Maule MXT-7-180 Star Rocket and M-7-235 Super STOL Rocket

	MXT-7-180	M-7-235 Super
Specifications		
Wingspan	30 ft 10 in	33 ft 8 in
Length	23 ft 6 in	23 ft 6 in
Gross weight, normal category	2,500 lb	2,500 lb
Empty weight	1,410 lb	1,500 lb
Useful load	1,090 lb	1,000 lb
Useful load, full fuel	730 lb (w/aux)	580 lb
Fuel capacity, standard tanks	40 gal (70 w/aux)	40 gal (70 w/aux)
Performance		
Cruise speed, 75% power, best altitude	140 mph	160 mph
Fuel consumption, 75% power	9.5 gph	12 gph
Range 45-min reserve, 75% power	891 mi	933 mi
Sea level rate of climb	1,200 fpm	2,000 fpm
Service ceiling	15,000 ft	20,000 ft
Stall, clean	N/A	N/A
Stall, full flaps	40 mph	34.5 mph
Takeoff over a 50-foot obstacle	600 ft	600 ft
Landing over a 50-foot obstacle	500 ft	500 ft

Figure 11.12. Maules are good but often overlooked airplanes. (Courtesy Maule Air)

Cub, getting into or out of a Maule can be a gymnastic exercise in the tail-draggers, but one that is not all that difficult once you get used to it. Open the three doors on the right side, and it looks like the whole side of the airplane is wide open (which it practically is). And the back seat easily folds forward and up out of the way for serious cargo hauling.

The Maule instrument panel is basic and utilitarian, with enough space for an IFR radio stack. The door knobs and some of the panel knobs look like they came from the bargain bin at the local hardware store (maybe they did down in Georgia), but rumor has it that if they break, Maule charges appropriately low replacement prices. The money and heft is put where it counts. The middle of new Maule panels looks like a cross between late-model Cherokee and Cessna 182 panels, with Cherokee-like rocker switches and big, solid, no-nonsense vernier-style throttle, prop, and mixture controls.

The Maule fuel system and fuel tank arrangement is a classic "good news, bad news" situation. The good news is that the standard airplane will hold a total of 70 gallons. The bad news is that you can't read the amount of fuel in all four tanks at once or even switch directly to the auxiliary tanks outboard in the wings. Fuel management can be challenging. The 30-gallon auxiliary tanks electrically transfer fuel to the 40-gallon main tanks. If you estimate wrong on your fuel consumption, you may transfer fuel out the overflow vents if you have more fuel in the mains than you thought. Maules are also justly criticized for their fuel selector. The short end of the pointer-shaped selector points toward the tank in use, when common sense tends to tell you that the long end of the selector should do so. The lack of positive selector detents isn't so great, either.

The strong suit of a Maule is its flying characteristics. This is an "honest" airplane, one with a nice feel and lots of built-in safety margin for real pilots. Lazy airplane drivers probably won't like them, though. You have to use a lot of well-coordinated rudder in a Maule to make it give you its best.

Maules are known for phenomenal short-field landing and takeoff perform-ance. Takeoffs and landings into fields of less than 1,000 feet with ground runs of only a couple hundred feet are not unusual.

The big, broad, vertical tail makes caution necessary on crosswind land-ings to avoid groundloops in the typical taildragger Maule. In the air, that big tail comes into its own. There's no fishtailing and no need for a Bonanza-style yaw damper in this airplane. The 7-degree up setting on the flaps actu-ally seems to work as claimed, with an additional 3.5 mph showing on the airspeed indicator at cruise power settings when the "up flap" setting is selected.

Approach stalls are docile, but there is a definite stall break with the nose dropping through the horizon. Departure stalls can be sharp, although the nose attitude in such a powerful, strong-climbing airplane will be very high in a power-on stall. Don't believe Maule airspeed claims, though. They come with bigger and draggier main gear tires than almost any other aircraft in their class, and they haven't discovered how to make a strut-braced steel-tube and fabric fuselage airplane go faster than a slick low-wing aluminum bird with the same engine, no matter what they claim!

A Maule can be a very good selection for a pilot who is willing to have his or her high performance packaged in a metal-winged, fabric-covered tail-dragger or new tricycle gear aircraft without a big name. For someone intending to operate off dirt strips, it could be a great choice, even in the new tricycle gear configuration. The price will probably be right, and 1977 and later models will come with very reliable Lycoming engines. Earlier models with Franklin engines should be avoided. The airframe is basically simple, but you should find a good steel-tube and fabric mechanic if you intend to buy one. And don't look for a mechanic who fastidiously follows the main-tenance manual. Maule manuals have been described as looking like copies of high school term papers!

Lake Buccaneer and Renegade

Live in an area with a lot of inland lakes and rivers? Are you looking for something really different in an airplane? Are you willing to accept less than average performance for exciting versatility? How about an airplane that can take off from your home airport and then cannot only land in the water once, but can even take off and do it again? And again and again! Except for ungainly Cessnas with super expensive and performance-destroying amphibious floats, you really have only one choice. And that choice is the small family of amphibians built by Lake.

Most people don't know it, but this modern-looking airplane is really a design that is nearly 60 years old! Grumman project engineer David Thurston designed a 125-hp, two-seat amphibian that at first glance looks nearly identical to a 1970s vintage LA-4. First flown in December 1944, Grumman abandoned the "Tadpole" and destroyed the aircraft and all data when the decision was made not to compete with Republic's postwar Seabee.

But details of the design were still fresh in Thurston's mind, and he joined Dave Lindblad and a small group of Grumman and Republic expatriates who developed the three-seat, 150-hp Lycoming O-320-powered Colonial C-1 Skimmer. Developed in the late '40s and produced in the early '50s, the C-1 Skimmer became the 180-hp, four-seat C-2 in 1958. Two years later, the Lake LA-4 was introduced, a long-nose, long-wing Skimmer variant. In 1970, the fuel-injected Lycoming 200-hp IO-360 engine made it the LA-4-200 Buccaneer. With airframes built by Lindblad's Aerofab in Sanford, Maine, most of the amphibians were finished and marketed by Houston-based Lake Aircraft.

In a classic case of a man liking the product so much he bought the company, New Hampshire real estate developer Armand Rivard bought Lake in 1979. He moved the corporate offices to an appropriate if out-of-the-way location in Laconia, New Hampshire, on the shores of large and scenic Lake Winnipesaukee. Eliminating corporate clutter, he later bought Aerofab, but left the production facilities in nearby Sanford, Maine. Son Bruce and daughter Cheryl helped manage the operation, which also had facilities in Kissimmee, Florida, and Renton, Washington.

Shortly after buying the company, the Rivards improved the breed with the 200EP, a Buccaneer with a 5-inch propeller extension, "batwing" trailing edge wing fillets, hull hydro boosters, an improved nacelle, and other small improvements. The package offered better performance on the water and on takeoff and landing, and quieter operation. The 200EPR option also offered a reversible propeller, quite useful when approaching obstacles on the water with no room to turn around.

Modest differences in the LA-4 line through the years include the use of troublesome Janitrol cabin heaters (requiring expensive overhauls every two years) until 1974 when Southwind heaters were introduced. Improved controllable Janitrols returned in 1983 (the Southwinds had only an on-off, cook or freeze, switch). Alodine and zinc chromate corrosion proofing was first used regularly in 1970, with an improved polychromate primer added starting in 1983.

The biggest change came in 1983, when the LA-4-250 Renegade with a big 250-hp IO-540 Lycoming engine driving a three-bladed Q-tip prop, six seats, and a big swept-back tail was introduced. In 1987, Lake brought out the turbocharged, 270-hp Turbo Renegade 270. Just to show they weren't messing around, Lake took the Turbo Renegade and set four world altitude records with the airplane. The Sea Fury, a beefed-up Renegade with salt water corrosion protection and originally intended for charter and patrol work, was introduced by Lake in late 1994. Rivard noted that the beefing up and salt water corrosion protection added approximately $70,000 to the cost of the already expensive amphibian. Want your own counter-insurgency patrol plane? The Seafury comes in a "Seawolf" version with a radar mounted on the front of the engine cowling and hardpoints under the wings for auxiliary fuel tanks (or bombs and rockets if you can get those for your plane!).

The end of an era came for Lake in 2002 and 2003. An aeronautical engineer/entrepreneur named Wadi Rahim bought the assets of Lake and Aerofab from Bruce Rivard in 2002. In 2003, Rahim announced that his company, LanShe Aerospace (www.lansheaero.com), would move Lake production from Maine and New Hampshire to a new 50,000 square foot production facility in Fort Pierce, Florida where the company also would build the high performance low-wing Micco SP-20 and SP-26 taildraggers. The 2003 Renegade 2 now cost $449,000 and the turbo Seafury now cost nearly three-quarters of a million dollars each, making them among the most expensive piston singles in production. One tantalizing item on the LanShe Aero Web site in 2003 promised that "a new entry level amphibian is to be announced later this year," possibly indicating that an upgraded Buccaneer might be headed back into production. In February 2004, a LanShe press release announced that LanShe Aerospace had reintroduced the LA-4-200 EP (EP) priced at $299,000.

These airplanes are decidedly different from all the usual Cessnas, Pipers, Beechcrafts, and Mooneys, but they are not difficult to get to know and love. You enter the airplane through clamshell doors (which are the windshield halves) hinged at the top of the cabin, and entry is not difficult. You cannot open both doors at once, however, which rules out romantic scenes of you and your beloved sitting in your Lake on calm waters with the windows open and dangling your hands in the water. The doors seal in the front on the top of the instrument panel with almost no room left to pile maps or headsets, so you'll have to be careful not to step on intercom wires and headsets as you enter most Lakes.

The four-seat Lakes are cramped, as are the six-seat Renegades and Seafurys. But the Renegades and Seafurys become spacious four-seaters with the back seats folded up. The baggage compartment is low but very long and spacious, extending for most of the length of the center fuselage under the wing and the engine. It'll take skis and even disassembled bicycles, but getting them in past the folding rear seats can be a chore. The Renegade has an

Table 11.13. Lake LA-4-200 Buccaneer and LA-250 Renegade 1989

	LA-4-200 Buccaneer	LA-250 Renegade
Specifications		
Wingspan	38 ft	38 ft
Length	24 ft 11 in	28 ft 2 in
Gross weight, normal category	2,690 lb	3,050 lb
Empty weight	1,700 lb	1,850 lb
Useful load	990 lb	1,200 lb
Useful load, full fuel	750 lb	744 lb
Fuel capacity, standard tanks	40 gal	76 gal
Performance		
Cruise speed, 75% power, best altitude	146 mph	153 mph
Fuel consumption, 75% power	9.5 gph	13.2 gph
Range 45-min reserve, 75% power	505 mi	766 mi
Sea level rate of climb	1,200 fpm	900 fpm
Service ceiling	14,000 ft	12,500 ft
Stall, clean	52 mph	64 mph
Stall, full flaps	45 mph	57 mph
Takeoff over a 50-foot obstacle	N/A	N/A
Landing over a 50-foot obstacle	N/A	N/A

additional big upward-opening center door, making loading passengers and cargo a lot easier than in the Buccaneers.

The main fuel tank in Lakes is a 40-gallon fuselage tank which feeds the engine directly. Post-1985 Renegades and 200EPs come with two additional 18-gallon tanks, one in each inboard wing leading edge, which flow by gravity to the main fuselage tank. There are gauges for the wing tanks and for the main fuselage tank. Optional wing float tanks are available in all models (generally retrofittable) with 7 gallons in each tank. There are no gauges for these tanks, and an electric pump is required to slowly transfer fuel from them. Just make sure you have room in the fuselage tank or you'll pump it overboard!

Checking the engine is easy once you climb up to it, with panels on each side of the cowling that drop down like an inverted Cherokee 140 cowling, giving excellent access to the engine. You'll also have to use an Allen wrench to check five fuselage drains plus one in each of the wing floats.

The first noticeable difference in the cockpit are the overhead controls for throttle, prop, and mixture. Surprisingly enough, they are easy to get used to. Ground taxiing can be a chore, since you have to use differential braking just like in a Tr-2 or Tiger, but this is a lot bigger and heavier airplane than the Grumman-Americans. Only the pilot has brake pedals. Gear, flaps, and trim are hydraulic. The trim is set by "pulsing" a handle located between the front seats.

Figure 11.13. The Lake Buccaneer is a fascinating airplane and a great speedboat!

Takeoffs from a runway are short, quick, and STOL-like, with a rapid climb-out. In the air, the Buccaneer feels like a boat-bottomed Cessna 182. Like the 182, it has a solid feel with smooth but not quick ailerons. Its elevator seems stronger than the 182's, though, and is not as ponderous as the 182 in pitch. The Renegade and Seafury is bigger and heavier, and its ailerons are best described as "vintage Mack truck." Stall breaks in Lakes are barely perceptible. Amazingly, they are even more benign than in a Cherokee, with even banked departure stalls causing only a shudder and a sink with little or no sharp pitchdown. In leisurely flight, as the aircraft gets too slow, you hear an odd sound which is prop cavitation just before the shudder of an impending stall. Visibility is generally excellent, although the shoulder-height wings do block rearward visibility in straight and level flight.

For retracs with 200 or more horsepower, these airplanes are not fast. But flying off the water is the element of these beauties. They are good airplanes, and damn good boats. A Renegade demonstration flight includes a landing in which the demo pilot kicks the rudder and yanks the ailerons, throwing the plane into a hard 90-degree turn immediately after landing on the water! The speedboat characteristics on the water are excellent, which can be useful in making circling step takeoffs from smaller lakes and ponds. One tricky characteristic of the aircraft, caused by its high mounted pusher engine, takes some getting used to, particularly when practicing "splashes and dashes" on the water. Applying full throttle will cause the nose to pitch down, not up, and this can be a real surprise as you nose down in the water at maximum power!

And oh yes, one other thing. It is even more important to remember to put the gear UP when landing on water than it is to put the gear down when landing on a runway. Lakes have successfully landed on their bellies, without damage, on grass and snow. But they will flip over and sink if landed gear-down on the water!

The main thing to look for in evaluating used Lakes is corrosion. An aircraft that has been used in salt water and poorly maintained may be just about worthless. Pre-1970 Lakes had little or no corrosion proofing, and are probably not a good buy. Early 1970s vintage LA-4-200s should be checked carefully to assure that the Lycoming IO-360 engine has had all the latest mods. Like the Piper Arrow, the LA-4-200's engine needed longer bearing dowels added in 1971 and a redesigned camshaft in 1973 to bring the TBO up from 1,200 hours to 1,800 hours.

The best used Lakes are good older ones which were refurbished by the factory when the factory was located in New Hampshire. Lake took back and refurbished older Lake aircraft, adding modifications and doing a very extensive annual prior to the resale of the aircraft. Lake 200s were upgraded by adding hull strakes that improve performance on the water, installing a new custom interior, and applying a corrosion inhibitor/lubricant that was "misted" or painted into the inside of all hull and wing cavities. The 200EP batwing modification was optional, and the Rivards recommended it only for owners who intended to regularly use the aircraft heavily loaded off the water.

Armand Rivard remains involved with marketing new and used Lake aircraft. His new company, Team Lake LLC (www.teamlake.com), like the old Lake production company, has offices in New Hampshire and

Figure 11.14. The Lake Renegade is a seaplane with power to spare—but it ain't cheap!

Kissimmee, Florida. Anyone considering the purchase of a Lake should look into the services offered by Rivard's Team Lake, because the organization retains at least some of the expertise and facilities of the old Lake company. Team Lake also offers comprehensive flight training programs and specialized insurance programs. Under Rivard, Lake had offered owner training programs which allowed the new owners to obtain insurance at a significant discount.

New Lakes are fantastic aircraft, running from $299,000 for an LA-4-200 EP to a half-million dollars for a Renegade 2 and nearly three-quarters of a million dollars for a new Seafury. (You could get a new Cirrus SR20 AND a Pitts biplane for that much. Of course they will only land on the water once. But a Maule dealer suggested that for the price of a Seafury you could get an SR22 or a Lancair Columbia and a Maule on floats, a comment which certainly wouldn't endear him to the folks at Lake!)

The Lake may not be a fast, efficient traveling machine, but it is a seabird that can quickly become a habit if you've got the money to buy one.

Aerospatiale Tobago and Trinidad

Tired of airplanes that were all designed in the '40s, '50s, and early '60s? Want an airplane that has a wild, exotic, sleek look or a modern airplane that was designed with all the latest in CAD/CAM computers and software? If so, you'll definitely want to look at a small family of French airplanes brought to you by Aerospatiale, "the people that brought you the Concorde." (Actually, they're built by Aerospatiale subsidiary SOCATA, the people who brought you the less-than-successful bug-eyed Rallye.)

The TB10 Tobago, the TB20 Trinidad, and the TB21 turbocharged Trinidad TC all share the same big, sleek, beautiful airframe. The Tobago is a fixed-gear airplane with a 180-hp Lycoming O-360 driving a constant-speed prop. The Trinidad has a 250-hp Lycoming IO-540 along with retractable landing gear, and the Trinidad TC adds turbocharging to the 250-hp engine. There is also a 160-hp TB-9 Tampico. The Tobago first flew in 1977, and entered production in 1979. The Trinidad was the first of the line to be imported to the United States in 1984, followed by the Tobago and Trinidad TC a year later.

In early 2000, SOCATA made significant changes to the cabin area of the fuselage, coming out with the "Generation Two" or GT line. A modified carbon fiber cockpit roof increased cabin volume and headroom. Combined with different windows and a swoopier paint job, the result is an even sleeker looking airplane.

Figure 11.15. The Aerospatiale Trinidad is sleek, modern, and comfortable. (Courtesy Aerospatiale General Aircraft Corporation)

The aircraft's sleek good looks is its main strong suit, followed closely by its wide and comfortable interior. You enter the cabin through a pair of gull-wing doors, which give the airplane much of its exotic look. The doors are a mixed blessing. There are two of them, allowing entry from either side. But the wing walk is a bit narrow, particularly back by the trailing edge, and trying to open the door while you stand on the wing leaves you with a bit of a clumsy feeling.

The 50-inch wide fuselage is one of the widest in its class, 8 inches wider than the basic Piper Cherokee series (but only an inch and a half wider than the Cherokee 6/Saratoga series) or the Mooney aircraft that are its closest competitors. The center console, holding the throttle, prop, and mixture controls, as well as the backup manual pitch trim wheel and the flap switch, can impinge a bit on the hip and leg room up front. The fancy reclinable and very comfortable front bucket seats make the plane look like an exotic European sports car. The original models were not airplanes for tall people, however. Headroom is barely adequate if you're more than six feet tall. But this shortcoming was fixed with the GT line's new roofline. All of the line are claimed to be five-seaters, with seating for three on the rear bench seat. It'd be a bit cramped for full-size, full-width adults back there, though.

The baggage compartment is accessible through a zipper panel in the rear of the cabin. Not a bad idea, considering the outside baggage door is a

Table 11.14. Aerospatiale TB10 Tobago and TB20 Trinidad

	TB10 Tobago	TB20 Trinidad
Specifications		
Wingspan	32 ft 1 in	32 ft 1 in
Length	25 ft	25 ft 4 in
Gross weight, normal category	2,535 lb	3,086 lb
Empty weight	1,554 lb	1,764 lb
Useful load	981 lb	1,333 lb
Useful load, full fuel	657 lb	816 lb
Fuel capacity, standard tanks	55.5 gal (54 usable)	88.8 gal (86.2 usable)
Performance		
Cruise speed, 75% power, best altitude	147 mph	190 mph
Fuel consumption, 75% power	9.5 gph	14 gph
Range 45-min reserve, 75% power	725 mi	1,027 mi
Sea level rate of climb	790 fpm	1,260 fpm
Service ceiling	13,000 ft	20,000 ft
Stall, clean	69.5 mph	81 mph
Stall, full flaps	61.5 mph	68 mph
Takeoff over a 50-foot obstacle	1,657 ft	1,950 ft
Landing over a 50-foot obstacle	1,394 ft	1,750

small and odd triangular hatch. Baggage capacity is rather limited for aircraft in this class, with a limitation of 143 pounds for the whole TB series.

The instrument panel is definitely a classy modern touch. Modular, it is built in three sections. Anyone who has removed the seats from a Cherokee or Skyhawk (or, God forbid, a Mooney!) and then lain on his or her back, "busting knuckles," working up behind the instrument panel of one of those aircraft will appreciate the Aerospatiale designer's handiwork. The left and right panels are hinged to allow quick and easy access to instrument wiring and connectors.

From the outside, the plane has a long-nosed beauty. With the whole line sharing the same airframe, there is a surplus of room under the Tobago's nose for a four-cylinder Lycoming in a space designed to comfortably hold a six-cylinder engine. The tail of these airplanes looks just a little strange, however, with the horizontal stabilator perched all by itself behind the vertical stabilizer and rudder.

Cockpit visibility from all seats (except maybe for somebody scrunched in the center of the rear seat) is good through the broad expanses of plexiglass, but wide cornerposts and too much plastic trim limit the pilot's vision. The long nose can hinder visibility forward in a climb-out at the best angle of climb, as well.

In the air, performance is good but not outstanding. Aerospatiale has succeeded in getting close to the same performance from these wide-cabin beauties that other manufacturers get with their narrow-cabin birds. In a head-to-head comparison with the Piper Archer II, for example, the Tobago is just a little slower than the Archer II but has longer range. The Tobago has a better rate of climb, but a lower service ceiling. Even with the latest in computer technology, one cannot engineer miracles. Unlike the Tobago, the Trinidad is in a class by itself, with only now-ancient Piper Comanches using a 250-hp engine. Its performance is good, and its big tanks give a pilot the rare ability to use it as a 1,000 nm tourer. It has a respectable cruising speed of 190 mph, and a 20,000 feet service ceiling, which should handle most Western mountain passes if you've got the oxygen on board to handle them yourself. If you fly long distances and have a cast-iron bladder, this is the bird for you! And of course, if you want to trade off a little range for more speed and altitude, the Trinidad TC has a cruising speed over 215 mph and a 25,000 feet service ceiling.

Unfortunately, the sleek good looks of these airplanes promise more excitement than the relatively large and heavy aircraft can deliver. Taxiing, it takes a lot of throttle to even get the airplane to move, and a lot to keep it moving. Acceleration on takeoff is nothing spectacular.

In the air, the airplane has a solid but unexciting feel. It's pushrod-driven ailerons feel a bit stiff at cruising speed, but the plane responds smoothly to the controls, even if it seems to require a bit of muscle to make it turn. In a head-to-head comparison of the Tobago and the Archer, the Archer has "quicker" ailerons and is likely to get the nod as being more satisfying to fly. And Tiger Aircraft's Tiger will be the most satisfying of all the 180-hp aircraft.

Figure 11.16. The Tobago shares the "signature" gull-wing doors with other TB-series aircraft. (Courtesy Aerospatiale General Aircraft Corporation)

Stalls are benign and Cherokee-like, but with some odd eccentricities. With full flaps and power off, the nose gently bobs, and it starts developing a high sink rate. But be careful if you pull the power back without dropping the flaps. With little or no warning shudder or buffet, a sink rate approaching 1,000 fpm can develop with the nose level or slightly above the horizon.

With their narrow wings, these planes can develop a high sink rate on approach with a full load and full flaps, so carry some power on final and be sure to keep your speed up. The Tobago's stall speed is more than 6 mph higher than its Piper Archer III competition. One very satisfying feature on the Trinidad and Tobago is the stall warning bell. Most airplanes have raucous stall warning horns. The Trinidad and Tobago have a bell that sounds so much like the old European telephones seen in old movies that when it goes off, it may make you think of Bogart and Bergman in the classic Casablanca!

Its landing characteristics are honest and predictable, so making the transition to one of these sleek birds should be no problem for any reasonably accomplished pilot. And the stable characteristics of the aircraft, though making it just a little dull in the air, are likely to make it a very capable aircraft for flying instrument approaches.

The airplane is well designed for maintenance, with lots of easy-to-remove access panels. The cowling is fastened with quick-release fasteners, and has plenty of room for maintenance even under the cowling of the big-engined Trinidads. For anyone worrying about spare parts from an organization that was less than spectacular in supporting the earlier Rallye, there may still be concerns. Aerospatiale replaced an excellent parts network arrangement with Aviall in favor of a support facility at North Perry Airport in Pembroke Pines, Florida. Anyone interested in one of these aircraft should also check the user group Web site at www.socata.org.

There are lots of American parts in key places in these airplanes, too. Among these are a Lycoming engine, Hartzell propeller, Cleveland wheels and brakes, Prestolite alternator, and American avionics.

But they may have carried copying American ideas one step too far. Unfortunately, in 1989 Aerospatiale copied one of the last of Cessna's "new and better" ideas, changing from a 14-volt to a 28-volt electrical system. Its too bad that the liability lawyers forced the suppliers of 14-volt electrical systems out of the market. If you live in the northern United States, a 28-volt system guarantees that you can't jump-start your plane from your car on a cold winter day!

If you're looking for a comfortable and sharp-looking airplane that will stand out in a crowd, give one of these European beauties a try! But don't expect them to fly rings around trusty old Cherokees, though—or to cost less, either!

Waco YMF Super

Do you long for the "good old days of flying," the ones that came before you were born? The days of biplanes, wind in the wires, leather helmets and goggles, and white silk scarves flying in the wind? And how about the unique rumble of a big round engine? Amazingly enough, if you are wealthy enough to ante up over $300,000, you can still buy one of those airplanes ... new! WACO Classic Aircraft Company (www.wacoclassic.com) in Lansing, Michigan, still builds big radial-engined, open-cockpit biplanes just like they used to build them around 1935, before "the Big War"—WWII. Well, maybe just a little bit better, actually.

FBO operators Richard Kettles and Michael Dow had a crazy idea to build classic biplanes again. They discovered that the type certificate to the Waco YMF-5 was in the public domain, with drawings and certification data in the Smithsonian Institution. With the help of their congressional representative to clear out some FAA bureaucratic inertia, they received approval in 1984 to begin production. By the time the decade of the '80s ended, they had nearly doubled Waco's original output of 18 YMFs!

These are beautiful masterpieces, built with classic steel-tube and fabric fuselages and fabric-covered wooden wings with Sitka spruce spars and ribs.

Figure 11.17. The Classic Aircraft Waco YMF-5 is a "classic" in the truest sense. (Courtesy Classic Aircraft Corporation)

Improvements have been made over the 1930s originals without compromising the classic feel. The steel tubing is bathed with hot linseed oil inside and painted with epoxy outside to prevent corrosion. Long-wearing Ceconite fabric is used, and Cleveland brakes and a steerable tailwheel make it more manageable on the ground than its '30s forebears. The engine up front is a Jacobs R-755 radial, a 275-hp engine derated to 245 hp. Amazingly enough, "new" radial engines are still built by Jacobs in Payson, Arizona. Some of the parts used to build the new engines may date back to 1944, though. But the engines are reliable, with a 1,200 hour TBO.

This is a big, beautiful biplane. The pilot in command flies from the single-seat rear cockpit, and up to two others can ride in the wider front cockpit. The plane isn't rated for aerobatics, but only because Aero Bulletin 7A under which the YMF-5 was originally licensed didn't address such things. The plane is rated for more than 5 Gs positive and 2 Gs negative, so go out and have a ball! This is a classic. It handles smoothly and somewhat serenely, but it isn't a hot Pitts, so don't expect to dogfight with the competition acro boys and girls. With a gross weight right up there with modern 180-hp four-seaters like the Archer and Tobago, this is a plane for lazy loops and rolls and spins and landing on grass strips. And for getting strange and admiring looks when you pull up at more modern FBOs, climb down from the cockpit, and pull off your goggles, helmet, and gloves.

Don't think that it can't be flown from modern fields, though. The plane can be outfitted for legal IFR, and the owners of some new Wacos have actually outfitted them with everything up to and including Garmin color map GPSs and Stormscopes! It can also be used as a working airplane, taking paying passengers up for scenic rides, or for glider or banner towing. But at a price of over $300,000 each, it's unlikely too many of these handcrafted beauties are likely to be used as workhorses.

Table 11.15. Classic Aircraft Waco YMF-5

Specifications	
Wingspan	30 ft
Length	23 ft 4 in
Gross weight, normal category	2,650 lb
Empty weight	1,905 lb
Useful load	745 lb
Useful load, full fuel	457 lb
Fuel capacity, standard tanks	49 gal (48 usable)
Performance	
Cruise speed, 75% power, best altitude	125 mph
Fuel consumption, 75% power	13 gph
Range 45-min reserve, 75% power	368 mi
Sea level rate of climb	1,250 fpm
Service ceiling	16,000 ft
Stall	57 mph

Aviat Husky

If Piper had modernized the Super Cub and brought it out with a 180-hp Lycoming engine, the result probably would have been identical to the Aviat Husky. The Husky was developed by Frank L. Christensen, the Christen Eagle developer who also bought the Pitts line when he was looking for another steel tube and fabric airplane to build on his Christen production line in Afton, Wyoming. Christen attempted to buy the rights to the Piper Super Cub, the Interstate/Arctic Tern, and the Aeronca Champion lines, but found the overall price and liability "tail" prohibitive. Teaming with agricultural aircraft designer Herb Andersen, Jr., Christensen set up Christen Industries and developed a new utility taildragger aircraft. The A-1 Husky was certificated in July 1987.

Christen Industries was purchased by Canadian Malcolm White in 1991, and the name of the company was changed to Aviat. Aviat, Inc. (www.aviataircraft.com) was purchased by New York businessman and real estate developer Stuart Horn in 1996. Horn aggressively pursued expanding the business and had tripled the company's sales as of 2000. Horn is also an aviation enthusiast, and made an abortive attempt in 2000 to produce an updated version of the high-wing 1930s Monoplane racer. The 2003 price for a new A-1B Husky was $148,000 without any avionics. (1994 models sold new for a base price of around $79,000, so like other new aircraft in production, the 2003 price shows a substantial increase for a period of otherwise low economic inflation.)

Table 11.16. Aviat Husky

Specifications	
Wingspan	35 ft 6 in
Length	20 ft 7 in
Gross weight, normal category	1,800 lb
Empty weight	1,190 lb
Useful load	610 lb
Useful load, full fuel	298 lb
Fuel capacity, standard tanks	52 gal (50 usable)
Performance	
Cruise speed, 75% power, best altitude	140 mph
Fuel consumption, 75% power	9.5 gph
Range 45-min reserve, 75% power	630 mi
Sea level rate of climb	1,500 fpm
Service ceiling	20,000 ft
Stall, clean	51 mph
Stall, full flaps	45 mph
Takeoff over a 50-foot obstacle	520 ft
Landing over a 50-foot obstacle	1,400 ft

In 2003 a 160-hp "little brother" to the Husky was announced. Called the Husky Pup, prices started around $116,000. The Husky Pup has no flaps and a fixed pitch propeller. It has the same maximum gross weight as the Husky and comparable cruise speeds, but has a longer takeoff and landing roll than its big brother.

The Husky looks and flies a lot like a Super Cub, with the Super Cub split door on the right with the top half opening up and the bottom half down and the same sliding windows on the left. It has improved 4130 chrome-moly steel tubing, a fuselage covered with metal to the rear of the cabin, three-position flaps, and ailerons with good control authority right down to stall speeds. The biggest change is the engine, a 180-hp Lycoming driving a constant-speed propeller. All A-1s are built with float attach fittings already installed, and the Husky is approved for skis as well as banner and glider tow hooks. Another improvement is toe rather than heel brakes. About the only negative is that the seats are not adjustable except by adding or removing seat cushions.

Handling is just slightly better than that of the typical taildragger. Takeoff and climb are in the STOL category with takeoff distance with full flaps an incredible 200 feet and sea level rate of climb 1,500 feet per minute. Aileron response and control coordination, while not acro quick, are better than average for this class of airplane. Cruising speed for the latest A-1B is a very respectable 140 mph at 75 percent power. Although it was certificated primarily as a VFR aircraft, post-2000 models come with a Garmin 430 and a surprising number of owners have even put in full IFR panels.

The Husky is a good, honest taildragger capable of hard work as well as fun. Don't expect to find a cheap one in decent condition, though. They hold their value, and in 2003 *Trade-A-Plane* prices for a Husky started around $69,000 for a 1988 model on up to over $160,000 for a new one.

Pitts S-2C

In the small western town of Afton, Wyoming, they build a totally different breed of biplane for pilots who aren't interested in slow, lazy, romantic aerial acrobatics. If you want to push your limits as a pilot in the controlled violence of competition aerobatics, you can own a biplane that took World Championships in unlimited aerobatics. For only slightly more than half the price of a Waco, you can own a Pitts!

You're talking about sheer power in a tiny airframe. And talk about growth of powerplants—this one started with a 55-hp Lycoming in Curtis Pitts' first airplane built in 1945. Its empty weight of 500 pounds has more than doubled in the modern Pitts S-2B, but the power has gone up by nearly a factor of five, too, with a big, mean, fuel-injected six-cylinder Lycoming AEIO-540-D4A5 in the nose!

Pitts fame grew with the legendary "Li'l Stinker," star of air shows and contests, built in 1947. By 1962, Pitts was selling plans to homebuilders. In 1971, the modern Pitts S-2A was introduced with symmetrical airfoils, four ailerons for instantaneous roll response, and two cockpits so that acro pilots could show their "steadies" and buddies what barf bags were really for. Also in 1971, the first production Pitts rolled off the line in Afton. Pitts left the company in 1977, when it was purchased by Christen Eagle developer and airplane perfectionist Frank L. Christensen. In 1991, Christensen sold the business to Aviat, Inc., a British company headed by Canadian Malcolm T. White, an active pilot and aviation enthusiast. It was announced after the sale that production of Pitts, Christen Eagle, and Cub look-alike Husky aircraft would continue uninterrupted at the Wyoming factory. Stuart Horn purchased Aviat, Inc. (www.aviataircraft.com) in 1996.

Pitts production models in 1990 included the single-seat 200-hp S-1T (the smallest of a line of tiny airplanes and reputed to have the best roll rates and snap roll characteristics), the 260-hp S-2S (better at maneuvers requiring speed and vertical penetration), and the two-seat 260-hp S-2B. The S-2C, a much improved version of the two-seat 260-hp S-2B, was introduced in the late 1990s and was the only production model available in 2003. Other single- and two-seat models are still available as kits. The 2003 price of a well-equipped new Pitts S-2C was in the neighborhood of $200,000.

The performance and handling characteristics of these airplanes are legendary for their ability to perform just about any maneuver in the air that a pilot can conceive of. Forget loops and rolls. Think horizontal and vertical

Table 11.17. Pitts S-2B (260 hp)

Specifications	
Wingspan	20 ft
Length	18 ft 9 in
Gross weight, normal category	1,625 lb
Empty weight	1,150 lb
Useful load	475 lb
Useful load, full fuel	307 lb
Fuel capacity, standard tanks	29 gal (28 usable)
Performance	
Cruise speed, 75% power, best altitude	176 mph
Fuel consumption, 75% power	12 gph
Range 45-min reserve, 75% power	279 mi
Sea level rate of climb	2,700 fpm
Service ceiling	N/A
Stall, clean	60 mph

hesitation rolls, snap rolls, vertical snap rolls, torque rolls. Also tail slides, whip stalls, negative-G outside maneuvers, inverted flat spins, and incredible to watch or perform lomcevaks. You strap this airplane on, and then it will seem to respond to your thoughts. But you'd better think fast to stay ahead of this beast!

It's also legendary for its difficulty in handling on the ground and on takeoff and landing. Taxiing, you have to use S-turns with lots of head bobbing and weaving. Forward visibility is about nil. Throw all that power to the tiny airframe, and you'll understand why Pitts pilots have a new meaning for "cross-country." To them it means heading to the weeds alongside the runway until they've mastered all that torque—or if they let their attention wander even once on takeoff, they wind up in the weeds, too!

Fortunately, with all that power, you'll be in the air, where this airplane belongs, very quickly. Landings are best made from a shallow, slipping approach. Otherwise, visibility to the runway is hard to come by and the descent path may be steep. The Pitts is also famous for bouncing. Flare too late, and you hit hard and bounce. Flare too soon, and you drop it in and bounce. And when the wheels are on the ground, you better stay sharp on those rudder pedals and brakes until you are in the hangar or tied down or it'll teach you a thing or two.

Cabin comfort was not a design factor. This is a windy, noisy, cold, and cramped airplane, particularly with a parachute and five-point harness. Cabin heat is provided by your body inside a thick flight suit.

The baggage space behind the rear seat in the S-2 models might hold your shaving kit for an overnight on the air show circuit if you're lucky. Hey, if you want cross-country comfort, buy a Piper Saratoga II HP, a Beech A36, or a Lancair Columbia 300!

This is a very strongly built airplane. The plane is built for +6 and -3 Gs, but the maneuvers pilots have been known to do in it can exceed even these limits. Structural cracks are a very real possibility. Buy a used one only after a VERY careful inspection by a mechanic who has worked on them before. And take engine times and TBO numbers with a grain of salt. These engines will have been screaming—literally. And remember that there are a lot of home-built Pitts out there. The best advice about buying one of them— don't! Not unless you know and would trust your life to the person who built it. If you're going to buy a used Pitts, your best bet probably would be to get one that's been thoroughly rebuilt by a Pitts expert and that has a new or newly custom-majored engine.

This is a truly amazing airplane. If you want to do some really macho flying that tests your limits, this is probably the plane for you. But you'd probably better line up some good instruction with somebody that has an S-

2 Pitts (or get instruction in yours, if you're buying one). And be sure to check with your insurance company to see if you're even insurable. After that, go out and kick it around the sky. And maybe even make a few bucks in the summer on the air show circuit.

Lancair Columbia 300, 350, and 400

Every time a new and exciting homebuilt was spotted at the annual EAA convention in Oshkosh, it would seem that someone would say that it would be wonderful if it would be put into production as a factory-built airplane. But in almost every case, the very expensive and rigorous FAA requirements for certificating a new production aircraft made it merely an idle dream. Lance Neibauer would be the one big exception. Neibauer started building sleek, slim, and very fast homebuilt/kitbuilt Lancairs at Neico Aviation in California in 1985. He would eventually move the company to Bend, Oregon, where the line of speedsters that started with the two-seat Lancair 235 would expand all the way up through a pressurized, four-seat Lancair IV-P.

Neibauer would take the Continental IO-550 powered Lancair ES and rework it into a completely new production airplane. The first new Columbia 300s came off the Lancair Company (www.lancair.com) assembly line in 1998. But cash flow problems kept production to a limited number of nearly hand-built airplanes until significant financing was received from Composite Technology Research Malaysia (CTRM) in early 2003. CTRM specialized in construction of composite aircraft components, and would mass produce major Lancair components to be shipped to Oregon for final construction. By mid-2003, approximately 70 Lancair Columbias were flying, and another 170 were on the order books. Neibauer would also make his commitment to the production Lancairs, selling off his interest in Lancair kitplanes.

The Lancair Columbia 300 may well be the most beautiful fixed gear single-engine production airplane ever built. Your first impressions seeing it are likely to be, "Very sleek ... very impressive ... beautiful ... ." Lancair company literature appropriately calls it "The Lexus of the Air." Seen from close up it feels solid and very well built, with excellent fit and finish. Very sleek with no rivet lines. A big polished spinner in front of a sculpted 3-blade prop. Vertical opening doors on the passenger compartment, with pneumatic door seals to eliminate wind noise. The spacious baggage compartment holds 120 pounds with a shelf that holds another 20. One unusual feature

Table 11.18. Lancair Columbia 300

Specifications	
Wingspan	36 ft
Length	25 ft 3 in
Gross weight, normal category	3,400 lb
Empty weight	2,250 lb
Useful load	1,150 lb
Useful load, full fuel	562 lb
Fuel capacity, standard tanks	98 gal
Performance	
Cruise speed, 75% power, best altitude	220 mph
Fuel consumption, 75% power	15 gph
Range 45-min reserve, 75% power	1,254 mi
Sea level rate of climb	1,225 fpm
Service ceiling	18,000 ft
Stall, clean	N/A
Stall, full flaps	66 mph
Takeoff over a 50-foot obstacle	1,250 ft
Landing over a 50-foot obstacle	2,350 ft

for this class of airplane: the back seats come out easily, either one at a time or both, adding to cargo space if necessary (assuming you have somewhere like a clean hangar to store the expensive leather seats).

Getting in is easy, but takes a little maneuvering not to step on the fancy leather seats. Early 300s had two UPSAT MX-20 multifunction displays fed by a GX-50 GPS. All future aircraft will be all-electric with dual electrical systems, with Avidyne Entegra displays an extra cost option. The 350 has the standard TCM IO-550 engine and a 2003 base price of about $370,000; the 400 is a turbocharged version with a base price of $437,000. Comm and nav radios and the transponder are in easy reach on the center console below the throttle, prop, and mixture. The fuel tank switch is a large circular knob in the middle of the center console. A small blue light under the tank gauge tells you which tank you have selected. One impressive option is a unique thermoelectric deicing system using laminated layers of heat tapes in the wing leading edges.

In 2003 Lancair announced that High Performance Aircraft Training had been hired to conduct flight training seminars and to offer individual flight instruction for Lancair pilots. The objective was to improve Lancair pilot proficiency and to help Lancair owners obtain lower insurance rates.

Like Tigers and Lake amphibians, the Lancair has a castering nose-wheel. Like the equally new and "clean sheet of paper" Cirrus, the Lancair has a sidestick controller. It is surprisingly easy to get used to, although at first there is a tendency to want to push down in a left turn and lift up in a right turn, the natural arm/wrist motion with a wheel. Otherwise, using the sidestick is so easy and natural that you probably won't thing about it at all.

Figure 11.18. The Lancair may be one of the most beautiful fixed-gear airplanes ever built.

There is more of a tendency to overcontrol in subtle situations like trying to maintain a specific altitude to IFR tolerances, for example, and a tendency to use the electric trim as a more integral part of flying the plane than in airplanes with typical control wheels. Elevator and aileron trim are controlled with a little ridged dome switch on top of the stick, and the radio push-to-talk is mounted on the back of the sidestick. Although visibility is quite good, the sidepost in front of the door is somewhat obtrusive. The headliner above the pilot is heavily padded and it doesn't seem like there would be enough headroom for tall pilots. The cabin is wide and spacious, although a high center console/divider between the two pilot's seats reduces the feeling of spaciousness.

Book value for sea level rate of climb with a full load is 1,225 fpm, and with lower loads you may see rates of climb as high as 1,800 fpm. A climbout speed of 139 mph is recommended for better visibility and engine cooling, faster than the cruise speed of many general aviation airplanes. The pushrod-connected ailerons are solid and responsive for a big airplane, although certainly not acro responsive. Elevator (pitch) response is also solid and so well balanced to not even be noticeable. At cruise power settings, you know this is one "go like hell" airplane. It has a cruise speed of 220 mph, just a little faster than V35 and F33 Bonanzas, and that's with fixed gear.

In flight the wings, which look long but narrow on the ground, look surprisingly small for such a big, fast bird. The outboard wings have a wider chord than the inboard section, which is part of what gives the plane its incredibly gentle stall characteristics. Adding to the safety in stalls is a rudder limiter which makes it nearly impossible for the plane to spin. This plane has some of the best manners in stalls of any airplane flying. Power off (approach) stalls are similar to those of a Cherokee, rocking up and down and losing only modest amounts of altitude if you keep the stick back. But departure stalls are the surprise. The Lancair 300 has a departure stall characteristic that can best be described as identical to the approach stall except the nose is high and the engine makes more noise. The nose bobs down and then back up again, going from around 30 degrees nose up, down to 10 to 15 degrees, and then back up again. There is no real nose or wing-dropping stall break. To recover, simply drop the nose to just above the horizon and resume normal flight.

Although the plane slows easily enough to allow the first notch of flaps to be put down at a relatively high 150 mph and then to slow further for good manners in the pattern, scissor-type speedbrakes that pop out of slots in the top of the wings at any speed are an $8,700 option. Not small change, but a reasonable enough number that anyone spending over $300,000 for a new airplane should add them so they will be available if you really need them. Landings are firm, not elegant. You won't make a squeaker. In aircraft design, there is "no free lunch," and the firm landings are likely due to limits on elevator travel that give the plane its excellent stall characteristics but make it difficult to make a good landing flare. This just might be a plane that gets a reputation for solid arrivals like the Piper Comanche, an earlier-era beautiful fast traveler.

If life has blessed you with a lot more money than the average pilot, you want a "go like hell" cruiser, and you're tired of warmed-over aluminum designs from the '50s and '60s put out by Cessna, New Piper, Beechcraft, and Mooney, this may be the plane for you. You'll love just looking at it every time you see it on the ramp. Just don't expect to impress anybody with your gentle landings.

Cirrus SRV, SR20, SR22

Cirrus Design (www.cirrusdesign.com), like Lancair, started out building a homebuilt. But unlike the generally small and sleek Lancair homebuilts, the Cirrus VK-30 was a big cabin class 4-seater powered by a 350-hp Continental engine with a pusher prop. The VK-30 first flew in February

1988. After selling several dozen VK-30 kits, in 1993 brothers Dale and Alan Klapmeier stopped selling VK-30s and began a secretive project in Duluth, Minnesota on what promised to be a revolutionary new certificated production aircraft. They also continued development of a turboprop version of the VK-30, the ST50, a design they sold to an Israeli consortium. The prototype of the revolutionary certificated aircraft, the Cirrus SR20, first flew in March 1995.

The Cirrus SR20 is a sleek, white fixed-gear four-seater in a standard configuration. Powered by a 200-hp Continental IO-360-ES engine and built with modern composite materials, it has performance matching or exceeding earlier metal retractables with a cruise speed of 186 mph. Entry into the spacious and modern cabin is through doors made so that both sides are hinged to swing up and forward. Early SR20s came with dual Garmin 430s and a large ARNAV multifunction display. Later SR20s replaced the ARNAV display with Avidyne displays.

In 2001, Cirrus added the bigger and more powerful SR22 to their lineup. Powered by the 310-hp Continental IO-550 driving a standard 3-blade propeller, the SR22 has a longer and stronger wing, carries 84 gallons of avgas versus 60.5 gallons in SR20, and carries a larger load with a faster rate of climb and a cruise speed of 210 mph while burning 18 gph.

Like Lancairs, Tigers, and Diamond aircraft, Cirrus aircraft have castering nosewheels and steer by differential braking while taxiing. The SR20 and SR22 have sidestick controllers. The sidesticks have self-centering spring

Table 11.19. Cirrus SR20 and SR22

	Cirrus SR20	Cirrus SR22
Specifications		
Wingspan	36 ft	38 ft 4 in
Length	26 ft	26 ft
Gross weight, normal category	3,000 lb	3,400 lb
Empty weight	2,070 lb	2,250 lb
Useful load	930 lb	1,150 lb
Useful load, full fuel	570 lb	646 lb
Fuel capacity, standard tanks	60 gal (56 usable)	84 gal (81 usable)
Performance		
Cruise speed, 75% power, best altitude	179 mph	207 mph
Fuel consumption, 75% power	10.5 gph	17.5 gph
Range 45-min reserve, 75% power	820 mi	803 mi
Sea level rate of climb	900 fpm	1,300 fpm
Service ceiling	16,000 ft	17,000 ft
Stall, clean	75 mph	79 mph
Stall, full flaps	62 mph	68 mph
Takeoff over a 50-foot obstacle	1,958 ft	1,575 ft
Landing over a 50-foot obstacle	2,040 ft	2,325 ft

cartridges in lieu of trim tabs. A "coolie hat" trim switch on top of the side-stick adjusts spring cartridge pressures. The centering springs mean that if you release the controls, movement stops immediately. The spring cartridges give the aircraft a different and not entirely pleasant feel. At times the springs seem to be opposing your control movements as you fly the aircraft. The springs are heavy enough that Cirrus reps claim you don't need to use gust locks on the controls on the ground. The result is that this is not a plane you will be able to fly with smooth, gentle, sensitive touches on the controls. Frequent trimming will be necessary.

Good transition training is essential in Cirrus aircraft. Landings are difficult to get used to at first. The approach is made nose down for what seems too long by normal standards, and the initial impression is that you are going to dive right into the runway. You can't see any part of the cowling from the pilot's seat, which is different from a lot of other aircraft. Most pilots will have learned to gauge their proper landing approach in training aircraft by sighting along part of the cowling, and that is not possible in the Cirrus. Developing peripheral vision is necessary for good landings in a Cirrus. Developing an intuitive feel for the Cirrus aircraft is difficult, particularly for those used to Piper, Cessna, or other typical aircraft. The SR22, at least, is too fast and too much of a handful to ever be used as a primary training aircraft, although it might make one hell of an instrument trainer for pilots intending to fly aircraft with advanced avionics systems.

The price for an IFR-equipped SR20, with an Avidyne Entegra display, one Garmin 430 plus one backup 250XL VFR GPS/COM plus a 55SR autopilot, was $229,900 in 2003. Expensive, but not that much more expensive than a fully-equipped "old technology" Skyhawk SP. The SR20s and SR22s are among the first aircraft to offer the Avidyne FlightMax Entegra primary flight display with an electronic attitude direction indicator (EADI), electronic horizontal situation indicator (EHSI), altitude, airspeed, vertical speed, moving map display, and a solid-state attitude reference heading system (AHRS).

The most impressive difference between the SR20 and the SR22 is that the SR22 has an all-electric panel. The SR20 had two vacuum pumps, but the SR22 is all electric with two alternators and batteries. There is a primary and an essential electrical bus. There are two alternators, with the main rated at 60 amps and the secondary at 20 amps. The essential bus is designed to allow one Garmin 430, the attitude indicator, turn coordinator, and autopilot to operate off the number two battery for 45 minutes even if both alternators and the first battery all have failed. The price for an IFR-equipped SR22 with an Avidyne Entegra display in 2003 was $313,900. The SR22 also offers another very impressive option for a fixed-gear single, an optional TKS "weeping wing" deicing system for the wings, horizontal stabilizer, and propeller, available for around $20,000. The TKS includes porous metal strips on the front of the wings and horizontal stabilizer, as well as on the inboard first quarter of prop. The prop deicer slings deicing fluid on the windshield to deice it after the deicing prop. Cirrus SR22s with TKS are not certified for flight into known icing. It is intended to be a safety feature for pilots who inadvertently encounter icing, not something to tempt pilots to take on icing in a single-engine aircraft.

Avidyne-Entegra-equipped Cirrus aircraft are probably the first true General Aviation "glass cockpit" single-engine airplanes. You fly by indications on the displays. Knowing how to use the Primary Flight Display (PFD) and Multifunction Displays (MFD) are essential in these aircraft. The PFD directly in front of the pilot has a large full-color artificial horizon on top, with an airspeed ribbon and digital readouts on the left and the same kind of indicators for altitude on the right. An HSI is on the lower half of the screen.

The MFD in the center of the console has an impressive array of screens, with logical touch screen controls along each side of the display screen. The primary display is a GPS color map, showing some terrain features, airports, route of flight, and even other aircraft in close proximity if the plane has the Skywatch function. Radar avoidance Stormscope information is another available option. When the GPS map is shown, an alphanumeric presentation of engine and systems data is presented on the upper left side of the screen. You can adjust percentage of power or inches of manifold pressure using just the information on the MFD. A fully redundant display of all engine gauges is also selectable. A full set of checklists is available, from start-up to in-flight emergency procedures, and a full database of information on nearby airports, VORs, ILSs, and even NDBs is readily available on selectable lists.

Cirrus, particularly given the depressed conditions of the modern general aviation market, has been a striking success, delivering its 1,000th production airplane in 2003. Cirrus is also planning to build the SR21 powered by a 230-hp SMA turbodiesel engine for the European market. In a rather strange move, in 2003 Cirrus also announced a stripped-down VFR SR20 called the SRV. The selection of avionics and other features on the aircraft is a bit strange, offering the Avidyne Entegra display but only a single Garmin 420 GPS/COM, meaning there is no backup navigation system and no VOR or ILS capability. Even a landing light is a $900 option. It is a bit hard to understand why Cirrus feels anyone would want to pay $189,900 for an aircraft not capable of IFR flight, unless they feel that some flight schools will be willing to pay that much for their day VFR rental fleets. Without VOR or ILS navigation capability, the SRV wouldn't even make a good trainer.

Figure 11.19. The Cirrus SR22 sets a new standard for in-flight safety.

The defining feature of the Cirrus aircraft, and perhaps its most controversial feature, is the Cirrus Airframe Parachute System (CAPS). In emergency situations, the pilot of a Cirrus can deploy the CAPS by reaching over his or her right shoulder and pulling a handle. A rocket fires the parachute out from behind the aft window. The parachute will lower the aircraft to the ground at descent rates for the SR20 of 24 fps/1,440 fpm and 28 fps/1,680 fpm for the SR22 with the same chute. The pilot and passengers should be able to walk away, but the plane will never fly again.

Cirrus is adamant that the CAPS is a plus. A Cirrus rep put it this way: "Think of the CAPS as the ultimate safety system in times of a potential pending disaster, such as a midair, worst-case engine failure, pilot incapacitation (stroke), bird through the windshield, etc. Cirrus feels so strongly about these types of events that the CAPS is included in all of the aircraft."

Is the parachute really an advance in safety, or may it even be a liability? Cirrus touts the parachute as a major advance in safety. But despite the parachute and other safety features, the early safety record of the Cirrus aircraft was questionable at best. In 2003, both *Aviation Consumer* and *Flying* magazines ran articles questioning the poor early safety record of Cirrus aircraft. Richard Collins in *Flying* noted that from April 2002 until January 2003 there were five fatal crashes in Cirrus aircraft, with approximately 500 Cirrus aircraft flying. By comparison, there were eleven Cessna 182 fatal crashes in the same period, out of an estimated 10,000 Cessna 182s flying. And the September 2003 *Aviation Consumer* article noted that the Diamond Katana fleet, with more than 800 aircraft flying since 1994, has had only two fatal crashes in that entire time.

By late 2003, Cirrus could claim only one life saved by CAPS activation. And that incident was one which could raise questions about the Cirrus design or maintenance practices. In October 2002, there was an in-flight separation of the left aileron on an SR22. The pilot chose to activate the CAPS and walked away from the crash uninjured. Most pilots, however, would probably prefer to have an aircraft in which all of the serious parts keep flying in close formation than to trash the plane by deploying a parachute after losing the parts. A review of NTSB records shows that most Cirrus fatals were what David Letterman might call "stupid pilot tricks." Uncontrolled flight into terrain, either in cruise flight or on approach, is common in all aircraft, including the Cirrus, and parachutes will not save any pilots who insist on killing themselves that way.

One SR22 crash, a flat spin accident which killed the two pilot co-owners, is particularly troubling and was the subject of another Richard Collins September 2002 *Flying* magazine article. Cirrus aircraft are supposed to be designed to have excellent stall- and spin-resistant characteristics. But the ill-fated pilots, both of whom had received type-specific training in a Cirrus, were practicing in-flight maneuvers in an SR22 and ended up in a flat spin. The parachute was not deployed, and the pilots were killed. The accident raises some interesting points. One question is whether a pilot of an aircraft in a flat spin would be capable of overcoming centrifugal forces and reaching over his or her shoulder and pulling a handle on the ceiling. The pilots of this aircraft did not.

The *Flying* article noted that "the certification of the Cirrus airplanes was allowed by the FAA without full spin testing based on the fact that the airplane has a ballistic whole-airplane parachute recovery system. The FAA spin recovery requirement for singles is basically a recovery from a one-turn spin in one additional turn. The Cirrus was exempt from this regulation because of the parachute." In short, the FAA gave Cirrus a "pass" on a certification requirement based on the CAPS. The NTSB report on the SR22 flat spin accident incorrectly claimed that the only approved and demonstrated method of spin recovery included in the SR22 Pilot Owner Handbook is the activation of the Cirrus Airframe Parachute System. This was not correct, and the SR22 POH does include standard spin recovery procedures to be tried before pulling the chute. And it should be noted that Cirrus aircraft are designed to avoid inadvertent entry into spins.

Both *Aviation Consumer* and Collins in *Flying* also question whether the Cirrus is attracting under qualified pilots who feel safer than they should flying what is really a complex aircraft with less than proper training. And Collins questions whether the parachute makes some pilots attempt dangerous flights that they might not be tempted to try in an aircraft not advertised as having advanced safety features.

Cirrus aircraft are excellent aircraft that advance the state of the art of general aviation. They are incredible traveling machines with some of the most advanced avionics in any single-engine aircraft flying. But be sure to fly one before you buy one, and be sure to get good transition training both on the avionics and on the aircraft's flight characteristics whether you buy it new or used. The sidestick controller has a different feel from any other aircraft (including the Lancair, which also has a sidestick controller, but without the centering springs), and not every pilot will like the way this plane flies.

With a properly trained pilot who is familiar with all of the features inherent in the Avidyne Entegra package at the controls, a Cirrus SR22 equipped with all of the available optional safety features may well be one of the safest piston single-engine airplanes ever built. Even without the dubious advantages of the CAPS, the TKS anti-icing, the Skywatch traffic avoidance system, and the Stormscope lightning avoidance system, combined with the unparalleled situational awareness inherent in the Garmin-driven Entegra displays, the SR22 provides for an impressive level of safety available in few other non-turbine aircraft.

Diamond DA40-180 Diamond Star

In 1999, Diamond converted its Katana to the sporty Diamond DA20-C1 Eclipse. It was pricey for a two-seater, and it had one big weakness for serious pilots that seriously limited its sales potential—it wasn't IFR capable. Introduced in 2000, Diamond brought out the real answer to the sport plane for serious pilots. They introduced the four-seat, soon to be instrument-capable Diamond DA40-180 Diamond Star. It looked like a DA20 on steroids, but it really was a whole new airplane. By August 2001, IFR certification was obtained, and the plane was ready for prime time, ready to fill a market niche just below the Lancairs and Cirrus SR22s. It has the potential to be a Skyhawk and Archer killer.

The DA40 has long, narrow carbon fiber wings with embedded metal strips for IFR certification. The wingspan is surprisingly large for an aircraft in this class, over 39 feet, which could be challenging when taxiing between lines of parked aircraft or snow banks or when putting it in a hangar. It has a fiberglass fuselage with an egg-shaped cabin and a narrow tail boom. It is an airplane that looks small but feels large inside. Getting into the airplane is unique and a little weird. You climb up the front, not the back of the wing. The pilot and front seat passenger enter under a forward hinged canopy, while rear-seat passengers swing up a side-hinged, upward opening door. Perhaps because there are control sticks rather than control wheels, the front seats are not adjustable, although the rudder pedals are. Like the Katana, Evolution, and Eclipse, and the Cirrus and Lancair as well, directional control while taxiing is with differential braking.

No Rotax engine here. A fuel-injected 180-hp Lycoming drives a three-blade MT composite constant-speed propeller. One unusual design feature is that the airplane's instruments are all electric, with no vacuum pump. An "essential bus" of one navcom, lights, and an electric attitude gyro can be driven by a battery good for one and one-half hours. A battery pack of 28 AA batteries will power the attitude gyro and panel lights for an additional hour. Most DA40s leave the factory with Garmin radios, many with a 430 and a 530. One oddity: showing its motorglider roots, the DA40 has a glider and banner tow package available. It can be a working airplane despite its almost delicate features. Standard fuel tanks are a little on the small side compared to the competition, with only 40-gallon tanks (39 gallons usable), although 50-gallon extended range tanks are available for about $4,000.

The DA40 is reasonably fast (quicker than the Archer III and Skyhawk SP, not as quick as the SR20, and certainly not as fast as the Lancair and SR22) and fun to fly. Visibility is excellent. Stalls in the DA40 are similar to those in Cherokees. Power-off approach stalls result in a bobbing motion

Table 11.20. Diamond DA-4-180 Diamond Star

Specifications	
Wingspan	39 ft 5 in
Length	26 ft 4 in
Gross weight, normal category	2,535 lb
Empty weight	1,543 lb
Useful load	992 lb
Useful load, full fuel	562 lb
Fuel capacity, standard tanks	41.2 gal (39.1 usable)
Performance	
Cruise speed, 75% power, best altitude	168 mph
Fuel consumption, 75% power	10 gph
Range 45-min reserve, 75% power	530 mi
Sea level rate of climb	1,070 fpm
Service ceiling	N/A
Stall, clean	54.5 mph
Stall, full flaps	52 mph
Takeoff over a 50-foot obstacle	1,150 ft
Landing over a 50-foot obstacle	1,070 ft

and little altitude loss, whereas departure stalls can result in some nose dropoff and some rolloff to one side. Like the Cherokees, stall recovery is straightforward. Like the Katanas, despite the long glider-like wings it will descend rapidly and with good manners when necessary. Like a Mooney, it can be a floater on landing if the approach airspeed isn't just right.

2003 prices for the DA40 put it in the same ballpark as the Cirrus SR20 when similarly equipped, although unlike the SR20 you can save money by buying a DA40 without an autopilot. DA40s come with three option packages and price ranges. The least expensive is with Bendix/King avionics. Base price with a GPS and single navcomm is $186,900. IFR avionics add $11,220, and a KAP 140 autopilot and a KCS 55A HSI add another $26,900. Next most expensive is with Garmin avionics. Base price with a single GNS 430 GPS/com/nav is $188,900, with IFR avionics adding $11,945 and the Bendix autopilot and HSI adding $26,900. The most expensive option is the same as the second option (base price of $188,900) but with an Avidyne FlightMax Entegra primary flight display available for an additional $39,000. An autopilot and additional GNS 430 costs $24,900, with separate HSI required with the Avidyne PFD.

Figure 11.20. The DA40-180 Diamond Star is the nicest-flying of the sleek new singles. (Courtesy of Diamond Aircraft)

But you will probably find few Avidyne-equipped DA40s around, because Diamond decided to go with the Garmin G1000 Primary Flight Display/Multifunction Display equipment with two large screens taking up most of the DA40 panel as their preferred top-of-the-line option for 2004. G1000 capabilities include HSI, WAAS-capable GPS; VHF and ILS nav; VHF comm with 8.33 kHZ spacing; and a Mode S transponder with Traffic Information Service. Weather and terrain data are extra cost options. The Diamond press release described the estimated price as "$25,000 over a conventional IFR-equipped DA40," which would put it right around a quarter of a million dollars. Damn expensive, but a bargain compared to similarly equipped Lancairs and Cirrus SR22s.

Another enhancement for the 2004 Diamond Stars was a 90 percent larger baggage compartment. Early Diamond Stars had good but not great baggage compartments. With the 2004 "4-Way Baggage Compartment" and Tiger-style folding rear seats, up to seven feet of space is available behind the front seats. Like the Tiger, this is an airplane you can take to Oshkosh and sleep in if you want to. A novel idea included in the "4-Way Baggage Compartment" is a full-width, under-floor compartment for hiding valuables out of sight.

Also announced for 2004 was the Diamond Star FP, powered by a carbureted 180-hp Lycoming engine turning a fixed-pitch metal Sensenich propeller replacing the standard Diamond Star's fuel-injected Lycoming with a constant-speed propeller. Intended as a relatively low-cost trainer for flight schools, the Diamond Star FP has a 2004 base price around $175,000, nearly $14,000 less than the Diamond Star. Other minor concessions to keep the price down include the lack of wheel pants, standard on the Diamond Star. Airspeed loss due to the changes is claimed to be less than 8 mph, meaning it is still faster than the Skyhawks and the Archer IIIs, but making it a little slower than the Skylanes and the Arrows. Diamond Aircraft announced that the Diamond Star FP would be available with "all currently available avionics configurations," but pushed the Garmin G1000 all-glass option as "the lowest-cost all-glass IFR certified trainer."

If you have the money to buy a new Skyhawk or Archer III, you definitely should take a look at this one. Many Diamond dealers also have fractional ownership plans available. But like the Cirrus and the Lancair, it is a really new airplane.

Where the aircraft are advertised

The following publications and their associated Web sites are good sources of planes that are advertised for sale:

AeroTrader
  www.aerotraderonline.com

Atlantic Flyer
  P.O. Box 668
  Litchfield, CT 06759
  E-mail: mail@aflyer.com
  www.aflyer.com

Aviation Digest
  P.O. Box 456
  Dalton, MA 01227-0456
  E-mail: aviationdigest@aol.com
  www.avdigest.net

The Controller
  P.O. Box 85310
  Lincoln, NE 68501-5310
  E-mail: feedback@controller.com
  www.aircraft.com

GA (General Aviation) News
  P.O. Box 39099
  Lakewood, WA 98439
  E-mail: comments@GeneralAviationNews.com
  www.GeneralAviationNews.com

Pacific Flyer
  3355 Mission Ave.
  Oceanside, CA 92054
  www.pacificflyer.com

Trade-A-Plane
 P.O. Box 509
 Crossville, TN 38557
 www.trade-a-plane.com

The following Web sites which advertise aircraft are not associated with print advertising:

Aircraft Shopper Online
 www.aso.com

Aircraft Owners and Pilots Association (AOPA)
 www.aopa.org
     (Click on "Aviation Classifieds" on HomePage)

AVWEB
 www.avweb.com
     (Click on "Classifieds;" scroll down to "READ Classified Ads")
     Note: You may have to enroll with AVWEB to use this site.

Aircraft classified ad abbreviations

As you read the ads for airplanes for sale, the following list should help you break the secret code:

AD: Airworthiness Directive. A design defect or fatigue/ wearout problem directly affecting the safety and/or airworthiness of an aircraft. The FAA sends out notification of the problem to all registered owners of the type of aircraft involved. The notification also specifies the time limit before the fix must be accomplished, depending upon the seriousness of the potential failure.

ADF: Automatic direction finder.

AH: Artificial horizon.

AP, A/P: Autopilot. May vary from a wing leveler to a complex autopilot with heading and altitude hold and VOR, ILS, and/or GPS coupling capability.

AS, ASI: Airspeed indicator.

B: Beacon. (See also RB.)

C: Clock.

CAT, CT: Carburetor air temperature gauge.

CDI: Course deviation indicator.

CEC: Ceconite (modern synthetic fabric).

CH, ch: Channel (as in "720-channel nav/comm").

CHT: Cylinder head temperature gauge.

CMOH: Chrome major overhaul. (See Chapter 7.)

COM, COMM: Communication (as in "360-channel nav/comm").

Cont.: Continental engine.

cont.: Control(s).

CTOH: Chrome top overhaul. (See Chapter 7.)

DF: Direction finder.

DG: Directional gyro.

DME: Distance measuring equipment.

EGT: Exhaust gas temperature gauge.

ELT: Emergency locator transmitter. (Because all typical private aircraft must have one, listing the ELT is an indication of someone trying to fatten up the equipment list, not a real extra!)

ex: Excellent condition.

facremfg: Factory remanufactured engine.

FD: Flight director (only found in the expensive singles and twins).

FGP: Full gyro panel. Generally refers to a panel with DG, AH, and TB; most aircraft built since 1960 are equipped with FGP.

FI: Fuel-injected. Generally used on 200-hp and larger engines.

Frank.: Franklin engine. No longer manufactured in the United States. Used in old Stinsons, some Bellancas, and older Maules.

FRMF: Factory remanufactured engine. (See Chapter 8.)

FWF: Firewall forward. Generally used to indicate that an overhaul includes overhauled accessories like mags, starter, and alternator, plus new hoses and cables.

GPH, gph: Gallons per hour. Take the present owner's claims with a touch of skepticism until you see the aircraft owner's manual.

GPS: Global Positioning System (state-of-the-art navigational receiver system).

GS, G/S: Glideslope.

GSI: Groundspeed indicator. Generally a function built into DMEs and GPSs.

GSP: Ground service plug. Allows safe, easy, winter battery jump starts. Check to see if the present owner is throwing in the cable.

HC: Heavy case. Generally refers to certain models of Franklin 165-hp engines or Continental O-520 series engines. A heavy case is generally a positive feature.

HF: High-frequency radio. Usually found in military (or military surplus) aircraft or ocean-crossing aircraft (like Voyagers).

HP: Heated pitot. A desirable feature for all IFR aircraft.

HP, hp: Horsepower.

HSI: Horizontal situation indicator. Combines VOR, GS, and DG in one indicator.

HT: See CHT.

IFR: Instrument flight rules.

ILS: Instrument landing system.

inst.: Instruments.

IVSI: Instantaneous vertical speed indicator.

ldg.: Landing.

LE: Left engine (multiengine aircraft).

LF: Low frequency (radio). Was obsolete, came back with LORAN, superceded again by GPS.

lgt.: Light.

LMB, 3LMB: Three-light marker beacon. May be incorporated in a switching panel.

LOC: Localizer. Most modern nav receivers have built-in localizer receivers.

LORAN: Long-range navigation. A family of navigation receivers using computer technology to provide amazing database capabilities. Generally superceded by GPS receivers.

LRT: Long-range tanks. Remember that fuel weight must be deducted from useful load if you intend to use full long-range capability.

Ly, Lyc: Lycoming engine(s).

MB: Marker beacon (receiver).

MC: Magnetic compass.

MFD: Multi-function display.

MDH: Major damage history. Stay away from this, particularly in Cherokee-series aircraft with recurring severe inspections recommended for damage history aircraft.

MKR: Marker beacon (receiver).

MO: Major overhaul. (See Chapter 8.)

MP: Manifold pressure gauge.

NAV, nav: Navigation (as in 200-channel nav/comm radio).

NDB: Non-directional beacon.

NDH: No damage history. May really mean "none we couldn't hide".

O: Overhaul. (See Chapter 8.)

OAT: Outside air temperature gauge.

OBS: Omni bearing selector.

OH, O/H: Overhaul. (See Chapter 8.)

OSFRM: Zero time since factory remanufactured (engine).

OSMOH: Zero time since major overhaul (engine).
PC: Positive control (Mooney wing leveler).
PFD: Primary flight display.
PWI: Proximity warning indicator.
RB: Rotating beacon.
RC: Rate of climb.
rcvr: Receiver.
reman.: Remanufactured.
RDF: Radio direction finder.
RDR: Radar.
RE: Right engine (multi-engine aircraft).
RG: Retractable gear.
RH: Right-hand (copilot's seat).
RMF: Remanufactured.
RMI: Remote magnetic indicator.
RNAV: Area navigation.
S: Strobe.
SCMOH: Since chrome major overhaul.
SCTOH: Since chrome top overhaul.
SFRM: Since factory remanufactured (engine).
SG: Slaved gyro.
SMOH: Since major overhaul.
SOH: Since overhaul. May be top or major; the difference is considerable.
SPOH: Since prop overhaul (variable-pitch propeller).
Sprhmr: Superhomer (a museum-piece old Narco radio).
STOH: Since top overhaul.
STOL: Short takeoff and landing.
surf.: Surfaces. Generally refers to fabric-covered aircraft.
SW: Stall warning.
TASI: True airspeed indicator.
TB, T&B: Turn and bank indicator (needle and ball).
TBO: Time between (major) overhaul.
TT: Total time.
TTAE: Total time, airframe and engine.
TTSN: Total time since new.
TXP: Transponder.
TW: Tailwheel.
UHF: Ultrahigh frequency (radio).
VHF: Very high frequency (radio).
VOR: Omni receiver/indicator.

VOR/LOC: Omni receiver/indicator with built-in or interfaced localizer.

V/STOL: Vertical/short takeoff and landing.

WAAS: Wide Area Augmentation System. Advanced ILS-like GPS upgrade.

XPDR: Transponder.

XTAL: Crystal.

Owner-performed maintenance allowed by FAR Part 43, Appendix A, Subpart (c)

1. Removal, installation, and repair of landing gear tires.
2. Replacing elastic shock absorber cords on landing gear.
3. Servicing landing gear shock struts by adding oil, air, or both.
4. Servicing landing gear wheel bearings, such as cleaning and greasing.
5. Replacing defective safety wiring or cotter keys.
6. Lubrication not requiring disassembly other than removal of nonstructural items such as cover plates, cowlings, and fairings.
7. Making simple fabric patches not requiring rib stitching or the removal of structural parts or control surfaces. In the case of balloons, the making of small fabric repairs to envelopes (as defined in, and in accordance with, the balloon manufacturer's instructions) not requiring load tape repair or replacement.
8. Replenishing hydraulic fluid in the hydraulic reservoir.
9. Refinishing decorative coating of fuselage, balloon baskets, wings, tail group surfaces (excluding balanced control surfaces), fairings, cowlings, landing gear, or cockpit interior when removal or disassembly of any primary structure or operating system is not required.
10. Applying preservative or protective material to components where no disassembly of any primary structure or operating system is involved and where such coating is not prohibited or is not contrary to good practices.
11. Repairing upholstery and decorative finishes of the cabin, cockpit, or balloon interior when the repairing does not require disassembly of any primary structure or operating system or interfere with an operating system or affect primary structure of the aircraft.
12. Making small, simple repairs to fairings, nonstructural cover plates, cowlings, and small patches and reinforcements not changing the contour so as to interfere with proper airflow.
13. Replacing side windows where that work does not interfere with the structure or any operating system such as controls, electrical equipment, etc.

14. Replacing safety belts.
15. Replacing seats or seat parts with replacement parts approved for the aircraft, not involving disassembly of any primary structure or operating system.
16. Troubleshooting and repairing broken circuits in landing light wiring circuits.
17. Replacing bulbs, reflectors, and lenses of position and landing lights.
18. Replacing wheels and skis where no weight and balance computation is involved.
19. Replacing any cowling not requiring removal of the propeller or disconnection of flight controls.
20. Replacing or cleaning spark plugs and setting of spark plug gap clearance.
21. Replacing any hose connection except hydraulic connections.
22. Replacing prefabricated fuel lines.
23. Cleaning or replacing fuel and oil strainers or filter elements.
24. Replacing and servicing batteries.
25. Cleaning of balloon burner pilot and main nozzles in accordance with the balloon manufacturer's instructions.
26. Replacement or adjustment of nonstructural standard fasteners incidental to operations.
27. The interchange of balloon baskets and burners on envelopes when the basket or burner is designated as interchangeable in the balloon type certificate data and the baskets and burners are specifically designed for quick removal and installation.
28. The installation of antimisfueling devices to reduce the diameter of fuel tank filler openings provided the specific device has been made a part of the aircraft type certificate data by the aircraft manufacturer, the aircraft manufacturer has provided FAA-approved instructions for installation of the specific device, and installation does not involve the disassembly of the existing tank filler opening.
29. Removing, checking, and replacing magnetic chip detectors.
30. The inspection and maintenance tasks prescribed and specifically identified as preventive maintenance in a primary category aircraft type certificate or supplemental type certificate holder's approved special inspection and preventive maintenance program when accomplished on a primary category aircraft provided: (i) They are performed by the holder of at least a private pilot certificate issued under part 61 who is the registered owner (including co-owners) of the affected aircraft and who holds a certificate of competency for the affected aircraft (1) issued by a school approved under § 147.21(e) of this chapter; (2) issued by the

holder of the production certificate for that primary category aircraft that has a special training program approved under § 21.24 of this sub-chapter; or (3) issued by another entity that has a course approved by the Administrator; and (ii) The inspections and maintenance tasks are performed in accordance with instructions contained by the special inspection and preventive maintenance program approved as part of the aircraft's type design or supplemental type design.

31. Removing and replacing self-contained, front instrument panel-mount-ed navigation and communication devices that employ tray-mounted connectors that connect the unit when the unit is installed into the instrument panel, (excluding automatic flight control systems, transpon-ders, and microwave frequency distance measuring equipment (DME)). The approved unit must be designed to be readily and repeatedly removed and replaced, and pertinent instructions must be provided. Prior to the unit's intended use, an operational check must be performed in accordance with the applicable sections of part 91 of this chapter.*

32. Updating self-contained, front instrument panel-mounted Air Traffic Control (ATC) navigational software data bases (excluding those of automatic flight control systems, transponders, and microwave frequen-cy distance measuring equipment (DME)) provided no disassembly of the unit is required and pertinent instructions are provided. Prior to the unit's intended use, an operational check must be performed in accor-dance with applicable sections of part 91 of this chapter.*

* 91.407

(b) No person may carry any person (other than crewmembers) in an aircraft that has been maintained, rebuilt, or altered in a manner that may have appreciably changed its flight characteristics or substantially affected its operation in flight until an appropriately rated pilot with at least a private pilot certificate flies the aircraft, makes an operational check of the mainte-nance performed or alteration made, and logs the flight in the aircraft records.

(c) The aircraft does not have to be flown as required by paragraph (b) of this section if, prior to flight, ground tests, inspection, or both show conclu-sively that the maintenance, preventive maintenance, rebuilding, or alter-ation has not appreciably changed the flight characteristics or substantially affected the flight operation of the aircraft.

Type clubs

Aeronca Aviators Club

Julie or Joe Dickey
55 Oakey Avenue
Lawrenceburg, IN 47025-1538
P: 812-537-9354
F: 812-537-9354
E-mail: jdickey@seidata.com

National Aeronca Association

P.O. Box 2219
806 Lockport Road
Terre Haute, IN 47802
812-232-1491
www.aeroncapilots.com

Aviat Husky Owners Group

Charles McDowell
E-mail: aviat@bigfoot.com

Bellanca-Champion Club

Robert Szego, President
P.O. Box 100
Coxsackie, NY 12051-0100
P: 518-731-6800
F: 518-731-8190
E-mail: szegor@bellanca-championclub.com
www.bellanca-championclub.com

American Bonanza Society

Nancy F. Johnson, Executive Director
P.O. Box 12888
Wichita, KS 67277
P: 316-945-1700
F: 316-945-1710
E-mail: bonanza2@bonanza.org
www.bonanza.org

Classic Bonanza Association
P.O. Box 868002
Plano, TX 75086
214-875-4279
www.classicbonanza.com

Cessna Pilots Association
P.O. Box 5817
Santa Maria, CA 93456
P: 805-922-2580
Fax: 805-922-7249
E-mail: info@cessna.org
www.cessna.org

Cessna Owner Organization
N 7450 Aanstad Road
P.O. Box 5000
Iola, WI 54945-5000
P: 888-692-3776 (1-888-MY-CESSNA)
P: 715-445-5000
F: 715-445-4053
E-mail: help@cessnaowner.org
www.cessnaowner.org

International Cessna 120/140 Association
Doug Corrigan, President
P.O. Box 830092
Richardson, TX 75083-0092
P: 815-633-6858
E-mail: DPCflyer@aol.com
www.cessna120.com

Cessna 150/152 Club
Royson Parsons, Executive Director
P.O. Box 1917
Atascadero, CA 93423-1917
P: 805-461-1958
F: 805-461-1035
E-mail: membership@cessna150-152.com
www.cessna150-152.com

International Cessna 170 Association Inc.
Velvet Fackeldey, Executive Secretary
P.O. Box 1667
Lebanon, MO 65536
P: 417-532-4847
F: 417-532-4847
E-mail: www.headquarters@cessna170.org
www.cessna170.org

Cessna 172/182 Club
Scott Jones, President
Wiley Post Airport
P.O. Box 22631
Oklahoma City, OK 73123
P: 405-495-8664
F: 405-495-8666
E-mail: membership@cessna172-182.com
www.cessna172-182.com

Cardinal Club
Phil Harrison, Secretary
1701 St. Andrew's Drive
Lawrence, KS 66047-1763
P: 785-842-7016
F:785-842-1777
E-mail: cardinalclub@juno.com

Cardinal Flyers Online
Paul Millner, Digest Editor
P.O. Box 532
Hampshire, IL 60140
P: 847-683-4799
E-mail: info@cardinalflyers.com
www.cardinalflyers.com

International 180/185 Club
Scott White, President
P.O. Box 639
Castlewood, VA 24224
P: 540-738-8134
F: 540-738-8136

Cirrus Owners and Pilots Association (COPA)
Martin Kent, President
9710 White Blossom Boulevard
Louisville, KY 40241-4178
P: 502-412-6500
F: 502-581-3919
E-mail: membership@cirruspilots.org
www.cirruspilots.org

Ercoupe Owners Club
Carolyn T. Carden
7263 Schooners Court S.W. A-2
Ocean Isle Beach, NC 28469-5644
P: 910-575-2758
F: 910-575-2758
E-mail: coupecaper@aol.com

Lake Amphibian Flyers Club
Marc Rodstein, Executive Director
7188 Mandarin Drive
Boca Raton, FL 33433
P: 561-483-6566
E-mail: lakeflyersclub@avweb.com

Continental Luscombe Association
Patti Sani
10251 E. Central Avenue
Del Rey, CA 93616
E-mail: cla-jim-patti@pacbell.net
www.luscombe-cla.org

Luscombe Association
John Bergeson
6438 West Millbrook
Remus, MI 49340-9625
P: 517-561-2393
F: 517-561-5101

Maule Aircraft Association
Dave and Kathleen Neumeister, Publishers
5630 South Washington Road
Lansing, MI 48911-4999
P: 800-594-4634, 517-882-8433
F: 800-596-8341, 517-882-8341
E-mail: aircraftnews@msn.com

Mooney Aircraft Pilots Association
140 Heimer Rd, Suite 560
San Antonio, Texas, 78232
P: 210-525-8008
F: 210-525-8085
E-mail: mapa@mooneypilots.com
www.mooneypilots.com

American Navion Society
Gary Rankin, President
PMB 335
16420 S.E. McGillivray #103
Vancouver, WA 98683-3461
P: 360-833-9921
F: 360-833-1074
E-mail: flynavion@yahoo.com
http://navionsociety.org/

Piper Owner Society
N7450 Aanstad Road
P.O. Box 5000
Iola, WI 54945-5000
P: 1-866-697-4737
E-mail: help@Piperowner.org
www.piperowner.org

Cherokee Pilots Association
Terry L. Rogers, Executive Director
P.O. Box 1996
Lutz, FL 33548
P: 813-948-3616
E-mail: terry@piperowner.com
www.piperowner.com

International Comanche Society, Incorporated
Bruce G. Berman, Managing Editor
Wiley Post Airport
Hangar 3
Bethany, OK 73008
P: 405-491-0321
F: 405-491-0325
E-mail: comancheflyer@compuserve.com
www.comancheflyer.com

Cub Club
Sharon and Steve Krog
1002 Heather Lane
Hartford, WI 53027
P: 262-966-7627
F: 262-966-9627
E-mail: sskrog@aol.com

Short Wing Piper Club
Halstead, Kansas
P: 316-835-3650
E-mail: swpn@southwind.net
www.shortwing.org

Supercub.org
Steve Johnson
953 S. Shore Drive
Lake Waukomis, MO 64151
P: 816-741-1486
F: 816-741-5212
www.supercub.org

Malibu-Mirage Owners and Pilots Association (MMOPA)
Russ Caauwe
280 N. Bluebird Drive
Green Valley, AZ 85614
P: 520-399-1121
F: 520-648-3828
E-mail: mmopa@uswest.net
www.mmopa.com

International Stinson Club
Tony Wright
2264 Los Robles Road
Meadow Vista, CA 95722
P: 530-878-0219
E-mail: stinson2@juno.com
www.aeromar.com/swsc.html

National Stinson Club
George Alleman
1229 Rising Hill Road West
Placerville, CA 95667
P: 530-622-4004
F: 530-622-4004
E-mail: nscgeorge@d-web.com

Taylorcraft Owners Club
12809 Greenbower Road
Alliance, OH 44601
P: 330-823-9748
E-mail: tcraft@taylorcraft.org
www.taylorcraft.org

International Taylorcraft Owners Club
Bruce Bixler
12809 Greenbower Road
Alliance, OH 44601
P: 330-823-9748
E-mail: bixlerbr@laa.ci.canton.oh.us
www.taylorcraft.org

American Yankee Association
Stewart Wilson, Secretary-Treasurer
P.O. Box 1531
Cameron Park, CA 95682
P: 530-676-4292
F: 530-676-3949
E-mail: sec@aya.org
www.aya.org

Aircraft manufacturers

American Champion Aircraft
P.O. Box 37
32032 Washington Ave.
Rochester, Wisconsin 53167

Phone: 262-534-6315
Fax: 262-534-2395
www.amerchampionaircraft.com

Aircraft	2003 Base Price	IFR Package (Basic)
7ECA Citabria Aurora	$73,900	Custom Order Approx. $25,000
7GCA Citabria Adventure	$84,900	Custom Order Approx. $25,000
7GCBC Citabria Explorer	$87,900	Custom Order Approx. $25,000
8GCBC Scout	$113,900	Custom Order Approx. $25,000
8KCAB Super Decathlon	$106,900	Custom Order Approx. $25,000

Aviat, Inc.
Box 1240
South Washington Street
Afton, Wyoming 83110

Phone: 307-885-3151
Fax: 307-885-9674
www.aviataircraft.com

Aircraft	2003 Base Price	IFR Package (Basic)
A-1B Husky	$148,000	Custom Order Approx. $30,000
Husky Pup	$116,000	Custom Order Approx. $30,000
Pitts S-2C	$200,000	N/A

**Beechcraft
(Raytheon Aircraft Company)**
P.O. Box 85
Wichita, KS 67201-0085

Phone: 316-676-5034
Fax: 316-676-6614
www.raytheonaircraft.com

Aircraft	2003 Base Price	IFR Package (Basic)
A 36 Bonanza	$644,030	IFR Std.

Cessna Aircraft Company
2603 South Hoover Road
Wichita, Kansas 67215

Phone: 316-517-6056
Fax: 316-332-0388
www.se.cessna.com

Aircraft	2003 Base Price	IFR Package (Basic)
172R Skyhawk	$155,000	$9,900
172S Skyhawk SP	$165,000	$9,900
182T Skylane	$260,000	$18,100
T182T Turbo Skylane	$299,000	$18,100
206H Stationair	$345,000	$18,500
T206H Turbo Stationair	$388,000	$18,500

Cirrus Design Corporation
4515 Taylor Circle
Duluth, MN 55811

Phone: 888-750-9927
Fax: 218-727-2148
www.cirrusdesign.com

Aircraft	2003 Base Price	IFR Package (Basic)
SRV	$189,900	N/A
SR20	$229,900	IFR Std.
SR22	$313,900	IFR Std.

Diamond Aircraft Industries
1560 Crumlin Sideroad
London, Ontario, Canada N5V 1S2

Phone: 888-359-3220
       519-457-4000
Fax: 519-457-4021
www.diamondair.com

Aircraft	2003 Base Price	IFR Package (Basic)
DA20-C1 Evolution	$125,900	N/A
DA20-C1 Eclipse	$139,900	N/A
DA40-180 Diamond Star	$188,900	$11,945
DA40-180FP Diamond Star FP	$175,000	$11,945

LanShe Aerospace, L.L.C.
3100 Airmans Drive
Fort Pierce, FL 34946

Phone: 772-465-9996
www.lansheaero.com

Aircraft	2003 Base Price	IFR Package (Basic)
Lake LA-4-200 EP	$299,000	N\A
Lake Renegade 2	$449,000	$15,500
Lake Seafury	$749,000	Included
Micco SP20	$219,000	Included
Micco SP26	$226,000	Included

Luscombe Aircraft Corporation
5333 N. Main St.
Altus, OK 73521

Phone: 580-477-3355
Fax: 580-477-3368
www.luscombeaircraft.com

Aircraft	2003 Base Price	IFR Package (Basic)
Luscombe 11E	$155,900	Custom Order Approx. $20,000

Maule Air, Inc.

2099 Ga. Hwy. 133S
Moultrie, GA 31678

Phone: 229-985-2045
Fax: 229-890-2402
www.mauleairinc.com

Aircraft	2003 Base Price	IFR Package (Basic)
MX-7-160 Sportsplane	$105,000	$20,400
MX-7-160C Sportplane	$110,400	$20,400
MX-7-180A Sportplane	$110,850	$20,400
MX-7-180AC Sportplane	$116,150	$20,400
MXT-7-160 Comet	$114,600	$20,400
MXT-7-180A Comet	$120,400	$20,400
MX-7-180B Star Rocket	$123,500	$20,400
MX-7-180C Star Rocket	$128,800	$20,400
MXT-7-180 Star Rocket	$134,600	$20,400
M-7-235B Super Rocket	$139,600	$20,400
M-7-235B Super Rocket	$147,750	$20,400
M-7-235C Orion	$145,800	$20,400
M-7-235C Orion	$153,950	$20,400
MT-7-235 Super Rocket	$160,200	$20,400
M-7-260 Super Rocket	$158,400	$20,400
M-7-260C Orion	$165,200	$20,400
M-7-260 Super Rocket	$170,850	$20,400
M-7-420AC (Turboprop)	$450,000	$20,400
MT-7-420 (Turboprop)	$470,000	$20,400
M9-230 (Diesel)	$200,000	$20,400

Mooney Airplane Company, Inc.
Louis Schreiner Field
Kerrville, TX 78028

Phone: 800-456-3033
Fax: 830-792-2054
www.mooney.com

Aircraft	2003 Base Price	IFR Package (Basic)
Ovation	$299,450	$20,000
Ovation 2 DX	$384,950	IFR Std.
Bravo DX	$434,950	IFR Std.

Renaissance Aircraft LLC
P.O. Box 596
Cape Girardeau, MO 63702

Phone: 573-651-3933
Fax: 573-651-3923
www.renaissanceaircraft.com

Aircraft	2003 Base Price	IFR Package (Basic)
Renaissance 8F (Luscombe Silvaire)	$77,500	N/A

Taylorcraft Aviation, Inc.
4495 W. State Hwy. 71
La Grange, Texas 78945-5150

Phone: 800-217-1399
www.taylorcraft.com

Aircraft	2003 Base Price	IFR Package (Basic)
F22	$59,995*	N/A
F22A	$63,995*	N/A
F22B	$69,995*	N/A
F22C	$73,995*	N/A

* Note: Base Price is with no radios and no gyro panel

The Lancair Company
22550 Nelson Road
Bend, Oregon 97701-9710

Phone: 541-318-1144
Fax: 541-318-1177
www.lancair.com

Aircraft	2003 Base Price	IFR Package (Basic)
Lancair Columbia 350	$370,000	IFR Std.
Lancair Columbia 400	$437,000	IFR Std.

The New Piper Aircraft, Inc.
2926 Piper Drive
Vero Beach, FL 32960

Phone: 772-567-4361
Fax: 772-978-6584
www.newpiper.com

Aircraft	2003 Base Price	IFR Package (Basic)
Warrior III	$175,300	$17,130
Archer III	$205,500	$33,500
Arrow	$271,600	$25,000
6X	$336,000	$25,000 (Est.)
6XT	$356,000	$25,000 (Est.
Saratoga II HP	$440,800	IFR Std.
Saratoga II TC	$472,200	IFR Std.

Tiger Aircraft LLC
226 Pilot Way
Martinsburg, WV 25401

Phone: 877-80-TIGER
      304-267-1000
www.tigeraircraft.com

Aircraft	2003 Base Price	IFR Package (Basic)
Tiger	$235,800	IFR Std.

Index